TO IMPROVE THE ACADEMY

TO IMPROVE THE ACADEMY

Resources for Faculty, Instructional, and Organizational Development

Volume 28

Linda B. Nilson, Editor

Judith E. Miller, Associate Editor

Professional and Organizational Development
Network in Higher Education

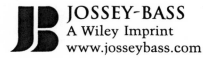

JOSSEY-BASS
A Wiley Imprint
www.josseybass.com

TO IMPROVE THE ACADEMY

To Improve the Academy is published annually by the Professional and Organizational Development Network in Higher Education (POD) through Jossey-Bass Publishers and is abstracted in ERIC documents and in Higher Education Abstracts.

Ordering Information

The annual volume of *To Improve the Academy* is distributed to members at the POD conference in the autumn of every year. To order or obtain ordering information, contact:

John Wiley & Sons, Inc.

One Wiley Drive

Somerset, NJ 08875–1272

Voice: (877) 762-2974

Fax: (317) 572-4002

Email: consumer@wiley.com

Web: www.josseybass.com

Permission to Copy

The contents of *To Improve the Academy* are copyrighted to protect the authors. Nevertheless, consistent with the networking and resource-sharing functions of POD, readers are encouraged to reproduce articles and cases from *To Improve the Academy* for educational use, as long as the source is identified.

Instructions to Contributors for the Next Volume

Anyone interested in the issues related to instructional, faculty, and organizational development in higher education may submit manuscripts. Manuscripts are submitted to the current editor in December of every year and sent through a blind peer-review process. Correspondence, including requests for information about guidelines and submission of manuscripts for Volume 29, should be directed to:

Judith E. Miller

Executive Director of Assessment

Office of Institutional Research

University of North Florida

1 UNF Drive

Jacksonville, FL 32224

Email: jmiller@unf.edu

Mission Statement

As revised and accepted by the POD Core Committee, April 2, 2004.

Statement of Purpose

The Professional and Organizational Development Network in Higher Education is an association of higher education professionals dedicated to enhancing teaching and learning by supporting educational developers and leaders in higher education.

The Professional and Organizational Development Network in Higher Education encourages advocacy of ongoing enhancement of teaching and learning through faculty, TA, instructional, and organizational development. To this end, it supports the work of educational developers and champions their importance to the academic enterprise.

Vision Statement

During the twenty-first century, the Professional and Organizational Development Network in Higher Education will expand guidelines for educational development, build strong alliances with sister organizations, and encourage developer exchanges and research projects to improve teaching and learning.

Values

The Professional and Organizational Development Network in Higher Education is committed to:

- Personal, faculty, instructional, and organizational development
- Humane and collaborative organizations and administrations
- Diverse perspectives and a diverse membership
- Supportive educational development networks on the local, regional, national, and international levels
- Advocacy for improved teaching and learning in the academy through programs for faculty, administrators, and graduate students
- Identification and collection of a strong and accessible body of research on development theories and practices
- Establishment of guidelines for ethical practice
- Increasingly useful and thorough assessment and evaluation of practice and research

Programs, Publications, and Activities

The Professional and Organizational Development Network in Higher Education offers members and interested individuals these benefits:

- An annual membership conference designed to promote professional and personal growth, nurture innovation and change, stimulate important research projects, and enable participants to exchange ideas and broaden professional networks
- An annual membership directory and networking guide
- Publications in print and in electronic form
- Access to the POD website and listserv

Membership, Conference, and Programs Information

For information contact:
Hoag Holmgren, Executive Director
The POD Network
P.O. Box 3318
Nederland, CO 80466 USA
Voice: (303) 258-9521
Fax: (303) 258-7377
Email: podoffice@podnetwork.org

CONTENTS

SECTION ONE
Improving Our Performance

SECTION TWO
Understanding Faculty

SECTION THREE

Understanding Students and Their Learning

SECTION FOUR

Enhancing Our Programming

ABOUT THE AUTHORS

The Editors

Linda B. Nilson is founding director of the Office of Teaching Effectiveness and Innovation at Clemson University. She is author of *Teaching at Its Best: A Research-Based Resource for College Instructors,* now in its second edition (2003; Jossey-Bass, 2007) and *The Graphic Syllabus and the Outcomes Map: Communicating Your Course* (Jossey-Bass, 2007). She is co-editor of *Enhancing Learning with Laptops in the Classroom* (with Barbara E. Weaver, Jossey-Bass, 2005), associate editor of Volumes 25 and 26 of *To Improve the Academy* (with Douglas R. Robertson, 2007, 2008), and editor of Volume 27 (with Judith E. Miller, Jossey-Bass, 2009). She is currently working on the third edition of *Teaching at Its Best.* In addition, Dr. Nilson has published many articles and book chapters and has presented conference sessions and faculty workshops both nationally and internationally on dozens of topics related to teaching effectiveness, assessment, scholarly productivity, and academic career matters. Before coming to Clemson, she directed teaching centers at Vanderbilt University and the University of California, Riverside, and was a sociology professor at UCLA. Dr. Nilson has held leadership positions in the Society for the Study of Social Problems, Toastmasters International, Mensa, and the Southern Regional Faculty and Instructional Development Consortium. She may contacted be at nilson@clemson.edu.

Judith E. Miller is executive director of assessment at the University of North Florida in Jacksonville. A former biology faculty member, her current teaching includes courses in college teaching for graduate students. In 1998 she received the Outstanding Undergraduate Science Teacher award from the Society for College Science Teachers; in 2002 she was named the Massachusetts CASE Professor of the Year by the Carnegie Foundation for the Advancement of Teaching; and in 2004 she won the Worcester Polytechnic Institute Trustees' Award for Outstanding Teaching. Dr. Miller is co-editor (with Jim Groccia and Marilyn Miller) of *Student-Assisted Teaching: A Guide to Faculty–Student Teamwork* (2001) and (with Jim Groccia) of *On Becoming a Productive University: Strategies for Reducing Costs and Increasing Quality* (2005). She has published and presented extensively on active and cooperative learning, learning outcomes assessment, team teaching, and educational productivity. She may be contacted at jmiller@unf.edu.

The Contributors

Eric Aoki is an associate professor in communication studies at Colorado State University. His teaching and research focuses on identity and diversity. His publications include "The Politics of Negotiating Public Tragedy: Media Framing of the Matthew Shepard Murder" (with Brian Ott) in *Rhetoric and Public Affairs* and "Making Space in the Classroom for My Gay Identity: A Letter I've Been Wanting to Write" in *Teaching Diversity: Challenges and Complexities, Identities and Integrity,* edited by William M. Timpson. He may be contacted at eric.aoki@colostate.edu.

Raoul A. Arreola is professor and associate dean for assessment in the College of Pharmacy at the University of Tennessee Health Science Center. He has held various faculty and administrative positions at three universities; has published on distance education, academic leadership, and assessment of faculty performance; and has served as a consultant to more than 320 colleges and universities on designing and implementing large-scale faculty evaluation and development systems. He may be contacted at raoularreola@utmem.edu.

Dorothe J. Bach is an assistant professor and faculty consultant at the University of Virginia's Teaching Resource Center. In her role as faculty developer, she facilitates events designed to enhance the university's teaching mission and supports incoming faculty through the Excellence in Diversity Fellows Program. She also teaches literature and culture courses in the German department and the Comparative Literature Program. Her publications include articles on teaching and learning and early career faculty. She may be contacted at bach@virginia.edu.

Daniel J. Bernstein is director of the Center for Teaching Excellence at the University of Kansas, where he is also professor of psychology. He served from 1999 to 2003 as director of a five-university project granting faculty fellowships to generate peer reviews of teaching materials. His recent writing has focused on representing the intellectual work in teaching, especially through external review of electronic course portfolios centered on student work (see www.cte.ku.edu/gallery/ and www.courseportfolio.org/). He may be contacted at djb@ku.edu.

Laurel Johnson Black is associate professor of English and the director of the Center for Teaching Excellence at Indiana University of Pennsylvania. For several years she has also served as a co-director of the Reflective Practice Project. She teaches courses in composition, creative writing, the paranormal, and sociolinguistics. Her research interests include student-teacher conferencing, faculty professional development, and social class and education. She may be contacted at laurel.black@iup.edu.

Phyllis Blumberg is director of the Teaching and Learning Center at the University of the Sciences in Philadelphia and a professor of social sciences. Over the past thirty years she has served in various capacities on many committees in five higher education settings. She is author of *Developing Learner-Centered Teaching: A Practical Guide for Faculty* (Jossey-Bass, 2009). She received her Ph.D. in educational and developmental psychology from the University of Pittsburgh and may be contacted at p.blumbe@usip.edu.

Stephen P. Bogdewic is executive associate dean for faculty affairs and professional development and George W. Copeland Professor and associate chair of family medicine at Indiana University School of Medicine. He received his Ph.D. in adult education and organizational development from the University of North Carolina and his M.A. in marriage, family, and child counseling from Santa Clara University. His interests include professional and leadership development, clinical teaching skills, and quality improvement of health care. He may be contacted at bogdewic@iupui.edu.

Allison P. Boye is director of the Teaching Effectiveness and Career Enhancement (TEACH) Program for the Teaching, Learning, and Technology Center at Texas Tech University. Her work at the center includes consulting with faculty and graduate students, running an intensive graduate student development program, and leading pedagogical seminars. Her current research focuses on the intersection of gender and faculty development, active learning across the disciplines, and generational differences. She may be contacted at allison.p.boye@ttu.edu.

Judy Britnell is director of Ryerson University's Learning and Teaching Office, which supports professional development of faculty members. Her research has addressed the needs of English as a second language students, suspended students, immigrant professors working in Ontario higher education, and faculty engagement in teaching development activities. A former executive member of the Society of Teaching and Learning in Higher Education, she is actively engaged in innovative opportunities for learning. She may be contacted at britnell@ryerson.ca.

Randy R. Brutkiewicz is assistant dean for faculty affairs and professional development and professor of microbiology and immunology at the Indiana University School of Medicine, where he has been a faculty member for more than ten years. His main efforts in the dean's office are focused on development of research faculty, both tenure track and non-tenure track. His NIH-funded laboratory investigates innate immunity, signal transduction pathways, and immune evasion by viruses and tumors. He may be contacted at rbrutkie@iupui.edu.

Susanna Calkins is an associate director at the Searle Center for Teaching Excellence at Northwestern University, where she leads several faculty development initiatives. She received her Ph.D. in European history from Purdue University. Her recent publications have focused on faculty conceptions of teaching and mentoring. She is coauthor of *Learning and Teaching in Higher Education: The Reflective Professional* (2009). She may be contacted at s-calkins@northwestern.edu.

Constance E. Cook is associate vice provost and executive director of the Center for Research on Learning and Teaching at the University of Michigan. She serves as clinical professor in the School of Education and adjunct associate professor of political science. She works on institutional transformation—that is, creating a culture of teaching at a research university, a topic on which she has been writing and lecturing for more than a decade. She may be contacted at cecook@umich.edu.

Amber Dailey-Hebert is executive director of the Center for Excellence in Teaching and Learning at Park University and associate professor of education. In addition to teaching, she offers enhancement opportunities to her institution's worldwide faculty and publishes on organizational change, faculty evaluation, and student engagement. She is currently researching integrative pedagogies and leadership in higher education. She was honored as the 2007 Ebadi Scholar of the Year and the Outstanding Graduate Faculty Member. She may be contacted at adailey@park.edu.

Mary E. Dankoski is assistant dean for faculty affairs and professional development, assistant chair for academic affairs, Lester D. Bibler Scholar, and associate professor of clinical family medicine at Indiana University. She earned her Ph.D. in marriage and family therapy and graduate minor in women's studies from Purdue University. Her scholarly interests include advancement of women and faculty of color, assessment of faculty vitality, and behavioral medicine education in family medicine. She may be contacted at mdankosk@iupui.edu.

Elise J. Dallimore is associate professor of organizational communication with a joint appointment in the College of Business Administration at Northeastern University. Her publications focus on organizational learning, cold calling and discussion, socialization, and quality-of-life issues. She teaches courses on organizational, interpersonal, and instructional communication, including the senior capstone course Consultation Skills. She may be contacted at e.dallimore@neu.edu.

Debra Dawson is director of Teaching and Learning Services and an adjunct research professor in the Faculty of Education at the University of Western Ontario in London, Ontario. An award-winning teacher, she has served on the boards of the Society for Teaching and Learning in Higher Education and the Canadian Society for Studies in Higher Education. Her research interests include student engagement, faculty and graduate student development, and the scholarship of teaching and learning. She may be contacted at dldawson@uwo.ca.

Michele DiPietro is associate director of the Eberly Center for Teaching Excellence and an instructor in the statistics department at Carnegie Mellon University. His scholarship focuses on diversity in the classroom, faculty responses to tragic events, statistics education, student ratings of instruction, and the teaching consultation process. He has served on the POD core committee and was the conference chair of the 2006 POD conference Theory and Research for a Scholarship of Practice. He may be contacted at dipietro@andrew.cmu.edu.

Emily Donnelli is assistant professor of English and faculty director of professional enhancement at Park University. She develops resources to support teaching excellence across the disciplines, working with faculty who teach in online, hybrid, and face-to-face modalities. In addition to her professional enhancement work, she teaches courses in writing and rhetoric; her research examines how public sphere theory can inform civic engagement pedagogies in first-year composition. She may be contacted at emilyd@park.edu.

Wesley H. Dotson is a doctoral student in the Department of Applied Behavior Analysis at the University of Kansas. He conducts research in the areas of undergraduate education and social skills instruction for children and adolescents with autism. He is also a graduate assistant at the Center for Teaching Excellence and acts as a writing partner for faculty who are creating electronic course portfolios. He may be contacted at wdotson@ku.edu.

Denise Drane is an associate director at the Searle Center for Teaching Excellence at Northwestern University, where she leads on several evaluation and research projects. She received her Ph.D. in speech and language pathology from Northwestern University. Her recent publications have focused on personal response systems and nanoscience education. She may be contacted at d-drane@northwestern.edu.

Steve Fifield is an associate policy scientist in the Delaware Education Research and Development Center at the University of Delaware, where he also holds a secondary appointment as assistant professor in the Department of Biological Sciences. He conducts research and evaluation studies of science curriculum reform and the sociocultural and organizational dynamics of interdisciplinary initiatives in science and medicine. His other interests include culture and identity at the intersections of science, religion, and sexuality. He may be contacted at fifield@udel.edu.

Alicia Hitchcock works as a research assistant for the Teaching Support Center at the University of Western Ontario in London, Ontario. She received her undergraduate degrees from the University of Western Ontario in political science and sociology. She plans to pursue graduate education, furthering her research into the development of educational developer competencies. She may be contacted at ahitchc2@uwo.ca.

Cassandra Volpe Horii is an associate director at the Derek Bok Center for Teaching and Learning at Harvard University, where she directs the Departmental Teaching Fellows Program; coordinates pedagogical inquiry, assessment, and dissemination; and consults with faculty and graduate students on teaching. With her Ph.D. in environmental science (atmospheric chemistry), she continues to teach engineering courses as a lecturer; she has also taught freshman expository writing. She may be contacted at cvhorii@post.harvard.edu.

Sally Kuhlenschmidt has been director of the Faculty Center for Excellence in Teaching at Western Kentucky University since 1994. She received her Ph.D. in clinical psychology from Purdue University. Her current research interests include assessing faculty development programs and services and using technology to enhance development. She may be contacted at sally.kuhlenschmidt@wku.edu.

Lia S. Logio, M.D., is assistant dean for faculty affairs and professional development, associate professor of clinical medicine, vice chair of graduate medical education, and program director of the residency in the Department of Medicine at Indiana University. A general internist, she practices both inpatient and outpatient medicine. She graduated from the Johns Hopkins School of Medicine and completed residency at Duke University Medical Center. Her interests include medical education, patient safety, leadership, and faculty development. She may be contacted at llogio@iupui.edu.

Pamela S. Lottero-Perdue is assistant professor of science education in the Department of Physics, Astronomy, and Geosciences at Towson University. In addition to her work on faculty mentoring, her research interests include studying children's critical analyses of text and technology and examining how elementary teachers learn to teach technology and engineering. She may be contacted at plottero@towson.edu.

B. Jean Mandernach is director for scholarly engagement in the Center for Excellence in Teaching and Learning at Park University. Her research focuses on enhancing student learning through assessment and innovative online instructional strategies. In addition, she has interests in examining the perception of online degrees and development of effective faculty evaluation models. She may be contacted at jean.mandernach@park.edu.

Susanne Morgan is a long-time faculty member in sociology at Ithaca College. She is assigned half-time to coordinate faculty development activities for her institution and in that role has built the virtual Center for Faculty Excellence. She may be contacted at morgan@ithaca.edu.

Bonnie Mullinix is senior consultant for faculty and educational development with the TLT Group and co-president of Jacaranda Educational Development. An adult educator with nearly thirty years of national and international experience, she set up and directed two teaching centers, one as assistant dean, and taught at Monmouth and Drexel universities. Her professional work has explored educational innovation, technologies, research, and evaluation as well as integration of participatory, learner-centered approaches. She may be contacted at mullinix@tltgroup.org.

Craig E. Nelson is professor emeritus of biology at Indiana University and a Carnegie scholar. He was founding president of the International Society for the Scholarship of Teaching and Learning. His teaching scholarship addresses critical thinking, mature valuing, diversity, active learning, evolution, and SoTL. His biological research was on evolution and ecology. His awards include the President's Medal for Excellence and Outstanding Research and the Carnegie/CASE Doctoral University Professor of the Year 2000. He may be contacted at nelson1@indiana.edu.

Amanda Stone Norton is an adjunct professor in the Department of Teacher Education at Texas Woman's University, where she teaches classes on diversity and gender equity in K–12 classrooms. She recently earned her Ph.D. in higher education from the University of Denver. Her research agenda includes Latina/Latino student persistence in the U.S. education system, multicultural education in teacher education, inclusive pedagogies, and white identity development. She may be contacted at astonenorton@twu.edu.

Chris O'Neal is associate director of the Teaching, Learning, and Technology Center at the University of California, Irvine. He received his Ph.D. in ecology and evolution from the University of Michigan in 2001. His current research interests include development of higher education administrators and the impact of instructors on student retention in the sciences. He may be contacted at coneal@uci.edu.

Megan M. Palmer is assistant dean for faculty affairs and professional development at Indiana University School of Medicine, director of faculty development in the health professions at Indiana University–Purdue University Indianapolis, and visiting assistant professor at Indiana University School of Education. She holds an M.S. in higher education from Colorado State University and a Ph.D. in higher education administration from Indiana University. Her research focuses on college teaching, faculty development, and faculty experience. She may be contacted at mmpalmer@iupui.edu.

Brian C. Pilling is a training facilitator and curriculum developer for a company in Riverton, Utah. While collecting data for the study in Chapter Thirteen, he was an assistant professor at Westminster College, where he coordinated the speech department and taught courses in speech, communication, and theater. Currently he designs and delivers management, communication, and diversity classes. His research focuses on interpersonal relationships and communication in learning environments. He may be contacted at briancpilling@hotmail.com.

Terry Ray was, until January 2009, a faculty member of the Eberly College of Business at Indiana University of Pennsylvania, where he taught courses in law. He has been involved in the Center for Teaching Excellence and the Reflective Practice Project for many years. He has recently published a novel, *The Avatar: God, Man, or the Anti-Christ?* and is working on a sequel. He may be contacted at tray@auxmail .iup.edu.

María del Carmen Salazar is assistant professor of education at the University of Denver. Her research and teaching fields include teacher education, linguistically diverse education, and inclusive excellence in K–12 and college classrooms. She has published numerous academic journal articles and has given national, state, and regional scholarly presentations. In addition, she is the lead author of the widely distributed policy document *The State of Latinos 2008: Defining an Agenda for the Future.* She may be contacted at msalazar@du.edu.

Mary Deane Sorcinelli is associate provost for faculty development and professor in the Department of Educational Policy, Research, and Administration at the University of Massachusetts Amherst. She is co-principal investigator of a grant from the Andrew W. Mellon Foundation to support mentoring for new and underrepresented faculty. She also is the founding director of UMass Amherst's award-winning Center for Teaching and the author of several resources on teaching and learning, faculty development, and early career faculty. She may be contacted at msorcinelli@acad.umass.edu.

Tasha J. Souza is professor of instructional communication and the faculty development coordinator for the Center for Excellence in Learning and Teaching at Humboldt State University. Her research interests lie in instructional communication, including gender-related communication and cold calling in the classroom. She teaches and provides professional development in the areas of gender, intercultural, and organizational communication as well as mediation, training and facilitation skills, classroom communication, active-learning pedagogies, and universal design for learning. She may be contacted at tasha@humboldt.edu.

Suzanne Tapp has worked at the Teaching, Learning, and Technology Center at Texas Tech University for the past thirteen years and currently serves as the associate director. Although she spends a great deal of her time planning events for the center, she prefers to be in the classroom observing good teaching. She is the 2009 chair of the Texas Faculty Development Network and is working with the 2009 POD conference planning team. She may be contacted at suzanne.tapp@ttu.edu.

Michael Theall is professor of education at Youngstown State University. He has directed teaching centers at four universities and has edited, published, or presented more than 230 books, monographs, papers, and workshops on college teaching, faculty evaluation and development, teaching improvement, and organizational development. Currently president-elect of POD, he has received three national awards for his research and scholarship. He may be contacted at mtheall@ysu.edu.

Franklin A. Tuitt is an assistant professor and director of the higher education program in the Morgridge College of Education at the University of Denver. His research explores access and equity in higher education, teaching and learning in racially diverse classrooms, and organizational transformation related to diversity. He is a co-editor and contributing author of *Race and Higher Education: Rethinking Pedagogy in Diverse College Classrooms,* as well as former cochair of the *Harvard Educational Review.* He may be contacted at ftuitt@du.edu.

Judith Villa teaches classes in English and women's studies at Indiana University of Pennsylvania and holds a Ph.D. in American studies from the University of New Mexico. Her areas of research are popular culture and empowering pedagogy. She is deeply committed to helping IUP undergraduates gain intern status as undergraduate teaching assistants, further promoting sharing of classroom authority. She has been active in the Reflective Practice Project for the past twelve years. She may be contacted at Judith.Villa@iup.edu.

Susan Weaver is director of the Center for Teaching and Learning, the Quality Enhancement Plan, and assessment at the University of the Cumberlands. Previously, she taught sociology at Marshall University, Atlantic Christian College, and Miami University of Ohio in various venues including traditional classrooms, satellite, T1 classrooms, the Internet, and prison. She received her B.A. and M.A. degrees in sociology from Marshall University and her Ed.D. in educational leadership from West Virginia University. She may be contacted at susan.weaver@ucumberlands.edu.

Susan Wilcox specializes in the field of adult and higher education, focusing on emancipatory education and transformative learning, learner-directed inquiry, the scholarship of postsecondary teaching, and continuing professional education. From 1992 to 2008 she was a faculty member in the Centre for Teaching and Learning at Queen's University. Currently she is in the Department of Women's Studies and the Faculty of Education at Queen's. She may be contacted at wilcoxs@queensu.ca.

Mary C. Wright is assistant research scientist and assistant director for evaluation research at the Center for Research on Learning and Teaching at the University of Michigan. Her research and teaching interests include teaching cultures, how graduate students learn about the academic job market, and qualitative research and evaluation methods. Her book about how chairs and faculty create cultures of teaching, *Always at Odds?*, was published in 2008. She may be contacted at mcwright@umich.edu.

Niki Young is director of teaching and learning at Western Oregon University. Her interest in faculty and instructional development emerged from her work with graduate students in communication studies on communication and pedagogy. She is especially interested in use of narrative to establish and communicate identity and on how we use narrative to form connections and relationships with others. She currently serves on the POD core committee and edits the POD newsletter. She may be contacted at youngn@wou.edu.

Sue Fostaty Young is an educational developer and a doctoral candidate in the Faculty of Education at Queen's University. Her dissertation, *The Transformative Effects of Learning/Assessment-Focused Educational Development*, is a collaborative heuristic inquiry into faculty members' conceptual development and professional learning when conversations and conceptions of assessment are featured elements. She may be contacted at fostatys@queensu.ca.

John Zubizarreta is professor of English and director of honors and faculty development at Columbia College. He publishes widely on modern literature, honors education, and faculty development. Foremost among his disciplinary publications is *The Robert Frost Encyclopedia* (2001). A South Carolina CASE professor, his recent books include *Inspiring Exemplary Teaching and Learning: Perspectives on Teaching Academically Talented College Students* (2008) and *The Learning Portfolio: Reflective Practice for Improving Student Learning* (2004; Jossey-Bass, 2009). He may be contacted at jzubizarreta@columbiasc.edu.

PREFACE

THE CHAPTERS IN THIS VOLUME fit under four themes. The first focuses on our profession: the competencies it requires and strategies for being more effective in it. The second adds to our knowledge of the faculty we serve: their roles and responsibilities, their reactions to feedback, and the effects of their beliefs. In the third section, we revisit our reason for being: students, along with how they learn and how we can have a positive impact on them. Finally, the fourth theme examines successful new programs, each of which offers elements that we can borrow and adapt to improve our own programming.

Section One: Improving Our Performance

Chapter One. Debra Dawson, Judy Britnell, and Alicia Hitchcock engaged groups of faculty developers in World Café, a collaborative discussion-based research method, to build a matrix of competencies for each of three teaching and learning center positions—entry-level, senior-level, and director—to determine how these competencies can be demonstrated. This is the first formal effort to identify the specific abilities, experiences, and traits necessary for success at career stages in the profession.

Chapter Two. Sally Kuhlenschmidt, Susan Weaver, and Susanne Morgan describe their three distinct approaches to developing a clear intellectual vision or plan for their very different types of centers. One unit operates under one unifying theme, a second is fashioned around faculty roles and level organizational impact, and the third focuses on systematically developing faculty teaching skills within a curriculum. Each model has its own strengths, challenges, and pattern of development.

Chapter Three. Pamela S. Lottero-Perdue and Steve Fifield propose a conceptual framework for faculty mentoring programs that they developed by identifying patterns in program design, implementation, and evaluation across colleges and universities. In addition to a thorough review of the literature, they provide a tool for administrators, participants, and evaluators to use in tailoring mentoring programs to their unique faculty and institutional needs.

Chapter Four. Phyllis Blumberg convincingly argues that faculty developers can enhance their institution's effectiveness by bringing their distinctive expertise and perspective to committee service. However, they must make strategic decisions about where and how they will serve. Blumberg lays out a framework for selecting committee membership and positions based on five criteria, pointing out the hazards of certain kinds of committees and roles.

Chapter Five. Wesley H. Dotson and Daniel J. Bernstein conducted an informal comparative analysis of teaching centers at larger state universities in the United States as part of their center's ten-year review. The dimensions they chose for comparison (programs, resources, size), along with their methods of data collection and analysis, serve as a model for center leaders who may be called on, or may independently decide, to conduct similar research.

Chapter Six. Niki Young revisits classroom observation, an individual teaching improvement service that most centers offer. Going beyond the literature of general guidelines for observations, she presents and deconstructs examples of her own observation narratives, recommending strategies to enhance the helpfulness of the observation to faculty and making our techniques and the reasons behind them more explicit, transparent, and replicable.

Section Two: Understanding Faculty

Chapter Seven. Michael Theall, Bonnie Mullinix, and Raoul A. Arreola present findings from an international study of faculty skills, roles, and responsibilities that are the basis for a metaprofessional model. Such data can inform organizational and professional development efforts as well as faculty evaluation policies. Although the authors come to general conclusions about faculty expertise and needs across roles and disciplines, they urge local replication of their study for basing local decisions.

Chapter Eight. Allison P. Boye and Suzanne Tapp address a topic that has received scant attention in the literature. Drawing on their faculty survey, in-depth interviews, and observations, they uncover patterns to negative feedback and the consultation process among male and female instructors. In addition to some gender differences, they find that a faculty developer needs empathy, time, and mastery of the SoTL literature to reach certain instructors and meet their individual needs.

Chapter Nine. Sue Fostaty Young and Susan Wilcox delve into the factors behind instructors' assessment practices. Their in-depth interviews reveal that faculty beliefs and values about teaching interact with the institutional context to shape assessment choices, and that faculty beliefs and teaching experiences mutually affect one another. The authors also identify consulting practices that prove particularly effective or ineffective in helping faculty understand and enhance their teaching.

Section Three: Understanding Students and Their Learning

Chapter Ten. Craig E. Nelson reflects back on nine beliefs about students and teaching that he held as a young professor. He now calls these beliefs "dysfunctional illusions"—*dysfunctional* because they hinder student learning and *illusions* because the scholarship of teaching and learning has shown them to be wrong. As he describes each such illusion, he corrects it with relevant research findings and a more realistic viewpoint.

Chapter Eleven. John Zubizarreta examines the often-made claim that students learn more and more deeply in small classes than in large ones. According to the research, they do, mainly because of the active, collaborative pedagogies, mentoring, reflection, feedback, and instructor-to-student and student-to-student interactions that small numbers make easily possible. By incorporating some of these components, large classes can stimulate significant learning, but they entail unrecognized costs that reduce their bottom-line efficiency.

Chapter Twelve. María del Carmen Salazar, Amanda Stone Norton, and Franklin A. Tuitt propose strategies for advancing from the prevailing fragmentary approach to diversity to infusing inclusive excellence into predominantly white institutions. The authors cite research that inclusive excellence improves student motivation and achievement, cultural awareness understanding, and civic involvement; they then suggest a range of methods that faculty and faculty developers can use to promote inclusive excellence in teaching and learning.

Chapter Thirteen. Tasha J. Souza, Elise J. Dallimore, Eric Aoki, and Brian C. Pilling test the commonly held belief that cold calling intimidates students and chills the communication climate. Yet it may be the only way instructors can equalize participation in discussion. This multi-institutional study finds that, in fact, cold calling enhances students' engagement in the classroom without making them uncomfortable, as long as the instructor maintains a supportive communication climate.

Chapter Fourteen. Michele DiPietro challenges higher education's current approach to academic dishonesty. He first describes the theoretical frameworks that institutions typically draw on to conceptualize cheating, along with each theory's predictions about dishonest behaviors and its supporting empirical evidence. He then identifies a major limitation of these frameworks and proposes new interpretations of academic dishonesty, as well as their implications for faculty development.

Section Four: Enhancing Our Programming

Chapter Fifteen. Susanna Calkins and Denise Drane capitalized on the new requirements of the National Science Foundation and other major funding agencies to incorporate educational activities into research grants; they introduced a faculty workshop on how to structure an education plan into grants. This workshop has enabled them to reach research-focused faculty and engage them in lively discussion about formulating and aligning learning objectives, educational objectives, pedagogical approaches, and assessment instruments.

Chapter Sixteen. Mary C. Wright, Constance E. Cook, and Chris O'Neal promote a broader view of faculty development to encompass academic leadership preparation. In addition to training new chairs, they developed a model program that fosters ongoing growth in institutional leadership. Initiated by the provost, it begins with an extensive needs assessment of the participants and progresses to a developmentally oriented leadership training program and performance evaluation.

Chapter Seventeen. Megan M. Palmer, Mary E. Dankoski, Randy R. Brutkiewicz, Lia S. Logio, and Stephen P. Bogdewic responded to the high stress and low satisfaction among their academic medical center faculty by establishing a model faculty development program. Such a comprehensive effort is rare in medical schools, and the authors detail how they did it: their collaborations, extensive needs assessment, vision and mission development, career-stage framework for faculty development, goal-setting and strategic planning, and ongoing assessments.

Chapter Eighteen. Dorothe J. Bach and Mary Deane Sorcinelli share lessons learned about an early career program for underrepresented faculty from two assessment studies: an internal survey of program graduates and an external evaluation using focus groups and interviews with faculty, staff, and administrators. The studies found that the program's success rested on creating a peer network, involving senior faculty and administrators, and offering useful events. They also identified issues of concern around which improvements were made.

Chapter Nineteen. Amber Dailey-Hebert, Emily Donnelli, and B. Jean Mandernach describe an ambitious new model for mentoring female faculty and administrators and developing them into academic leaders. Initiated by their university president, this effective, proactive approach is built on networking opportunities, guest mentoring by influential women from many professions, peer mentoring in a group setting, collaborative problem solving, and a capstone "legacy project" designed to advance the status of women in academe.

Chapter Twenty. Laurel Johnson Black, Terry Ray, and Judith Villa conducted in-depth interviews with faculty in their reflective practice program to assess exactly what the participants were gaining from the program. Soundly grounding their evaluation in theory, the authors determined the extent of reflection by comparing the participants' comments to the elements of reflection posited by Dewey and Rodgers. They also identified three important needs the program met for the faculty involved.

Chapter Twenty-One. Cassandra Volpe Horii reports the results of a four-year assessment study of a program that has employed Ph.D. students as department-based teaching mentors to their peers. These mentors seized the opportunity to effect several improvements in their department's intellectual culture, including the value, support, and discussion given to teaching, the frequency of exchange of teaching materials, and the quality and quantity of graduate student–faculty interactions.

To Improve the Academy allows our colleagues to share some of their most extraordinary accomplishments. A few have examined our profession and what it takes to be successful. Some have devised strategies to make us more effective in our jobs, including initiating impressive programs. Others have conducted research that offers novel insights into faculty or have revealed new facets of learning and ways to reach students. By virtue of their broad application, the contributions of our colleagues can make our work easier, more exciting, and more rewarding.

Through us, our colleagues' wisdom can do the same for our faculty, and in turn for our students. We all have taught and typically still do. As instructors we often get a thrill realizing the effect we have on the world through our students. As faculty developers, we should also get a thrill over the broad *indirect* effects we have on that world. For every faculty member who leaves our office or workshop more knowledgeable about learning, more understanding of students, and inspired to teach better in large or small ways, thousands of learners benefit over the years.

ACKNOWLEDGMENTS

MANY MINDS MADE LIGHT WORK this year as I distributed just over 130 reviews across eighty reviewers. Almost all the forty-five reviewers from Volume 27 of *To Improve the Academy* served again for this volume, and dozens of new colleagues volunteered to join us. I was amazed at the quality of the vast majority of the reviews: detailed and specific, helpful to the authors, methodologically savvy, substantively rich covering content to wording, and long (one to four pages single-spaced). Although the reviewers didn't always agree about a given manuscript, they explained the values and standards they used to arrive at their recommendations.

Those who worked so diligently to bring you the best possible *To Improve the Academy* include Dorothe Bach, Gabriele Bauer, Danilo Baylen, Laurie Bellows, Lillian Benavente-McEnery, Jim Benner, Donna Bird, Phyllis Blumberg, Jim Borgford-Parnell, Carolyn Brown, Jeanette Clausen, Eli Collins-Brown, Jodi Cressman, Bonnie Daniel, Cynthia Desrochers, Michele DiPietro, Sally Barr Ebest, Bonnie Farley-Lucas, Kim Fielding, Clifford ("Kip") Finnegan, De Gallow, Chris Garrett, Francine Glazer, Judy Grace, Stacy Grooters, Elizabeth Yost Hammer, Jace Hargis, Nira Hativa, Sue Hines, Eric Hobson, Linda Hodges, Katherine Hoffman, Sallie Ives, Wayne Jacobson, Doug James, Kathleen Kane, Bruce Kelley, Diana Kelly, Joseph ("Mick") LaLopa, Bruce Larson, Marion Larson, Jean Layne, Virginia S. Lee, P. Rachel Levin, Deandra Little, Alice Macpherson, B. Jean Mandernach, Jean Martin-Williams, Leslie McBride, Daniel Mercier, Sal Meyers, Cheryl Chute Miller, Stephen Moore, Theresa Moore, Bonnie Mullinix, Ed Neal, Linda Noble, Ed Nuhfer, Leslie Ortquist-Arhens, Patrick O'Sullivan, Pratul Pathak, Donna Petherbridge, Susan Polich, Nancy Polk, Michael Potter, Edwin Ralph, Gerald Ratliff, Ann Riley, Stewart Ross, Brian Rybarczyk, "Beez" Lea Ann Schell, Jen Schoepke, Ike Shibley, Jennifer Shinaberger, Julie Sievers, Suzanne Tapp, Brigitte Valesey, Karen Ward, and Mary Wright. In addition, thanks are due to Hoag Holmgren, executive director of the POD Network, for supporting my efforts, and to David Brightman and Aneesa Davenport of Jossey-Bass for gently keeping me on track. I am also grateful to my husband, Greg, for being so good about my working longer hours to get this job done properly.

Associate editor Judith E. Miller is about the best collaborator one can have. She brought to the task her impressive talents as a scholar, especially her probing intelligence and precision communication skills, and as an administrator, which includes organization, tact, time management, and the ability to stay on top of everything. Her comments on, recommended revisions to, and close editing of just over half the accepted manuscripts were constructive and right on target, and she never missed any of the tights deadlines we had to meet. She is going to make a stellar editor of the next two volumes of *To Improve the Academy*. Jim Groccia is fortunate to have been selected as her associate editor; he will be learning from a master.

Clemson University's Office of Teaching Effectiveness and Innovation is a one-person office, so I do not have staff members to thank for their assistance in preparing this volume. But I do want to express my deep appreciation to William Weathers, Geraldine Hunter, and Sheilah Bagwell for the assistance and the wonderful company they give me, even though they belong to the instructional technology unit.

Linda B. Nilson

Clemson University

Clemson, South Carolina

April 2009

ETHICAL GUIDELINES FOR EDUCATIONAL DEVELOPERS

Preamble

EDUCATIONAL DEVELOPERS, AS PROFESSIONALS, HAVE a unique opportunity and a special responsibility to contribute to improving the quality of teaching and learning in higher education. As members of the academic community, we are subject to all the codes of conduct and ethical guidelines that already exist for those who work or study on our campuses and in our respective disciplinary associations. In addition, we have special ethical responsibilities because of the unique and privileged access we have to people and information, often sensitive information. This document provides general guidelines that can and should inform the practice of everyone working in educational development roles in higher education.

Individuals who work as educational developers come from various disciplinary areas. Some of us work in this field part-time, or for a short time; for others, this is our full-time career. The nature of our responsibilities and prerogatives as developers varies with our position in the organization; with our experience, interests, and talents; and with the special characteristics of our institutions. This document attempts to set out general ethical guidelines that should apply to most developers across a variety of settings.

Ethical guidelines indicate a consensus among practitioners about the ideals that should inform our practice as professionals, as well as those behaviors that we would identify as misconduct. Between ideals and misconduct is the area of dilemmas: where a choice seems equally right or wrong, or where our roles and responsibilities place competing—if not incompatible—demands on us, or where certain behaviors may seem questionable but there is no consensus that those behaviors are misconduct.

It is our hope that these guidelines will complement individual statements of philosophy and mission and that they will be useful to educational developers in three ways:

1. In promoting ethical practice by describing the ideals of our practice
2. In presenting a model for thinking through situations that contain conflicting choices or questionable behavior
3. In identifying those specific behaviors that we agree represent professional misconduct

Responsibilities to Clients

- Offer services to everyone within our mandate, provided that we are able to serve them responsibly
- Treat clients fairly, respecting their uniqueness; their fundamental rights, dignity, and worth; and their right to set objectives and make decisions
- Continue services only as long as the client is benefiting, discontinuing service by mutual consent; suggest other resources to meet needs we cannot or should not address
- Maintain appropriate boundaries in the relationship; avoid exploiting the relationship in any way; be clear with ourselves and our clients about our role
- Protect all privileged information and get informed consent from our client before using or referring publicly to his or her case in such a way that the person could possibly be identified

Competence and Integrity

Behavior

- Clarify professional roles and obligations
- Accept appropriate responsibility for our behavior
- Don't make false or intentionally misleading statements
- Avoid distortion and misuse of our work
- When providing services at the behest of a third party, clarify our roles and responsibilities with each party from the outset

- Model ethical behavior with coworkers and supervisees and in the larger community
- Maintain appropriate responsibility for the behavior of those we supervise

Skills and Boundaries

- Be reflective and self-critical in our practice; strive to be aware of our own belief system, values, biases, needs, and the effect of these on our work
- Incorporate diverse points of view
- Know and act in consonance with our purpose, mandate, and philosophy, integrating them insofar as possible
- Ensure that we have the institutional freedom to do our job ethically
- Don't allow personal or private interests to conflict or appear to conflict with professional duties or the client's needs
- Continuously seek out knowledge, skills, and resources to undergird and expand our practice
- Consult with other professionals when they lack the experience or training for a particular case or endeavor and to prevent and avoid unethical conduct
- Know and work within the boundaries of our competence and time limitations
- Take care of our personal welfare so we can take care of others

Others' Rights

- Be receptive to differing styles and approaches to teaching and learning and to others' professional roles and functions
- Respect the rights of others to hold values, attitudes, and opinions different from our own
- Respect the right of the client to refuse our services or to ask for the services of another
- Work against harassment and discrimination of any kind, including race, ethnicity, gender, class, religion, sexual orientation, age, and nationality

- Be aware of various power relationships with clients (for example, power based on position or on information); don't abuse our power

Confidentiality

- Keep confidential the identity of our clients, as well as our observations, interactions, or conclusions related to specific individuals or cases
- Know the legal requirements regarding appropriate and inappropriate professional confidentiality (for example, in case of murder, suicide, or gross misconduct)
- Store and dispose of records in a safe way; comply with institutional, state, and federal regulations about storage and ownership of records
- Conduct discreet conversations among professional colleagues; don't discuss clients in public places

Responsibilities to the Profession

- Attribute materials and ideas to their authors or creators
- Contribute ideas, experience, and knowledge to colleagues
- Respond promptly to requests from colleagues
- Respect your colleagues and acknowledge their differences
- Work positively for the development of individuals and the profession
- Cooperate with other units and professionals involved in development efforts
- Be an advocate for your institutional and professional missions
- Take responsibility when you become aware of gross unethical conduct in the profession

Conflict Arising from Multiple Responsibilities, Constituents, Relationships, Loyalties

We are responsible to the institution, faculty, graduate students, undergraduate students, and our own ethical values. These multiple responsibilities and relationships to various constituencies, together with competing loyalties, can lead to conflicting ethical responsibilities, for example:

- When an instructor is teaching extremely poorly and the students are suffering seriously as a result
- Conflict: responsibility of confidentiality to client teacher versus responsibility to students and institution to take some immediate action
- A faculty member wants to know how a TA, with whom we are working, is doing in his or her work or in the classroom
- Conflict: responding to faculty's legitimate concern versus confidentiality with TA
- We know firsthand that a professor is making racist or sexist remarks or is sexually harassing a student
- Conflict: confidentiality with professor versus institutional and personal ethical responsibilities, along with responsibility to students
- A fine teacher is coming up for tenure, has worked with our center or program for two years, and asks for a letter to the tenure committee
- Conflict: confidentiality rules versus our commitment to advocate for good teaching on campus and in tenure decisions

In such instances, we need to practice sensitive and sensible confidentiality:

- Consult in confidence with other professionals when we have conflicting or confusing ethical choices
- Break confidentiality in cases of potential suicide, murder, or gross misconduct
- Inform the other person or persons when we have to break confidentiality, unless to do so would be to jeopardize our safety or the safety of someone else
- Decide cases of questionable practice individually, after first informing ourselves, to the best of our ability, of all the ramifications of our actions; work to determine when we will act or not act, while being mindful of the rules and regulations of the institution and the relevant legal requirements

Conflict Arising from Multiple Roles

As educational developers, we often assume or are assigned roles that might be characterized as, for example, police officer, doctor, coach, teacher, or advocate among others. We endeavor to provide a "safe place" for our clients; we are at the same time an institutional model and a guardian for a conscience for good teaching. These multiple roles can also lead to ethical conflicts.

Some educational developers, for example, serve both as faculty developers and faculty members. As faculty we are on review committees, but through our faculty development work we have access to information that probably is not public but important to the cases involved. Given these multiple roles, it is essential to always clarify our role for ourselves, and for those with whom we are working. When necessary, we rescue ourselves.

A particular case of multiple roles needing guidelines is summative evaluation of teaching. Faculty and administrators (chairs, deans, and so on) have the responsibility for assessment of teaching for personnel decisions.

In general, we educational developers do not make summative judgments about an individual's teaching. In particular, we should never perform the role of developer and summative evaluator concurrently for the same individual, other than with that person's explicit consent and with proper declaration to any panel or committee. However, we may supply assessment tools, collect student evaluations, help individuals prepare dossiers, educate those who make summative decisions, and critique evaluation systems.

Conclusion

These guidelines are an attempt to define ethical behavior for the current practice of our profession. The core committee welcomes comments and suggestions as we continue to refine this document in light of the changes and issues confronting us as educational developers in higher education. The guidelines will be updated periodically.

We would like to thank our many colleagues who offered their thoughtful comments on earlier drafts.

In creating this document, we have referred to and borrowed from the ethical guidelines of these organizations: American Psychological Association, American Association for Marriage and Family Therapy, Guidance Counselors, Society for Teaching and Learning in Higher Education, and Staff and Educational Development Association.

Prepared by Mintz, Smith, and Warren, January 1999. Revised March 1999, September 1999, and March 2000.

TO IMPROVE THE ACADEMY

SECTION ONE

IMPROVING OUR PERFORMANCE

I

DEVELOPING COMPETENCY MODELS OF FACULTY DEVELOPERS

USING WORLD CAFÉ TO FOSTER DIALOGUE

Debra Dawson, The University of Western Ontario
Judy Britnell, Ryerson University
Alicia Hitchcock, The University of Western Ontario

Recent research by Chism (2007); Sorcinelli, Austin, Eddy, and Beach (2006); and Taylor (2005) speaks to the critical roles that faculty developers play in ensuring institutional success. Yet we have not as a profession identified the specific competencies necessary for success at different career stages. Our research generated these competencies for three faculty developer positions—entry-level, senior-level, and director—within a teaching and learning center. We used World Café, a collaborative discussion-based technique, to engage developers in building a matrix of competencies for each position and in determining how these competencies could be demonstrated.

The roles of faculty developers are rapidly evolving as teaching and learning centers grow in size, evolving from one-person operations to centers employing several developers (Sorcinelli, Austin, Eddy, & Beach, 2006). Increasingly centers are being seen as central rather than peripheral to a university's success (Gosling, McDonald, & Stockley, 2007; Harland & Staniforth, 2008; McDonald & Stockley, 2008). As Chism (2007) maintains, it is critical that we recruit new faculty developers and identify the skills and knowledge they require, given the worldwide expansion of university enrollment and the need for developers to facilitate change and innovation in higher education. However, the developer's roles must be clearly delineated for these centers to operate effectively. Furthermore, if we are to attract new members to our profession, we must identify the competencies necessary for success at different stages of the career.

In recent years, only a few scholars have researched how individuals enter our emerging profession (Gosling, 2001; McDonald & Stockley, 2008). McDonald and Stockley (2008) found no clear pathway into the field of faculty development either in North America or internationally. Rather, they uncovered myriad ways in which individuals became faculty developers. They argued that, for the profession to continue to flourish, we need a clearer idea about why and how academics become involved in faculty development activities, what facilitates their progress, and whether they would choose this as their primary occupational identity. However, we surmise that part of the reason for the faculty developers' weak occupational identity may be that we have not yet clearly articulated the competencies necessary for success. As a result, some people believe that almost anyone can be a faculty developer and marginalize practitioners within the academy (Harland & Staniforth, 2008).

Chism (2007) argues that, as an evolving profession, we have moved beyond an apprenticeship model of development and that we can now specify the skills and knowledge needed for entry. Her survey of more than 560 developers from around the world found that her respondents rated their content knowledge at entry to the profession as *some* to *moderate* for most categories, with the highest ratings going to knowledge of instructional design and active learning and the lowest to organizational change and faculty development. Both Taylor (2005) and Gosling et al. (2007) see faculty developers playing the role of change agents. Perhaps it is not surprising that those in entry-level positions know little about organizational change and do not see it as a necessary component of success for beginning faculty developers. Chism's research represents the most comprehensive overview of self-assessed skill and knowledge of faculty developers to date and makes a compelling argument for more formal career preparation. But her research does not differentiate skills, knowledge, and abilities of developers dependent on their role in the center; nor does earlier work by Wright and Miller (2000), which proposed fourteen action verbs to describe the developer's roles and responsibilities.

As centers grow in size, faculty developers may be expected to assume a variety of roles. This is exactly what Sorcinelli et al. (2006) found in both American and Canadian institutions, particularly research-doctoral or comprehensive universities. According to Wright (2002), campuswide centers typically have a director, associate director, faculty developers, and support staff. In this structure, each level requires its own skills, knowledge, abilities, and competencies.

The importance of clarifying these roles is underscored by the recent international research of Harland and Staniforth (2008), who reveal that faculty development may have many goals and vary dramatically from institution to institution in terms of the work. As some centers emphasize teaching and others research, the skills and expertise required of their employees may be quite disparate.

Our research on competencies focuses on identifying the knowledge, skills, abilities, and experiences that are demanded in three typical positions in faculty development centers, as well as demonstration of competency useful in assessing performance. According to the U.S. Department of Education, competency is "a combination of skills, abilities, and knowledge needed to perform a specific task" (U.S. Department of Education, 2002, p. 1, in Voorhees, 2001). Their competency model (see Figure 1.1) depicts the four levels that constitute a foundation for learning: traits and characteristics; skills, abilities, and knowledge; competencies; and finally demonstrations (for assessing the competencies through performance). Voorhees states that "each of the rungs of the ladder is thought to influence those rungs that appear above and underneath" (2001, p. 8). Ability can be understood as the individual's capacity to perform a task, and skills as expertise developed through practice or formal training or education. Traits constitute the innate make-up of individuals. Skills, abilities, and knowledge are acquired through many

Figure 1.1. U.S. Department of Education Competency Model

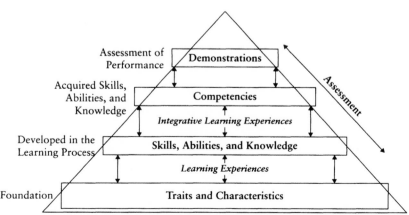

Source: U.S. Department of Education (2002); Voorhees (2001).

learning experiences. Competencies result from integrative learning experiences within numerous contexts (Voorhees, 2001).

Given the many functions that faculty developers are expected to perform—from facilitating curriculum review to enhancing teaching and learning methods within an institution, to engaging in research on the scholarship of teaching and learning (Gosling, 2001; Harland & Staniforth, 2008)—the required job competencies are problematic. The hierarchy of positions available in campuswide centers in research and comprehensive universities offers employees opportunities for career progression. This is a radical shift from a common past practice of appointing a teaching award winner as center director without recognition of the breadth of competencies required.

We believe we need to examine faculty developer roles now for two reasons. The first is to help centers expand and flourish. The second is to plan for succession during the wave of retirements we anticipate over the next decade. We need to facilitate the entry of new members into our profession. We focus here on identifying the competencies of three distinct faculty developer roles found in one type of center. We recognize that this center represents only the centralized model of faculty development and that the type of institution, its mission, and its culture all influence the nature and structure of a faculty development unit. But most of our results should extend across institutions.

Research Methodology

Like the work of Mullinix (2008), our research took "an active, constructivist approach" (p. 174) to gathering data on faculty developer competencies. We used World Café, a group work method, to facilitate discussion among our participants (Brown, 2005). Although World Café has not appeared in the literature as a research method, Heron and Reason (2001) point out that "good research is research conducted *with* people rather than *on* people" (p. 179). Cornwall and Jewkes (1995) refer to the distinctiveness of participatory research as being in the methodological context of how it is applied. The participants had a vested interest in the outcome of this work because of their affiliation with the issue being studied. Their experience also made them informants, so they were co-creators of the competency models. We have supported the notion of ownership of the findings by sharing the results of each session's discussions and the new models of representation with participants.

Our methodology differs from action research in that we, the researchers, are also affiliated with the topic being studied. However, consistent with action research, our intent was to find answers of major importance to the stakeholders, our participants. We also added cooperative inquiry into the process as a method used to inform practice (Heron & Reason, 2001). In this case, faculty developers shared knowledge about common practice, thereby creating new knowledge. It is a process of creative action that can ultimately transform our practice.

Phases to the Research

Data were collected from several sources, including Internet listservs, a roundtable discussion, and three additional discussions guided by the principles of World Café that involved faculty developers in the data analysis and interpretation. In the first stage of the research, we reviewed twenty-five short descriptions of faculty developer positions that had been gathered electronically from Canadian faculty development listservs between 2002 and 2008. All of the job descriptions were from research-intensive or comprehensive universities of middle to large size (more than fourteen thousand students, with some graduate students). We eliminated positions that focused on technology (for instance, instructional designers) or that were discipline-specific (such as a teaching and learning center for a medical school). The descriptions fell into three position categories: director of a teaching and learning center (N = 10), associate director/senior faculty developer (N = 8), and entry-level faculty developer (N = 7). We distilled the common responsibilities and typical activities for each position type. These three generic job descriptions are presented in the Appendix.

In the second phase of the research, we determined how we would collect data from as many faculty developers as possible, selecting World Café as the best way to engage many participants in a purposeful, collaborative dialogue (Brown, 2005). The method relies on a café-like atmosphere created with round tables, tablecloths, music, and food. Each table has up to six participants and a table host who stays at her table when a new group of participants joins her in the second or third round of conversation. She also summarizes each group's ten-to-fifteen-minute conversation. In this welcoming setting, each participant "has the opportunity to share what is true and meaningful" (Cunningham, 2007, p. 4). In addition to creating a hospitable environment, World Café is premised on exploring questions that matter; encouraging everyone's contribution; connecting diverse people and ideas; listening for insights, patterns, and deeper questions; and making collective knowledge visible (Brown, 2005).

Findings

Our data collection process was an iterative one in which previous sessions guided later ones, so we will present the findings for each session. We held four data-gathering sessions during 2008, at four faculty development conferences. The participants were self-selected. The first, third, and fourth sessions followed the World Café model, while the second session was a roundtable discussion. All participants granted us explicit permission to include their work (the competency models) in our research.

Session One

During a national Canadian conference (Educational Developers Caucus 2008), fourteen faculty developers participated in a ninety-minute group-work session using World Café. First, we reviewed the competency development model of the U.S. Department of Education and the rules of World Café (World Café, 2008), fielding the questions that arose. Participants then dispersed among three tables, where they were to read one of the generic job descriptions and address these questions:

- What are competencies necessary for individuals to succeed in this position?
- How would they acquire them?
- What questions do you want the next group to consider?

Each table selected a table host to facilitate the discussion and stay at the table for all three rounds of discussion. Participants were given markers and a large piece of paper for writing key words and developing a competency model for each position. Because this was World Café, participants had candy and cookies to eat during the sessions and were encouraged to work collaboratively. After fifteen minutes, they moved individually to new tables (rather than as a group) for the next discussion round in order to maximize opportunities for unique contributions to the models. After three rounds, the table hosts presented their model to the whole group, which then identified differences among the models and raised questions to refer to an international group of developers, who would assess the models for their global validity (session two). As researchers, we answered participants' questions but did not contribute to their development of the competency models.

This first session generated dramatically different models for each of the three faculty developer positions. As shown in Figure 1.2, the director's model emphasized three perceived roles, which the participants

Figure 1.2. Competency Model for the Director of a Faculty
Development Center from Session One

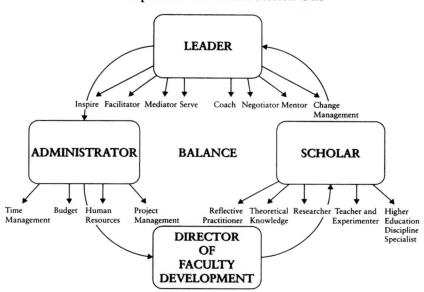

defined as leader, administrator, and scholar. For each role they also delineated several competencies, traits, and skills. Their model included as well a pathway between the roles and key word "balance" in the center of the diagram. For the entry-level position, depicted in Figure 1.3, the participants focused on all levels of the competency model (from traits to competencies) but emphasized traits and characteristics. In fact, the participants agreed that entry-level positions required incumbents with certain traits and that skills and abilities could be acquired later with training. The model for the senior faculty developer position, shown in Figure 1.4, placed high importance on the abilities the individual had developed and listed fewer competencies than the director's model.

Session Two

The next session was a sixty-minute roundtable discussion among seven faculty development experts attending an international conference (International Consortium of Educational Development 2008). The participants were asked to review the competency model of the U.S. Department of Education and then use it as a tool for analysis of the three group-developed models. They also reviewed the position descriptions.

Figure 1.3. Competency Model for the Entry-Level Faculty Developer Position from Session One

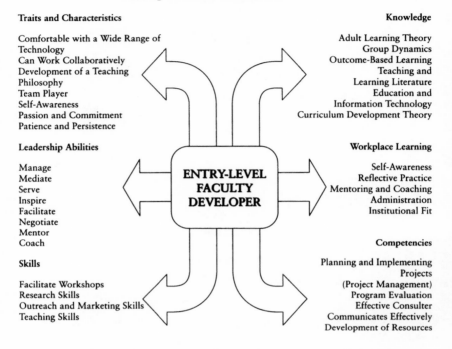

Traits and Characteristics

Comfortable with a Wide Range of
Technology
Can Work Collaboratively
Development of a Teaching
Philosophy
Team Player
Self-Awareness
Passion and Commitment
Patience and Persistence

Leadership Abilities

Manage
Mediate
Serve
Inspire
Facilitate
Negotiate
Mentor
Coach

Skills

Facilitate Workshops
Research Skills
Outreach and Marketing Skills
Teaching Skills

ENTRY-LEVEL FACULTY DEVELOPER

Knowledge

Adult Learning Theory
Group Dynamics
Outcome-Based Learning
Teaching and
Learning Literature
Education and
Information Technology
Curriculum Development Theory

Workplace Learning

Self-Awareness
Reflective Practice
Mentoring and Coaching
Administration
Institutional Fit

Competencies

Planning and Implementing
Projects
(Project Management)
Program Evaluation
Effective Consulter
Communicates Effectively
Development of Resources

Their primary tasks were to identify gaps in the group-developed models and ensure their broad cultural applicability. For each model, the participants expanded the lists of required skills, traits, knowledge, abilities, and competencies, generating such lengthy lists that we wondered if all the additions were equally valued. Fortunately, our participants suggested that we use the third session for ranking the top three traits, skills, knowledge, abilities, and competencies.

Session Three

This seventy-five-minute session was held at an international conference of faculty developers (Professional and Organizational Development Network in Higher Education 2008). We again returned to the World Café methodology, including colorful tablecloths and candy. As in session one, we first described the World Café process, reviewed the U.S. Department of Education competency model, and then asked our nineteen participants to review, in light of the original job descriptions, the competency models developed in session two. As in the first session, they had fifteen minutes

Figure 1.4. Competency Model for the Senior Faculty
Developer from Session One

for each round to explore one of the models. In addition to identifying any gaps or omissions, they were asked to rank the three most important skills, abilities, knowledge, competencies, and traits for each model.

Table 1.1 displays these rankings. A score of ten or higher designates the items that the participants perceived to be most important. For the entry-level position, it was most important to be a team player, exhibit reflective practice, communicate effectively, and have strong learning skills, knowledge of curriculum development theory, and leadership abilities in the area of facilitation. For the senior faculty developer, the most important trait was being passionate about faculty development, followed by strong interpersonal skills in working with others. In addition, the successful incumbent would demonstrate educational leadership, have formal graduate education in pedagogy, possess strong competencies as an educator, and be able to develop and implement programs. For the director's position, skill at balancing the three roles became paramount, making time management skills critical, along with competencies in facilitation, advocacy, and change management. The role of leader also within the institution gained prominence.

Table 1.1. Ranked Competencies for Faculty Developer Positions

	Entry-Level Faculty Developer	Senior-Level Faculty Developer	Director of Faculty Development
		Will Demonstrate the Following:	
Traits and Characteristics	• Team player (12) • Passion and commitment to professional development (10) • Self-awareness (8) • Can work collaboratively (6) • Open to new experiences (6) • Quick to learn and grow (6) • Creativity (4) • Patience and persistence (2) • Institutional fit (1)	• Passionate (15) • Creativity (6) • Initiative (6) • Lifelong learner (4) • Open to criticism (3) • Persistence (2) • Adaptable (1)	• Inspirer (3) • Constantly learning (1)
Skills	• Reflective practice (14) • Learning skills (10) • Teaching skills (8) • Outreach and marketing (4) • Facilitate workshops (4) • Administration (4) • Research skills (3) • Effective listening (2)	• Interpersonal skills: conflict resolution, negotiation, mediation, diplomacy, trust, listening, empathy (27) • Educational leadership (15) • Self-reflective (9) • Peer mentor/coach (3) • Model (2) • Consultation (1)	• Balance of multiple roles—leader, scholar, manager (14) • Time management (14) • Strategic planning and prioritizing (4) • Project management and assessment (2) • Delegation (2) • Financial management (2)
Knowledge	• Curriculum development theory (11) • Teaching and learning literature (9) • Adult learning theory (6)	• Formal education in pedagogy—Ph.D. or M.A. (21) • Organizational behavior (8)	• Higher education (5) • Human resources (2) • Theoretical knowledge (2)

	• Group dynamics (4) • Outcome-based learning (2) • Philosophies of education (1) • Understanding organizational culture using multiple frameworks (1)	• Literacies—information, media, technology (3)	
Abilities	Leadership abilities: • Facilitation (13) • Coach/mentor (7) • Management (6) • Service (4) • Inspire (1)		
Competencies	• Communicate effectively (13) • Planning and implementation (7) • Facilitate change and development (5) • Project management (3) • Team building (3) • Effective consultant (2) • Selection of appropriate teaching and learning strategies (1)	• Educator: course design, instructional strategies, program development strategies, evaluation strategies (29)	• Facilitator (12) • Advocacy and change management agent (11) • Relationship management (8) • Teaching (8) • Policy developer (7) • Community building (6) • Mentor; internal and external to institution (6) • SoTL research (3) • Staff and faculty coach (2) • Mediator and negotiator (2)

Note: Ranked 1st = 3 points, 2nd = 2 points, 3rd = 1 point.

The participants suggested that they would find it easier to detect gaps in the models if all of them looked like the competency model developed by the U.S. Department of Education as presented in Figure 1.1.

Session Four

For our fourth and final session, we reformatted the information in Table 1.1 into the models presented in Figures 1.5, 1.6, and 1.7. Twenty Canadian faculty developers and one international developer participated in this final ninety-minute World Café session (Council of Ontario Educational Developers 2008), complete with refreshments and background music. As in sessions one and three, we first described World Café, reviewed the U.S. Department of Education competency model, and then asked our participants to review, in light of the original job descriptions, the competency models developed thus far. At the first fifteen-minute round of discussions, participants were asked to identify *large* gaps in the traits and characteristics, skills, abilities, knowledge, and competency levels. During the second and third rounds, they were to decide, beyond the position description given, how they would expect an individual to demonstrate that he or she had achieved these competencies.

Participants developed a variety of demonstrations of competence, all listed in Table 1.2. To document reflective practice (a skill seen as especially essential for the senior faculty developer and director's positions), they recommended a portfolio. For the entry-level position, they favored the performance feedback of peers and faculty. Finally, at the director's level an incumbent must demonstrate competence in strategic planning and implementation, which requires documentation as well as integration of sound management principles.

Session four's discussions raised problematic issues and questions. How can one assess resilience, tolerance for uncertainty, and rapport and effectiveness in confidential interactions with clients—all critical competencies for the entry-level position? Is teaching experience or formal education in pedagogy more important at the senior faculty developer level? The answer may be context- or institution-dependent. Some participants believed that a director should be capable of doing the work of the other two positions, which meant having many of their traits, skills, knowledge, and competencies. Perhaps our participants required fewer traits, characteristics, abilities, and knowledge of the highest-level position (see Table 1.2) because they assumed the director would have many of them already. The session four participants identified integrity, a sense of agency, being a people person, and responsiveness as crucial director

Figure 1.5. Competency Model for the Director of a Faculty Development Center from Session Three

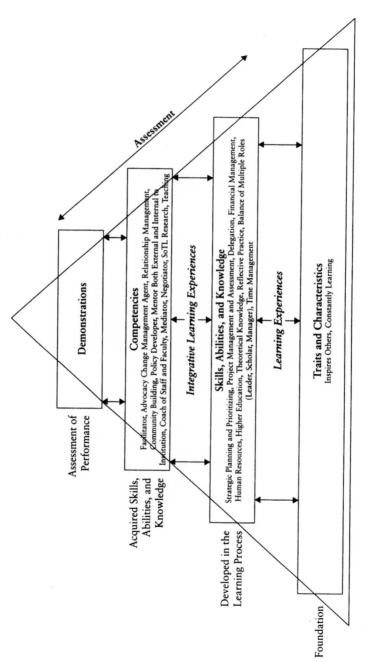

Figure 1.6. Competency Model for the Entry-Level Faculty Developer from Session Three

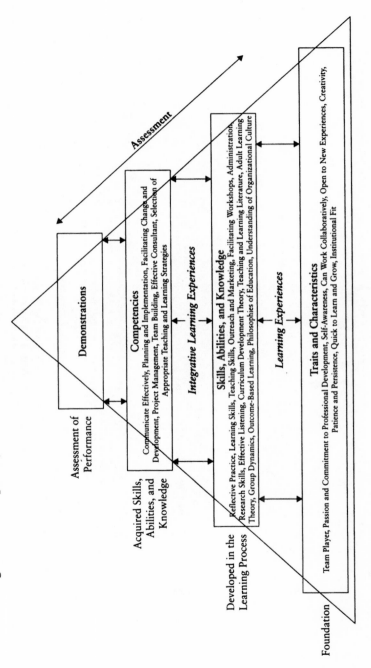

Figure 1.7. Competency Model for a Senior-Level Faculty Developer from Session Three

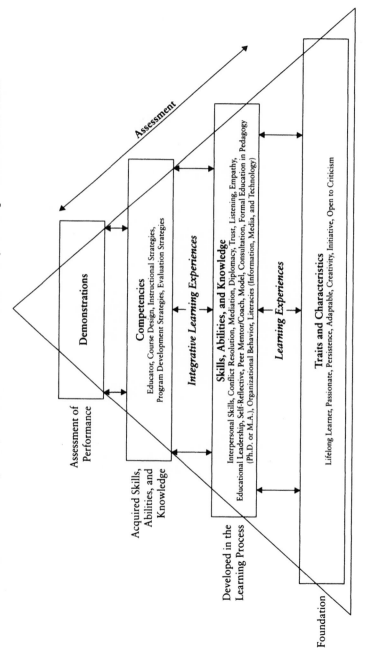

Table 1.2. Demonstration of Competency for Faculty
Developer Positions

Position	Demonstration of Competencies
Director of faculty development center	• Show evidence of self-reflection and strategies practice through a director's portfolio • Evidence of the ability to respectfully manage relationships with staff, faculty, and administration • Visible strategic plan and alignment with the university's strategic plan • Staff satisfaction as evidenced by low turnover rate • Qualitative artifacts • Performance plan with stated goals and evidence of performance
Senior-level faculty developer position	• Portfolio of reflective practice such as a teaching portfolio • Evidence of improvement in teaching development • Show evidence of ability to operate programs effectively and with good outcomes (participant evaluations) • Show evidence of program growth • Demonstrate competencies through establishing goals/ objectives and assessment • Demonstrate cultural competency • Show evidence of ability to work well with various campus groups
Entry-level faculty developer position	• Presentations with formal peer assessment • Feedback from faculty after consultation (interviews, evaluation forms) • Evidence of commitment to learning such as seeking mentorship, participation in educational programs • New programs initiated and sustained and the ability to redevelop existing programs • Teaching experience in relevant environment

traits. They also recommended assessing the values and attitudes of individuals for all three of these positions.

Discussion

Our research involving experienced faculty developers allowed multiple voices to be heard, which we believe enhanced the quality and depth of the competency models created. Using World Café as our research method—although this is uncommon—generated a richer discussion over less time than traditional discussion techniques or surveys could have accomplished. Because it maximized inclusion, this form of participatory action research was well suited to developing the three competency models (Kemmis & McTaggart, 2005). Each session we held validated and elaborated the models. Adding the voices of multiple global experts ensured broad cultural representation.

Our results delineate three distinctive competency sets necessary for success at the stages of a faculty developer's career. Those specifically from session three recommend that entry-level faculty developers be hired largely on the traits they possess, such as creativity, and a few competencies, such as project management. Senior faculty developers, on the other hand, require more fully developed interpersonal and leadership skills. At the director level, the needed competencies are much more complex: change management, facilitation, relationship management, and policy development. In contrast to Wright and Miller's study (2000), our participants speculated that directors are assuming the new role of change agent, which expands the position to advocate, policy developer, and change manager. Both Chism (2007) and Sorcinelli et al. (2006) emphasize this emerging role of developers as change agents.

Our session four participants outlined several ways to demonstrate faculty developer competencies, from peer performance review to developers' portfolios. Interestingly, Wright and Miller (2000) recommended some time ago that developers use such a portfolio to document their accomplishments. The portfolio would resemble a teaching portfolio, with a section on faculty development responsibilities and a philosophy statement. It would generate critical documentation for developers at all levels.

Conclusion

The faculty development profession is emerging, so we expect the role to change and evolve within our institutions. Arreola, Theall, and Aleamoni (2003) conceptualize that the role of faculty now must encompass discipline-specific skills and knowledge plus metaprofessional skills related to teaching, service, administration, and creative activities. Therefore, the competencies required for developers will need to expand accordingly.

In their discussion of the current "age of the network," Sorcinelli et al. (2006) posit that the rising expectations of students, faculty, and institutions are pushing the developer role toward greater complexity. They suggest that the function may move beyond institutional leader to leadership developer of new administrators. If they are correct, one or more faculty development positions will take on yet another new required competency.

Many questions about our practice raised by our participants remain to be answered:

- How well do these competency models reflect the requirements of these faculty development positions across institutional settings?
- Given different cultural perspectives on their work, how do faculty developers weigh abilities, skills, knowledge, traits, and competencies in hiring for these positions?
- As values and attitudes are seen as the human and social capital needed for the positions, what roles do they play in shaping traits and characteristics?
- What are those values and attitudes?

Defining competencies is a first step in creating the faculty developer's occupational identity, and only continuing dialogue among developers can further validate these models. We are grateful to the sixty contributors who participated in the process thus far. If these models prove viable, we must ensure that developers have the opportunities to develop the competencies identified. Without a clear career path, individuals may find it difficult to anticipate and acquire the competencies necessary for career progression. We hope this line of research will support the diverse work of developers and enhance the credibility of their work worldwide. These models should also help clarify the roles that faculty developers can play in advancing institutional missions and mandates.

Appendix A: Faculty Developer Job Descriptions
Entry-Level Faculty Developer
Overview of Responsibilities

- Participates in development, planning, implementation, and evaluation of both new and ongoing programs to support teaching and learning excellence at the university
- Under the direction of the director or senior faculty developer, collaborates with the faculties and academic units to offer discipline-specific programs as well as instruction in centralized programs offered through the teaching and learning center
- Identifies and develops opportunities for teaching project collaboration between the faculties and the teaching and learning center
- Collaborates with faculty on research related to the scholarship of teaching in various disciplines

- Promotes and supports activities and events that concern the university community on teaching and learning issues

Specific Activities

- Conducts workshops and other programs both in the center and in specific faculties on request (this will take up to 60 percent of the individual's time)
- Supports departmental teaching programs through consultations, facilitation, and workshop development
- Develops and updates the center's website content
- Identifies and creates teaching and learning resources
- Performs administrative duties related to faculty programming, including preparation of reports, scheduling, and advertising
- Assists the senior faculty developer in designing and implementing new programs
- Edits the center's newsletter
- Conducts research on the scholarship of teaching
- Offers a leadership role on specific projects

Associate Director/Senior Faculty Developer

Overview of Responsibilities

- Reports to the director
- Performs confidential consultations with faculty, graduate students, and academic units on teaching and learning issues
- Develops and implements educational programs and activities
- Facilitates curriculum development and evaluation
- Conducts and disseminates research on teaching and learning

Specific Activities

- Takes the lead on one of the center's programs, such as the graduate education initiative; develops, implements, and administers a universitywide program to support graduate student education, to include both TA training and development of other competencies related to graduate student success (for example, academic and nonacademic career preparation and advanced presentation skills)

- Plans, facilitates, and implements workshops within the center as well as educational development sessions in specific departments when requested
- Takes a leadership role in coordinating one of the center's initiatives such as new faculty orientation
- Contributes to development of print and Web-based teaching and learning resources and is expected to contribute to the field of faculty development through conducting research related to teaching and learning
- Supports faculty in their scholarship of teaching and learning
- May teach in the graduate course Theory and Practice of University Teaching
- May sit on university committees related to teaching and learning
- Aids in preparation of budgets, plans, and reports
- Collaborates with the director and staff to plan, coordinate, implement, and evaluate a variety of programs and activities to support teaching and learning at all levels
- Establishes and maintains effective networks with the regional, national, and international faculty development communities

Director of Faculty Development Center

Overview of Responsibilities

- Supervises the work of the other staff and reports to the academic VP
- Exercises leadership in visioning, planning, developing, and administering educational development programs
- Works collaboratively with the faculty of graduate studies and the university's academic and administrative units to support and advance teaching and learning initiatives on campus
- Plays an active role in research on the scholarship of teaching and learning
- Actively participates and where possible takes a leadership role in national and international associations dealing with educational development issues
- Controls the unit's budget

Specific Activities

- Consults with faculty, academic administrators, and academic units on learning and teaching issues
- Oversees development and implementation of specific educational development programs for faculty, graduate students, and postdocs
- Fosters, conducts, synthesizes, and disseminates research on teaching and learning
- Performs confidential consultations with faculty, deans, and chairs on curriculum design and strategies to enhance teaching and learning within the university
- Networks to further advance the role of faculty development in higher education
- Sits on policy-making committees related to teaching and learning within the university
- Participates on the teaching awards committee
- Coordinates the graduate course Theory and Practice of University Teaching
- Oversees the budget planning of the unit

REFERENCES

Arreola, R. A., Theall, M., & Aleamoni, L. M. (2003). *Beyond scholarship: Recognizing the multiple roles of the professoriate*. Paper presented at the 83rd annual meeting of the American Educational Research Association, Chicago.

Brown, J. (2005). *The World Café: Shaping our futures through conversations that matter*. San Francisco: Berrett-Koehler.

Chism, N.V.N. (2007, October). *A professional priority: Preparing future developers*. Paper presented at the 32nd annual meeting of the Professional and Organizational Development Network in Higher Education, Pittsburgh, PA.

Cornwall, A., & Jewkes, R. (1995). What is participatory research? *Social Science and Medicine, 41*(12), 1667–1676.

Cunningham, S. (2007). Reflections of an innovative teaching or group-work method: The World Café. *STLHE Teaching and Learning in Higher Education, 47*, 4–5.

Gosling, D. (2001). Educational development units in the UK: What are they doing five years on? *International Journal for Academic Development, 6*(1), 74–90.

Gosling, D., McDonald, J., & Stockley, D. (2007). We did it our way! Narratives of pathways to the profession of educational development. *Educational Developments, 8*(4), 1–5.

Harland, T., & Staniforth, D. (2008). A family of strangers: The fragmented nature of academic development. *Teaching in Higher Education, 13*(6), 669–678.

Heron, J., & Reason, P. (2001). The practice of co-operative inquiry: Research with rather than on people. In P. Reason & H. Bradbury (Eds.), *Handbook of action research: Participative inquiry and practice* (pp. 179–188). London: Sage.

Kemmis, S., & McTaggart, R. (2005). Participatory action research: Communicative action and the public sphere. In N. K. Denzin & Y. S. Lincoln (Eds.), *Handbook of qualitative research* (3rd ed., pp. 559–604). Thousand Oaks, CA: Sage.

McDonald, J., & Stockley, D. (2008). Pathways to the profession of educational development: An international perspective. *International Journal for Academic Development, 13*(3), 213–218.

Mullinix, B. (2008). Credibility and effectiveness in context: An exploration of the importance of faculty status for faculty developers. In D. R. Robertson & L. B. Nilson (Eds.), *To improve the academy: Vol. 26. Resources for faculty, instructional, and organizational development* (pp. 173–195). San Francisco: Jossey-Bass.

Sorcinelli, M. D., Austin, A. E., Eddy, P. L., & Beach, A. L. (2006). *Creating the future of faculty development: Learning from the past, understanding the present.* Bolton, MA: Anker.

Taylor, K. L. (2005). Academic development as institutional leadership: An interplay of person, role, strategy, and institution. *International Journal for Academic Development, 10*(1), 31–46.

U.S. Department of Education, National Center for Education Statistics. (2002). *Defining and assessing learning: Exploring competency-based initiatives* (NCES 2002–159). Prepared by Elizabeth A. Jones and Richard A. Voorhees, with Karen Paulson, for the Council of the National Postsecondary Education Cooperative Working Group on Competency-Based Initiatives. Washington, DC: Author.

Voorhees, R. A. (2001). Competency-based learning models: A necessary future. In R. A. Voorhees (Ed.), *New directions for institutional research: No. 110. Measuring what matters: Competency-based learning models in higher education* (pp. 5–13). San Francisco: Jossey-Bass.

World Café. (2008). *The World Café presents café to go: A quick reference guide for putting conversation to work.* Retrieved February 14, 2008, from www.theworldcafe.com/articles/cafetogo.pdf

Wright, A., & Miller, J. (2000). The educational developer's portfolio. *International Journal for Academic Development, 5*(1), 20–29.

Wright, D. L. (2002). Program types and prototypes. In K. H. Gillespie, L. R. Hilsen, & E. C. Wadsworth (Eds.), *A guide to faculty development: Practical advice, examples, and resources* (pp. 24–34). Bolton, MA: Anker.

2

A CONCEPTUAL FRAMEWORK FOR THE CENTER

GOING BEYOND SETTING PRIORITIES

Sally Kuhlenschmidt, Western Kentucky University

Susan Weaver, University of the Cumberlands

Susanne Morgan, Ithaca College

Management of faculty development centers can be made more effective and efficient by following a clearly articulated conceptual framework. This chapter examines three centers organized around distinct approaches. At one center, a single theme guides the choice of activities. At a second, primary faculty roles and organizational level of impact determine programming choices. At a third, a curriculum of teaching skills shapes planning and assessment. In each case, working from an explicit conceptual framework enables the center staff to more effectively prioritize competing demands and retain perspective in a changing higher education environment.

Faculty development centers often grow from some combination of the immediate needs of a particular institution, the strategic plan of the institution, and the particular talents of the director (Gillespie, Hilsen, & Wadsworth, 2002). Typically, the center offers workshops, resources, consultation, and organizational engagement and may choose those activities simply on the basis of what other centers are doing (Hellyer & Boschmann, 1993) or on serendipity. In the ideal world, center staff advocate for faculty members to plan their curriculum around a coherent framework that is explicit to students. To what extent do faculty developers employ that same level of planning in the overall curriculum of center offerings and resources?

Center directors should be intellectually proactive. They should identify overall learning objectives for the entire program, develop a global approach that reflects those objectives, and then apply that approach to all decisions, from seminar selection to assessment priorities, from book purchasing to center database management. This chapter identifies the programmatic and administrative advantages of a conceptual framework for center management. Although some level of flexibility and responsiveness to the moment will always be necessary, deeper and long-term learning by faculty will best be accomplished if the staff has an intellectual basis for center offerings and daily choices.

The staff at three centers have started the process of structuring planning, activities, and assessment around a conceptual framework. After introducing the idea of a conceptual framework for center programs, we will review how each institution has begun to realize this goal. The three programs represent differing degrees of conceptual complexity. A small private college uses a single theme from which all activities and decisions follow. A medium-sized private comprehensive has devised a plan based on faculty role and organizational level of impact to decide what is critical for the institution. A large public comprehensive institution uses a curriculum to categorize, select, and assess activities. We recount the development of each institution's approach as well as the specifics of implementation, the assessment potential of the approach, and special issues for that particular approach.

A Conceptual Framework

As education specialists, faculty developers appreciate the value of objectives for advancing student learning. In a well-designed course the objectives direct selection of activities and the nature of assessments. Well-written objectives advance student motivation and help the instructor sustain interest and direct energies. At the end of the term, the success or failure of the course is judged against the learning objectives. Without learning objectives the instructor will waste time on nonproductive activities. Similarly, a faculty development center can benefit from a conceptually structured program to guide the focus of services. Hellyer and Boschmann (1993) approached the task of planning center actions by seeking normative data on what most centers did. However, a normative approach fails to match local needs, misses unique opportunities, and focuses on actions rather than learning outcomes. Cox (2001) proposed using faculty learning communities as a major center activity, arguing for the value of their intellectual power, an advantage of a conceptual framework. Without a guiding vision, the center ends up defined by others or implicitly self-defined as remediating or "preaching to the converted"

(Chism & Szabo, 1996). Everley and Smith (1996) point out that transitioning from soft to hard money works best when the center serves the values and goals of the institutional mission. Center staff need to make the institutional connection explicit as part of their planning process.

What is a conceptual framework? It is a coherent, selective vision relevant to the particular situation that guides the faculty development program over time and through changing trends. Although responsive to themes of current significance, a conceptual framework is grounded in research, best practice, or logical structures that are likely to endure. The goal of such a framework is meeting the long-term learning needs of the target population. It reflects truth, as currently understood, about what faculty members need.

A conceptual framework is not a laundry list of unrelated activities. It is not everything and anything that might fall within a description of a faculty development unit. Just as a theory that explains everything is useless, so too is an approach that fulfills every intellectual agenda. It is probably not simply a scaled-down version of the institution's strategic plan but a plan with center ownership.

Why adopt a conceptual framework in contrast to reacting only to external influences? Because moving toward a clear goal is a source of power. Having a framework grounded in what is researched or logically understood enables the unit to present a coherent plan to faculty and to persuade by ideas. A clear rationale for center activities enables the developer to think of the program as a whole and then identify parts that should be strengthened or abandoned. It invites complex assessments, such as appropriate balance among activities. It allows center staff to be proactive and thus drive conversation on campus. It enables more effective marketing and more persuasive arguments for resources. It also guides decisions about what direction *not* to pursue. A conceptual framework enables the center mission to absorb new ideas but still make progress on established ideas.

Of course, adopting a conceptual framework brings challenges. The most obvious one is how to create or select that framework. Who has the responsibility for choosing? Is it a leadership task for the director or a collaborative one for an advisory council? What factors should be considered in identifying the framework? How local should it be? How much of the larger society should it reflect? Will it be research-based or theoretical? Will it emphasize the ideal or the real?

Having a framework makes some aspects of center work easier. It eases directional decision making and sets a standard against which to measure decisions, from purchasing choices to the content of administrative reports. It should influence the content of center educational messages (for example, emphasizing critical thinking or technology) as well as their form (for instance, face-to-face seminars versus online workshops). At a minimum, a conceptual framework can lend coherence to center activities.

The relationship of the framework to the institution's goals is also important. If the framework diverges too much from those goals, the center staff will find itself at odds with administrative expectations and resources. If it overlaps with current institutional goals too much, it may lack the flexibility to adapt to changes in administrators who bring new interpretations of institutional goals. If nothing else, thinking through these issues prepares the center staff to respond more immediately and more substantively to queries and complaints. Having a conceptual framework means the unit has considered the institutional mission deeply and broadly and will be better prepared to deal with changing administrations—to retain what is critical to the unit and adapt to what is new and worthwhile.

The Central Theme Approach: Critical Thinking Across the Curriculum

The University of the Cumberlands is a private liberal arts college with about fifteen hundred undergraduate and eight hundred graduate students. The Center for Teaching and Learning (CTL) was established in August 2005 as part of the Quality Enhancement Plan (QEP) required for reaffirmation of accreditation by the Southern Association of Colleges and Schools. The CTL staff consists of a half-time administrative assistant and a full-time director who also serves as director of the QEP in cooperation with the QEP Steering Committee. The five-year QEP emphasizes critical thinking in reading and writing during the first two years, adding information literacy and oral communication in later years. The central organizing theme, Critical Thinking Across the Curriculum, grew out of two years of meetings with various stakeholders across campus.

Three mandates drive CTL programming. The first is to support faculty efforts to enhance critical thinking in the classroom. The second, in recognition that critical thinking involves both skills and dispositions (Leamnson, 1999), is to furnish cocurricular student programming that nurtures affective dispositions such as truth seeking and fair-mindedness (Facione, 1990). The third is to organize complementary professional development, including a summer retreat for a cadre of eight to ten faculty each year. Cadre members are charged with infusing their courses with critical thinking in reading, writing, oral communication, and information literacy, and then assessing their efforts.

Although a few CTL programs are specifically for either faculty or students, most are open to faculty, staff, and students. Inclusiveness characterizes the campus culture and serves to increase the number of participants, enhance dynamics, and showcase efforts that incorporate critical thinking into areas of special interest and expertise. For example, every semester the CTL organizes a series of critical thinking seminars in which students and faculty discuss a chosen theme from among disciplinary perspectives. This semester, the subject of food is being examined from political, biological, health, and literary perspectives. Another example is an annual debate team event that features a short video about a controversial topic, followed by formal debate of the issue. In addition to reinforcing critical thinking as a campuswide initiative, these events promote networking that can lead to future collaborations or consultations.

ASSESSMENT OF THE APPROACH. Formative and summative assessments are built into the QEP plan. The CTL director uses feedback from the steering committee, workshop evaluations, email questionnaires, anonymous online surveys, focus groups, and informal communications to prepare an annual assessment report that reflects on the goals, outcomes, assessments, results, and recommendations. In addition, the university measures global success in advancing critical thinking through standardized testing of first-year students and juniors to track progress in reading, writing, and critical thinking.

The main difficulty in evaluating the Central Theme Model is isolating programming effects from confounding factors such as the students' natural transition from adolescence to young adulthood and their experience of living away from home, taking college classes, holding a job, or having new friends. Attendance and survey responses are suspect as measures because they are not direct assessments, and given a modest response rate the small student population yields a low number of responses. Further, even faculty who do not attend a workshop can spawn student reflection and growth. In reality, decisions to add or drop a program are based on best fit for the theme, stated needs and interests, or perceived needs.

CHALLENGES AND ISSUES. The theme affords the CTL name recognition and branding. The university's long-term commitment to critical thinking and the center's reputation for excellence make the Central Theme Model ideal. However, living up to varied expectations can be challenging, especially as the university establishes new programs and hires new faculty. As new needs and initiatives emerge, the director is tempted to overextend. On the other hand, the QEP mission plays heavily into development of these new programs and into assessment of the general education curriculum, thus granting the CTL security.

Faculty Roles by Organizational Level Approach

Ithaca College is a private comprehensive college with six thousand undergraduate and five hundred graduate students. Begun as a music conservatory, it has strong professional schools and liberal arts majors. Most of the 450 faculty members are full-time. The Center for Faculty Excellence (CFE) is a virtual center consisting of a webpage and activities implemented solely by a half-time faculty member.

Simply providing workshops to interested faculty was inefficient and ineffective in creating systemic change. Faculty perceived teaching as fundamental but expressed greater concern about accomplishing scholarship. The actions of department chairs and other leaders (Wergin, 2007) did not consistently reflect institutional priorities. The faculty culture varied dramatically from school to school, and institutional identity was weak.

Addressing these issues entailed systematic intervention focused on the roles in which faculty were required to succeed. Setting faculty roles by organizational level approach is designed to build a faculty of effective teachers, productive scholars, and engaged institutional citizens by supporting them at the individual, departmental, and institutional levels (see Table 2.1).

When previous CFE activities were mapped onto the table, it became clear that most were for individuals and focused on teaching, and few supported other areas. Now each event must fit in a cell, and the director monitors the grid to ensure impact on all faculty roles and at all levels. In place of the previous ad hoc workshops are structured public conversations about one of the three professional areas, scheduled on faculty request. Rather than the occasional faculty colloquium of the past, the CFE offers a half-day conference featuring faculty research in each of the faculty handbook's five types of scholarship, an important institutional concern. In addition, all faculty participating in key all-college programs

---

Table 2.1. Choices in Faculty Development Activities

Organizational Level/ Faculty Role	Individual	Departmental	Institutional
Teaching			
Scholarship			
Service and citizenship			

must attend a four-day, year-end workshop themed around an institutional priority. At the department level, chairs now have their own series of events designed to increase the consistency and effectiveness of their work. Addressing the individual and institutional levels are two programs: a seminar for tenure-eligible faculty that supports their teaching, scholarship, and citizenship; and an all-college, group-based mentoring program, supplemented by departmental efforts, designed to create an institution-wide faculty culture.

ASSESSMENT OF THE APPROACH. The approach highlights a broad definition of faculty development and permits analysis of the institutional relevance of individual support. By categorizing activities in terms of the grid, a center that adopts this approach can quickly identify imbalances across cells and areas for further attention. It may discontinue some activities if too many occupy the same cell. Or it can reframe activities to serve at another organizational level. The grid can also facilitate conversation with administrators about expanding the center's mission to increase its organizational impact.

CHALLENGES AND ISSUES. This approach might suggest that a center be all things to all people—an unfeasible goal in a time of limited resources. However, the grid can inform reduction or redirection of services as well as expansion. For example, it guided the CFE's decision to discontinue ad hoc workshops and increase support for department chairs.

The Curriculum Approach

Western Kentucky University is a public master's-level institution with about nineteen thousand students. Its Faculty Center for Excellence in Teaching (FaCET) has been in existence about seventeen years and has a full-time staff of three, plus a part-time faculty associate and student workers. Its recent initiatives have addressed civic engagement and internationalism.

About six years ago the director became concerned that FaCET seminars were scattered in content and its programming might be overemphasizing some key aspects of instruction at the expense of others. So she devised a checklist of topics that the staff initially used for program assessment. The goal was to offer training, either a seminar or a print product, in each major area at least once during a three-year period. As part of a database overhaul, the staff decided to update the checklist and integrate it into the new database, devising a tool to qualitatively evaluate the depth and breadth of the program.

The FaCET staff started from the existing checklist and added topics, developing a large number of themes. Then the professional staff plus two faculty associates individually sorted the themes into general categories. The group resolved discrepancies and revised categories until all members agreed the system contained essential, enduring components of instruction. The staff then took this curriculum to the FaCET faculty advisory council, which approved the system with very little discussion.

The system has seven major curricular areas, each with subcategories (the reporting protocol focuses on the major areas but uses the subcategories for some activities):

1. Understanding the student (major student variables or characteristics that influence learning; student diversity)

2. Teacher issues (career development issues; teaching assessment; special needs of faculty subgroups)

3. Preparing to teach (principles of effective teaching; learning basics; legal and ethical issues; course structuring; lesson structuring; class types)

4. Course in progress (active learning theory and methods; teaching methods; student behavior management; learning assessment; interdisciplinary content, such as writing)

5. Course technology (distributed education; technology applied to teaching)

6. Curriculum development (integrating courses with university and department objectives; managing outcomes)

7. Administrative experiences (academic leadership; departmental leadership; policies and procedures)

Staff members use the curriculum to plan FaCET programs and activities. Each event, resource item, and consultation is entered in the database within one of the seven categories. Individual faculty receive a report of their FaCET activities, called a Teaching Development Record. The seminars they attend are classified into the seven topic areas, showing the areas in which a faculty member was active or inactive. The goal of this reporting is to increase the complexity the faculty's and department heads' thinking about instruction. In planning the seminar schedule every year, FaCET staff members review the distribution of seminars across the seven categories with an eye on addressing each area over the set three-year period. Although university goals sometimes encourage heavy emphasis in one area for a year, the staff is able to restore balance in subsequent years. This planning process revealed that civic engagement activities did not fit into the curriculum, so the director gave up significant responsibility for a university civic engagement program.

The consultation data showed that FaCET staff members were doing a considerable amount of career planning with faculty. The data also made evident that a large number of the consultations fell in the category of course technology. This emphasis, along with faculty hiring trends, enabled the director to advocate successfully for a new position.

The database overall also presented the opportunity to bring more order and accessibility to the books, equipment, and other materials that had accumulated in the FaCET resource library. A skilled graduate student updated the library database and categorized all resources by the seven curricular areas. A report showed the neglected topics and guided later purchasing decisions. The database also enabled production of bibliographies for each area of resource. When the Teaching Development Records were mailed out, these bibliographies were offered to anyone wanting to find resources for an empty category.

ASSESSMENT OF THE APPROACH. FaCET staff members have found the curriculum approach to be a useful intellectual and administrative tool. It has given them a new perspective on activities and has allowed more precise planning and purchasing. Because they can compare the curriculum against the goals, accountability is inherent in the system. Review of the curriculum with each activity keeps these goals uppermost in staff thinking and offers a far more satisfying form of accountability than reporting seminar attendance or number of books checked out.

FaCET personnel are still exploring the potential of the curriculum approach. Beyond usage counts, they can track the content areas that appeal most and least to faculty and decide whether to offer more events and resources on popular topics or promote the neglected one. These data can then buttress requests for more resources in particular areas. They also allow the staff to compare the resources being provided with those the faculty want, and to customize activities accordingly. When faculty or administrators ask the center to organize an activity, the staff can compare activity to the curriculum to determine its appropriateness as a center project.

The greatest assessment limitation of this approach may be too much information, leading to difficulties interpreting the data and underuse of the data. In addition, if the curriculum fails to accommodate a new initiative, the available data may be useless for responding to that need.

CHALLENGES AND ISSUES. Developing a locally relevant, well-structured curriculum takes time. Adopting an existing curriculum is easier and faster, but it may not meet local needs. The developers also have to keep in mind the durability of the curriculum. Can it incorporate current trends? Should it be designed for long-term or short-term goals? Another major issue is whom to involve in determining the curriculum. Although it is tempting to get input from advisory councils and administrators, perhaps even the whole faculty, this effort is simply not practical in many circumstances. Too much input can impede the process and produce a compromised curriculum. On the other hand, insufficient input can yield a curriculum that is divorced from real needs or tied too closely to an individual director's style.

The curriculum itself and how it is communicated can also help or hinder the project. If the curriculum is not easy to use and clear to all concerned parties, inconsistent implementation or conflicting understandings will doom the project. Although it may be tempting to incorporate every possible topic into the curriculum, no center can keep such broad promises. In addition, curricular categories must be consistent, reliable, mutually exclusive, and as simple as possible because new staff will have to be trained to use them.

The final challenge is addressing change. One reason to have a curriculum-based approach is to track changes in center activities over time. But change will come to the curriculum as well, interfering with that tracking. Ideally, a strong curriculum endures with minimal changes to permit long-term comparisons and trend mapping. The areas should be general enough to accommodate changes and minimize loss of long-term data. However, new presidential initiatives, major teaching innovations, and the like will eventually force restructuring of the curriculum.

Conclusion

Center staff wishing to adopt a conceptual framework will have to consider several factors. The approach chosen must fit within the overall campus strategic plan, which should in turn flow from the institutional mission. Accreditation expectations may also play a role in selecting an approach. The viability of the plan in the eyes of administrators and faculty is another consideration. If the approach is to be used beyond the confines of the center, then consider how it will appear to all constituencies and fit into campus culture. However, do not let fear of constituencies undermine the truth of the vision. In addition, the available resources and other constraints on center staff will influence which type of approach is selected. If only limited resources are available, then a more focused approach is desirable.

If the clientele are diverse, then the approach needs to support them and may be correspondingly more layered.

Sometimes center staff may not have a choice in their approach. The specific conceptual framework may be chosen by another, and the center is expected to fulfill the initiative. In these cases, it may be possible to reconcile needs behind the scenes. For example, a center may have a two-tiered approach. That is, it may have core concepts described with language unlikely to change (such as objectives, activities, and assessments) and then have a marketing approach laid over this deeper set of concepts (for example, civic engagement). The marketing approach may change for the sake of novelty and currency, but the staff understand what the deeper message is and infuse it into the surface idea.

Of course, a conceptual framework may become obsolete with time. New circumstances may call for a new theme, or the approach's language and concepts may not keep pace with changes in understanding. Center staff should review the framework regularly and adapt it as necessary. Finally, a strategy for assessing the approach requires advance planning. How will a director know if the approach is working for the center? How well is it meeting the goals and needs of the unit? What are the criteria for success? The fact that the approach must change eventually does not invalidate its usefulness for the next five to ten years, or even longer.

Whether a center's framework is based on one of the approaches outlined in this chapter, is a hybrid, or is grown from local needs, working from an explicit conceptual framework imparts a structure that offers perspective and prioritizing for daily activities and a strong mission for long-term success.

REFERENCES

Chism, N.V.N., & Szabo, B. (1996). Who uses faculty development services? In L. Richlin & D. DeZure (Eds.), *To improve the academy: Vol. 15. Resources for faculty, instructional, and organizational development* (pp. 115–128). Stillwater, OK: New Forums Press.

Cox, M. (2001). Faculty learning communities: Change agents for transforming institutions into learning organizations. In D. Lieberman & C. Wehlburg (Eds.), *To improve the academy: Vol. 19. Resources for faculty, instructional, and organizational development* (pp. 69–93). Bolton, MA: Anker.

Everley, M. L., & Smith, J. (1996). Making the transition from soft to hard funding: The politics of institutionalizing instructional development programs. In L. Richlin & D. DeZure (Eds.), *To improve the academy: Vol. 15. Resources for faculty, instructional, and organizational development* (pp. 209–230). Stillwater, OK: New Forums Press.

Facione, P. (1990). *Critical thinking: A statement of expert consensus for purposes of educational assessment and instruction.* Millbrae, CA: California Academic Press.

Gillespie, K. H., Hilsen, L. R., & Wadsworth, E. C. (Eds.). (2002). *A guide to faculty development: Practical advice, examples, and resources.* Bolton, MA: Anker.

Hellyer, S., & Boschmann, E. (1993). Faculty development programs: A perspective. In D. L. Wright & J. P. Lunde (Eds.), *To improve the academy: Vol. 12. Resources for faculty, instructional, and organizational development* (pp. 217–224). Stillwater, OK: New Forums Press.

Leamnson, R. (1999). *Thinking about teaching and learning: Developing habits of learning with first year college and university students.* Sterling, VA: Stylus.

Wergin, J. F. (Ed.). (2007). *Leadership in place: How academic professionals can find their leadership voice.* Bolton, MA: Anker.

3

A CONCEPTUAL FRAMEWORK FOR HIGHER EDUCATION FACULTY MENTORING

Pamela S. Lottero-Perdue, Towson University

Steve Fifield, University of Delaware

There is considerable variability in conceptions of faculty mentoring in higher education. Rather than view this diversity as a problem, we see it as a potential resource that can inform design, implementation, and evaluation of faculty mentoring. To learn from this diversity, we review the literature on faculty mentoring in higher education to create a conceptual framework of mentoring. The conceptual framework is a tool that program administrators, participants, and evaluators can use to adapt mentoring to the unique needs of particular faculty and institutions.

Claims about the benefits of mentoring are widespread in professional and career development literature (Allen, Eby, Poteet, Lentz, & Lima, 2004; Luna & Cullen, 1995; Morrison-Beedy, Aronowitz, Dyne, & Mkandawire, 2001; Spencer, Tribe, & Sokolovskaja, 2004). But a close reading of conceptual, programmatic, and empirical studies reveals considerable variability in how mentoring is understood and put into practice

This publication was made possible by Grant Number 2 P20 RR016472-06, under the INBRE program of the National Center for Research Resources, a component of the National Institutes of Health (NIH). Its contents are solely the responsibility of the authors and do not necessarily represent the official views of NIH. This publication was also based upon work supported by the National Science Foundation (NSF) under Grant Nos. EPS-0408729 and EPS-0814251. Any opinions, findings, and conclusions or recommendations expressed in this material are those of the authors and do not necessarily reflect the views of the NSF. Thanks to Gabriele Bauer and three anonymous reviewers.

(Borisoff, 1998; Davidson & Foster-Johnson, 2001; Goodwin, Stevens, Goodwin, & Hagood, 2000; Healy & Welchert, 1990; Mertz, 2004; Sands, Parson, & Duane, 1991; Wunsch, 1994a). The many meanings and practices collected under the term *mentoring* suggest that we take care when looking to the literature for help in designing, implementing, and evaluating mentoring.

One response to variable conceptions of mentoring is to develop a single definition broad enough to cover all circumstances. A few mentoring researchers have proposed consensus definitions or unifying models of mentoring (Carmin, 1988; Galbraith, 2001; Healy, 1997; Healy & Welchert, 1990; Mertz, 2004). For instance, Carmin (1988), citing Kram (1980), Levinson (1978), and Parham (1981), suggested that "a mentoring relationship occurs in a learning context and is a continuing, one-to-one relationship between an older and/or more experienced individual and a younger and/or less experienced person" (p. 10). This attempt to define common ground embodies the paradox of putatively universal definitions of mentoring: for some settings they are too broad, while for others they are too narrow. Carmin's definition seems to combine the roles of mentor and counselor, which some have argued are distinct relationships (Mertz, 2004). On the other hand, peer and multiple mentoring (deJanasz & Sullivan, 2004; Pololi, Knight, Dennis, & Frankel, 2002) are excluded by the hierarchical and dyadic nature of mentoring in this definition.

Rather than seek a single conception of mentoring, in this chapter we review recent literature on faculty-to-faculty mentoring in higher education (hereafter referred to as "faculty mentoring") to build a conceptual framework that systematically identifies and connects key components of mentoring as reflected in a variety of programs. The framework is analytic and synthetic, not prescriptive or predictive. It captures diverse conceptions of faculty mentoring and is an interpretive structure through which to understand and use this richness in local reinvention of mentoring.

The framework facilitates critical reading of mentoring literature with pointed questions: Who or what is the intended beneficiary? Who or what initiates and sustains mentoring? What is the relationship between the mentor(s) and mentee(s)? What topics do they engage in their interactions? What actions do they take in regard to one another? The framework does not dictate how one ought to conceive of faculty mentoring in any particular setting. Instead, it synthesizes the literature to foreground alternative perspectives on and possibilities for mentoring. As we discuss in the Implications section, the framework can contribute to more effective and purposeful choices in designing, participating in, and evaluating faculty mentoring.

Methods

The work that led to this chapter began with what we thought would be a straightforward literature review for an evaluation of a university science faculty mentoring program. We simply wanted to know how others defined *mentoring*. Reading broadly in foundational literature on mentoring (Allen et al., 2004; Cohen, 1995; Eby, Lockwood, & Butts, 2006; Kram, 1985; Levinson, 1978) and about mentoring in educational settings (Boice, 1990; Bova, 1995; Luna & Cullen, 1995; Sands et al., 1991; Wunsch, 1994b), we soon realized that there was no simple answer to our question. In response, we created a provisional conceptual framework for mentoring definitions to identify patterns in the literature. For us, a mentoring definition provides insight into what authors explicitly or implicitly understand mentoring to be. Using a qualitative, grounded-theory approach (Charmaz, 2000; Glaser & Strauss, 1967), we identified recurrent themes across definitions of mentoring.

We then returned to our initial concern with the nature of faculty mentoring in higher education. Using online databases and reference lists in publications, we narrowed and deepened our literature review to include peer-reviewed articles, edited book chapters, and reports on faculty mentoring in higher education from 1996 to 2007. We also included a few widely cited publications dating back to the 1980s. We identified eighty-eight articles, book chapters, books, and reports for analysis. (A full bibliography is available from the first author.) Moving iteratively between these publications and the provisional framework, we extended and refined the framework to reflect clear patterns in how faculty mentoring is conceptualized in the literature.

Results and Discussion

The resulting conceptual framework of faculty mentoring contains five dimensions: (1) intended beneficiaries, (2) locus of control, (3) relationship characteristics, (4) topics, and (5) actions. We describe these dimensions with the aid of six diagrams that reflect the range of conceptions of faculty mentoring that we found in the literature. Each diagram is a visual outline that illustrates elements or options within the key dimensions of faculty mentoring identified in our literature review. Lines and arrows in each diagram are organizational tools to represent how one element might be broken into subelements. For example, Figure 3.1, discussed in detail in the following section, depicts the intended beneficiaries of a mentoring relationship. Arrows emanating from the central "intended beneficiaries" box identify these beneficiaries as institutions, groups, and

**Figure 3.1. Intended Beneficiaries in the Mentoring
Relationship or Program**

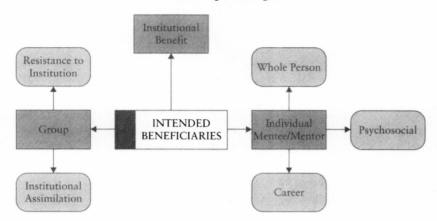

individuals. Further, individuals may be intended to receive career-related
or psychosocial benefits, or benefits better described as addressing the
whole person.

Intended Beneficiaries

Certain people, groups, and institutions are intended beneficiaries of faculty
mentoring (see Figure 3.1). Mentees, who are usually junior faculty members, are the primary intended beneficiaries (Gray & Birch, 2007; Luckhaupt
et al., 2005; Schrodt, Cawyer, & Sanders, 2003). Statements about providing
"support [for] new faculty" (Reder & Gallagher, 2007, p. 327) are common
in descriptions of the purposes of mentoring. Many mentoring definitions
suggest that mentors, who are usually senior faculty, can also benefit from
reciprocal mentoring relationships (Gibson, 2004; Jackson et al., 2003;
Steiner, Curtis, Lanphear, Vu, & Main, 2004; Yun & Sorcinelli, 2009).

Kram (1983, 1985) was the first to describe mentoring as involving
both career and psychosocial functions. Henry, Stockdale, Hall, and
Deniston (1994) described reciprocal mentoring as involving an exchange
of career-related and psychosocial benefits. Intended career-related benefits
of academic mentoring include gaining knowledge, improving teaching,
acquiring grants, collaborating and networking, developing a research
program, publishing, and achieving tenure (St. Clair, 1994). Intended psychosocial benefits include feeling accepted by the academic community,
becoming familiar with the campus climate, and receiving social support.
Career-related benefits for mentees are the dominant or exclusive focus of

most faculty mentoring programs and relationships (Berk, Berg, Mortimer, Walton-Moss, & Yeo, 2005; Hardwick, 2005; Illes, Glover, Wexler, Leung, & Glazer, 2000; Morzinski, 2005). Faculty mentoring is also intended to provide psychosocial benefits for mentees (Cawyer, Simonds, & Davis, 2002; deJanasz & Sullivan, 2004; Snelson et al., 2002). Less frequently, mentoring is seen as a source of psychosocial (Gammack et al., 2004; Morzinski, 2005; Pierce, 1998) and career-related benefits (Campbell, 1992; Smith, Smith, & Markham, 2000) for mentors. A few articles dissolve the longstanding dualism of career versus psychosocial benefits to describe mentoring in which participants are treated as whole people with intersecting career, psychosocial, and personal worlds (Angelique, Kyle, & Taylor, 2002; Jordan-Zachery, 2004; McGuire & Reger, 2003).

Institutional entities (that is, universities, colleges, departments, disciplinary associations) can be the intended beneficiaries of faculty mentoring. Mentoring in these cases is intended to help advance an unspoken contract between institutions and people in which "each expects to give and receive something in the relationship" (Campbell, 1992, p. 75). Institutions may expect mentoring to aid socialization of faculty into organizational culture (Fayne & Ortquist-Ahrens, 2006; Kirchmeyer, 2005; Snelson et al., 2002), and these institutions may expect to benefit from mentoring by increasing faculty retention (Johnsrud, 1994; Wunsch, 1994b), faculty diversity (Blackwell, 1989; Davidson & Foster-Johnson, 2001), and scholarly productivity (Bergen & Connelly, 1988; Mundt, 2001; Olson & Connelly, 1995).

Groups within institutions are also sometimes conceived as beneficiaries of faculty mentoring. These groups include those who are or have been minorities in academia, including women (Wunsch & Johnsrud, 1992), African Americans (Green & King, 2002), and Hispanic women (Bova, 1995). In these instances mentoring is intended to help members of minority groups cope with and challenge inequality in academia (Moody, 2004). This conception sometimes explicitly resists mentoring-as-assimilation and envisions mentoring as a means for participants "to evolve as change agents in the institution" (Angelique et al., 2002, p. 197).

Locus of Control

Locus of control concerns who has influence over mentoring relationships (see Figure 3.2). In the general literature on mentoring, locus of control is often referenced through the distinction between formal programs (administered by third parties as an institutional program) and informal (managed by mentoring participants) (Chao, Walz, & Gardner, 1992; Ragins & Cotton, 1999). Reflecting a pattern in the literature we reviewed,

Figure 3.2. Locus of Control of the Mentoring Relationship or Program

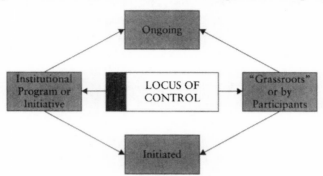

we refine the formal–informal dichotomy by considering who initiates mentoring and who manages it as it proceeds.

In formal mentoring programs, administrators generally have a role in both initiation and ongoing management (Boice, 1990; Lemel & Sullivan-Catlin, 2000; Levy et al., 2004; Pololi et al., 2002; Tracy, Jagsi, Starr, & Tarbell, 2004). There is considerable variation within this generalization. In some cases participants and administrators co-initiate and co-manage mentoring (Gray & Birch, 2007; Mundt, 2001). Other mentoring programs are so highly structured that they resemble administered faculty development programs (Morzinski, 2005). In practice, many faculty members (including the authors of this chapter) experience formal mentoring when they are assigned a mentor by a supervisor or administrator, and the pair is then left to their own devices to work out the relationship.

In informal mentoring, participants find one another and create relationships. We found few explicit accounts of this kind of mentoring in the literature, though it is a deeply rooted notion of how mentoring develops (cf., Levinson, 1978). One notable example is the New Scholars Network, a program designed and maintained by its participants, not university administrators (Angelique et al., 2002). Morrison-Shetlar and Heinrich (1999); Limbert (1995); and Jacelon, Zucker, Staccarini, and Henneman (2003) describe other mentoring programs that were created and managed by the participants.

Relationship Characteristics

Relationship characteristics are about the participants and how they interact (see Figure 3.3). The key characteristics we draw from the literature are (1) number of participants, (2) relationship between participants,

Figure 3.3. Characteristics of the Mentoring Relationship or Program

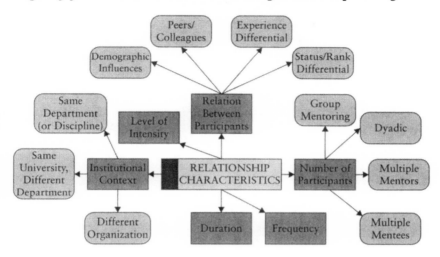

(3) role fluidity, (4) institutional context, (5) level of intensity, (6) frequency, and (7) duration.

NUMBER OF PARTICIPANTS. Mentoring relationships can be dyadic or involve multiple mentors, multiple mentees, or groups. Dyadic mentoring relationships are the most common in the foundational literature on mentoring (Carmin, 1988; Kram, 1980, 1983, 1985; Levinson, 1978). Accounts of faculty mentoring often include explicit statements about the one-on-one, coupled, or paired nature of mentoring, as well as implicit assumptions that two faculty members form the relationship (Boice, 1990; Gibson, 2004; Jackson et al., 2003).

Some scholars suggest that faculty mentees often need multiple mentors simultaneously (Cawyer et al., 2002; Dixon-Reeves, 2003; King & Cubic, 2005) to "construct a mentoring community based on a diverse set of helpers instead of relying on a single mentor" (Chesler & Chesler, 2002, pp. 51–52). Less common are descriptions of one mentor with multiple mentees (Harnish & Wild, 1994; Levy et al., 2004).

Group mentoring occurs when many faculty members come together to form a mentoring community. Most often this involves junior faculty helping one another as peer mentors (Gammack et al., 2004; Gray & Birch, 2007; Waitzkin, Yager, Parker, & Duran, 2006), but it also includes groups of senior and junior faculty members (Cox, 1997; Lemel & Sullivan-Catlin, 2000). Group mentoring occurs as a stand-alone approach (Green & King, 2002) and in combination with mentor-mentee pairs (Fayne & Ortquist-Ahrens, 2006).

RELATIONSHIP BETWEEN PARTICIPANTS. The mentoring literature describes mentees, mentors, and their relationship in several ways. Mentees and mentors can differ or be similar to one another in terms of rank, experience, and demographics. Further, mentoring participants might have stable roles as either a mentor or a mentee, or fluid roles that alternate among or combine the characteristics of mentors and mentees.

The most common distinction between mentors and mentees is a difference in rank or tenure (August & Waltman, 2004; Boice & Turner, 1989; Smith et al., 2000). Johnsrud (1994) suggested that "mentoring for faculty means coupling those who have been successful in achieving tenure and promotion with those aspiring to reach these traditional milestones for academic achievement" (p. 53). Typically, untenured assistant professors are the population of concern (Girves, Zepeda, & Gwathmey, 2005; Nielson & Eisenbach, 2001; Woodd, 2001). Mentors are usually tenured associate or full professors (Fong, 2000; Illes et al., 2000; Lemel & Sullivan-Catlin, 2000). Associate professors, it seems, could benefit from mentoring by senior colleagues, but few papers in our sample included associate professors in the target population (Goodwin et al., 2000; Green & King, 2002; Morrison-Shetlar & Heinrich, 1999).

Some programs associate mentors' higher rank with achievements in research and teaching (Bergen & Connelly, 1988; Boice, 1990; Fong, 2000). Others recognize that mentors with "useful experience, knowledge, skills and/or wisdom" (Berk et al., 2005, p. 67) may not be of higher rank than their mentees (Gibson, 2004; Snelson et al., 2002; Woodd, 2001; Yun & Sorcinelli, 2009). Knowledge may move from a lower to a higher rank, with junior faculty members sharing their experience with more senior members. For example, Morrison-Shetlar and Heinrich (1999) described group mentoring focused on a technique called experiential teaching, in which mentors' pedagogical expertise, not rank, was most important.

In peer mentoring, those of similar rank or status mentor one another, exchanging experiences, ideas, and concerns (Chesler & Chesler, 2002; deJanasz & Sullivan, 2004). In this approach, individuals play multiple and fluid roles as both mentors and mentees (Harnish & Wild, 1993; McGuire & Reger, 2003). Peer mentoring usually occurs in groups (Angelique et al., 2002; Benson, Morahan, Sachdeva, & Richman, 2002; Pololi et al., 2002), and peer mentors are often included among the multiple mentors had by mentees (Grant & Ward, 1992; Lewellen-Williams et al., 2006; Woodd, 2001).

Conceptions of mentoring may also be shaped by concerns about the demographic characteristics of participants. Studies of demographic factors in mentoring have examined the experiences of minorities and women (Bova, 1995; Solorzano, 1998; Tillman, 2001) and compared the outcomes of homogeneous (by sex and minority status) and heterogeneous mentoring relationships (Boice, 1990; Boice & Turner, 1989; Smith et al., 2000). Some mentoring programs have been designed exclusively for women and minorities (Green & King, 2002; Jordan-Zachery, 2004; Wunsch & Johnsrud, 1992). Many of these use peer mentoring to deemphasize power differentials (McGuire & Reger, 2003) or build empathic communities of support (Chesler & Chesler, 2002; Green & King, 2002). Programs for general faculty populations have been designed to address similar concerns by pairing mentors and mentees of the same sex (Lemel & Sullivan-Catlin, 2000), and by encouraging mentors to be sensitive to the particular challenges faced by women and minorities (Fong, 2000; King & Cubic, 2005; Waitzkin et al., 2006).

INSTITUTIONAL CONTEXT. Most mentoring programs are interdepartmental (Fong, 2000; Lemel & Sullivan-Catlin, 2000; Reder & Gallagher, 2007) or include both intra- and interdepartmental relationships (Cox, 1997; Gray & Birch, 2007; Hardwick, 2005). Although many faculty members encounter intradepartmental mentoring, few exclusively intradepartmental programs are described in the literature we examined (Tracy et al., 2004). The putative benefits of intradepartmental mentoring include "ease of daily contact" (Hardwick, 2005, p. 24) and the ability to provide "concrete guidance that is specific to the discrete unit" (Borisoff, 1998, p. 87). Interdepartmental mentoring may be motivated by a limited pool of mentors in a department (Herr, 1994), or by the belief that mentees may be better able to share frustrations and failures with mentors outside their departments (Fayne & Ortquist-Ahrens, 2006).

Cross-institutional mentoring generally aims to connect mentees and mentors who are in the same discipline or demographic group. The External Mentor Program described by Mundt (2001) sought out external mentors with strong research records in mentees' areas of study to help the mentees increase their research productivity. Other mentoring programs have spanned institutional boundaries to link biomedical scholars and leaders (King & Cubic, 2005; Lewellen-Williams et al., 2006), geographers (Hardwick, 2005), and ethnic minorities (Waitzkin et al., 2006). Cross-institutional mentoring also happens when faculty members maintain mentoring relationships that were established earlier in their career at other institutions (Grant & Ward, 1992; Kirchmeyer, 2005).

LEVEL OF INTENSITY. Mentoring relationships vary in intensity (Kirchmeyer, 2005), but accounts in the literature either do not explicitly address intensity or suggest that mentoring ought to be a markedly intense experience for all participants. In favor of high-intensity relationships, Campbell (1992) suggests that faculty mentoring is "not for the timid or casual" (p. 77), and Pierce (1998) states that mentors ought to be "the most personal and intimate point of contact that the new faculty member has with the organization" (p. 9). Others suggest that faculty mentoring involves trust (Blackwell, 1989), intense exchange (Smith et al., 2000), genuine caring and concern for mentees' well-being (Chalmers, 1992; Gibson, 2004; Snelson et al., 2002), nurturing and protection (Girves et al., 2005), and creation of a home place (hooks, 1989) in which faculty are safe and free from marginalization (Jordan-Zachery, 2004).

DURATION AND FREQUENCY. Some descriptions of mentoring refer to its duration and frequency. Authors often treat duration as a continuum, ranging from short- to long-term, having no distinct end point, and being determined by the needs of the participants (Berk et al., 2005; Gammack et al., 2004; Hardwick, 2005). Luckhaupt and colleagues (2005) suggest that mentoring should continue "over an extended period of time" (p. 1015), and Souba (1999) describes most "worthy" mentoring relationships as "infrequently short-term" (p. 113). Mentoring programs typically specify a minimum length of participation, from four months to six years, beyond which participants may choose to continue the relationship (Fox, Waldron, Bohnert, Hishinuma, & Nordquist, 1998; Golding & Gray, 2002; Mundt, 2001).

Like duration, prescriptions for the frequency of mentoring interactions vary widely. Accounts that address this issue suggest that participants meet frequently (Benson et al., 2002; Boice, 1990; Mundt, 2001), specify just how frequently participants are expected to meet (Illes et al., 2000; Limbert, 1995; Pololi, Knight, & Dunn, 2004), or leave it to participants to decide (Chesler & Chesler, 2002; Wunsch & Johnsrud, 1992). Programs that call for frequent meetings seem to favor once per week (Boice, 1990; Golding & Gray, 2002; Green & King, 2002).

Topics

In the literature we reviewed, the most important topics (see Figure 3.4) for mentors and mentees to address are how to balance research, teaching, and service; and how to navigate the politics and procedures of academia on the way to promotion and tenure (Angelique et al., 2002; Benson et al.,

Figure 3.4. Topics of Focus in the Mentoring Relationship or Program

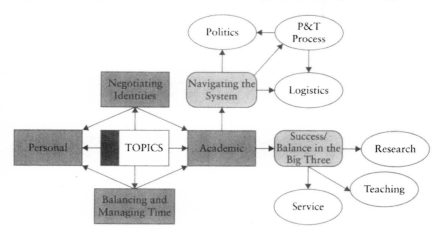

2002; Gray & Birch, 2007). Some faculty mentoring programs focus more on teaching (Chism, Fraser, & Arnold, 1996; Golding & Gray, 2002; Reder & Gallagher, 2007) or research (Jacelon et al., 2003; Mundt, 2001; Waitzkin et al., 2006). Service was included as part of the larger concern about time management and workload (Fayne & Ortquist-Ahrens, 2006; Hardwick, 2005; Smith et al., 2001).

Personal issues are also a common topic in accounts of faculty mentoring (Chalmers, 1992; Fox et al., 1998; Jordan-Zachery, 2004). Campbell (1992) wrote: "No one will be surprised that mentoring includes reviewing drafts of manuscripts or revising the design of a research project; less obvious is that mentoring can include dealing with terminal illness, unplanned pregnancy, and financial distress" (p. 77).

The challenges of balancing personal concerns and academic life are addressed in many conceptions of faculty mentoring (King & Cubic, 2005; Levy et al., 2004; McGuire & Reger, 2003). Some authors suggest that faculty mentoring is part of negotiating personal and professional identities (Jordan-Zachery, 2004; Tillman, 2001; Wunsch & Johnsrud, 1992) and thus includes exploring such issues as what it means to be both a Hispanic woman and an academic (Bova, 1995).

Actions

The final dimension in our conceptual framework of faculty mentoring is about what mentors and mentees do in mentoring relationships (see Figures 3.5 and 3.6). We avoid using the broad terms for mentoring roles

Figure 3.5. Mentor Actions in the Mentoring Relationship or Program

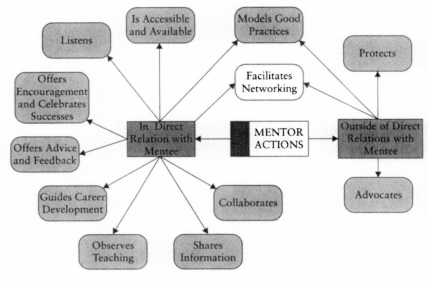

Figure 3.6. Mentee Actions in the Mentoring Relationship or Program

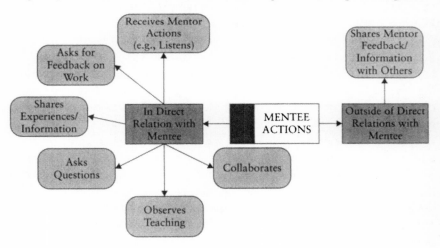

that are common in the literature, such as teacher or counselor, and instead focus on concrete actions.

MENTOR ACTIONS. In most accounts, mentors have the active, causal role in the relationship. Mentors can interact directly with mentees or take actions with other people that indirectly affect mentees (see Figure 3.5). In direct interactions with mentees, mentors make themselves available (Lemel & Sullivan-Catlin, 2000; Pierce, 1998; Souba, 1999), listen (Angelique et al., 2002; Borisoff, 1998; Fox et al., 1998), offer encouragement and celebrate successes (Berk et al., 2005; Blackwell, 1989; Smith et al., 2001), give advice and feedback on specific work and ideas (Jacelon et al., 2003; King & Cubic, 2005; Lewellen-Williams et al., 2006) or overall career development (Benson et al., 2002; Morzinski, 2005; Sands et al., 1991), observe mentees' teaching (Golding & Gray, 2002; St. Clair, 1994), share information (Dixon-Reeves, 2003; Limbert, 1995; Souba, 1999), and collaborate with mentees (Goodwin et al., 2000; Pololi et al., 2004; Reder & Gallagher, 2007). Working indirectly, mentors may facilitate networking with or on behalf of mentees (Gammack et al., 2004; King & Cubic, 2005; Mundt, 2001); model good teaching, research, and service practices (Bova, 1995; Dixon-Reeves, 2003; Golding & Gray, 2002); protect mentees from being overloaded with extraneous obligations (Girves et al., 2005; Sands et al., 1991; Snelson et al., 2002); and advocate on behalf of mentees (Borisoff, 1998; Lewellen-Williams et al., 2006; Wunsch & Johnsrud, 1992).

MENTEE ACTIONS. Descriptions of mentoring address mentor actions more than mentee actions (Blackwell, 1989; Goodwin & Stevens, 1998; Knox & McGovern, 1988). Perhaps this is not surprising for an activity called mentoring, but mentoring is also conceived as an interaction among participants. The mentee action we call "receiving mentor actions" (see Figure 3.6) could include listening to and engaging mentors' advice. Some authors offer a more complex picture of actions entailed in being a mentee, repositioning mentees from passive recipients to "agents in their own development" (Yun & Sorcinelli, 2009, p. 369). In direct interactions with mentors, mentees may share their experiences, ask for feedback on work, and pass along information (Jacelon et al., 2003; Morrison-Shetlar & Heinrich, 1999; Pololi et al., 2002); ask questions (Benson et al., 2002; Jacelon et al., 2003; St. Clair, 1994); observe mentors' classes (Golding & Gray, 2002; Lemel & Sullivan-Catlin, 2000); collaborate with mentors (Goodwin et al., 2000; Pololi et al., 2004; Reder & Gallagher, 2007); and participate in networking facilitated by the mentor (Benson et al., 2002). Beyond face-to-face interactions with their mentors, mentees may extend mentoring relationships by sharing what they have gained with others. For example, mentees in hierarchical, dyadic mentoring relationships can use peer mentoring to share experiences and reflect on challenges with one another (Gray & Birch, 2007).

Implications

Wunsch (1994a) cautioned that those involved in faculty mentoring programs "will get little conclusive guidance about definitions from the literature or from observing working programs" (p. 28). Our framework is meant to help those who administer, participate in, and evaluate mentoring programs thoughtfully consider key dimensions of mentoring that emerge from published accounts. Because the framework reflects diverse conceptions of faculty mentoring, it can inform design decisions in very different kinds of approaches. For example, a grassroots group of junior faculty members could use the framework to envision group peer mentoring as a way to help one another cope with the entangled responsibilities of their professional and personal lives. But the framework also reflects the characteristics of institutionally administered mentoring programs that connect senior and junior faculty members to help junior colleagues achieve promotion and tenure.

We developed a worksheet (see Exhibit 3.1) to help mentoring program developers, participants, and evaluators use the framework in Figures 3.1 through 3.6. The worksheet leads users through key issues and the range of responses that we found in the literature we reviewed. Additional space is provided for novel responses and adaptations of the framework. The worksheet does not prescribe what mentoring programs ought to look like. Instead, it organizes the diverse ways that faculty mentoring has been conceptualized, making it easier, hopefully, for those involved in mentoring to thoughtfully consider a variety of possibilities. Depending on the context in which the worksheet is applied, some of the questions will be more relevant than others.

The worksheet may be used differently by mentoring program developers, participants, and evaluators. Mentoring program developers and administrators can use it to think systematically about program design. For example, the lead author's department chair asked her to develop a proposal for a departmental mentoring program to help first- and second-year faculty enhance their teaching. She used the worksheet to sketch out key characteristics of such a program (see Exhibit 3.2). If used by participants, the worksheet offers prompts for critical reflection about what mentees and mentors want to make of their relationships. The worksheet might help them uncover assumptions so they can more explicitly consider what they want to gain from the experience and what they are willing to contribute to it. Evaluators can adapt the worksheet to characterize what mentoring experiences are like in practice, in comparison to the intentions of programs and participants. For instance, in evaluating the science faculty mentoring

Exhibit 3.1. Faculty Mentoring Program Worksheet

Question	Response(s): Check all that apply
1. How many participants are there in the mentoring relationship?	☐ One mentee with one mentor (dyadic) ☐ One mentee with multiple mentors ☐ One mentor with multiple mentees ☐ A group in which individuals mentor one another ☐ Other: _____
2. How are these participants related to one another with respect to rank, experience, and status?	☐ Difference in rank, specifically: _____ (e.g., mentor is associate professor or higher, and mentee is assistant professor) ☐ Difference in experience, specifically: _____ (e.g., teaching) ☐ Similar status as peers/colleagues, specifically: _____ (e.g., associate professors) ☐ Other: _____

3. To what extent are participants intentionally matched with respect to demographic characteristics?	☐ Demographic similarity of participants, specifically, _____ (e.g., same sex), is:
	   ☐ required
	   ☐ preferred
	   ☐ not a matter of consideration
	☐ Other: _____

4. How are mentoring participants related with respect to the institutional context?	☐ In the same department: _____ ☐ In the same university/college, but in different departments, specifically: _____ ☐ In different universities/institutions, specifically: _____ ☐ Other: _____

5. Who stands to benefit from mentoring?	Individuals:
	   ☐ mentees, who benefit by _____
	   ☐ mentors, who benefit by _____
	   ☐ other: _____
	☐ Institution, specifically _____ (e.g., university, college, department) that benefits by _____
	☐ Group, having this defining characteristic: _____ (e.g., women), benefits by _____
	☐ Other: _____

6. What is the scope of individual benefit?	☐ Career benefits are the primary focus ☐ Career and psychosocial benefits ☐ The whole person and his or her needs will be attended to ☐ Other: _____

(Continued)

Exhibit 3.1. (*Continued*)

Question	Response(s): Check all that apply

Question

Response(s): Check all that apply

7. Who is responsible for initiating the mentoring relationship(s)?

Individual participants, namely:
  ☐ mentees
  ☐ mentors
  ☐ the group
☐ The institutional program/initiative (i.e., those other than participants), namely: _____
☐ Other: _____

8. Who is responsible for ongoing management and control of mentoring relationship(s)?

Individual participants, namely:
  ☐ mentees
  ☐ mentors
  ☐ the group
☐ The institutional program/initiative (i.e., those other than participants), namely: _____
☐ Other: _____

9. How often do participants interact?

Face-to-face meetings: _____
(e.g., once per month)
Electronic/phone contact: _____
(e.g., as needed)

10. How long does the relationship last?

Duration: _____
(e.g., for one year)

11. How would the intensity of an ideal mentoring relationship be described?

☐ Casual
☐ Caring, involving genuine concern
☐ Other: _____

12. What are the major topics to be addressed in the mentoring relationship?

Success in (check all that apply):
  ☐ Research
  ☐ Teaching
  ☐ Service
  ☐ Balance among/between some combination of the above: _____
Navigating the system, specifically:
  ☐ Promotion and tenure process (i.e., logistics and politics)
  ☐ Other logistics, specifically:
    _____ (e.g., navigating the department)
  ☐ Politics
☐ Balancing personal/academic responsibilities and managing demands on personal/academic time

☐ Negotiating personal/academic identities, specifically: _____ (e.g., being a Hispanic faculty member)

☐ Other: _____

13. What does a mentor do?	☐ Is accessible and available ☐ Listens ☐ Offers encouragement ☐ Celebrates success ☐ Guides career development ☐ Observes teaching ☐ Shares information ☐ Offers advice and feedback ☐ Collaborates ☐ Models good practices ☐ Facilitates networking ☐ Protects ☐ Advocates	Space to elaborate checked items and add others:
14. What does a mentee do?	☐ Asks for feedback on work ☐ Shares experiences/information ☐ Asks questions ☐ Observes teaching ☐ Collaborates ☐ Shares feedback with others	Space to elaborate checked items and add others:

Exhibit 3.2. Using the Faculty Mentoring Program Worksheet

Question	Response(s)
No. of participants	☑ One mentee with multiple (two to three) mentors
Experience, rank, status difference?	☑ Difference in experience, specifically pedagogical or pedagogical content knowledge (PCK) Note: likely to be of different rank, but that is not as important as experience
Demographics	Demographic similarity among participants, specifically, same sex or ethnic minority status is: ☑ preferred (i.e., will try to find demographically similar mentors for mentees)

(Continued)

Exhibit 3.2. (*Continued*)

Question	Response(s)
Institutional context	☑ In the same department
Beneficiaries	☑ Mentees who benefit by learning from experienced teachers, and improving pedagogical and PCK (primary beneficiary) ☑ Mentors who benefit by learning from other mentors, the mentee, and self-reflection (improve pedagogical knowledge and PCK) ☑ Institution, specifically the department, which benefits from higher quality teaching
Scope of individual benefit	☑ Career and psychosocial benefits (teaching is inherently psychosocial endeavor)
Initiation of relationship	☑ The institutional program (those other than participants); department chair and program developer recruit teaching mentors
Ongoing management of relationship	Individual participants, that is, ☑ mentees and ☑ mentors, who communicate flexibly (in addition to required activities) ☑ The institutional program (those other than participants), requires certain activities (for example, face-to-face meetings, teaching observations; see frequency section)
Frequency of interaction	Face-to-face meetings: twice each semester (minimum) Electronic/phone contact: as needed Teaching observations: mentee is observed by mentors in second year; mentee observes mentors once each semester in first and second year
Duration	Two years (first and second year for mentee) and beyond as desired by participants
Intensity	☑ Caring, involving, genuine concern for mentees' and students' success
Topics	Success in ☑ teaching and in ☑ balancing teaching and other responsibilities
What does a mentor do?	☑ Is accessible and available ☑ Listens ☑ Offers encouragement ☑ Celebrates success ☑ Observes teaching ☑ Shares information	"Collaborates" refers to working together to enact pedagogical ideas; collaboration may continue into the future; sharing information includes syllabi, activities, demonstrations, ideas, etc.

☑ Offers advice and feed-
back
☑ Models good practices
☑ Facilitates networking
☑ Collaborates

| What does a mentee do? | ☑ Asks for feedback on work
☑ Shares experiences/information
☑ Asks questions
☑ Observes teaching
☑ Collaborates | "Collaborates" refers to working together to enact pedagogical ideas; collaboration may continue into the future |

program that motivated this literature review, we discovered highly variable understandings and manifestations of mentoring rooted in a weakly conceptualized program. The leaders of the program have since directed more attention to developing a shared vision of mentoring by considering some of the issues identified in the conceptual framework and the worksheet. In this way, we hope the conceptual framework we have presented will contribute to more successful mentoring experiences across the diverse settings of higher education.

REFERENCES

Allen, T. D., Eby, L. T., Poteet, M. L., Lentz, E., & Lima, L. (2004). Career benefits associated with mentoring for protégés: A meta-analysis. *Journal of Applied Psychology, 89*(1), 127–136.

Angelique, H., Kyle, K., & Taylor, E. (2002). Mentors and muses: New strategies for academic success. *Innovative Higher Education, 26*(3), 195–209.

August, L., & Waltman, J. (2004). Culture, climate, and contribution: Career satisfaction among female faculty. *Research in Higher Education, 45*(2), 177–191.

Benson, C. A., Morahan, P. S., Sachdeva, A. K., & Richman, R. C. (2002). Effective faculty preceptoring and mentoring during reorganization of an academic medical center. *Medical Teacher, 24*(5), 550–557.

Bergen, D., & Connelly, J. (1988). The collegial research mentor project: A model for faculty research and scholarship development. *Career Planning and Adult Development Journal, 4*(2), 3–8.

Berk, R. A., Berg, J., Mortimer, R., Walton-Moss, B., & Yeo, T. P. (2005). Measuring the effectiveness of faculty mentoring relationships. *Academic Medicine, 80*(1), 66–71.

Blackwell, J. E. (1989). Mentoring: An action strategy for increasing minority faculty. *Academe, 75*(5), 8–14.

Boice, R. (1990). Mentoring new faculty: A program for implementation. *Journal of Staff, Program, and Organizational Development, 8*(3), 143–160.

Boice, R., & Turner, J. L. (1989). The FIPSE-CSULB mentoring project for new faculty. In S. Kahn (Ed.), *To improve the academy: Vol. 8. Resources for student, faculty, and institutional development* (pp. 117–129). Stillwater, OK: New Forums Press.

Borisoff, D. (1998). Strategies for effective mentoring and for being effectively mentored: A focus on research institutions. *Journal of the Association for Communication Administration, 27*(2), 84–96.

Bova, B. M. (1995). Mentoring revisited: The Hispanic woman's perspective. *MPAEA Journal of Adult Education, 23*(1), 8–19.

Campbell, W. H. (1992). Mentoring of junior faculty. *American Journal of Pharmaceutical Education, 56*(1), 75–79.

Carmin, C. N. (1988). Issues in research on mentoring: Definitional and methodological. *International Journal of Mentoring, 2*(2), 9–13.

Cawyer, C. S., Simonds, C., & Davis, S. (2002). Mentoring to facilitate socialization: The case of the new faculty member. *Qualitative Studies in Education, 15*(2), 225–242.

Chalmers, R. K. (1992). Faculty development: The nature and benefits of mentoring. *American Journal of Pharmaceutical Education, 56*(1), 71–74.

Chao, G. T., Walz, P. M., & Gardner, P. D. (1992). Formal and informal mentorships: A comparison on mentoring functions and contrast with non-mentored counterparts. *Personnel Psychology, 45*(3), 619–636.

Charmaz, K. (2000). Grounded theory: Objectivist and constructivist methods. In N. K. Denzin & Y. S. Lincoln (Eds.), *Handbook of qualitative research* (2nd ed., pp. 509–536). Thousand Oaks, CA: Sage.

Chesler, N. C., & Chesler, M. A. (2002). Gender-informed mentoring strategies for women engineering scholars: On establishing a caring community. *Journal of Engineering Education, 91*(1), 49–55.

Chism, N.V.N., Fraser, J. M., & Arnold, R. L. (1996). Teaching academies: Honoring and promoting teaching through a community of expertise. In R. J. Menges & M. D. Svinicki (Eds.), *New directions for adult and continuing education: No. 65. Honoring exemplary teaching* (pp. 25–32). San Francisco: Jossey-Bass.

Cohen, N. H. (1995). The principles of adult mentoring scale. In M. W. Galbraith & N. H. Cohen (Eds.), *New directions for adult and continuing education:*

No. 66. Mentoring: New strategies and challenges (pp. 15–32). San Francisco: Jossey-Bass.

Cox, M. D. (1997). Long-term patterns in a mentoring program for junior faculty: Recommendations for practice. In D. Dezure (Ed.), *To improve the academy: Vol. 16. Resources for faculty, instructional, and organizational development* (pp. 225–268). Stillwater, OK: New Forums Press.

Davidson, M. N., & Foster-Johnson, L. (2001). Mentoring in the preparation of graduate researchers of color. *Review of Educational Research, 71*(4), 549–574.

deJanasz, S. C., & Sullivan, S. E. (2004). Multiple mentoring in academe: Developing the professional network. *Journal of Vocational Behavior, 64*(2), 263–283.

Dixon-Reeves, R. (2003). Mentoring as a precursor to incorporation: An assessment of the mentoring experience of recently minted Ph.D.s. *Journal of Black Studies, 34*(1), 12–27.

Eby, L. T., Lockwood, A. L., & Butts, M. (2006). Perceived support for mentoring: A multiple perspectives approach. *Journal of Vocational Behavior, 68*(2), 267–291.

Fayne, H., & Ortquist-Ahrens, L. (2006). Learning communities for first-year faculty: Transition, acculturation, and transformation. In S. Chadwick-Blossey & D. R. Robertson (Eds.), *To improve the academy: Vol. 24. Resources for faculty, instructional, and organizational development* (pp. 277–290). Bolton, MA: Anker.

Fong, B. (2000). Toto, I think we're still in Kansas: Supporting and mentoring minority faculty and administrators. *Liberal Education, 86*(4), 56–60.

Fox, E. C., Waldron, J. A., Bohnert, P., Hishinuma, E. S., & Nordquist, C. R. (1998). Mentoring new faculty in a department of psychiatry. *Academic Psychiatry, 22*(2), 98–106.

Galbraith, M. W. (2001). Mentoring development for community college faculty. *Michigan Community College Journal of Research and Practice, 7*(2), 29–39.

Gammack, J. K., Rudolph, J. L., Adedokun, A., Hirth, V., Kevorkian, R., & Misra, S. (2004). Perceptions of geriatric medicine junior faculty on success in academic medicine: The Saint Louis University Geriatric Academy (SLUGA) Faculty Development Program. *Journals of Gerontology Series A: Biological Sciences and Medical Sciences, 59*(10), M1029–M1035.

Gibson, S. K. (2004). Being mentored: The experience of women faculty. *Journal of Career Development, 30*(3), 173–188.

Girves, J. E., Zepeda, Y., & Gwathmey, J. K. (2005). Mentoring in a post-affirmative action world. *Journal of Social Issues, 61*(3), 449–479.

Glaser, B., & Strauss, A. (1967). *The discovery of grounded theory.* Hawthorne, NY: Aldine de Gruyter.

Golding, T. L., & Gray, E. D. (2002). Mentoring mathematics faculty: A model. *Primus, 12*(1), 87–95.

Goodwin, L. D., & Stevens, E. A. (1998). An exploratory study of the role of mentoring in the retention of faculty. *Journal of Staff, Program, and Organizational Development, 16*(1), 39–47.

Goodwin, L. D., Stevens, E. A., Goodwin, W. L., & Hagood, E. A. (2000). The meaning of faculty mentoring. *Journal of Staff, Program, and Organizational Development, 17*(1), 17–30.

Grant, L., & Ward, K. B. (1992). *Mentoring, gender, and publication among social, natural, and physical scientists. Final report.* Washington, DC: Office of Educational Research and Improvement.

Gray, T., & Birch, A. J. (2007). Team mentoring: An alternative way to mentor new faculty. In D. R. Robertson & L. B. Nilson (Eds.), *To improve the academy: Vol. 26. Resources for faculty, instructional, and organizational development* (pp. 230–241). Bolton, MA: Anker.

Green, C. E., & King, V. G. (2002). Sisters mentoring sisters: Africentric leadership development for black women in the academy. *Journal of Negro Education, 70*(3), 156–165.

Hardwick, S. W. (2005). Mentoring early career faculty in geography: Issues and strategies. *Professional Geographer, 57*(1), 21–27.

Harnish, D., & Wild, L. A. (1993). Peer mentoring in higher education: A professional development strategy for faculty. *Community College Journal of Research and Practice, 17*(3), 271–282.

Harnish, D., & Wild, L. A. (1994). Mentoring strategies for faculty development. *Studies in Higher Education, 19*(2), 191–201.

Healy, C. C. (1997). An operational definition of mentoring. In H. T. Frierson, Jr. (Ed.), *Diversity in higher education: Mentoring and diversity in higher education* (Vol. 1, pp. 9–22). Greenwich, CT: JAI Press.

Healy, C. C., & Welchert, A. J. (1990). Mentoring relations: A definition to advance research and practice. *Educational Researcher, 19*(9), 17–21.

Henry, J. S., Stockdale, M. B., Hall, M., & Deniston, W. (1994). A formal mentoring program for junior female faculty: Description and evaluation. *Initiatives, 56*(2), 37–45.

Herr, K. U. (1994). Mentoring faculty at the department level. In M. A. Wunsch (Ed.), *New directions for teaching and learning: Vol. 57. Mentoring revisited: Making an impact on individuals and institutions* (pp. 81–90). San Francisco: Jossey-Bass.

hooks, b. (1989). *Talking back: Thinking feminist, thinking black.* Boston: South End Press.

Illes, J., Glover, G. H., Wexler, L., Leung, A.N.C., & Glazer, G. M. (2000). A model for faculty mentoring in academic radiology. *Academic Radiology, 7*(9), 717–724.

Jacelon, C. S., Zucker, D. M., Staccarini, J.-M., & Henneman, E. A. (2003). Peer mentoring for tenure-track faculty. *Journal of Professional Nursing, 19*(6), 335–338.

Jackson, V. A., Palepu, A., Szalacha, L., Caswell, C., Carr, P. L., & Inui, T. (2003). "Having the right chemistry": A qualitative study of mentoring in academic medicine. *Academic Medicine, 78*(3), 328–334.

Johnsrud, L. K. (1994). Enabling the success of junior faculty women through mentoring. In M. A. Wunsch (Ed.), *New directions for teaching and learning: Vol. 57. Mentoring revisited: Making an impact on individuals and institutions* (pp. 53–63). San Francisco: Jossey-Bass.

Jordan-Zachery, J. S. (2004). Reflections on mentoring: Black women and the academy. *PS: Political Science and Politics, 37*(4), 875–877.

King, C. A., & Cubic, B. (2005). Women psychologists within academic health systems: Mentorship and career advancement. *Journal of Clinical Psychology in Medical Settings, 12*(3), 271–280.

Kirchmeyer, C. (2005). The effects of mentoring on academic careers over time: Testing performance and political perspectives. *Human Relations, 58*(5), 637–660.

Knox, P. L., & McGovern, T. V. (1988). Mentoring women in academia. *Teaching of Psychology, 15*(1), 39–41.

Kram, K. E. (1980). *Mentoring process at work: Developmental relationships in managerial careers.* Unpublished doctoral dissertation, Yale University, New Haven, CT.

Kram, K. E. (1983). Phases of the mentor relationship. *Academy of Management Journal, 26*(4), 608–625.

Kram, K. E. (1985). *Mentoring at work: Developmental relationships in organizational life.* Glenview, IL: Scott, Foresman.

Lemel, R., & Sullivan-Catlin, H. (2000). The Kean University mentoring program: A model for integrating new faculty. *Journal of Staff, Program, and Organizational Development, 17*(1), 51–55.

Levinson, D. J. (1978). *The seasons of a man's life.* New York: Knopf.

Levy, B. D., Katz, J. T., Wolf, M. A., Sillman, J. S., Handin, R. I., & Dzau, V. J. (2004). An initiative in mentoring to promote residents' and faculty members' careers. *Academic Medicine, 79*(9), 845–850.

Lewellen-Williams, C., Johnson, V. A., Deloney, L. A., Thomas, B. R., Goyol, A., & Henry-Tillman, R. (2006). The POD: A new model for mentoring underrepresented minority faculty. *Academic Medicine, 81*(3), 275–279.

Limbert, C. A. (1995). Crysalis, a peer mentoring group for faculty and staff women. *NWSA Journal, 7*(2), 86–99.

Luckhaupt, S. E., Chin, M. H., Mangione, C. M., Phillips, R. S., Bell, D., Leonard, A. C., et al. (2005). Mentorship in academic general internal medicine. *Journal of General Internal Medicine, 20*(11), 1014–1018.

Luna, G., & Cullen, D. L. (1995). *Empowering the faculty: Mentoring redirected and renewed* (ASHE-ERIC Higher Education Report No. 3). Washington, DC: George Washington University, Graduate School of Education and Human Development.

McGuire, G. M., & Reger, J. (2003). Feminist co-mentoring: A model for academic professional development. *NWSA Journal, 15*(1), 54–72.

Mertz, N. T. (2004). What's a mentor anyway? *Educational Administration Quarterly, 40*(4), 541–560.

Moody, J. (2004). *Faculty diversity: Problems and solutions.* New York: RoutledgeFalmer.

Morrison-Beedy, D., Aronowitz, T., Dyne, J., & Mkandawire, L. (2001). Mentoring students and junior faculty in faculty research: A win–win scenario. *Journal of Professional Nursing, 17*(6), 291–296.

Morrison-Shetlar, A., & Heinrich, K. T. (1999). Mentoring at the edge: A faculty group fosters experiential teaching. *Journal of Experiential Education, 22*(1), 5–11.

Morzinski, J. A. (2005). Mentors, colleagues, and successful health science faculty: Lessons from the field. *Journal of Veterinary Medical Education, 32*(1), 5–11.

Mundt, M. H. (2001). An external mentor program: Stimulus for faculty research development. *Journal of Professional Nursing, 17*(1), 40–45.

Nielson, T. R., & Eisenbach, R. J. (2001). Mentoring in academia: A conversation with Lyman Porter. *Journal of Management Inquiry, 10*(2), 183–189.

Olson, R. K., & Connelly, L. M. (1995). Mentoring through predoctoral fellowships to enhance research productivity. *Journal of Professional Nursing, 11*(5), 270–275.

Parham, W. D. (1981). *Mentors and protégés: Stages of development in a mentoring relationship.* Unpublished doctoral dissertation, Southern Illinois University, Carbondale.

Pierce, G. (1998). Developing new university faculty through mentoring. *Journal of Humanistic Education and Development, 37*(1), 13–40.

Pololi, L. H., Knight, S. M., Dennis, K., & Frankel, R. M. (2002). Helping medical school faculty realize their dreams: An innovative, collaborative mentoring program. *Academic Medicine, 77*(5), 377–384.

Pololi, L. H., Knight, S., & Dunn, K. (2004). Facilitating scholarly writing in academic medicine: Lessons learned from a collaborative peer mentoring program. *Journal of General Internal Medicine, 19*(1), 64–68.

Ragins, B. R., & Cotton, J. L. (1999). Mentor functions and outcomes: A comparison of men and women in formal and informal mentoring relationships. *Journal of Applied Psychology, 84*(4), 529–550.

Reder, M., & Gallagher, E. V. (2007). Transforming a teaching culture through peer mentoring: Connecticut College's Johnson Teaching Seminar for incoming faculty. In D. R. Robertson & L. B. Nilson (Eds.), *To improve the academy: Vol. 25. Resources for faculty, instructional, and organizational development* (pp. 327–344). Bolton, MA: Anker.

Sands, R. G., Parson, L. A., & Duane, J. (1991). Faculty mentoring faculty in a public university. *Journal of Higher Education, 62*(2), 174–193.

Schrodt, P., Cawyer, C. S., & Sanders, R. (2003). An examination of academic mentoring behaviors and new faculty members' satisfaction with socialization and tenure and promotion processes. *Communication Education, 52*(1), 17–29.

Smith, J. O., Whitman, J. S., Grant, P. A., Stanutz, A., Russett, J. A., & Rankin, K. (2001). Peer networking as a dynamic approach to supporting new faculty. *Innovative Higher Education, 25*(3), 197–207.

Smith, J. W., Smith, W. J., & Markham, S. E. (2000). Diversity issues in mentoring academic faculty. *Journal of Career Development, 26*(4), 251–262.

Snelson, C. M., Martsolf, D. S., Dieckman, B. C., Anaya, E. R., Cartechine, K. A., Miller, B., et al. (2002). Caring as a theoretical perspective for a nursing faculty mentoring program. *Nurse Education Today, 22*(8), 654–660.

Solorzano, D. G. (1998). Role models, mentors, and the experiences of Chicana and Chicano Ph.D. scientists. *Diversity in Higher Education, 2,* 91–103.

Souba, W. W. (1999). Mentoring young academic surgeons, our most precious asset. *Journal of Surgical Research, 82*(2), 113–120.

Spencer, C., Tribe, K., & Sokolovskaja, J. (2004). *Mentoring made easy: A practical guide.* Retrieved January 3, 2009, from www.eeo.nsw.gov.au/publications_and_resources/publications/publication_list_-_new#26618

St. Clair, K. L. (1994). Faculty-to-faculty mentoring in the community college: An instructional component of faculty development. *Community College Review, 22*(3), 23–36.

Steiner, J. F., Curtis, P., Lanphear, B. P., Vu, K. O., & Main, D. S. (2004). Assessing the role of influential mentors in the research development of primary care fellows. *Academic Medicine, 79*(9), 865–872.

Tillman, L. C. (2001). Mentoring African American faculty in predominantly white institutions. *Research in Higher Education, 42*(3), 295–325.

Tracy, E. E., Jagsi, R., Starr, R., & Tarbell, N. J. (2004). Outcomes of a pilot faculty mentoring program. *American Journal of Obstetrics and Gynecology, 191*(6), 1846–1850.

Waitzkin, H., Yager, J., Parker, T., & Duran, B. (2006). Mentoring partnerships for minority faculty and graduate students in mental health services research. *Academic Psychiatry, 30*(3), 205–217.

Woodd, M. (2001). Learning to leap from a peer: A research study on mentoring in a further and higher education institution. *Research in Post-Compulsory Education, 6*(1), 97–104.

Wunsch, M. A. (1994a). Developing mentoring programs: Major themes and issues. In M. A. Wunsch (Ed.), *New directions for teaching and learning: Vol. 57. Mentoring revisited: Making an impact on individuals and institutions* (pp. 27–34). San Francisco: Jossey-Bass.

Wunsch, M. A. (1994b). Giving structure to experience: Mentoring strategies for women faculty. *Initiatives, 56*(1), 1–10.

Wunsch, M. A., & Johnsrud, L. K. (1992). Breaking barriers: Mentoring junior faculty women for professional development and retention. In D. H. Wulff & J. D. Nyquist (Eds.), *To improve the academy: Vol. 11. Resources for faculty, instructional, and organizational development* (pp. 175–187). Stillwater, OK: New Forums Press.

Yun, J. H., & Sorcinelli, M. D. (2009). When mentoring is the medium: Lessons learned from a faculty development initiative. In L. B. Nilson & J. E. Miller (Eds.), *To improve the academy: Vol. 27. Resources for faculty, instructional, and organizational development* (pp. 365–383). San Francisco: Jossey-Bass.

4

STRATEGIC COMMITTEE INVOLVEMENT

A GUIDE FOR FACULTY DEVELOPERS

Phyllis Blumberg, University of the Sciences in Philadelphia

Faculty developers should seek purposeful involvement in committee service because committees are essential to the functioning of higher education institutions. The unique expertise and perspectives that faculty developers bring to the table help committees execute their tasks and benefit faculty development efforts. Given the number of possible institutional committees and limitations on time, developers should decide carefully about their service. Offered here is a framework for making strategic decisions about committee membership on five criteria: committee characteristics, individual's impact on the committee, personal characteristics, conditions that should discourage service, and pitfalls to consider before deciding to serve.

Committees and task forces represent the sharing of governance between administrators and faculty (Marshall, 1999). They can alter the culture and policies of an institution, thereby influencing teaching and learning, institutional practices, and educational programs (Schroeder, 2006). As they consider important initiatives regarding student assessment, curriculum revision, and course and faculty evaluation, they can act as change agents themselves and can attract people interested in change. Because committees and task forces (henceforth, I use "committee" to mean both) play such an essential role in the functioning of institutions of higher education, faculty developers should seek purposeful involvement in them (Gillespie & Zinsmeister, 2004; Schroeder, 2006) and view committee service in the context of their normal consultative and educational roles with faculty.

Yet many developers do not embrace committee service. They may believe that committee work takes time away from other pressing responsibilities. Indeed, such service is time-consuming, which is why Diamond (1995) advises faculty to limit it to less than 20 percent of their time. However, his guideline may not be appropriate for faculty developers, who have different responsibilities. Manuals on faculty development (for example, Gillespie, Hilsen, & Wadsworth, 2002) are silent on both the importance of committee service and the proportion of time it is worth. In addition, few sessions at the annual POD Network conferences address the subject of committee involvement for faculty developers; nor do orientations for new faculty developers. Perhaps the profession regards committee work as ancillary because of its traditional service and support roles emphasizing one-on-one consultation with faculty and small-group workshops (Lieberman & Guskin, 2003).

However, POD Network leaders are now fostering another model of faculty development with an institutional focus (Baron, 2006; Chism, 1998; Lieberman & Guskin, 2003; Schroeder, in press). Chism (1998) calls this a paradigm shift in faculty development, from reactive individual consultation and training to proactive organizational development. With this new paradigm, faculty developers need easy access to governance bodies, decision makers, and the faculty at large, which committee participation affords (Chism, 1998). Lieberman and Guskin (2003) contend that developers now need to be seen as change agents who work to transform their institutions to support not only faculty but administrators and faculty leaders as well. When engaged in institutionwide activities, they work collaboratively with a variety of campus units and can serve as catalysts and active participants of institutional change (Baron, 2006).

To determine the extent and channels of the institutional influence of faculty developers, Schroeder (in press) surveyed 149 center directors across all types of institutions. She classified their responses about their centers on a continuum from marginalized to acting as leaders within the central functions of their institutions. She found that centers she defined as marginalized focused their attention on individual faculty, in sharp contrast to those centers that she classified as key leaders. More than 61 percent of the latter had an institutional focus, while only 12 percent of the marginalized centers did. Virtually all of the centers in leadership roles were involved in committee work, often with heavy responsibilities, which was one of thirty-six factors that enhanced their institutional impact. Committee involvement, then, is a key component of the new proactive, leadership model of the profession.

Faculty developers can forge a reciprocal exchange of benefits between the institutional committees on which they serve and their own centers. For their own benefit, they can network and establish trust and rapport with a range of faculty and administrators whom they might not otherwise meet through their center work. They also gain a sense of how faculty members and administrators think about issues, adding other perspectives to those acquired through center-based contacts. For the institution's benefit, they can offer their unique expertise and knowledge to the decision-making process. In fact, when committees are charged with developing new initiatives or directions, the presence and leadership of a faculty developer may have a greater influence on the outcomes than all of the workshops and learning communities that may grow out of these new initiatives (Schroeder, 2006).

Roles on Committees

How an individual comes to serve on a given committee has implications for faculty developers. If he or she is elected, this usually signifies a vote of faculty confidence. If administrators or faculty leadership ask a faculty developer to serve on a committee as a regular, ex-officio, or staff member, it is usually because that individual has special, needed expertise. In some cases, faculty developers automatically serve on certain committees because of their expertise, knowledge, perspective, or job responsibilities. Their supervisor may request or recommend membership on a specific committee for the same reason.

However, faculty developers can actively seek committee membership by volunteering, self-nominating, or talking to decision makers about the value they can bring to the committee (expertise, knowledge, perspective) or their interest in learning more about its work. Even if faculty developers do not hold faculty rank and may not be eligible for academic committees, they can still participate on the committee in a number of ways: by seeking out the chairperson and presenting background or literature on a topic, by asking to sit in at meetings or present relevant information, and by attending open meetings, especially those where the agenda pertains to what they do.

Despite the benefits that can mutually accrue, faculty developers should make wise committee-service choices. Most focus on improving the quality of instruction (Diamond, 2002), which involves improving instructor teaching knowledge and behavior, courses and curriculum, and organizational processes related to the teaching mission. Therefore, faculty developers should target committees congruent with these purposes. For example, committees that plan an outside speaker series or determine policies related to workload or class size can help instructors improve how they teach. Curriculum committees address ways to improve instruction, such as innovative types of courses, active learning strategies, and more valid assessment methods. Strategic planning and program development shape organizational processes. Student and program assessment committees are also linked to the faculty developer's domains.

Framework to Guide Decisions About Serving on Specific Committees

Given the number of possible committees and limitations on time, faculty developers may find a framework for seeking or selecting committee involvement helpful. The one I propose here rates the value of their involvement on five criteria: committee characteristics, potential impact of the faculty developer on the committee, personal characteristics, conditions that should deter faculty developers from serving, and pitfalls to consider before deciding to serve, as shown in the table (4.1) in the appendix. Alone or in consultation with others, faculty developers can apply this framework to any potential committee assignment, including whether to continue or end membership. In the next few pages, I explain each section of the framework and furnish examples of applying the framework to specific committee service options.

I used a modified critical incidents method to assign positive, negative, and neutral points as a soft indicator of whether to serve on a particular committee; therefore, the numbers given are value judgments. The number of total positive point considerations for serving on a committee is about the same as the total negative point considerations against serving. When a scale is given, the individual completing the framework should assess the appropriate rating for the committee being considered. Then, after completing this framework, he or she should add up the positive and the negative points, count the number of points given as neutral, and examine the balance among these categories. The greater the total positive points, the potentially more valuable this committee service; the greater the total negative points, the potentially less value or more hazardous the service, or the less visible one's role should be.

Rather than recommending cutoff scores for deciding about committee work, I leave the individual to decide on the basis of the institutional culture. Sometimes a particular committee may have a low positive score, but one may be required to serve on it. In this case, one may want to limit visibility or try to change the role to that of an advisor, resource person, or nonvoting member.

Committee Characteristics

Committee characteristics (Section A in Table 4.1) include its mission and perceived institutional prestige. For instance, committees that prepare materials for accreditation or steering committees for accreditation review relate to essential faculty development functions and carry considerable prestige and visibility, so they are good candidates for the faculty developer's service (Gillespie, in press). In contrast are committees that determine scholarships, graduation awards, athletic conferences, and other matter unconnected to faculty development.

Potential Impact of the Faculty Developer on the Committee

Potential impact (Section B in Table 4.1) encompasses a dozen ways in which faculty developers can add value (sometimes uniquely so) to a committee. For example, unlike faculty members, faculty developers often have the expertise and funding to invite outside speakers to campus, promote dialogues on topics, and support faculty travel to relevant meetings. They might consider serving on a facilities or teaching environment committee because it has the power to improve the quality of teaching and learning (Gillespie, in press). Marilla Svinicki of the University of Texas at Austin (personal communication, May 4, 2003) recounted her success promoting active learning in large classrooms when she convinced her university to replace the theater-style bolted-down seating with movable chairs. Facilities committees often address this type of topic, and faculty developers can research how other institutions have designed learning spaces and bring relevant articles or websites into committee discussions on classroom design. They can also promote dialogue on designs for learning among faculty and administrators, describe new approaches to learning spaces, and help people to think creatively about merging laboratories and classrooms into studio science classrooms, for example (Beichner & Saul, 2003). Faculty developers can meet with the chair or influential members one-on-one outside of formal meetings to teach them about flexible learning environments. They can also encourage others to question the status quo. Finally, they can help translate architects' ideas to committee members and vice versa.

Whether or not faculty developers use the framework for committee work decisions, they can enhance their overall impact on a committee by performing as many of the roles listed in Section B, Table 4.1 as appropriate. These roles furnish opportunities to display proactive leadership and educate committee members and the institution at large. Some of them also have an impact on the committee's ability to effect change and promote more effective and efficient institutional operations—for example, by providing process consultation or proposing alternative ways to run the committee if an impasse occurs.

Personal Characteristics

Personal characteristics (Section C, Table 4.1) refer to what faculty developers bring to a committee, including the role they might play on the committee, their job-related expertise, and other areas of expertise arising from their background or strengths. Because of their position, they have tremendous knowledge about pedagogy, instructional technology, curriculum development, and assessment of student learning at the course and program level. They may also be skilled in group facilitation and can apply this to the committee process. Faculty developers are familiar with current controversies and trends in higher education in general and in specific areas such as faculty roles, responsibilities, and academic governance. They typically can describe the local context and the institutional culture, its history, and its unspoken norms and taboos. They often have well-honed skills in oral and written communication, quantitative and qualitative research, and development of assessment tools that can help committees charged with data gathering and producing a report.

Individual faculty developers can bring unique skills to committees because of their disciplinary background and special areas of expertise and interest, and they may volunteer to serve or run for election on the basis of these skills. For example, being an educational psychologist with a strong background in learning and curriculum development, I choose to serve on committees responsible for developing new educational programs and curricula or conducting the self-study needed for professional program accreditation. While reviewing course or program proposals in committee deliberations, I often highlight the importance of active learning, student engagement, and learning-centered teaching. An instructional designer with distance learning experience may serve more effectively on a technology committee.

Conditions That Should Deter Faculty Developers from Serving

Two overriding conditions should deter faculty developers from serving on a committee (Section D, Table 4.1). The first is a conflict of interest between the faculty development mission and the committee charge. For example, faculty developers should not serve on promotion and tenure committees. They must avoid the appearance of serving as judge, lest they lose the trust of faculty. The second condition arises when faculty perceive a committee as undermining their best interests. For example, if the administration wants to change the terms under which faculty serve the university, and faculty see the change as an antifaculty move, then faculty developers should not be associated with any committee promoting the change. Because a committee either does or doesn't subvert faculty interests, I did not assign a range to this item.

Conditions That Should Cause Faculty Developers to Reconsider

Section E in Table 4.1 lists conditions that should cause faculty developers to reconsider serving but that are not as severe as the conditions that should deter service. Individuals who are new to the institution or to faculty development might consult with others about the potential risks or pitfalls of specific committees.

People can make enemies by serving on controversial committees or by taking an unpopular stand. Unfortunately, some faculty members and administrators do not confine disagreements to the topic at hand and may extend them to estimate the individual's total value or worth to the institution. Thus, taking a controversial stand could damage one's credibility and even that of an entire faculty development effort. For example, while serving on a task force to revise the general education program, I recommended a major reform that required assessing many cross-disciplinary outcomes, such as information literacy and the ability to work in teams. Many faculty thought the program was unworkable, and some believed I was trying to marginalize their currently required courses in the proposed curriculum. Chairs and faculty alike criticized me (and some of them still hold it against me). I have heard that they trust my center less because of my stand.

Another condition that justifies reconsideration of service is how time-consuming a committee may be. Numerous meetings with little in the way of concrete progress can be frustrating, whether due to poor leadership, too sweeping a charge, or too ill-defined a task. Some faculty developers might be able to advise the chair in private on how to make the committee more productive, but otherwise they should consider becoming less active. In any case, faculty developers should balance the benefits against the time commitment. A time-consuming committee with a potentially major impact may be a good time investment.

If any pitfall or condition applies to one of their committee memberships, faculty developers should reassess their serving or look into changing their role. For instance, they might replace member status on a controversial committee with a staff position. Certainly they should avoid chairing such a committee.

Applying the Framework to an Example

In Table 4.1, I use the framework to illustrate how I decided to continue serving on a curriculum committee. I chose this committee because its charges—reviewing and deciding on new courses and educational programs and conducting periodic program reviews to ensure that all requirements are met—are consistent with many faculty development missions. In my institution, the universitywide curriculum committee oversees the general education curriculum and universitywide graduation requirements, and it reviews new educational programs. As expected, I have contributed my knowledge of curriculum development, pedagogy, and assessment to the committee's deliberations.

The third column in the table describes my rationale for my ratings, which appear in column four. The totals for my decisions about this committee indicate many more positives (sum of forty-three points) than negatives (sum of minus ten points), plus five neutral items. My membership could have a greater potential impact if this committee had more of a policy-making mandate than an approval function, or if it were more involved with developing new programs or a new general education curriculum. However, given the potential negative impacts of the committee, it may be wisest for faculty developers to serve on it, but not chair it. One year, I did serve as chair and found that this position gave me (and therefore the Teaching and Learning Center) *too much* visibility when courses were not approved or had to be revised repeatedly.

Conclusion

Faculty developers have good reason to seek institutional committee involvement. It enhances the credibility and visibility of their own efforts and broadens their influence among faculty and administrators. By contributing their unique expertise, knowledge, and perspectives to the discussion, they improve the functioning of the committees they join. Acting as change agents, they can influence the committee's outcomes and thus the entire institution.

As faculty developers expand their focus from individual faculty to the institution, serving on or helping to lead university- or collegewide committees and task forces becomes a more essential facet of their work. With this institutional orientation, they must ensure they are represented on key committees that affect the education of students. Through strategic committee involvement, faculty developers can transition from playing reactive, supportive roles to assuming proactive, leadership responsibilities. In fact, their being proactive on key committees may have an impact on teaching and learning at the institution more than can the one-on-one consultations and small-group workshops that they normally offer.

Because institutions of higher education have so many committees, faculty developers must select their committee participation with care. The framework introduced here can help them make strategic decisions about whether or not to serve, and in what role to serve on a given committee. Further, the framework is useful for teaching center staff as well. In fact, staff deliberations about committee memberships can lead to important related discussions about the center's direction, mission, and vision.

Appendix

Table 4.1. Framework to Help Faculty Developers Decide If They Should Serve on a Specific Committee

Committee Name: Universitywide Curriculum Committee

Characteristic	Possible Ratings	Comments and Description	Personal Rating
A. *Committee characteristics as they relate to service priorities*	Rating 1 (low priority to serve) to 5 (high priority to serve)		
1. Prestige of service—consider type of committee (standing, ad hoc, etc.); scope; reporting relationship; how people come to serve	Rating 1 (low) to 5 (high)	• Type: Standing committee of the faculty council • Scope: Review and approve all new courses for general education, review all programs • Reporting relationships: Chair reports to executive committee and faculty council at large • Come to serve: Elected or appointed by the president of the faculty council	3
2. Participation or leadership will promote the visibility and credibility of the center or faculty development efforts	Rating 1 (low) to 5 (high)	• Membership includes faculty across the campus • Opportunity to work with people who do not seek consultants or attend faculty development events • Potential to influence how courses are developed and implemented • Knowledge of whom to ask to present at faculty development programs	4

3. Closeness of fit of charge of the committee to the institution's mission	Rating 1 (low) to 5 (high)	• University's mission is to educate students, largely achieved through courses; the approval process helps maintain quality of courses	5
4. Closeness of fit of the charge of the committee to the mission of your center or faculty development efforts	Rating 1 (low) to 5 (high)	• Being part of the curriculum review process serves many faculty development functions	4
B. *Potential impact of the faculty developer on the committee*	1 point each if you might affect the ability of the committee to do the job well		
1. Provide committee with alternative approaches by describing alternative teaching and learning approaches elsewhere and researching similar programs at other institutions	1	• I bring insights into how other programs, both at my institution and elsewhere, are handling similar situations	1
2. Invite outside speakers to campus or disseminate appropriate literature	1	• Educate curriculum committee members on current trends, authentic assessment, or learner-centered teaching	1
3. Inform faculty and administrators about relevant national organizations, encourage association membership and conference attendance	1	• Inform administrators and faculty members about AAC&U and its relevance to general education • Encourage chief academic officers to join this association • Allocate funding for committee members to attend conferences	1

(Continued)

Table 4.1. (*Continued*)

Committee Name: Universitywide Curriculum Committee

Characteristic	Possible Ratings	Comments and Description	Personal Rating
4. Work with individual committee members outside of formal meetings to educate them or assist other individuals as needed	1	• Meet often with the committee chair to expedite committee meeting time or assist in the review process • Consult with faculty who submit course proposals that are not yet ready for approval • Assist faculty in preparing course proposals that contain relevant and appropriate information	1
5. Play devil's advocate to help others question the status quo or what they experienced; help team members recognize why traditional methods may be ineffective	1	Through my questions, the committee members have a broader view of different ways to conduct classes, assess students, and more objectively evaluate students on class participation	1
6. Provide support to try other approaches or pilot projects	1	Assist in the approval process for innovative courses; after approval I work with faculty who are developing innovative courses to offer further assistance	1
7. Help committee members think creativity	1		

8. Offer process consultation or propose alternative ways to run the committee if an impasse occurs	1		
9. Help experts translate their ideas about programs or policies to novices or those outside the discipline or program	1	Faculty members often write course proposals and curriculum in the vernacular of their discipline, which may be hard for outsiders to understand; I help faculty rewrite documents so others can understand them	1
10. Host public forums that are widely promoted to allow the committee to share examples of successful implementation across the institution	1		
11. Encourage or assist committee members to disseminate their successful ideas beyond your institution	1		
C. *Personal characteristics*		These are guides, not hard-and-fast rules: observe = 1; voice but not voice, if this committee makes decisions through votes = 2; advisor, consultant to committee, but not on committee = 3; voting member or staff or resource to committee = 4; chair = 5	
1. Your potential role on the committee		Rating 1 to 5 None = 1; little = 2; some = 3; moderate amount = 4; a great deal = 5	Voting member and staff or resource to committee	4

(*Continued*)

Table 4.1. (*Continued*)

Committee Name: Universitywide Curriculum Committee

Characteristic	Possible Ratings	Comments and Description	Personal Rating
2. What knowledge, skills, or expertise can you offer?	Rating 1 (low) to 5 (high)	I bring knowledge of best practices of curriculum development and revision, pedagogy, national trends in higher education	5
3. How much impact will you have on the committee?	Rating 1 (low) to 5 (high)	Raise profile of the importance of pedagogy; I have been instrumental in the development of a new course approval template that shows how teaching and learning activities engage the students, assessment methods, learning outcomes, and course alignment; I will continue to offer comments as this template is reviewed periodically	4
4. Personal interest in the topic, potential to advance your career	Rating 1 to 5	I have always been interested in curriculum development; my knowledge of courses across the curriculum has helped me understand the variety of educational programs this university offers	5
D. *Conditions that should discourage service*			

Item	Rating	Explanation	Score
1. A conflict of interest among the mission of your center, faculty development efforts, and the charge of the committee	Rating 0 (no conflict) to –5 (serious conflict)	No conflict exists	0
2. The committee is seen as promoting the interests of faculty	Rating 0 (not applicable or perceived as serving faculty interests) or –10 (perceived as subverting faculty interests)	Committee serves in the interest of faculty roles	0
E. *Pitfalls or conditions that should cause you to reconsider serving or consider having a less visible role on the committee*			
1. Is this a controversial topic at your institution? Are there polarizing factions of faculty members?	Rating 0 (not applicable or not controversial) to –10 depending on the extent of the controversy	Not a controversial topic in general; sometimes individual courses are controversial	–2
2. By serving, might you make enemies among the faculty?	Rating 0 (not applicable or no potential for making enemies) to –10 (high potential)	Faculty do not like revising their course proposals; they can take this personally and resent the person who required the revisions	–5
3. What is the ratio of time investment to impact?	Rating –6 to 6; see table note[a] for explanation of ratio ratings	Course approval and program review influence the direction of the university, but change occurs slowly and incrementally	2
4. Can you remain in turf battles, or be seen as neutral by faculty and administrators?	Rating –5 (cannot be neutral), 0 (can be neutral), or 5 (if being seen as neutral is an asset)	I can remain neutral in turf battles because they rarely come to this committee	

(Continued)

Table 4.1. (*Continued*)

Characteristic	Possible Ratings	Comments and Description	Personal Rating
	Committee Name: Universitywide Curriculum Committee		
How much does serving on the committee undermine your best interests or those of the center, or faculty development efforts? This may happen if others ask you to serve on the committee, including your direct supervisor, and you do not think it is in your own or your center's best interests	Rating 0 (not applicable or no conflict of interest) to –5 (severe conflict of interests)	This committee is not in conflict with my interests or that of the center's faculty development efforts	0
5. The chair of the committee has a bad reputation or is hard to work with	Rating = 0 (easy to work with to –3 (hard to work with)	The chair of the committee has a good reputation and is easy to work with	0
Totals			
Subtotal positive	Possible total positive score = 63		43
Subtotal negative	Possible total negative score = 59		–10
Subtotal number of neutrals	Possible total of neutrals = 7		5

Recommendations and decision

I should continue serving on this committee while avoiding chairing this committee; this is an elected committee with additional appointments from the president of the faculty council, so I should try to be elected or continue to seek appointment

[a]Ratio table to explain ratings for Section E, item 4:

Time ↓ Impact →	Low Impact	Medium Impact	High Impact
High total time	−6	3	4
Medium total time	−3	2	5
Low total time	−1	1	6

REFERENCES

Baron, L. (2006). The advantages of a reciprocal relationship between faculty development and organizational development in higher education. In S. Chadwick-Blossey & D. R. Robertson (Eds.), *To improve the academy: Vol. 24. Resources for faculty, instructional, and organizational development* (pp. 29–43). Bolton, MA: Anker.

Beichner, R. J., & Saul, J. M. (2003). *Introduction to the SCALE-UP (student-centered activities for large enrollment undergraduate programs) project.* Retrieved December 5, 2008, from www.ncsu.edu/PER/Articles/Varenna_SCALE_Paper.pdf

Chism, N.V.N. (1998). The role of educational developers in institutional change: From the basement office to the front office. In M. Kaplan & D. Lieberman (Eds.), *To improve the academy: Vol. 17. Resources for faculty, instructional, and organizational development* (pp. 141–153). Stillwater, OK: New Forums Press.

Diamond, R. M. (1995). *Preparing for promotion and tenure review: A faculty guide.* Bolton, MA: Anker.

Diamond, R. M. (2002). Faculty, instructional, and organizational development: Options and choices. In K. H. Gillespie, L. R. Hilsen, & E. C. Wadsworth (Eds.), *A guide to faculty development: Practical advice, examples, and resources* (pp. 2–8). Bolton, MA: Anker.

Gillespie, K. H. (in press). Administrative and organizational development. In K. H. Gillespie & D. R. Robertson (Eds.), *A guide to faculty development: Practical advice, examples, and resources* (2nd ed.). San Francisco: Jossey-Bass.

Gillespie, K. H., Hilsen, L. R., & Wadsworth, E. C. (Eds.). (2002). *A guide to faculty development: Practical advice, examples, and resources.* Bolton, MA: Anker.

Gillespie, K. H., & Zinsmeister, D. (2004, November). *Exploring organizational development: Getting involved in decision-making.* Paper presented at the 29th annual meeting of the Professional and Organizational Development Network in Higher Education, Montreal.

Lieberman, D. A., & Guskin, A. F. (2003). The essential role of faculty development in new higher education models. In C. M. Wehlburg & S. Chadwick-Blossey (Eds.), *To improve the academy: Vol. 21. Resources for faculty, instructional, and organizational development* (pp. 257–272). Bolton, MA: Anker.

Marshall, W. J. (1999). University service. In V. Bianco-Mathis & N. Chalofsky (Eds.), *The full-time faculty handbook* (pp. 113–128). Thousand Oaks, CA: Sage.

Schroeder, C. (2006, October). *Coming in from the margins: Redefining faculty development's institutional role.* Paper presented at the 31st annual meeting of the Professional and Organizational Development Network in Higher Education, Portland, OR.

Schroeder, C. (in press). *Coming in from the margins: Redefining faculty development's institutional role.* Sterling, VA: Stylus.

5

A MODEL FOR PUTTING A TEACHING CENTER IN CONTEXT

AN INFORMAL COMPARISON OF TEACHING CENTERS AT LARGER STATE UNIVERSITIES

Wesley H. Dotson, Daniel J. Bernstein, University of Kansas

An informal comparative analysis of teaching centers at larger state universities around the United States was conducted as part of a self-initiated ten-year review of our center. We compared centers along several dimensions, among them programs, resources, and size. This chapter offers our methods, results, and general impressions of the process as an example for others who might decide to conduct a similar analysis.

"So what are you doing, and how does that fit into the context of other teaching centers across the country?" The Center for Teaching Excellence at the University of Kansas considered that question last year when it was asked by our faculty advisory board while we were conducting a self-initiated ten-year review of the center. The advisory board wanted to know how the center compared to peer institutions along several dimensions, among them size, audience, types of services offered, resources, and faculty involvement.

We knew from informal conversations with peer institutions and being a part of the POD Network that teaching centers exist in a variety of forms and sizes. Some centers are small, with directors and staff splitting appointments with other departments. Other centers have dedicated directors and

First and foremost, we would like to thank all of the centers and their staff who shared their time and effort in gathering this information. Without them this project would not exist. Many thanks also to Judy Eddy for her patience and guidance throughout this project.

a staff of dozens of people. Centers play a role in technology support on campus, the formal teaching evaluation process, or participation in campus and systemwide teaching initiatives. Knowledge of the diversity of teaching center structure and philosophy presented a daunting challenge in answering our advisory board's question. To attempt to describe all of the various approaches to running a teaching center across the many types of academic environments in which they exist was beyond both the scope of our inquiry and our resources as a single center. Therefore, we hoped only to situate ourselves into the narrower context of teaching centers at large, state universities. We hoped that the process could be expedited by locating a central database of information about how centers of various sizes and types existed within their academic contexts, but such a resource could not be located. We did not find any published comparative reviews of similar teaching centers along the dimensions identified by our advisory board; nor did we locate an online database with any comprehensive information about centers of any size or type. Instead, we relied on the generosity of our colleagues at other centers to help us answer the question.

Fortunately, the review occurred in the context of strong local support for the center, and we were able to use the process of answering the question as a reflective and formative experience. We offer a description of our work here as an example of a method other centers might adapt to their needs to engage in similar projects, not as a definitive database or comprehensive resource. We undertook this analysis to answer our own specific questions, but the approach could be used by others, or it might suggest development of an ongoing collaborative pool of information about centers.

Collection of Information

We identified an initial pool of thirty-five teaching centers at peer institutions from which to gather information. We selected peer institutions on the basis of demographic similarity (larger state universities) and other characteristics (schools in the conference, presence of programs comparable to and complementary to our center goals). We chose our sample to allow us to gather the information our advisory board wanted in a timely fashion, not to compile an exhaustive list (we did not include many fine centers). Including many additional centers in the comparison would have offered small marginal benefit in our minds relative to the large increase in time and effort required to gather the information.

Following identification of the target centers, we developed a list of the information we needed from each center to answer the question posed by our advisory board. The advisory board wanted to know how our center compared to others around the United States in several areas. To facilitate finding that information, we developed a series of questions to be answered about each target center (see Exhibit 5.1). We designed the questions as a guide for exploring target centers and as a prompt for dialogue with a representative of each comparison center. The information

---

Exhibit 5.1. Interview Questions for Teaching Centers

Programs
- What three or four programs do you and your staff spend the most time on?
- What percentage of your staff's time is spent on these key programs?
- What audiences do you serve (tenure-track faculty, adjuncts, GTAs)?
- Do you offer grants or funding for course and teaching development? If so, how do they work?
- Do you have a role in technology training or support for faculty? If so, what percentage of your budget and staff time is spent on this?
- Do you have a role in administering or analyzing teacher evaluations for your university? If so, what percentage of your budget and staff time is spent on this?

Faculty Connections
- Do any faculty members have paid appointments with your center? If so, how do they work?
- Are faculty members reimbursed or paid for participating in your programs? If so, how does that work?

Staffing
- How many full-time staff members work at your center?
- How many part-time, and what is the full-time equivalent of all of them?

Resources and Budget
- What percentage of your budget is spent on your key programs (from Programs questions)?
- Are any of these programs funded by private sources?
- What percentage of your total budget is supplied by your institution, and what percentage by private funds (if any)?

GTA Preparation
- Is a course on teaching offered by your center for GTAs?
- If yes, do you design and oversee the course, or is it taught in partnership with another department or administrative unit?

Communication
- How do faculty members find out about what you're doing? What avenues of communication do you have in place?
- How do you communicate your work to your institution's administrators?

Conclusion
- Is there any other information you'd like for us to know about your center?

requested and gathered reflected the unique goals of our self-study and the advisory board's question. Other centers doing similar work would customize the questions they ask to elicit conversations about the issues and information they want to explore.

After creating our list of questions, we visited each center's website to gather as much information as possible. We did this both as a means of familiarizing ourselves with each center's programs and philosophy and as a way to answer as many questions as we could before asking colleagues to spend time talking to us. As the review of the websites progressed, it became apparent that the detailed information required to make an accurate comparison among centers could not be gathered by browsing alone. In addition, we discovered that four of the target universities did not have a currently active teaching center, so those universities were excluded from the study.

We then contacted the directors of the remaining thirty-one centers, explained the purpose of our review, and asked if they would be willing to converse by email or phone to fill in the gaps in the information we had collected about their center. If they responded positively, then we arranged a contact time and sent the directors copies of our questions (with a note about the information we still needed to gather) to allow them time to prepare relevant materials and facilitate an efficient conversation. Some interviewees e-mailed answers to the questions, while others spent twenty to thirty minutes on the phone with a graduate assistant to provide the requested information.

Seventeen centers completed the interview questions either by email or by phone. Several other centers that indicated willingness to share information could not be included in the final analysis, because of inability to schedule an interview time before the deadline for completing the self-study for our advisory board. Overall, eighteen centers (including ours) are represented in the comparative data reported here. Because responding centers had the option of not answering every interview question, some comparisons do not include all of the responding centers.

Centers Represented in Comparative Information

University of Arizona: University Teaching Center

Arizona State University: Center for Learning and Teaching Excellence

University of Georgia: Center for Teaching and Learning

University of Illinois at Urbana–Champaign: Center for Teaching Excellence

Indiana University–Purdue University Indianapolis: Center for Teaching and Learning

Iowa State University: Center for Excellence in Learning and Teaching

University of Kansas: Center for Teaching Excellence

Kansas State University: Center for Advancement of Teaching and Learning

Kennesaw State University: Center for Excellence in Teaching and Learning

University of Michigan: Center for Research on Learning and Teaching

University of Minnesota: Center for Teaching and Learning

University of North Carolina: Center for Teaching and Learning

Ohio State University: Faculty and TA Development

University of Oklahoma: Program for Instructional Innovation

University of Oregon: Teaching Effectiveness Program

Penn State University: Schreyer Institute for Teaching Excellence

Texas Christian University: Koehler Center for Teaching Excellence

Texas Tech University: Teaching, Learning, and Technology Center

Analysis of Information

In general, we present our findings as the percentage of centers meeting certain criteria related to the information our advisory board wanted to know. We used functional criteria, such as the presence of certain types of programs and audiences served, and also resource criteria, such as staffing size or budget sources. See Tables 5.1, 5.2, and 5.3 for a detailed explanation of the comparative criteria used in our self-study report. Evaluations of each criterion reflect binary decisions (yes or no only) rather than a nuanced spectrum of services that centers might offer. For example, a center offering a single $2,500 grant program would receive the same *yes* for the criterion "offers grant funding for programs" that a center with six grant programs would receive. Because of the diversity in approaches across centers, however, such simplification was necessary to bring coherence to the data.

In evaluating centers according to size, we compared centers according to the ratio of full-time equivalent (FTE) staff each center had per thousand students (both undergraduate and graduate). This measure yielded a more comparable representation of center size. We attempted to calcu-

Table 5.1. Criteria for Program-Based Comparison

Criterion	Definition
Role in technology support or training	We scored a *yes* if the center had any programs or staff dedicated to installing, maintaining, or training staff in the use of educational technology such as overheads, software, computer networks, etc.
Role in administration or analysis of teacher evaluations	We scored as *yes* any center that played an active part in the formal teacher evaluation process on their campus. We scored as *no* any center that simply consulted with individual faculty about their teacher evaluations.
Serves GTAs as well as faculty	We scored a *yes* for a center if it had any programs open to GTAs or marketed to them. Such programs might include beginning-of-year orientation, consulting services, or inclusion on campus mailing lists about center activities.
Offers a course on college teaching for GTAs	We scored a *yes* for a center if such a course was present and being offered through the center, or a center staff member was responsible for the teaching of the course through other campus departments.
Furnishes annual report to university administration	We scored a *yes* for a center if it submitted a yearly report to someone in the university administration. We did not distinguish types, length, or content of the report.

late the same proportion relative to the number of faculty members at the university, but universities defined their faculty positions differently so the reported numbers were ambiguous and difficult to compare. Division of centers by FTE into three groups was an arbitrary decision made to allow us to more easily represent data visually.

It proved difficult to gather information about the specific operating budgets of the cooperating centers. Rather than a comparison of resources measured in dollar amounts, we simply gathered information about various types of indicators (grants, faculty reimbursement, faculty appointments in the center, outside funding sources, and so on) as indicators of the functions served by resources allotted to the center.

Summary of Results

Table 5.4 shows that most centers use financial incentives to support faculty participation in programming. Although the funding is sometimes in grants to support particular projects, there are also funding programs that give a stipend or access to operating budgets as a thank-you to

Table 5.2. Criteria for Resource-Based Comparisons

Criterion	Definition
Offers grant funding for programs	We scored a *yes* if the center had programs for which faculty received grant funding through the center. We did not score programs in which centers assisted faculty in securing grants from other organizations or outside funding agencies.
Have faculty partners who assist in meeting center goals	We scored a *yes* if the center had faculty members working with them who received either a teaching release or a portion of their salary for time spent in the center working directly on meeting center goals.
Reimbursement for faculty participation in programs	We scored a *yes* if the center offered any monetary compensation to faculty for participating in center programs. Such compensation might include stipends for completing workshops, travel reimbursements to attend conferences, and the like.
Any part of budget comes from noninstitutional sources	We scored a *yes* if the center received any money from noninstitutional sources such as foundations, endowments, or private donations.
More than 10 percent of budget from noninstitutional sources	We scored a *yes* if more than 10 percent of the center's operating budget (as reported by the center) came from noninstitutional sources.

Table 5.3. Criteria for Size-Based Comparisons

Criterion	Definition
Center has 0.10–0.25 FTE per 1,000 students	We scored a *yes* if the center had no more than the equivalent of one full-time position for every 4,000 students at the university.
Center has 0.26–0.50 FTE per 1,000 students	We scored a *yes* if the center had no more than the equivalent of one full-time position for every 2,000 students at the university and no less than one full-time position for every 4,000 students at the university.
Center has > 0.50 FTE per 1,000 students	We scored a *yes* if the center had more than the equivalent of one full-time position for every 2,000 students at the university.

Note: We distinguished among three sizes of center arbitrarily to allow us to draw comparisons about types of programs offered relative to center size.

Table 5.4. Summary Report of Teaching Center Functions

Descriptor	Percentage of Centers
Offers grant funding for programs	72 (13 of 18)
Have faculty partners who assist in meeting center goals	56 (10 of 18)
Reimbursement for faculty participation in programs	50 (9 of 18)
Provides role in technology support or training	72 (13 of 18)
Role in administration or analysis of teacher evaluations	33 (3 of 9)
Serves GTAs as well as faculty	89 (16 of 18)
Offers a course on college teaching for GTAs	72 (13 of 18)
Annual report to university administration	83 (15 of 18)
Any part of budget comes from noninstitutional sources	47 (8 of 17)
More than 10% of budget from noninstitutional sources	18 (3 of 17)

faculty for engaging in workshops or ongoing faculty communities in the center. The data also show that the vast majority of centers work with graduate teaching assistants as well, sometimes in collaboration with the local graduate school or with departments. Further, the data show that even though almost half of the responding centers receive some portion of their budget from noninstitutional sources, few of them rely on such funding as a significant portion of their resources.

Figure 5.1 shows the percentage of centers in three categories of size, expressed as the ratio of staff positions to the number of students on a campus. There is no absolute meaning to any of these categories, but the range of personnel resources is interesting to note. It was useful to us in our self-study, because we were able to place our own center in the context of what other universities provided in support of faculty development.

Figure 5.2 shows the percentage of centers with a role in technology support or training by the size of the center, measured by a staff-per-student ratio. Within our sample, an increasingly larger proportion of centers had a role in technology as the size of the center increased. It is likely that the higher allocation of staff positions in larger centers may be partially a result of keeping several staff members in the center whose primary responsibilities revolve around training in and maintaining educational technology. Figure 5.2 also shows one way we represented our data to the advisory board, as a quick visual reference for one of our primary findings.

Figure 5.1. Percentage of Centers by Size

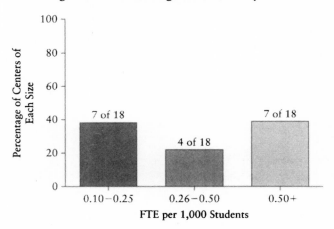

**Figure 5.2. Percentage of Centers with Role in Technology
Support or Training, by Size of Center**

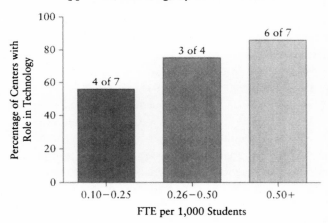

Figure 5.3 shows the percentage of centers that have responsibility for evaluation of teaching, as a function of the size of the center, again measured by a staff-per-student ratio. This graph shows that there is no simple relation between size of the center and its responsibility for student evaluations. This is different from the relationship for technology, suggesting that centers may have assumed this responsibility if it was part of their mission, defined by either a center's own staff, or by the university administration.

Figure 5.3. Percentage of Centers with Formal Role in
Evaluation of Teaching, by Size of Center

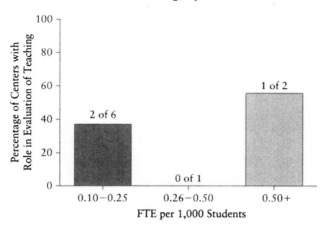

Discussion

We conducted this comparative review of teaching centers at peer institutions as a response to a question asked by our faculty advisory board. We have made both our methods and our findings public as a result of discussions with colleagues who suggested such an example might be useful for other centers choosing to undertake a similar inquiry. Though there were several limitations to the work, the original purpose of the process revolved around answering a question about several peer institutions—a situation many centers are likely to encounter at some point.

The process of creating this report gave us an opportunity to learn about other centers and reflect on our own practice in a way that we continue to find valuable. A pleasant by-product of the initial report was identification of interesting, novel, and successful programs undertaken by the various centers. We prepared an addendum to the original report containing highlights from the various programs we reviewed and shared those program highlights with our advisory board. In addition, we also took the opportunity to identify website features at various centers that we found helpful while browsing for information. See the Appendix to this chapter for additional information about program highlights and website features, with links to specific center sites so you can explore them for information as well. The work of several centers not represented in the comparative report was part of our initial thirty-five target centers, and it also appears in the program highlights.

We learned several things throughout this process that we want to pass on to centers considering a similar project. First, decide what you want to know before you start gathering information. The amount of material on most center websites can be overwhelming, and knowing what you are looking for helps streamline the search process. Second, identify for comparison only institutions that have characteristics similar to yours and programs you find compatible and in line with what you want your center to accomplish. Our center's specific needs within the self-study drove our selection of both desired information and comparison centers.

Third, do your homework before contacting the other centers. We wanted to minimize inconvenience to the other centers by gathering in advance as much information as possible. Our goal was to find every bit of public information possible, so all our colleagues had to do was fill in the blanks. Several center directors expressed appreciation for our consideration of their time in doing so, and we also found that being familiar with each center through browsing its website facilitated much more efficient and enjoyable conversation when we talked directly with center staff members. Fourth, recognize the inherent limitations in an inquiry like ours. Any small sample will not likely represent all teaching centers. The centers responding to our inquiry were only those we could contact and successfully interview in a short period of time, roughly six weeks, and the sample does not include centers from small liberal arts colleges or community colleges. Furthermore, the data represent only a single point in time. Several centers reported that their programs, budgets, or staffing had just changed or was likely to change in the near future, thus making these summary data reflective of the state of affairs at each center only at the time of the interview (spring 2008).

A more overarching consideration, and one that should drive all of your activities in conducting a review such as ours, involves the purpose for which you are conducting your review. Are you doing so to get ideas about programs or center structure? Are you attempting to leverage resources for desired programs or structural changes? Are you trying to situate yourself in the context of other, similar centers so you can identify realistic expectations for what your center can accomplish? By clearly defining your purpose in advance, you can approach the review and set realistic expectations for what information you need and the form it should take.

An additional type of information we wish we would have formally gathered was more qualitative data. Questions such as "What are the three things you are most proud of accomplishing in the last three years?" or "What are two or three things you hope to achieve in the next three years?" would have allowed us to get a better feel for the direction of the various centers, and it could have been another source of ideas for developing our own center. These topics sometimes came up in the course of follow-up conversation, but systematically prompting them would have been valuable.

Comparative information similar to that contained in this chapter has been willingly shared among centers in the past, and it appears in annual reports to administrators and in conversation with colleagues and advisory boards. After completing our survey, we learned of similar regional projects undertaken by universities connected by an athletic conference (Big Ten, SEC). The data do not appear to have been published, but this suggests the value of such information. Summary data of this form could be a resource for the entire teaching center community. We hope that, by sharing our data and our methods with the community, we will inspire similar work and its distribution through publication by others. In that way we can all better document what it is we do, and analyze how our work relates to what other centers are doing. It is also conceivable that a collaborative effort with the POD Network could begin the accumulation of a public database of information about some of these features of center functions and resources. If each center contributed its own information, other centers could sort the data by various institutional characteristics and get a comparison set of data quite readily. Such a database could also address the two limitations mentioned earlier, by allowing larger samples to be explored in more detail more quickly. Also, if contributing centers updated the database regularly (say, once a year), then the comparative information gathered would be more likely to reflect current circumstances. The first steps in this effort would involve a thorough and thoughtful consideration of what characteristics of centers and our work should be included and how they could be best represented. The present case is one example only, though it could be a useful starting point for that larger conversation.

Appendix: Selected Program Highlights and Website Features

Program Highlights

Teaching as Intellectual Work

Teaching Portfolio Gallery (University of Kansas)
www.cte.ku.edu/gallery/

- Visible examples of the intellectual work of college teaching
- Tangible product that can be referenced for tenure reviews and job interviews

Peer Review of Teaching (Kansas State University)
www.k-state.edu/catl/peerreview/

- Two-semester program that results in a course portfolio
- Faculty members paired with peer mentors who have already created a course portfolio

Department Level Development Grant (Iowa State University)
www.celt.iastate.edu/grants_awards/TEACHProposal2008
.html

- One-time grant to support improvement of teaching for an entire department
- Must go toward faculty development, not for technology

Faculty Learning Communities (University of Georgia and University of Minnesota)
www.ctl.uga.edu/resources/resources.htm#flc
www1.umn.edu/ohr/teachlearn/faculty/mid/index.html

- Foster dialogue among faculty
- Targeted toward specific audiences (e.g., midcareer faculty, pretenure faculty)

Workshops, Outreach, Teaching Resources

Workshops on Demand (University of Arizona)
nfc.arizona.edu/UTC/workshoprequest.html

- Workshops offered only when requested
- Online request form allows interested parties to request a workshop
- Workshop then planned and notice sent out to potential attendees via precreated email lists of instructors interested in particular topics

Workshops Open to the Community (Texas Christian University and University of Oregon)
www.cte.tcu.edu/workshopsevents.html
http://tep.uoregon.edu/workshops/index.html

- Open to audiences outside the hosting university
- Includes high school teachers, faculty at local community colleges, and businesses

Thank a Teacher (University of Iowa)
   http://centeach.uiowa.edu/thanks/index.shtml

- Online form students can complete to tell a professor or GTA something they enjoyed or appreciated
- Comments delivered following end of semester

TeachingTalk 2.0/Teaching Blogs (University of Iowa and University of Oregon)
   http://at-lamp.its.uiowa.edu/cft/teachingtalk/
   http://tepblog.uoregon.edu/blog/

- Online blog dedicated to conversation about teaching
- Informal and relaxed, with a range of topics covered

Podcasts/Teaching Tube (Arizona State University and University of Oregon)
   http://clte.asu.edu/podcasts/
   http://clte.asu.edu/teachingtube/
   http://tep.uoregon.edu/resources/facultyshowcase.html

- Online video and multimedia presentations about teaching
- Prepared and presented by faculty

Distance Learning, Technology of Teaching

Hybrid Courses (University of Oklahoma)
   http://pii.ou.edu/content/view/58/56/

- Replace some portion of classroom time with online experiences
- Variety of educational tasks can supplement lectures and seat work

Funding for Online Course Development (Indiana University–Purdue University Indianapolis)
   ctl.iupui.edu/Programs/jumpstart.asp

- Grant program to design and implement an online or hybrid course
- Support also offered in technical aspects of design such as programming, video support, graphic design, and so on

Online Certificate in College Teaching (University of New Hampshire)
www.unh.edu/teaching-excellence/Academic_prog_in_coll_teach/index
.html

- Open to students from around the United States
- Faculty who teach courses also from several universities

GTA Services

Graduate Teaching Consultants (University of Michigan)
www.crlt.umich.edu/gsis/gtc.php

- Experienced GTAs act as consultants for their peers
- Confidential and outside the departments

TA Mentors (University of Georgia)
www.ctl.uga.edu/teach_asst/ta_mentors/ta_mentors_long_description
.htm

- Mentors are experienced GTAs selected to participate in Future Faculty Program
- One aspect of program is to take leadership role in discussion of teaching within their department, including leading seminars, mentoring peers, and documenting their intellectual work

College Teaching Certificate Programs (University of Illinois at Urbana–Champaign, Ohio State University, and Texas Tech University)
www.cte.uiuc.edu/Did/Faculty/index.htm
http://ftad.osu.edu/gis/
www.tltc.ttu.edu/teach/about.asp

- Allow graduate students to document their teaching ability
- Requirements have various forms but usually involve a series of recommended courses and teaching experiences

Website Features

Navigation bars clearly located on the page (Kennesaw State University)
www.kennesaw.edu/cetl/

- Stay in place regardless of which page in the site the visitor is on
- Quick visual reference to various areas of the site

Site-specific search engine (University of Kansas)
www.cte.ku.edu/

- Allows visitor to look for keywords only on the center's site
- Quickly locate information of interest (for example, grant programs)

Site map link (Penn State University)
www.schreyerinstitute.psu.edu/sitemap/

- Single page with index of all site areas visible as a series of organized links
- Allows quick identification of scope of site and also easy locating of information within it

Audience-specific navigation bars (University of Michigan)
www.crlt.umich.edu/

- Allows quick identification of relevant services

6

THE VALUE OF THE NARRATIVE TEACHING OBSERVATION TO DOCUMENT TEACHING BEHAVIORS

Niki Young, Western Oregon University

A central mission of teaching and learning centers is to help faculty members improve their teaching. The teaching observation is an established tool to support this effort. Although educational developers have created general guides and forms for conducting teaching observations, the literature contains few examples of observation narratives. This chapter offers detailed examples of these narratives, deconstructing the process and demonstrating the value of narrative to document teaching behaviors. This chapter extends and develops the literature, showing how—and making explicit why—we do what we do, in the interest of making our work transparent and replicable.

> *I am a teacher at heart, and there are moments in the classroom when I can hardly hold the joy. When my students and I discover uncharted territory to explore, when the pathway out of a thicket opens up before us, when our experience is illuminated by the lightning-life of the mind—then teaching is the finest work I know.*
>
> —Parker Palmer

> *Dear Fellow Teachers, What do you do when silence breaks out in your class, the times when you suddenly forget everything you were going to say, or you ask a question no one answers, and you sit there wishing you were dead, blush rising from the throat, face hot, throat clenched?*
>
> —Jane Tompkins

No monuments record the bravery of teachers.

—Jane Tompkins

College teaching can, at times, be joyful and exhilarating, or painful and frustrating. One of the most important responsibilities of faculty developers, and a central mission of teaching and learning centers, is to "help faculty members develop, assess, and refine their teaching skills" (Frantz, Beebe, Horvath, Canales, & Swee, 2005, p. 73). Classroom observation is an established tool for this purpose (Chism, 2007; Frantz et al., 2005; Jacobson, Wulff, Grooters, Edwards, & Freisem, 2009; Jenson, 2002; Jones, Sagendorf, Morris, Stockburger, & Patterson, 2009; Lewis, 2002; Millis, 2006; Wehlburg, 2005; Wilkerson & Lewis, 2002) and "a powerful and effective faculty development strategy" (Wilkerson & Lewis, 2002, p. 74). "Classroom observations powerfully document teaching activities, encourage reflection, foster constructive dialogues, and strengthen teaching," observes Millis (2005, p. 34).

Research demonstrates that teaching observations are an effective means of professional development (Hatzipanagos & Lygo-Baker, 2006; Jacobson et al., 2009) that enable "ideas and techniques to be examined in more detail" (Hatzipanagos & Lygo-Baker, 2006, p. 100). Hatzipanagos and Lygo-Baker found that the teaching observation process enhanced faculty members' understanding of learning and teaching strategies and deepened their knowledge. In their study of the long-term value and effects of teaching center observations, Jacobson et al. (2009) reported that faculty consultations led faculty to change their teaching practices, change their teaching perspective, and learn to work constructively with student feedback.

Educational developers have created general guides on conducting teaching observations (for example, Chism, 2007; Lewis, 2002; McKeachie, 2002; Millis, 2005, 2006; Wilkerson & Lewis, 2002), devised a variety of forms (such as Chism, 2007), and offered tips on the process (for instance, Brinko, 1993; Jenson, 2002; Lewis, 2002), but the literature contains few examples of observational narratives that document what this powerful professional development process looks like. Chism (2007) includes a one-page example of a double-entry narrative log in her chapter on classroom observation, Wilkerson and Lewis (2002) offer suggestions on method, and Lewis (2002) gives an example of how to analyze participation in case study discussion. Jenson (2002) goes a step further in describing her method: "I drew a line down the notebook page and used one-half page for notes I thought the students would be taking and the other half for my observations" (p. 94). Although these examples are wonderful beginnings, none of the authors deconstructs the narrative to make explicit not only *how* we document what we do but also *why* we document what we do. This chapter seeks to fill that gap in the literature, demonstrating the value of a written record of teaching behaviors.

In the pages that follow, I review the generally agreed three-part process for conducting teaching observations as outlined by Chism (2007), McKeachie (2002), Millis (2006), and Wilkerson and Lewis (2002), which begins with a preobservation meeting, is followed by the observation itself, and concludes with a postobservation meeting. I describe the preparation necessary before the observation and the observation process in detail. Further, I identify an additional step in the process, the postobservation write up and analysis, in which the raw data or field notes from the observation are *transformed* into information for the faculty member. The transformation process has hitherto been a hidden and implicit part of the analysis, and the previous literature has failed to offer an interpretive frame that grounds our comments in the language of teaching and learning. Just as the art instructor I observed encouraged students to "use the vocabulary" in offering feedback on their peers' three-dimensional designs, we too need to couch our descriptions in our professional language and urge faculty to use our vocabulary to describe their work. This is appropriate use of an interpretive frame, and it gives faculty a new way of viewing their actions. To demonstrate the value of this approach, I give several examples of detailed observation narratives drawn from my experiences at several colleges and universities. Then I discuss communication and the postobservation meeting, and finally I draw some conclusions on the benefits of these narratives.

Phase One: Preparing to Enter the Field (Preobservation)

"Knowing what to look for is in fact a general principle applying to observations," notes McKeachie (2002, p. 324). During the preobservation meeting, educational developers ask questions of the faculty member, such as, "Do you have any areas of concern?" and "What questions would you like answered?" They should also request copies of relevant instructional materials such as the course syllabus, assignments, handouts, and other materials to support instruction such as PowerPoint slides. These materials are the blueprint of the course. Finally, this meeting is an opportunity to discuss the observation process in more detail, fleshing out when and where the observation will occur, and what it will look like.

Reviewing the course materials prior to the observation gives me a better sense of where the class has been and where they are going. These materials also offer me a fuller sense of the educational context, the relationship of this course to others in the department, and its relationship to the major. In addition, I am able to give the instructor feedback on instructional design, whether the course goals and learning outcomes are being met, and whether the methods are appropriate to the goals and outcomes. As Jones et al. (2009) learned while developing a learning-focused classroom observation form, "effective course design is critical" (p. 209). Fink (2003) and Richlin (2006) also advise us to ask what we want students to know or be able to do as a result of our instruction and then design activities and assignments to achieve those outcomes. An added benefit of offering feedback on instructional materials, such as the syllabus or course assignments, is that the onus is not on the instructor per se, and thus he or she is less apt to take this feedback personally or as criticism. Assignments and syllabi can be easily modified. Taking care to frame comments as questions or suggestions can also help to reduce the appearance of evaluation. Once I have reviewed the course materials, I am ready to observe the class.

Phase Two: Collecting the Data (the Observation)

What do you document when you observe a class? I try to document everything using the narrative approach of a social scientific researcher. I try to record, as fully as possible, what the instructor says and does during the class, as well as student responses and behaviors. Thus, the teaching observation narrative resembles the field notes or diaries recorded by anthropologists.

Why use a written record, when one could create a digital or video record instead? As McKeachie (2002) observes, "Videotaping would seem on the face of it to be especially helpful. . . . Nonetheless, videotaping may not be the best feedback" (p. 324). As he notes, subjects who are videotaped tend to focus so much on their own appearance and mannerism that they lose the larger point or purpose of the feedback. Videotaping can present a "more complete record of classroom events," Wilkerson and Lewis found; "[h]owever, it is more obtrusive, with both students and faculty reporting uneasiness and modification of their behavior to some extent" (2002, p. 74). In her analysis of the literature, Brinko (1993) refers to the process as "video self-confrontation" (p. 576) and remarks, "Video feedback is not for everyone. In many cases it can be a useful tool; in other cases it can be a threatening and stressful experience" (p. 582).

I find that despite trying to observe the course from the students' point of view, I cannot fully remove my consultant's hat, although conducting multiple observations can counteract this tendency. Lewis (2002) describes how she takes on the typical student's role in the initial observation: "I take notes, may or may not read/do the assignment prior to class, try to make sense of the lecture, and write down whatever questions come to mind" (p. 67). In subsequent observations she shifts her role to educational developer.

Deciding what aspects of the classroom experience are worth attending to and recording is a skill (Lewis, 2002). The first part of the task is to describe what we see—specifically, the instructor behaviors we observe—with as much precision as possible, for example, differentiating among "Professor A. *said* . . . " "Professor A *asked* . . . " "Professor A *explained* . . . " "Professor A *showed* . . . " and "Professor A *demonstrated*." We should then do our best to write down what the instructor said, asked, explained, showed, or demonstrated, documenting both the action and the content. For instance:

> Professor B connected student comments to one another, "That is like what Russ said," summarized, "It is a great focusing technique," and elaborated on student comments, as well as invited additional comments, asking: "Does anyone want to add to that?" and "Anybody else?" and "Who else?" She did not jump in to answer her own questions but rather waited for students to answer.

Likewise, we should record the student behaviors we observe. When the instructor poses a question, how do students react? Do they raise their hands, shout out an answer, consult their textbook or notes, or remain silent? What do they say, ask, note, comment on? Examples:

> Professor C said, "Your role is to be a mentor." He asked, "What does it mean to be a mentor?" A student said, "A mentor is someone you look up to." A student offered, "Someone with wisdom and knowledge." Professor C repeated student comments and wrote them on the board. Professor C called on students by name. "Jaycee?" Jaycee replied, "Someone who offers encouragement." Professor C asked, "What else?"
>
> Professor D asked, "What is plagiarism? Who can tell me?" He waited for students to respond and repeated the question three times. When students still did not respond, he added, "It's on your handout." Students still did not respond. Finally, Professor D wrote the answer on the white board.
>
> Students discussed bias and their reactions to the readings. A student commented, "This reminds me of something I saw on the Olympics—narrated by Oprah Winfrey, on Emmanuel." A student

asked, "So how do you advocate for somebody and still have your own self-motivation? I see this all happen all the time. This is a very simple example. . . ." A student gave an example of experiencing strong prejudice at Wal-Mart.

Another useful technique is to count specific behaviors: how many questions an instructor asked during a given class period, how many times students asked questions of the instructor, how many times students responded to the instructor, how many times the instructor called on students by name. For instance:

> Throughout the class Professor E referred to students by name, using 20 names in the course of the class I observed. Professor E was very polite and treated students with respect. When she needed to read from a student's handout, she asked, "May I read from yours? Thank you." She explicitly thanked students seven times for their contributions to discussion throughout the class. She gave explicit feedback in discussions, noting, "I heard you say . . . " "And I noticed you also said. . . ." She also gave students positive feedback on their responses in discussion, commenting, "Great." "Fantastic." "Interesting." "Lovely. I really like those." "Great." "Fantastic." "I really like that."
>
> Professor F asked over 76 questions in the class I observed, generating more than 66 student responses.
>
> Professor G asked 25 questions during the course of the lecture. Students responded to Professor G's questions, with some students calling out answers so the rest of the class could hear, and many students responding quietly in their seats.
>
> Several students participated in the discussion (I counted 19 responses), with students responding to Dr. H's questions (7), students posing their own questions (2), students responding to other students' questions (2), students interjecting their own opinion (3), and students offering alternative theories and interpretations about the painting under discussion (5). Students referenced the text and readings in their responses.

Phase Three: Interpreting and Analyzing the Data (the Write-up)

After sitting in on a class and taking detailed notes, I compose a chronological narrative of everything that occurred. Depending on the nature and structure of the class, this narrative description is approximately three to seven (sometimes more) typed pages, single-spaced. This functions as what anthropologist Clifford Geertz called "thick description"

(1973, p. 14). This detailed record of teaching behaviors and student responses can be one route to discovery. Many faculty have not seen themselves in action. The descriptions present snapshots or freeze frames of what they do and say in the classroom. Faculty can refer to them as they reflect on their teaching later.

Many faculty are grateful for this kind of detailed information. "This is so much more than I expected," is a typical comment. One faculty member added, "I will read through this a few more times to digest it all." Another wrote, "I can't thank you enough for the extensive work you have done for me in reviewing my teaching and the wonderful information to help me improve my ability to make a difference in the educational process of my students! I truly never expected so much effort on your part or the potential that I see in this document. I am amazed!"

These raw-data descriptions support the interpretation and analysis contained in the narrative and help keep the educational developer focused on the goal of "an observation that is developmental and not judgmental" (Hatzipanagos & Lygo-Baker, 2006, p. 96). "Whatever observational system is chosen, the major criterion should be that the approach provides for the fullest description possible of classroom events with the least amount of observer inference and judgment required" (Wilkerson & Lewis, 2002, p. 79). A variety of systems are available. What the best method is depends on the instructor, the situation, and the goals of the particular observation. Those with limited experience conducting observations can turn to Chism's *Peer Review of Teaching: A Sourcebook* for options and advice (2007).

Teaching observations should help faculty evaluate the effectiveness of their teaching behaviors (Wilkerson & Lewis, 2002). Judgment should be kept limited, but offering an interpretive frame and grounding our comments in the language of teaching and learning is important, because it gives faculty a new way of looking at their actions. As Fink (2003) observed, "A consultant can be an important resource by providing informed, personalized feedback as well as general information about teaching and learning" (p. 55).

The next examples illustrate how the addition of interpretive comments strengthens the feedback, starting with this one:

> Professor I began the class by explaining that she had altered the color scheme on her PowerPoint slides per the request of a visually impaired student. Instead of using a light background and dark letters (her usual approach), she used a dark background and light letters to help the student see better.

Adding the interpretation, "Professor I displayed concern for student learning," helps faculty members recognize this behavior as student-centered. Here is a second example:

> Professor J distributed blank note cards to the class and asked them to write down their responses to the questions: "What are you excited about? What do you have anxiety about? What are you nervous about?" He instructed students to write anonymously, "No names." He collected the cards and shuffled them, then asked, "Who wants to read one? What's out there?"

Adding the interpretive comment, "This classroom assessment technique [CAT] was useful in making students' anxieties visible, in an interactive manner" helps instructors see their teaching behaviors in a new way. Finally, consider this third example:

> Each student took a turn reading a card, so that all voices were heard. Professor K, said, "All feedback is valid." He summarized comments. He asked students, "What themes did you hear?" Common themes included being nervous about being interviewed, videotaped, and recorded. Professor K asked, "How does knowing about these concerns help you?" A student commented, "It is weird to watch yourself on tape." Professor K agreed, "It is weird," and displayed humor. A student commented, "When you watch yourself, you focus on 'ums,' 'likes,' etc."

Following this description with an interpretation, "Professor K demonstrated concern for student learning by explicitly seeking student feedback on their affective learning and addressing those concerns in class," explains the teaching behaviors and their impact on student learning and classroom climate.

An interpretive comment can also make the purpose of the teaching behavior more explicit, as in this example:

> When a student asked a question about the F.M. device, Professor L responded: "Let me summarize what you said and rephrase it." This allowed Professor L to repeat the content information in another way for the benefit of the whole class.

The description and the interpretation may even occur simultaneously:

> Professor M integrated student comments as he guided the discussion. For example, when discussing support for new interpreters, he remarked, "Another issue both you and Michelle touched on is what do you do when you have limited apprenticeship and mentoring?"

Framing the observation in the vocabulary of teaching and learning can give faculty a new, more professional understanding of their teaching. They may learn that one of their instructional activities has a name in the college-teaching literature: as in the next example, a CAT (Angelo & Cross, 1993):

> Professor N used two classroom assessment techniques. During the class he used several scenarios to check student understanding. For instance, he asked: "What if you are a service provider and ___ happens? What do you do?" These questions promoted higher-order thinking as students had to apply the information learned to situations that were drawn from real-life experience. Professor N ended the class with a quiz that also checked students' understanding. The questions were on the PowerPoint slide and could be seen by all, and served as a summation of the lecture material.

In addition, faculty may not be aware of the multiple uses of their teaching behaviors. Questions, for example, can be used in a variety of ways.

> Professor O used questions effectively to maintain student interest, to keep students involved and engaged with the material, and to propel the lecture forward. In the class I observed, Professor O asked 25 questions during the course of the lecture. His questions connected the course content to theory and readings when he asked "What is the theory called?" or "Is that why it's only a theory?" He asked students about the chemical reactions that occur to produce movement: "What does ATP do here?" and "What do we need for muscle tension to develop?" and "What has to happen to the nerve stimulus?" He used questions to elicit higher-order thinking on Bloom's taxonomy, asking "Why?" "What is the difference between this graph and the previous graph?" "What about the overall tension?" He used questions to get students to make predictions: "What's going to happen to the myosin head? What's it going to do? Have we moved at all?" "Now what will happen? What's going to happen next?" and "What is the next phase? What is happening at this time?" He used questions to get students to reflect on the course content: "Is this the way you move?" Professor O also used questions as transitions: "Now we know how it works. What happens when it doesn't work?" Professor O used questions to connect with students' experiences. "Who here has never had the hiccups?" and "When the medical examiner on TV examines a corpse, what are they checking for? What is rigor mortis? What's going to happen to the body?" and "What muscle do you *not* want affected by

bacterial tetanus?" He also incorporated students' questions into his own questions: "Now it comes back to what was brought up by Katelyn—are twitches useful?"

In another class, I noted:

Professor Q's questions were sequenced and built on one another, sometimes following a pattern such as "How did we . . . ?" "Why did we . . . ?" "What did we learn?" "How else can we do this?" "What might be the problem?" "Can anyone see a difficulty?" "Could we do this better?" "What does the research tell us?"

For another faculty member, it was helpful to furnish a typology of the questions she asked to help her understand how they influenced learning. Probing questions:

At the next piece, a student commented, "It is an interesting piece." Professor R replied, "Because?" The student elaborated, "Because of the negative space." Professor R asked, "What has happened here because of the negative space? Where is the dominant?" Professor R used questions to focus students' attention and get them to think critically about each piece.

Elaborating questions:

A student commented, "My eye gets stuck at the top [of the piece]." Professor R probed more deeply, asking, "What would you suggest?" urging the student to elaborate and make the comment more specific. At the next piece Professor R asked, "What do you have to say about this?" A student replied, "I like the corner." Professor R replied, "Because?" asking the student to elaborate and be more specific. The student explained that the piece "moved to flat surface to show the angles." Professor R explained, "It creates a focal point. The negative space is activated, really lovely differential."

Narrative teaching observations also allow educational developers to focus on teachable moments. For example, in an art class:

The instructor asked, "Was that supposed to be a piercing?" The artist replied, "I changed my mind." The instructor commented, "That's smart thinking." She probed, "Why would you think it might not work? What's happening here that isn't happening in anyone else's work? What form?"

I prefer to use a naturalistic process and let the data guide me. When I go back over the field notes or raw data, I often use different colored pens and highlighters to help me identify topics, categories, or themes. As I review the chronological record, I consider how the class is organized, where the instructor spent the most time, how students responded, what the learning outcomes were and the degree to which they were met, what stood out to me as an observer, what worked well, and whether the instructor encountered any difficulties or challenges. These general questions guide my interpretation and analysis.

When the purpose of the observation is to improve poor performance, I find it helpful to begin with a description, such as, "I noted that the directions for the activities were given orally and at times students were unclear about the directions." I then ask questions or make corrective suggestions. In this case, I asked: "Are there other ways to give directions or ways to help visually repeat them so students understand them more readily? Would it be helpful to have the directions written on a handout you distribute when you put students in groups or display them on in your PowerPoint slides or on the document camera at the beginning of the activity so that everyone can see?"

In another course, where students showed confusion over similarly titled assignments, I suggest a quick way to differentiate the tasks: copying them on colored paper. The instructor could then remind students, "The blue one is due today, and the yellow one is due next week." The next term the instructor could retitle them.

Another way to begin a narrative targeted to improve teaching is by acknowledging the difficulty of the situation. For example, late afternoon and early evening classes can be challenging for students and faculty because they are tired. Commenting on a difficulty we all share removes some of the onus from the instructor and communicates empathy. Offering examples of how other faculty have dealt with a problem can also be helpful. For instance, I shared that low energy was a problem in another late afternoon class I recently observed. The faculty member noticed that students were fading and not paying attention.

> Instead of scolding them, she explained, "For the next thirty minutes we will be offering feedback to one another on the projects. This is a really important part of the course, and it is really important for everyone to give this task their full attention and energy. We need to give everyone's work the respect it deserves. I notice that several people are tired and not very focused. Let's take a two-minute break. Get up, walk around, walk up and down the hall, get a drink, and come back so that we can all give our best effort to our peers."

In addition to asking questions and making suggestions, it is helpful to include details to support one's conclusions, as in this example:

> Are there ways to adjust the pacing of this class so that things move along more quickly? For instance, students worked in groups creating graphic organizers for some 20 to 30 minutes while you graded their journal responses. Students appeared to have completed the task in 10 to 15 minutes. How could this extra time be best used?

To supply additional resources for improvement, I often append a Part B to my observations that includes suggestions, models, and references tailored to solving the teaching problems the faculty member may have. As Jones et al. (2009, p. 209) advise, "Teaching cannot be boiled down to a recipe."

Phase Four: Meeting with the Instructor (the Postobservation Meeting)

The final step in the process is the face-to-face postobservation meeting with the faculty member. Complementing the written narrative, it brings together two professionals to engage in discussion and a process of problem solving: identifying a problem, identifying possible reasons for it, and exploring strategies to address it (DiPietro, 2008). The teaching observation can be an effective means of professional development as long as we remember its true purpose, to "build a relationship, not a case" (Jenson, 2002, p. 97). Our relationships with faculty rest on trust (Hatzipanagos & Lygo-Baker, 2006), and as professionals we have ethical obligations to treat faculty fairly and respect confidentiality. For a detailed explanation of these responsibilities, please refer to the Ethical Guidelines for Faculty Developers forwarded by the POD Network, printed near the front of this volume.

Conclusion

The detailed examples in this chapter illustrate the many benefits of narrative teaching observations. First, because narratives furnish detailed snapshots of given moments in time, they document effective (and less effective) teaching behaviors. Second, because they are written, they afford a permanent record that can be referred back to later. Third, because they supply an interpretive frame that videotapes and digital recordings cannot, they help faculty recognize and understand their own behavior. Fourth, because they can accommodate suggestions, models, and references, they help faculty members solve problems they may be encountering. Fifth, the narrative is flexible and useful in a variety of contexts and situations. As each class is a unique event: "Teaching observations involve complex social situations with large numbers of variables that cannot be controlled" (Hatzipanagos & Lygo-Baker, 2006, p. 99).

One final benefit these narratives offer is the opportunity for us to describe teaching behaviors using our professional vocabulary. Our agreed-on terminology reflects our in-depth understanding of these behaviors and allows us to integrate our knowledge of their pedagogical impacts. Therefore, it serves not to obfuscate but to illuminate the teaching process and make it more transparent (Hatzipanagos & Lygo-Baker, 2006). Given its high utility, our vocabulary merits broader dissemination across the academy. Our using it helps the narrative teaching observation make the *how* and the *why* of our professional practice more explicit and our contribution as faculty developers more evident.

REFERENCES

Angelo, T. A., & Cross, K. P. (1993). *Classroom assessment techniques: A handbook for college teachers* (2nd ed.). San Francisco: Jossey-Bass.

Brinko, K. T. (1993). The practice of giving feedback to improve teaching: What is effective? *Journal of Higher Education, 64*(5), 574–593.

Chism, N.V.N. (2007). *Peer review of teaching: A sourcebook* (2nd ed.). Bolton, MA: Anker.

DiPietro, M. (2008, October). *An online tool for teaching consultations.* Paper presented at the 33rd annual meeting of the Professional and Organizational Development Network in Higher Education, Reno, NV.

Fink, L. D. (2003). *Creating significant learning experiences: An integrated approach to designing college courses.* San Francisco: Jossey-Bass.

Frantz, A. C., Beebe, S. A., Horvath, V. S., Canales, J., & Swee, D. E. (2005). The roles of teaching and learning centers. In S. Chadwick-Blossey & D. R. Robertson (Eds.), *To improve the academy: Vol. 23. Resources for faculty, instructional, and organizational development* (pp. 72–90). Bolton, MA: Anker.

Geertz, C. (1973). *Thick description: Toward an interpretive theory of culture.* New York: Basic Books.

Hatzipanagos, S., & Lygo-Baker, S. (2006). Teacher observations: A meeting of minds? *International Journal of Teaching and Learning in Higher Education, 17*(2), 97–105.

Jacobson, W., Wulff, D. W., Grooters, S., Edwards, P. M., & Freisem, K. (2009). Reported long-term value and effects of teaching center consultations.

In L. B. Nilson & J. E. Miller (Eds.), *To improve the academy: Vol. 27. Resources for faculty, instructional, and organizational development* (pp. 223–246). San Francisco: Jossey-Bass.

Jenson, J. D. (2002). If I knew then what I know now: A first-year faculty consultant's top ten list. In K. H. Gillespie, L. R. Hilsen, & E. C. Wadsworth (Eds.), *A guide to faculty development: Practical advice, examples, and resources* (pp. 92–98). Bolton, MA: Anker.

Jones, S. K., Sagendorf, K. S., Morris, D. B, Stockburger, D., & Patterson, E. T. (2009). Lessons learned from developing a learning-focused classroom observation form. In L. B. Nilson & J. E. Miller (Eds.), *To improve the academy: Vol. 27. Resources for faculty, instructional, and organizational development* (pp. 199–222). San Francisco: Jossey-Bass.

Lewis, K. G. (2002). The process of individual consultation. In K. H. Gillespie, L. R. Hilsen, & E. C. Wadsworth (Eds.), *A guide to faculty development: Practical advice, examples, and resources* (pp. 59–73). Bolton, MA: Anker.

McKeachie, W. J. (2002). *McKeachie's teaching tips: Strategies, research, and theory for college and university teachers* (11th ed.). Boston: Houghton Mifflin.

Millis, B. J. (2005, October). *Conducting effective classroom observations.* Paper presented at the 30th annual meeting of the Professional and Organizational Development Network in Higher Education, Milwaukee, WI.

Millis, B. J. (2006). Peer observations as a catalyst for faculty development. In P. Seldin & Associates, *Evaluating faculty performance: A practical guide to assessing teaching, research, and service* (pp. 82–95). Bolton, MA: Anker.

Palmer, P. J. (1998). *The courage to teach: Exploring the inner landscape of a teacher's life.* San Francisco: Jossey-Bass.

Professional and Organizational Development Network in Higher Education. (2007). *Ethical guidelines for educational developers.* Retrieved March 2, 2009, from www.podnetwork.org/faculty_development/ethicalguidelines.htm

Richlin, L. (2006). *Blueprint for learning: Constructing college courses to facilitate, assess, and document learning.* Sterling, VA: Stylus.

Tompkins, J. (1993). Postcards from the edge. *Journal of Advanced Composition, 13*(2), 449–457.

Wehlburg, C. M. (2005). Using data to enhance college teaching: Course and departmental assessment results as a faculty development tool. In S. Chadwick-Blossey & D. R. Robertson (Eds.), *To improve the academy: Vol. 23. Resources for faculty, instructional, and organizational development* (pp. 165–172). Bolton, MA: Anker.

Wilkerson, L., & Lewis, K. G. (2002). Classroom observation: The observer as collaborator. In K. H. Gillespie, L. R. Hilsen, & E. C. Wadsworth (Eds.), *A guide to faculty development: Practical advice, examples, and resources* (pp. 74–81). Bolton, MA: Anker.

SECTION TWO

UNDERSTANDING FACULTY

7

PROMOTING DIALOGUE AND ACTION ON META-PROFESSIONAL SKILLS, ROLES, AND RESPONSIBILITIES

Michael Theall, Youngstown State University

Bonnie Mullinix, Teaching Learning and Technology Group

Raoul A. Arreola, University of Tennessee Health Science Center

Collecting and using information about faculty skills can serve as an organizational development activity to guide faculty evaluation and professional development policy and practice with the goal of leading to improved teaching and learning. This chapter presents findings from a study with international, local, quantitative, and qualitative components. Readers are encouraged to explore data patterns and consider courses of action that these imply, and to reflect on the potential usefulness of the Meta-Profession model for furthering reflection, dialogue, and action on development and evaluation processes on their own campus.

What is it that faculty *do,* and how should they be supported to excel at their core work? This central question permeates the academy and serves as the foundation for the work of those who support faculty to excel and succeed. The Meta-Profession Project was designed to address this question and has been doing so for nearly a decade. Results and experience over this period indicate that the model and findings from quantitative international survey research and qualitative context-grounded explorations can inform and promote dialogue, discussion, and action that will enhance the understanding and the experience of the professoriate.

History and Background of the Study

The past twenty years have seen many efforts to define the nature of the professoriate. Ernest Boyer's redefinition of scholarship (1990), the AAHE Forum on Faculty Roles and Rewards led by Gene Rice, and Diamond and Adam's books (1995, 2000) about disciplinary perspectives on faculty work have supplied a conceptual basis and real-world data for our thinking about what it means to be a college professor. However, to completely understand the work that the profession demands, we must also explore the skills that the work requires (Arreola, Theall, & Aleamoni, 2003; Theall, 2002; Theall & Arreola, 2006). Until we identify the generic and specific skills necessary to succeed in the four basic professorial roles (*teaching, scholarly and creative activities, service,* and *administration*), we cannot hope to evaluate that work effectively or offer meaningful support for those who do it. Equally important in times when the status of the professoriate has been diminished, it is critical to demonstrate that being a college professor involves much more than presenting one's expertise in a classroom for a few hours a week. We view college teaching as a "meta-profession," that is, a profession that requires expertise in a variety of complex professional skills *beyond* that of content expertise.

Our work in this area is called the Meta-Profession Project. The survey and integrated study (quantitative and qualitative) and action-oriented process presented herein are part of an ongoing effort to describe, define, explore, and support the professoriate. The Meta-Profession Project is described in detail at www.cedanet.com/meta (and in various papers and articles available at that Web location). By way of an introductory summary, the Meta-Profession Project has four main objectives:

> Engage college faculty in providing more precise information about the frequency with which the various identified skills are required in their work.
>
> Gather information that will permit the determination as to whether faculty expertise in, and patterns of use of, the skill sets vary from institution to institution and as a function of other variables.
>
> Present a structure (the meta-professional matrices) that can be used effectively in faculty development and evaluation, policy decision making, research, and important campus dialogue.
>
> Gather information on, and constitute, a central source for resource materials about the various skill sets in support of improved faculty evaluation, faculty development, research,

and campus policies and practices affecting the professoriate. Ultimately, the goals of the Meta-Profession Project are to contribute to systematic improvement of teaching and learning, enhance the effectiveness of higher education institutions, and promote recognition of the professoriate as a truly complex and higher calling.

A first step in the project was development of a framework that defined the Meta-Profession concept. Table 7.1 summarizes twenty skill sets required of faculty. These meta-professional skills include designing, constructing, and operating a complex environment that facilitates and supports student learning; working with and leading others; mastering the use of complex technologies; and representing one's work and institution to a variety of academic colleagues and to the public.

Frequency estimates for each skill set were originally developed on the basis of evidence in existing literature, on our own work in faculty development and evaluation over the past three decades, and in consultation with colleagues in these and other fields. Discussions of faculty work exist (Braskamp & Ory, 1994; Gappa, Austin, & Trice, 2007), but explorations of the actual skills required to do that work were not available. Table 7.2 thus presents estimates of the frequency of need for each skill set in four roles (teaching, scholarly and creative activities, service, and administration). These estimates use the terms "almost always," "frequently," "occasionally," and "almost never" (abbreviated as "always," "freq," "occa," and "never").

One finding that has been constantly identified as immediately apparent in the matrix is that graduate school training focuses extensively on the "base profession" but rarely supports preparation for the many other requirements of the meta-profession. The twenty skill sets identified in Table 7.2 indicate the range of capabilities necessary for faculty to succeed in their four primary roles. Additional matrices that examine subsets or application of skills within each faculty role may be seen at the Meta-Profession Project website (for example, the need for various skill sets associated with seven teaching situations, from large classes to online instruction to tutoring). These additional matrices, along with color versions of Tables 7.2 through 7.7, can be viewed at www.cedanet.com/meta.

An International Study

In 2007, the Professional and Organizational Development (POD) Network in Higher Education and the Special Interest Group in Faculty Teaching, Evaluation, and Development of the American Educational

Table 7.1. Meta-Professional Skill Set Definitions

Skill Set	Brief Definition or Description
Base Profession Skill Sets	
Content expertise	The formally recognized knowledge, skills, and abilities a faculty member possesses in a chosen field by virtue of advanced training, education, or experience.
Practice and clinical skills	Those skills in translating content expertise into actions so as to carry out a process, produce a product, or offer a service.
Research techniques	Those skills in acquiring existing knowledge, or creating or discovering new knowledge, within one's area of content expertise.
Meta-Profession Skill Sets	
Instructional design	Those technical skills in designing, sequencing, and presenting experiences that induce learning. Requires knowledge and skill in task analysis, the psychology of learning, the conditions of learning, and development of performance objectives.
Instructional delivery	Those human interactive skills that promote or facilitate learning in face-to-face instruction, as well as those skills in using various forms of instructional delivery mechanisms.
Instructional assessment	Those skills in developing and using tools and procedures for assessing student learning (including test construction, questionnaire and survey construction, grading practices, and grading procedures).
Course management	Those organizational and bureaucratic skills involved in maintaining and operating a course.
Instructional research	Those technical skills and techniques associated with scholarly inquiry into all aspects of instruction, teaching, and education.
Psychometrics and statistics	Psychometrics and statistics is concerned with measurement of human characteristics and design and analysis of research based on those measurements.
Epistemology	The branch of philosophy that studies the nature and limits of knowledge as well as examining the structure, origin, and criteria of knowledge. Its application can often be seen in course or curriculum design in which the structure of the knowledge to be acquired by the student is taken into account in designing instructional events or experiences.
Learning theory	Learning theory deals with various models to explain how learning takes place and to furnish a frame of reference for designing, developing, and delivering instruction.

Human development	Theories and models of human intellectual, ethical, social, cultural, and physical development. Knowledge and expertise in the theories of human development are often required in designing and developing the entire educational experience.
Information technology	Information technology (IT) encompasses all forms of technology used to create, store, exchange, and use information in its various forms (business data, voice conversations, still images, motion pictures, multimedia presentations).
Technical writing	Delivery of technical information to readers (or listeners or viewers) in a manner that is adapted to their needs, level of understanding, and background. The primary skill is to write about highly technical subjects in such a way that a beginner (learner) or a nonspecialist can understand.
Graphic design	Graphic design is the process and art of combining text and graphics to produce an efficient and effective means of visually communicating information or concepts.
Public speaking	Public speaking is generally defined as speaking to a large group of individuals, in a formal setting, for the purpose of imparting information or persuading others to a particular point of view.
Communication styles	Individuals have various preferences for both communicating with others and interpreting communications from others. Numerous models have been developed that describe how to recognize people's preferred style of communicating and what strategy to use in communicating most effectively with them.
Conflict management	The practice of identifying and handling conflict sensibly, fairly, and efficiently. Conflict management requires such skills as effective communicating, problem solving, and negotiating with a focus on interests.
Group process, team building	Groups of individuals, gathered together to achieve a goal or objective, either as a committee or some other grouping, go through several predictable stages before useful work can be done.
Resource management	Management of material resources so as to ensure their effective and efficient use in meeting specific purposes. Involves skills associated with inventory control procedures, replacement and maintenance scheduling, cost control, etc.
Personnel management	Skills in communicating effectively, developing teams, managing diversity, managing conflict, delegating responsibility, coaching and training, giving and receiving constructive feedback, and motivating and guiding either individuals or groups to achieve specific goals.

(Continued)

Table 7.1. (*Continued*)

Skill Set	Brief Definition or Description
Financial and budget development	Requires understanding of a variety of economic and monetary concepts, including cash flow, direct and indirect costs, debt management, depreciation, etc.; the ability to read and understand financial reports; and the ability to interpret and respond appropriately to federal, state, and local regulations and policies affecting expenditure of funds.
Policy analysis and development	Those skills necessary for understanding the political constraints faced by policy makers, assessing the performance of alternative approaches to policy implementation, evaluating the effectiveness of policies, and the role that values conflict has on development of policies.

Note: The term *skill set* is used to indicate a combination of knowledge, experience, proficiency, and skill in a specific area.

Research Association (AERA–SIGFTED) agreed to cosponsor a research project intended to validate the Meta-Profession conceptual model and to explore several issues surrounding its application in faculty development and evaluation. The survey was international in scope and circulated by professional organizations to their members, by some of those members to faculty and administrators at their individual campuses, and by individuals interested in the research. Requests for participation were disseminated in the United States and several other countries. There were 415 responses from the United States and 114 from other countries, primarily Canada. Additional data were collected at one institution in a separate survey, and seventy-four persons responded.

One of the first questions addressed was the extent to which the original model (see Table 7.2) was accurate in its estimates of the need for the skill sets. The data essentially validated the summary matrix representation of the need for the skill sets, and Theall et al. (2008) reported preliminary analyses. However, an equally important question was the extent to which faculty possessed expertise in the skill sets. Thus, in the same survey faculty were asked to self-report their expertise, and administrators were asked to report their estimates of the skills of the faculty with whom they worked. Because "base-profession" skills (content expertise, clinical and practical skills, and research techniques) are the focus of graduate education and prime criteria for entry into the professoriate, a high level of expertise was expected and the assumption was made that faculty would regularly need these skills. Thus, further analysis concentrated only on the meta-professional skill sets.

Table 7.2. An Overview of the Meta-Professional Model: Estimated General Frequency of Need for Each Skill Set in Four Traditional Faculty Roles

The META-PROFESSION of College Teaching				
		Faculty	Roles	
FACULTY SKILL SETS	Teaching Role	Scholarly and Creative Activities Role	Service Role	Administrative Role
BASE-PROFESSION SKILLS				
Content Expertise	Always	Always	Occa	Never
Practical-Clinical Skills	Freq	Freq	Occa	Never
Research Techniques	Occa	Freq	Never	Never
META-PROFESSION SKILLS				
Instructional Design	Always	Occa	Occa	Never
Instructional Delivery	Always	Occa	Occa	Never
Instructional Assessment	Always	Occa	Occa	Never
Course Management	Freq	Occa	Occa	Never
Instructional Research	Never	Freq	Occa	Never
Psychometrics/Statistics	Occa	Freq	Occa	Never
Epistemology	Occa	Occa	Occa	Never
Learning Theory	Freq	Occa	Occa	Never
Human Development	Occa	Occa	Occa	Never
Information Technology	Freq	Freq	Occa	Occa
Technical Writing	Occa	Freq	Occa	Never
Graphic Design	Occa	Occa	Occa	Never
Public Speaking	Freq	Freq	Occa	Freq
Communications Styles	Freq	Freq	Occa	Freq
Conflict Management	Occa	Never	Occa	Freq
Group Process	Occa	Never	Occa	Always
Resource Management	Occa	Never	Occa	Always
Personnel Supervision and Management	Never	Never	Occa	Always
Financial and Budget Development	Never	Never	Occa	Always
Policy Analysis and Development	Never	Never	Occa	Freq
Legend	Almost Always = "Always"; Frequently = "Freq"; Occasionally = "Occa"; Almost Never = "Never"			

Although there were many directions the analysis could take, the focus of this initial analysis centered around three areas that seemed to have the greatest potential for application:

1. Differences between ratings of expertise and need

2. Differences of opinion between administrators and faculty

3. Differences of opinion across disciplinary groups

Table 7.3. Expertise and Need: International Survey Data

SIGNIFICANT DIFFERENCES BETWEEN EXPERTISE AND FREQUENCY OF NEED				
Meta-Profession Skill Sets	Teaching Role	Scholarship Role	Service Role	Administrative Role
Instructional Design	Need	Expertise	Expertise	Expertise
Instructional Delivery	Need	Expertise	Expertise	Expertise
Instructional Assessment	Need	Expertise	Expertise	Expertise
Course Management	Need	Expertise	Expertise	Expertise
Instructional Research			Expertise	Expertise
Psychometrics/Statistics	Expertise		Expertise	Expertise
Epistemology	Need		Expertise	Expertise
Learning Theory	Need	Expertise	Expertise	Expertise
Human Development	Need	Expertise	Expertise	Expertise
Information Technology	Need	Expertise	Expertise	Expertise
Technical Writing			Expertise	Expertise
Graphic Design	Need		Expertise	Expertise
Public Speaking	Need	Expertise	Expertise	Expertise
Communications Styles	Need			Need
Conflict Management		Expertise	Expertise	Need
Group Process	Need	Expertise		Need
Resource Management	Expertise	Expertise	Expertise	Need
Personnel Supervision and Management		Expertise	Expertise	Need
Financial and Budget Development	Expertise		Expertise	Need
Policy Analysis and Development	Expertise	Expertise		Need

Expertise = Expertise rating significantly stronger than need (<.05 in all cases)
Need = Need rating significantly stronger than expertise (<.05 in all cases)
Blank = No significant difference

To retain focus on local campus applications, other differences of opinion in the data are omitted. To further facilitate an applied perspective, the data in Tables 7.3 through 7.7 are best viewed with respect to particular faculty evaluation and development issues and strategies for using data to promote dialogue. For example, if one takes the perspective of a faculty development and evaluation committee or the staff of a teaching center, then collection of such campus-specific meta-professional data could be used to initiate open discussion about whether existing policy and practice accurately reflect emphasis on skills that are critical to faculty success. The underlying questions to guide such discussions would include:

- What are "our" expectations for faculty performance?
- What skills are needed to perform well?
- Is the emphasis of evaluation on skills agreed to be critical?
- Are development resources allocated to critical skill areas?

Further on in this chapter, such an approach will be described to underscore how structured qualitative exploration could be used to clarify differences within an institution and across disciplinary departments. A perspective grounded in local consensus presents the opportunity to actively engage with the data and to make it *speak* to a specific context, illustrating the core premise of this research: that use of the Meta-Profession model to open campus dialogue about faculty roles, work, and skills can lead to a more supportive environment for faculty and to enhanced teaching and learning.

Faculty Expertise: Need Ratings

Table 7.3 presents aggregated data from the survey. The skill sets are arrayed on the left with the next four data columns showing the rated frequency of need for each skill set in each role. Frequency of need was rated as "almost always" (1.0), "frequently" (2.0), "occasionally" (3.0), and "almost never" (4.0).

The words *expertise* and *need* in the cells indicate which rating was significantly stronger. Shading is used to further distinguish need from expertise. Blank cells indicate no significant difference. All significance findings were at alpha levels more stringent than .05, and most were well below alpha .01. Similar graphic profiles are displayed in subsequent tables for consistency and readability.

Need and expertise ratings from all respondents were combined and means were compared using t tests. These were used because each respondent furnished a pair of ratings. However, because the two concepts are different, further analyses will be done using correlations or nonparametric tests such as chi square to cross-check the results. The primary question is whether a match between expertise and need exists. If, for example, a skill is "almost always" needed, one would hope that faculty expertise would approach the "advanced" level. If not, then caution is required in the evaluation of that skill, and it would be wise to allocate development resources to enhancing faculty expertise. Expertise ratings ranged from "advanced" through "moderate" and "basic" to "none," with most choices "moderate" or "basic," while the need ratings varied from "almost always" to "almost never." Table 7.3 reveals that the greatest needs are in the teaching and administrative roles in several skill areas. Respondents appear to feel comfortable that skill levels are sufficient to meet needs in the scholarship and service roles. These results are not unexpected because "base profession" training in graduate schools focuses on training in the areas of scholarship but seldom concentrates on teaching and administrative skill sets, except in a few disciplines (for example, education, business, psychology). Service appears to be a category where all respondents "almost always" feel fully qualified to carry out their responsibilities.

What these data suggest with respect to faculty development is the importance of using data to drive faculty development activities. Given that resources are often limited (this being an almost universal case in current times), they should target areas of greatest need. When data are collected and analyzed at the institutional level and patterns are found (either similar to or discrepant from the generalized findings), the institution should support professional enrichment activities that focus on the teaching role in certain skill sets and possibly in the administration role for other skill sets. Indeed, separate institutional datasets reveal that this pattern of results is consistent.

The data also make clear that faculty evaluation of certain kinds of skills must be tempered by the realization that a high level of expertise cannot be expected across all faculty, particularly on entry into the profession. Refined expertise cannot be assumed, and comparisons of individuals must thus avoid pitting experienced faculty who may have had the opportunity for training and skill development against those who have not had such opportunities. In other words, evaluation using inappropriate criteria and standards for performance is both poor methodology and unfair practice.

Perhaps more important, if these kinds of data are collected at the institutional level, their first and most important use would be as information to promote open dialogue and discussion about institutional context and realities related to the expectations for faculty work, existing policies and practices in evaluation and development, and identification of areas of need and improvement.

Faculty Versus Administrator Ratings

The international survey also explored possible differences in the ratings given by faculty (54 percent of the respondents) and administrators (46 percent of the respondents). Table 7.4 displays skill sets at the left, overall expertise ratings, and then four sets of needs ratings. As in Table 7.3, the words in the cells indicate which rating was significantly stronger, shading is used to supplement this distinction, and blank cells indicate no significant differences. T-tests were used because different groups furnished ratings of the two concepts, and the hypothesis was that there would be no cross-group differences. Each pair of ratings was independent and t-tests

Table 7.4. Administrator and Faculty Ratings: International Survey Data

SIGNIFICANT DIFFERENCES BETWEEN FACULTY AND ADMINISTRATORS					
Meta-Profession Skill Sets	Expertise	Teaching Role	Scholarship Role	Service Role	Administrative Role
Instructional Design	Faculty				Admin
Instructional Delivery			Faculty		Admin
Instructional Assessment				Admin	Admin
Course Management			Faculty		
Instructional Research	Faculty				Admin
Psychometrics/Statistics				Admin	Admin
Epistemology					Admin
Learning Theory				Admin	Admin
Human Development				Admin	Admin
Information Technology	Faculty				Admin
Technical Writing	Faculty	Faculty			Admin
Graphic Design	Faculty		Faculty		Admin
Public Speaking	Faculty	Faculty	Faculty		Admin
Communications Styles			Faculty		Admin
Conflict Management	Faculty		Faculty		Admin
Group Process			Faculty		Admin
Resource Management					Admin
Personnel Supervision and Management					Admin
Financial and Budget Development					Admin
Policy Analysis and Development					Admin
Faculty = Faculty ratings significantly stronger than administrators' (<.05 in all cases)					
Admin = Administrator ratings significantly stronger than faculty (<.05 in all cases)					
Blank = No significant difference					

could be used without fear of increasing the chance of type II error. The same rationale applies to Tables 7.5 through 7.7. All significant differences in Table 7.4 were at alpha .05, and most were well below alpha .01.

The most striking results are that (1) in no case did administrators rate faculty expertise in any skill sets significantly stronger than did faculty; and (2) in every skill set but one in the administrative role, administrator ratings of need were significantly higher than those of the faculty. The graphic dramatically displays this dichotomous result. A possible explanation for the result is that the demands of the roles are so different that one's perspectives about the importance of skills changes as one moves between roles. If this is the case, when administrators evaluate faculty performance they may assume a higher level of faculty skill than can realistically be expected. However, given that administrators do not rate faculty expertise higher in any instance, this concern may be unwarranted.

Table 7.5. Disciplinary Differences in Ratings: International Survey Data

SIGNIFICANT DIFFERENCES BETWEEN ED/SOC AND STEM FACULTY					
Meta-Profession Skill Sets	Expertise	Teaching Role	Scholarship Role	Service Role	Administrative Role
Instructional Design	ED/SOC				
Instructional Delivery	ED/SOC				
Instructional Assessment	ED/SOC			ED/SOC	ED/SOC
Course Management	ED/SOC				ED/SOC
Instructional Research	ED/SOC		ED/SOC		ED/SOC
Psychometrics/Statistics	ED/SOC	ED/SOC	ED/SOC	ED/SOC	ED/SOC
Epistemology	ED/SOC	ED/SOC	ED/SOC	ED/SOC	ED/SOC
Learning Theory	ED/SOC	ED/SOC	ED/SOC	ED/SOC	ED/SOC
Human Development	ED/SOC	ED/SOC	ED/SOC	ED/SOC	ED/SOC
Information Technology					
Technical Writing		STEM			
Graphic Design					
Public Speaking		STEM			
Communications Styles	ED/SOC			ED/SOC	ED/SOC
Conflict Management	ED/SOC	ED/SOC		ED/SOC	ED/SOC
Group Process	ED/SOC	ED/SOC		ED/SOC	
Resource Management	ED/SOC				
Personnel Supervision and Management					
Financial and Budget Development					
Policy Analysis and Development	ED/SOC	ED/SOC			

ED/SOC = ED/SOC faculty ratings significantly stronger than STEM (<.05 in all cases)
STEM = STEM faculty ratings significantly stronger than ED/SOC (<.05 in all cases)
Blank = No significant difference

Preliminary review of qualitative data suggests this is true, but this is a tentative explanation at best and further investigation is ongoing.

Disciplinary Differences in Ratings

The international survey included respondents from more than twenty-four disciplinary areas, but the two largest groups of related disciplines were science, technology, engineering, and math (STEM, 30 percent of the sample) and education and social science (ED/SOC 40 percent). These two groups were chosen for additional analysis. Table 7.5 uses the same graphic patterns as previous tables. Significant differences are indicated by the presence of words in the cells and by shading, and blank cells indicate no significant differences. Alpha levels are all at .05 or lower, and most differences are at alpha levels below .01. T-tests were used in this analysis because two groups were rating the same concepts.

One result is somewhat predictable: ED/SQC faculty would rate their expertise in teaching-related skill sets higher than would STEM faculty. However, the noticeable differences extend beyond those skill sets into many other skill sets and almost thirty of the frequency-of-need ratings. STEM ratings were significantly stronger than ED/SOC ratings in only two cases (need for technical writing, and public speaking in the teaching role). Apparently, disciplines have very different perspectives, values, and criteria for performance, as found in other studies (for example, Biglan, 1973; Franklin & Theall, 1992; Smart, Feldman, & Ethington, 2000). Two important implications for evaluation arise: (1) that the values and performance criteria of one discipline should not be used to judge performance of a person in another discipline, and (2) that exploration of disciplinary differences should be part of good evaluation practice on every campus.

Institutional Data and Contextually Grounded Perspectives

As suggested here, the most effective application of the Meta-Profession model will take place at the institutional level. It is there that the concept and associated tools can be used to increase understanding of unique institutional identity and dynamics that define the professoriate. This understanding can directly result in improvements in policy and practice in faculty development and evaluation as well as related improvements in teaching and learning, organizational effectiveness, and institutional performance.

To support application of the model, two institutions—one in Canada and the other in the United States—contributed to a contextually grounded dataset by prioritizing participation in the survey. The focus of the next section is on the U.S. institution, the survey findings, and their relationship to the international dataset.

A Local Institutional Study: Expertise and Needs Ratings

A local data collection effort essentially identical to the international survey was conducted concurrently with the international survey. Seventy-four responses were received (approximately 25 percent of full-time faculty) and analyzed in the same way as those in the large survey. The first analysis compared expertise and need ratings. Table 7.6 presents the local data in the same manner as did Table 7.2. T-tests were used as before with alpha levels at .05 or less and most below .01. These results present a close match with the international data with respect to frequency of need for the skill sets across the four roles. The number of significantly stronger expertise ratings differs by only one. The number of

Table 7.6. Expertise and Frequency of Need Ratings: Institutional Data

SIGNIFICANT DIFFERENCES BETWEEN INSTITUTIONAL EXPERTISE AND NEED RATINGS				
Meta-Profession Skill Sets	Teaching Role	Scholarship Role	Service Role	Administrative Role
Instructional Design	Need	Expertise	Expertise	Expertise
Instructional Delivery	Need	Expertise	Expertise	Expertise
Instructional Assessment	Need	Expertise	Expertise	Expertise
Course Management	Need	Expertise	Expertise	Expertise
Instructional Research			Expertise	Expertise
Psychometrics/Statistics	Expertise		Expertise	Expertise
Epistemology			Expertise	Expertise
Learning Theory		Expertise	Expertise	Expertise
Human Development		Expertise	Expertise	Expertise
Information Technology		Need	Expertise	
Technical Writing			Expertise	Expertise
Graphic Design		Expertise	Expertise	Expertise
Public Speaking	Need	Expertise	Expertise	
Communications Styles				
Conflict Management		Expertise	Expertise	
Group Process	Need	Expertise		
Resource Management	Expertise	Expertise	Expertise	Need
Personnel Supervision and Management		Expertise		Need
Financial and Budget Development	Expertise	Expertise	Expertise	Need
Policy Analysis and Development	Expertise	Expertise	Expertise	Need
Expertise = Expertise ratings significantly stronger than need (<.05 in all cases)				
Need = Need ratings significantly stronger than expertise (<.05 in all cases)				
Blank = No significant difference				

cells showing significantly stronger needs ratings is only slightly fewer. This reflects some differences in the expertise mean scores (not displayed here). The expertise ratings are stronger in the local data, yielding fewer differences with need ratings in the teaching and administration roles. The mean scores for local versus international were not analyzed for significant differences, but in some cases (for example, psychometrics/statistics and resource management) the numeric differences were large (almost a full point weaker in the international sample).

This might be expected, however, because a previous analysis (Theall et al., 2008) found significant differences across four institutional types based on Carnegie classification. The international sample would have homogenized the results from all types of institutions, and thus a mean expertise score at any one institution might differ considerably from the overall sample score in any skill set and role combination. Further, the respondent pool changes within this context, and the potential for increased

Table 7.7. Disciplinary Differences in ED/SOC and STEM: Institutional Data

SIGNIFICANT DIFFERENCES BETWEEN ED/SOC AND STEM FACULTY					
Meta-Profession Skill Sets	Expertise	Teaching Role	Scholarship Role	Service Role	Administrative Role
Instructional Design		ED/SOC	ED/SOC	ED/SOC	
Instructional Delivery	ED/SOC		ED/SOC		
Instructional Assessment	ED/SOC	ED/SOC	ED/SOC		
Course Management					
Instructional Research		ED/SOC		ED/SOC	
Psychometrics/Statistics					
Epistemology					
Learning Theory	ED/SOC	ED/SOC	ED/SOC		
Human Development	ED/SOC	ED/SOC			
Information Technology					
Technical Writing					
Graphic Design					
Public Speaking				ED/SOC	ED/SOC
Communications Styles		ED/SOC	ED/SOC	ED/SOC	ED/SOC
Conflict Management		ED/SOC			
Group Process					
Resource Management					
Personnel Supervision and Management					
Financial and Budget Development					
Policy Analysis and Development					
ED/SOC = ED/SOC faculty ratings significantly stronger than STEM (<.05 in all cases)					
No cases of STEM faculty ratings significantly stronger than ED/SOC					
Blank = No significant difference					

percentages of faculty respondents as compared to administrator/faculty developer responses may also shift the findings. In all cases, the local data become critical and comparison with the international profiles is useful primarily to prompt reflection and dialogue.

A Local Institutional Study: Disciplinary Difference Ratings

Data from the local institution were analyzed for disciplinary differences using the same disciplinary groups as in the international survey. Fortunately, the local sample contained the same disciplinary diversity as the international sample. Of the seventy-four respondents, ten were from STEM disciplines and thirteen from ED/SOC disciplines. Data from the analysis are presented in Table 7.7 in the same manner as before. Analysis was similar, and significant results were at the same alpha levels.

As in the expertise–need analysis, results from the local institution were very similar to those in the international survey, though not as pronounced in terms in the number of significant differences. ED/SOC expertise and need ratings were significantly stronger in some cases and in similar cells. The more coherent nature of the local sample and regression toward the mean in the larger sample may account for this. STEM ratings were not significantly stronger in any case. As before, established disciplinary differences may account for the results, but more investigation is necessary before reaching firm conclusions.

A Qualitative Extension of the Research

Ultimately, the interest in this study is fueled by its capacity to serve as a lever for change: to be a mechanism for reflection and dialogue that can help to unveil the professoriate and reveal context-specific issues that have an impact on faculty success. This implies a process of qualitative, participatory research that begins by referencing relevant data, such as that collected and presented above. Further, although the results of the local study were very interesting in their own right and informative when considered in relation to the international results, the local data analysis raised several questions not directly answerable through examination of quantitative data. Review of the local results coupled with prior review of the literature (for example, Birnbaum, 1988, on institutional types; Hativa & Marincovich, 1995) suggested that there would be unique characteristics but that the quantitative survey methodology was insufficient to unearth the reasons for the differences. To dig more deeply, a qualitative follow-up study and process was initiated. Its intention: to use the quantitative survey findings as a prompt for active exploration of a contextually grounded interpretation of the Meta-Profession model given local institutional realities.

This portion of the study is ongoing, and the discussion here represents preliminary results emerging from two initial interviews and one focus group. Thus far, respondents include three administrators from ED/SOC disciplines and one faculty member in education. Participants spent roughly one hour with the interviewer, were introduced to the local and international results, and were asked to reflect on them and consider how these points related to open-ended questions that served as discussion prompts: What are the most important skills faculty members in your department need to succeed? How do they acquire these skills? How are the skills evaluated?

Methodologically, this took an action research approach and was designed to engage key stakeholders in collaboratively exploring information that may expand their understanding and suggest action at the individual, departmental, or institutional level. Established qualitative research protocols were employed with grounded theory informing the initial coding and analysis of these interviews, as author-researchers identified emergent themes to allow their growth and ongoing validation (Strauss & Corbin, 1998). Periodic informal and formal discussions among author-researchers served as an inductive base to identify themes of topic impact that were further enhanced and explored using NVivo Qualitative Software (QSR International, 2007). Recoding strategies were used to increase validity by generating *initial free nodes* (stand-alone indicators) and subsequently exploring relationships by establishing *tree-noded categories* (related categories of indicators), supporting each with quotations and emergent analysis (Richards, 1999). Though preliminary and limited in scope, as anticipated, the results begin to echo, reinforce, and reveal differences reflected in the quantitative data while revealing some important distinctions.

A Summary of Emergent Themes

Small focus group conversations with three department chairs from education and social science and an individual interview with a faculty member in education revealed a consistency in categories of opinions expressed. For the sake of brevity, we present these emergent themes in Table 7.8.

The tone, focus, and content of faculty and administrator responses continued to differ within these interview contexts sufficiently to justify their separation (making them easier to consider with respect to the quantitative survey results, such as those in Table 7.4). We also found that the contributions seemed to fall into three primary categories of consideration: faculty skills, faculty development, and departmental needs. These reflected both the initial prompt questions and the specifics of the context. Although the summary terms used here are drawn from the phrases offered by interviewees, the majority of the faculty skills cited are directly reflected in the Meta-Professional skill set, either directly (for example, communication) or indirectly with a term that encompassed several skill sets (diplomatic and people skills, drawing from conflict management, communication, group process and team building, personnel management, and so on). There were also emergent themes that were not readily reflective of existing skills sets that have context-specific and disciplinary relevance and will be mentioned later. First, here are some revealing and illustrative quotes that help to clarify the motivations and perspectives of respondents vis-à-vis the themes we have noted.

Table 7.8. Emergent Themes from Qualitative Study

	Faculty Skills	Faculty Development	Department Needs
Administrator responses	Communication skills Knowledge of local area and people* Diplomatic skills (dealing with people) Teaching and scholarship (traditional) Specific teaching experience in a program area Teaching skills (for cross-appointed faculty)*	Mentoring (chair or others) Formative feedback (years 1–3) Collaboration with peers Institutional programs Professional programs	Areas of specialization of candidates Balance of skills across department Mix of skills and experience Collaborative potential "Team members" Public relations and external influence (collegiality?)
Faculty responses	Teaching skills most important Scholarship skills related to the discipline Service distracting Personal challenges and finding balance	Mentoring Laissez faire, "trial and error"	Administrator expectations— need for clarity, implications for success, fairness and consequences Public relations and external advocacy and influence

Note: = Pertains to ED/SOC but not necessarily to all disciplines.

Administrators shared these, regarding:

- What they look for when hiring new faculty:
  - Teaching and scholarship, mix of skills and experience: "As a chair, I look for success in teaching, but the university looks for publications."
  - Communication, public relations, collegiality: "I look for someone who has diplomatic skills and good personal relations skills."
  - Balance of skills: "I try to assemble a group of people who meet all the needs of the department."
- How they support faculty professional development:
  - Mentoring and formative feedback: "In the new faculty member's first three years, my role is as a mentor and someone

who can provide formative feedback about performance and growth, so that in the ensuing years, the person has the best chance to prepare for and to succeed in the promotion and tenure process."

The first faculty member mentioned:

- Faculty needs, skill areas:
  - On teaching: "If I had to categorize what's most important to me, I would like to suggest being an effective teacher."
  - On scholarship: "I would also say that scholarship is critical. I am constantly expanding my awareness and my sense of what is important in education. Both from the standpoint of theory and practice and where we live, in terms of what is impacting the educational sector."
  - On service: "Service is important, but I will be honest with you, sometimes it deters, it mitigates against my ability to really dive into the scholarship, and hence to make the greatest impact that I would like to in the teaching."
  - Personal challenges and finding balance: A difficult issue is "making the transition between negotiating the roles of single parent and the commitments that are nonnegotiable with the expectations and the mandates . . . for promotion and/or other benefits that go with the role of one who is on a tenure track. . . . There is a tension there. . . . And how I successfully engage those two has been very difficult."
- Faculty development:
  - On support to faculty: "Now should there be a commitment to ensure that the faculty have the best opportunity to develop the expected skills? In all fairness, yes, especially if the evaluation process suggests that my moving forward has been beneficial to me."
  - Intermittent lack of support: "A lot has been left to trial and error except for maybe the conversations that occur between myself and mentors. . . . I feel, maybe more is going to be unveiled . . . as I continue on here. But I think there's this silent understanding that it's supposed to 'just happen.'"
  - A suggestion: "[It] would be meaningful to have a formal opportunity even if it's just two . . . or one a semester, to actually have a meeting . . . in terms of what the administration expects: what you know in general, down to the specifics of 'Here it is, and

these are some possibilities to explore to how to get to [the] goals.'"

- Administrator stance and opinions (department needs):

  - Public relations and external advocacy, influence: "They [administrators] want to present the best picture that their faculty members are on top."

  - Departmental expectations: "I got a pretty good sense . . . from your survey, that they [administrators] are expecting more than I thought or at least there is . . . a sense that you should know something about these pieces [the skills]. . . . I think . . . it challenges me to balance it [the skills-roles demands] and so I'm mindful . . . because if I don't, it could result in negative action . . . although the beginning instructor may not have a handle of the skills beyond the basic level, the expectation that . . . as you matriculate somehow you will be endowed. . . . I feel that I've still been held accountable. . . . Is that fair? I don't know."

There are several emergent themes embedded in both Table 7.8 and the quotes offered by interviewees. They move beyond the task-focused Meta-Profession skills and present us with both suggestions and insights into context-influenced issues. Three of these themes that surface from faculty and administrator conversations are collegiality, balance, and community connections and networks. Collegiality is the elusive term that benefits from open discussion and collaborative definition. Additional interviews will undoubtedly help to flesh this term out for the study and for institutional participants. Balance emerges in multiple forms: from the classic balance challenge associated with teaching, scholarship, and service to administrators projecting the need to broadly consider their faculty's skills and expertise to create a balanced departmental profile, to faculty referencing the challenge of balancing professional and personal lives.

Limitations and Future Research

Beginning with the survey, it is relevant to note that even though the current international sample is sufficiently large to allow some analysis, many issues require further exploration. For example, accurate description of disciplinary differences would require a substantially greater number of responses from each disciplinary area. A gender breakdown in the current sample (66 percent female, 33 percent male) would allow some analysis, but the numbers are too small to explore whether gender differences (if they exist) hold across disciplines, academic ranks, years of experience, type of appointment, or location in different Carnegie institutional types. Thus, one practical and logistical problem is that the current sample is limited in terms of its representativeness, and this fact would likewise limit the analysis that can be done. Should resources become available that would support a coordinated effort to gather a truly large sample of faculty and administrator responses, this would allow such enhanced analysis and mark a next step toward understanding the effects of many variables on opinions about faculty roles, skills, and needs. In addition, expanded analyses of expertise and needs ratings should be considered (for example, chi-square analysis may prove more suitable than significance testing for mean score differences in comparisons of expertise and need).

A second limitation relates to the intended use of the survey and other mechanisms to collect unique institutional data. Again, even if overall results from analyses of gender, rank, and so on were available, local samples may be too small to examine whether or not they agree with the general results. Qualitative research approaches may well help to resolve questions, but such collaborative data collection, analysis and interpretation, though potentially transformative, is generally a time- and cost-intensive process.

Tentative Conclusions and Recommendations

The potential of this model, survey, and process for promoting community conversations around faculty roles, responsibility, development, and evaluation continues to hold promise. Whereas limitations exist, the ability to overlay an integrated research approach and action research methodology allows us to propose a process that consolidates efforts and moves more quickly from findings to action. We have developed and pretested a promising process whereby quantitative data is coded into visible patterns in profiles and used to prompt discussions that reveal qualitative insights regarding contextualized meaning while simultaneously promoting action.

Recognizing that institutional patterns differ, effective use of a meta-professional approach requires local data collection and analysis with particular attention to context-sensitive variables that could affect results. To date, preliminary analysis suggests such factors include the Carnegie classification of the institution and its size, location, mission, and resources. Disciplinary focus appears to be a variable of influence, and further examination of the current sample may suggest that other variables can affect opinions, perceptions, and understanding as well.

In general, the current results present sufficient and consistent patterns of responses that suggest a number of conclusions and recommendations.

For Findings

- *Faculty expertise and need across roles.* In skills related to teaching and administration, faculty expertise may be less than desired. The strongest areas of need for meta-professional skills are in teaching and administration. The teaching role is designated as having greater frequency of need and thus is a more likely first target for faculty development intervention and support. In remaining areas, expertise in the meta-professional skill sets is generally considered to be sufficient both for service activities (where the weakest felt need for the skills exists) and for scholarly and creative activities (where base profession preparation is strongest). Institutional determinations may differ.

- *Differing perspectives by roles.* Administrators and faculty differ considerably in their ratings of faculty expertise and in their perceptions about the need for almost every skill in the administrative role. The perceptions of administrators are both colored and broadened by the demands of their positions, and thus they ascribe more importance to almost all skill sets with respect to the administrative role. The perceptions of department-chair-level administrators are influenced by their views on the needs of their departments; they look for a balance of skills across their faculty rather than a full set of skills in every member of the faculty.

- *Differing perspectives by affiliation and status.* Opinions differ about both expertise and need for skills across at least some disciplines. The perceptions of pretenure faculty center on meeting the perceived needs and expectations of the department and the administration, and these expectations cut across all roles and skill sets.

Recommendations for Process

- The Meta-Profession model can be used as a vehicle for exploration of institutional issues as they relate to the professoriate and as a mechanism to prompt targeted improvement.

- An integrated approach, strategically using quantitative and qualitative data collection, can give a more complete picture of institutional perspectives on faculty skills and roles than either process alone.

- Data collection must be followed by ongoing dialogue about both the results and the topics. In other words, collecting data purely as a research effort will not promote improved policy and practice or institutional and organizational development.
- Community dialogue is well informed by data and results in additional qualitative insights.
- Engagement and deliberation are required for actionable outcomes to emerge.
- Dialogue on organizational improvement must be a continuous process.

As evident from the approach put forth, the strength of this research and the model will come from its expansion and contextually grounded application by scholar-practitioners in the field. The opportunity to share this research model with POD colleagues under the banner of the Menges Honored Presentation Award at the POD 2008 Conference further affirmed the findings and expanded the conception of ways it could be used. It prompted suggestions ranging from various ways to envision the model graphically to assorted applications such as guided mentoring, clarification of tenure and promotion expectations, frameworks for evaluation, and more. The Meta-Profession Project is open to continued investigation and to more interested, thoughtful, and reflective colleagues joining the journey to explore and support the professoriate and the advancement of teaching and learning in the academy.

REFERENCES

Arreola, R. A., Theall, M., & Aleamoni, L. M. (2003, April). *Beyond scholarship: Recognizing the multiple roles of the professoriate*. Paper presented at the 83rd annual meeting of the American Educational Research Association, Chicago.

Biglan, A. (1973). The characteristics of subject matter in different academic areas. *Journal of Applied Psychology, 73*(3), 195–203.

Birnbaum, R. (1988). *How colleges work: The cybernetics of academic organization and leadership*. San Francisco: Jossey-Bass.

Boyer, E. L. (1990). *Scholarship reconsidered: Priorities of the professoriate*. San Francisco: Jossey-Bass.

Braskamp, L. A., & Ory, J. C. (1994). *Assessing faculty work: Enhancing individual and institutional performance*. San Francisco: Jossey-Bass.

Diamond, R. M., & Adam, B. E. (1995). *The disciplines speak: Rewarding the scholarly, professional, and creative work of faculty.* Washington, DC: American Association for Higher Education.

Diamond, R. M., & Adam, B. E. (2000). *The disciplines speak II: More statements on rewarding the scholarly, professional, and creative work of faculty.* Washington, DC: American Association for Higher Education.

Franklin, J. L., & Theall, M. (1992, April). *Disciplinary differences, instructional goals and activities, measures of student performance, and student ratings of instruction.* Paper presented at the 73rd annual meeting of the American Educational Research Association, San Francisco.

Gappa, J. M., Austin, A. E., & Trice, A. G. (2007). *Rethinking faculty work: Higher education's strategic imperative.* San Francisco: Jossey-Bass.

Hativa, N., & Marincovich, M. (Eds.). (1995). *New directions for teaching and learning: No. 64. Disciplinary differences in teaching and learning: Implications for practice.* San Francisco: Jossey-Bass.

QSR International. (2007). *NVivo 8 fundamentals* and *Moving on with NVivo 8.* Cambridge, MA: Author.

Richards, L. (1999). *Using NVivo in qualitative research.* London: Sage.

Smart, J. C., Feldman, K. A., & Ethington, C. A. (2000). *Academic disciplines: Holland's theory and the study of college students and faculty.* Nashville, TN: Vanderbilt University Press.

Strauss, A., & Corbin, J. (1998). *Basics of qualitative research: Grounded theory, procedures, and techniques.* Thousand Oaks, CA: Sage.

Theall, M. (2002, April). *Leadership in faculty evaluation and development: Some thoughts on why and how the meta-profession can control its own destiny.* Invited address at the 82nd annual meeting of the American Educational Research Association, New Orleans, LA.

Theall, M., & Arreola, R. A. (2006). The meta-profession of teaching. *NEA Higher Education Advocate, 22*(5), 5–8.

Theall, M., Arreola, R. A., Mullinix, B., Franklin, J., Svinicki, M., & Chism, N.V.N. (2008, March). *The roles and skills of faculty in US and UK higher education institutions: What faculty need to succeed.* Paper presented at the 87th annual meeting of the American Educational Research Association, New York.

8

MACGYVERS, MEDEAS, AND
BIONIC WOMEN

PATTERNS OF INSTRUCTOR RESPONSE

TO NEGATIVE FEEDBACK

Allison P. Boye, Suzanne Tapp, Texas Technological University

Few studies have examined instructor responses to negative feedback and their interplay with gender, but faculty developers must be cognizant of and sensitive to the needs of the instructors with whom they work. This chapter identifies six general patterns of response among male and female instructors to negative feedback from students and consultants, based on survey results, interviews, and observations. A combination of empathy, resources, and time is the key to understanding and responding to those patterns and meeting the needs of individual instructors. Further, comparisons across gender reveal interesting differences related to language use, internalization versus externalization of feedback, and holistic versus specific approaches to reflective teaching.

We have all observed patterns of behavior in our colleagues, students, and faculty members such as common ways of speaking or dressing, patterns of anger, and similar responses to stress or excitement. As faculty developers, we have identified several response patterns from instructors as they reflect on negative feedback about their teaching. As such, we began to take note of how instructors, both male and female, react to the consultation process and negative feedback. Some instructors meet the feedback with flatness or indifference, while others adopt an emotional progression from devastation and anger to acceptance and action. Although instructors of both genders demonstrated some commonalities, they also demonstrated some very distinct differences in how they perceive and react to student feedback and the consultation process in general.

According to Diamond (2002), faculty developers must judge how sensitive an instructor will be to receiving student and consultant commentary. This becomes complicated when the dynamics of gender and potential conflict come into play. Our primary questions here are:

- How do instructors perceive the feedback they receive from students and consultants?

- How do instructors of both genders respond to feedback from students or consultants?

- How can faculty developers adjust their practice to respond to these patterns of response from instructors?

Context

Little research has been conducted on instructor responses to feedback across gender, particularly in relation to faculty development practice; much research, however, has investigated the reliability of student evaluations along gender lines, as well as faculty responses to stress. Much of the research conducted in the area of formal student evaluations of instructors reveals mixed results in regard to gender. Many, among them Centra and Gaubatz (2000) and Theall and Franklin (2001), report that, despite naysayers, standard student evaluations are generally reliable and indicate no strong gender-based bias; more specifically, students "do not favor instructors on the basis of gender alone" (Theall & Franklin, 2001, p. 50).

However, other studies (Andersen & Miller, 1997; Bachen, McLoughlin, & Garcia, 1999; Basow, 2000; Meyers, Bender, Hill, & Thomas, 2006; Sprague & Massoni, 2005) show that students often maintain different behavioral expectations of male and female instructors, usually related to gender-based stereotypes. For instance, some students expect female instructors to exhibit nurturing qualities, and they may penalize those who do not exhibit those qualities in student–teacher interactions. Franklin and Theall (1994); Laube, Massoni, Sprague, and Ferber (2007); and Theall (2005) call attention to other gender-based factors—such as how departments assign teaching responsibilities or how students interpret instructors' delivery—that can influence student evaluation of or behavior toward female instructors, as well as instructors' experiences in the classroom, which are often not easily detectable on traditional evaluation scales.

Regarding change and reaction to student evaluations, Schmelkin, Spencer, and Gellman (1997) show that faculty appear to view student feedback differentially. Instructors were not necessarily resistant to student feedback, as anticipated, yet they viewed feedback on interaction as most valuable while paying less heed to other elements. Nasser and Fresko (2002) indicate that few faculty reported changing instruction significantly as a result of student evaluations. However, studies by Piccinin (1999) and Piccinin, Cristi, and McCoy (1999) report that focused individual teaching consultations, including direct student feedback elicited privately by a consultant, are effective in influencing change and improving the quality of consultees' teaching. Interestingly, Roberts and Nolen-Hoeksema (1989) find that males and females exhibit subtle differences in their reactions to performance feedback. Their study suggests that negative and positive feedback more readily influences women's self-assessment of their own abilities.

Our Investigation

We surveyed instructors at our institution who participated in the small-group instructor diagnostic (SGID) process over the past three years (solicited n = 84, respondent n = 41). Our sample included male and female graduate teaching assistants, lecturers, and tenure-track and tenured faculty from all disciplines.

The survey gathered demographic data from the instructors such as gender, rank, and teaching experience, as well as their reflections on the SGID experience and responses to feedback. The survey used both open-ended and Likert scale questions, such as: How did you feel about your teaching after receiving the SGID feedback? How did you feel toward your students after receiving the SGID feedback? How often, if at all, did your students express frustration or satisfaction with the class *before or after* the SGID? How satisfied were you with the helpfulness of your consultant in evaluating students' feedback?

As part of our investigation, we also conducted individual interviews (n = 7) with male and female instructors from a variety of disciplines and ranks who initiated contact with us on the basis of their experiences with student evaluations, classroom incivility, sheer frustration, or simple desire for feedback. We included these faculty as well as survey respondents (described below), although the survey responses remained anonymous. To preserve confidentiality, we have also changed all names included in this chapter. Although the quantitative survey data did not show significant differences between male and female responses, the qualitative data and interviews revealed differences in how male and female instructors responded to negative feedback.

Our Discoveries

Some general patterns of response from male and female instructors emerged from the data that call to mind memorable cultural icons (summarized in Table 8.1). These patterns fall into three general categories: emotional responses ("Medea" and "Mr. Inconceivable"), detached responses ("Scarlett" and "Nero"), and action-oriented responses ("Bionic Woman" and "MacGyver"). These icons or archetypes may seem like light-hearted jokes or jabs, or even faculty bashing to amuse ourselves and our faculty development peers. However, at their core they could help faculty developers anticipate instructor responses to the consultation process and interact more effectively with individuals. We are not seeking to pigeonhole or offend, but rather to offer some unforgettable representations of possible behaviors. As with any imposed category, the lines between some of these patterns are often blurred, mutable, and not even always gender-specific. Regardless of inevitable overlap, recognizing the paradigms in some form, whether male or female, may help faculty developers prepare for and facilitate consultations.

Emotional Responses

Medea: "I felt that some of the comments were a little too critical. It seemed that some students were whining because they had to read and do homework for a college class." The first pattern we identified in some female instructors is the Medea, the protagonist in the classic story of a betrayed woman's revenge. The behavior we associate with this archetype belongs to instructors who get angry at the negative feedback, sometimes blaming their students for classroom struggles. We also include in this category instructors who demonstrate utter despair in response to feedback, who lament the work they have done as teachers and feel betrayed by the students to whom they have revealed their souls. They do not necessarily lash out at their students or consultants, but like those instructors who get angry they bring with them deep pain. Certainly this reaction is understandable given the amount of work many faculty and teaching assistants pour into their teaching.

One example of an instructor whose response fit into this pattern was Jennifer, a graduate instructor from the College of Education who requested our services near the end of a long and contentious semester with her students. She initiated contact with us via a long email in which she adopted a "victim's stance" in referring to her students, already exuding a great deal of anger toward them and blaming them for the majority, if not all, of the problems she was experiencing as their instructor.

Table 8.1. Archetypal Feelings and Responses

Response category	Archetype	Possible Feelings Expressed by Instructor					Possible Actions Taken by Instructor					Possible Processing of Feedback by Instructor			
		Angry	Sad	Defensive	Indifferent	Interested	Blames others	Shuts down	No action	Argues	Adopts changes	Internal	External	Holistic	Specific
Emotional	Medea	X	X	X			X	X	X	X		X		X	
	Mr. Inconceivable	X		X			X	X	X	X			X		X
Detached	Scarlett			X	X			X	X			X			
	Nero			X	X				X				X		
Action-oriented	Bionic Woman					X					X			X	
	MacGyver					X					X				X

Student complaints ranged from grading practices to course content. During her SGID, student descriptions of her erratic classroom behavior and their extreme malcontent alarmed us, and our initial expectations were confirmed when Jennifer displayed great anger and then sadness during the consultation, even pounding her fist on the table and eventually crying and laying her head on her hands.

Another initial Medea response came from Erin, an assistant professor in human development and family studies, whose negative student feedback took her by surprise. Having received a significant amount of pedagogical training, she was shocked and dismayed to learn that her students were dissatisfied with her expectations. She too responded with anger and sadness during her consultation, shedding tears and raising her voice, ultimately deciding to conduct her own SGID, which questioned her students' role in and commitment to the class.

Yolanda, a full professor from human sciences with an impressive research agenda, called on us after years of negative student evaluations that she described as "really hurtful." Unlike Jennifer, whose primary response was anger, Yolanda initially expressed deep sadness at her students' responses, remarking, "I get so discouraged and feel I should just not teach" (personal communication, January 30, 2007). Similarly, Denise, another Medea, expressed to us, "They [student comments] are just so mean. Why can't they see how much I invest in my teaching?" (personal communication, October 13, 2008).

Several comments from our survey also appear to reflect this pattern. For instance, one respondent wrote, "[I felt] somewhat exasperated . . . they [the students] were commenting on things that I had no control over." Another respondent commented, "I was a little hurt by a few of the comments," while another revealed, "It was insightful but slightly disappointing because the feedback I'd get from them regarding my teaching was generally positive and the SGID showed more negative feedback from them—something I wasn't really expecting and which made me question the disparity." These instructors clearly found the feedback to be meaningful and were processing it in a very personal way.

Mr. Inconceivable: "I was pretty happy with [my students'] responses, but had to wonder how honest many of them were." One response pattern we identified in some male instructors harkens back to the memorable Sicilian kidnapper Vizzini from the now-classic film *The Princess Bride*, who proclaims his own brilliance with the remark, "Let me put it this way. Have you ever heard of Plato? Aristotle? Socrates? . . . Morons!" Like this well-loved character who met every revelation or contention from others with the unforgettable declaration "Inconceivable!" these instructors often bring palpable skepticism to their consultations and might meet negative feedback with argumentation.

Jeff, a young philosophy instructor, was the perfect example of the Mr. Inconceivable response. He requested multiple classroom observations over several semesters, and during several consultations a number of consultants encouraged him to try harder to connect with his students and engage in faculty immediacy (Kearney & Plax, 1992; Meyers, 2003; Pogue & AhYun, 2006) to increase his students' motivation and participation. Despite the extremely small size of his two discussion sections (each ten to fifteen students), Jeff argued that he had too many students to learn and use their names during class. It took a great deal of consultation time and many references to push Jeff to *begin* to realize the importance—and feasibility—of learning his students' names.

Donald, a history instructor, embodied another example of devoted skepticism. His consultant initially observed a meeting of Donald's introductory history course, during which he presented dozens of PowerPoint slides during the short fifty-minute class. Later, his consultant advised him to consider incorporating simple active learning strategies and class discussion to augment his enthusiastic lectures and get his students more engaged with the material. At the outset, Donald vigorously questioned the practicability of these suggestions, voicing the classic concern that they would interfere with his ability to "cover" the necessary course content. Even as he made attempts to apply some of the suggestions, he continued to express doubts about their effectiveness, going so far as to forward to his consultant an email from a student dropping his class: "Guess the active-learning approach is hard for her too!" (personal communication, January 22, 2008).

Our survey contained some comments that reflected this approach to feedback. "I would like to have the person conducting the SGID ask the students what *they* could do to improve the class," wrote one Mr. Inconceivable, who clearly questioned the validity of the students' assessments. Mr. Inconceivable instructors often enjoyed talking about their own classroom experiences but were initially skeptical in response to feedback from others.

Detached Responses

Scarlett: "I was glad for the honest feedback, but I came away from it feeling like there was no way to make all of the students happy. What one student liked, another student hated. I felt that there is no way to please all of them." The second archetype we identified in some female instructors was the Scarlett O'Hara response, the seemingly apathetic "fiddle-dee-dee" reaction to negative feedback. These are the instructors who may shrug their shoulders and appear noncommittal. As Scarlett says in *Gone with the Wind*, these instructors may seem to believe "there is no war" and don't want to be bothered by it. They'd prefer to just walk away, outwardly content to go about their business when faced with the difficulty of hearing negative feedback.

One Scarlett example was a lecturer from health, exercise, and sports sciences who contacted us regarding her teaching. Although Lauren entered her teaching career with enthusiasm, classroom incivility issues and difficulty connecting with students soon soured her experience. Clearly she was affected by the turmoil she experienced with her students and the feedback she received from them. In her own words, her description of the "blood, sweat, and tears" she put into her teaching indicated that this was indeed an emotional Medea experience for her (personal communication, October 2, 2008). However, what she perceived as "constant opposition" quickly led her to shut down, to throw up her hands in the Scarlett fashion and declare that she could never make anybody happy, no matter what she did. Lauren commented that "this has really taken a toll on me and makes me look as if I am this mad black woman with an attitude" (personal communication, February 19, 2008). Regrettably, she left teaching after a few semesters, choosing to pursue another career path.

An associate professor from chemistry also demonstrated the classic Scarlett pattern. A classroom observation revealed that students blatantly cheated on a quiz, entered and left the room throughout the class, and talked to each other with little regard for her lecture. The faculty developer also noted that the instructor lectured nonstop using PowerPoint slides crammed with text and equations that literally ran off the screen. In the follow-up consultation, the instructor's response was decidedly ambivalent; her comments were almost nonresponsive and consisted of "hmm" and "OK." Despite strong encouragement, she has made no further requests for consultations or attempts to solicit feedback.

Yet another Scarlett emerged from the English department. In spite of receiving numerous emotional comments from students over several semesters about overly time-consuming components of the class, the instructor refused to make adjustments to her syllabus or her teaching. Some of her student comments were quite thoughtful (for example: "I don't like that everyday we come to class and she just lectures. The benefit of a small class is that we can all discuss and have a more personal environment. I didn't feel like I got a chance to connect well with my peers or the works studied in this class."). Yet the instructor brushed off such remarks as signs of student laziness or lack of understanding (personal communication, April 7, 2006).

The survey also contained Scarlett-type responses, such as those in answer to the question, "What changes did you make to your teaching?" One Scarlett admitted, "I did consider changing some policies/scheduling, but I decided against it." Another replied, "I think most of the things that were brought up were things which really couldn't be changed at that point in the semester." These comments demonstrated the tendency to shut down in response to feedback.

Nero: "I am not sure how the SGID changed my teaching." Another response pattern we identified in male instructors reflects the mentality of Nero, who fiddled while Rome burned. When faced with negative feedback from students or faculty developers, this instructor might display a similarly indifferent or seemingly unconcerned response. Like Mr. Inconceivable, Nero may argue against the student responses or the faculty developer's observations but also convey some underlying arrogance or disinterest in struggling to process the feedback.

Ned, a knowledgeable lecturer in history, confronted critical comments from his SGID, such as, "I don't think a class that is strictly lecture works because it's boring. One gets better results when they interact with the class" and "Sometimes he can go over too much information at one time. It's hard to get all of his points down at times. It would help if he didn't squeeze in so much information at the end of class" (personal communication, October 24, 2004). These remarks mirrored suggestions from a faculty developer who had observed him in the classroom on multiple occasions and offered ways to help him slow down his rapid-fire storytelling delivery and encourage student questions. But Ned literally responded, "Interesting. What else have you got?" Repeated comments over two semesters of SGID feedback were met with flat indifference and lack of recognition of any problems with the current classroom dynamic.

Another Nero example was a graduate student from marketing, Mark, who incorporated use of blogs in his classes. Student comments from the SGID concurred in their dissatisfaction with this use of the blog as an emerging technology. As one student put it, "I am not a big fan of the class blog. It doesn't really help me learn and it's just people posting their opinions" (personal communication, February 24, 2006). Yet the instructor believed that the blog worked beautifully and achieved his goal of student engagement, despite students saying that it "was just a task to always check the blog." He continued to use blogs in all subsequent classes he taught at our university and disregarded the feedback that students were not connecting with the technology. Following a classroom observation, faculty developers noted that his use of a forced cold call participation strategy seemed to be counterproductive to his desire to engage students. But he ignored comments on his SGID such as, "Stop randomly calling on people. Making people look foolish doesn't promote learning—it promotes fear!" and "he should do something else to involve everyone besides calling on random people" (personal communication, February 24, 2006).

We also noticed a few aloof survey responses from male respondents that sounded like Nero responses, such as, "I believe my students were being honest and trying to help me, and their evaluations did not affect my feelings towards them" and "I really felt no differently towards my students after the SGID, compared to before the SGID, though I did appreciate their willingness to provide candid feedback." Students often perceived Nero instructors as knowledgeable but disconnected.

Action-Oriented Responses

Bionic Woman: "I think that I am a good teacher overall but I have been able to make some changes based on comments from the feedback that I think have made me better." A third response pattern we recognized in female instructors is what we like to think of as the Bionic Woman. Like Jamie Summers, who suffered a parachuting accident in the popular television show of the 1970s, these instructors, in spite of suffering the "trauma" or "injury" of negative student or consultant feedback, ultimately rebuild themselves, their teaching strategies, and their relationship with their students, and become stronger than ever. They take action based on the feedback they receive to positively reshape their classroom.

One recent Bionic Woman example on our campus was an associate professor in health, exercise, and sports science who incorporated a significant service-learning project into her course that frustrated her students one semester because of problems in communication. On receiving somewhat harsh SGID feedback, she met with her community partners and worked hard to improve communication, rather than deeming the project a disaster and calling it quits. She approached the criticism graciously, took the feedback in stride, and made some important changes to meet her students' needs.

Further, although both Yolanda and Erin likewise began the consultation process with the Medea response pattern, they eventually transformed themselves into Bionic Women. Both of them worked through the initial pain of the feedback and took action to make significant changes in their teaching approach. Erin, for instance, chose to talk to her students directly about their comments and solicited even more feedback from them. Through this process she realized the error in her assumptions about their abilities and motivation, and she now starts each semester by clearly explicating her expectations. Taking a quieter approach, Yolanda thoughtfully analyzed each suggestion from her consultant and the feedback from her students with slight reluctance. But eventually she warmed to the process and began incorporating new teaching strategies. Yolanda's changes met with great success; the semester following her consultations, she wrote to us in an email:

> I just received my student evaluations for Fall of 07 and almost sobbed!!! I am attaching a copy of them so that you can see how great they were!!! I am soooooooooooooooo thankful to you for helping me improve my teaching skills. I did not think I had it in me to do. You have made an incredible difference in me professionally and I want you to know how much I appreciate all the help you gave me last year. Thank you, thank you, thank you. [personal communication, January 23, 2008]

The Bionic Women in our survey wrote comments such as these: "I've learned that as a teacher, you must continually assess your performance in order to be most effective. I found myself in a 'teaching rut' and I believe that the evaluation process opened my eyes to new ideas." And "Becoming aware of areas of improvement helped me address the issues which I could work on to make the classes more worthwhile." These responses demonstrated a clear desire to engage in reflective teaching and make changes that work toward improvement.

MacGyver: "My teaching changed because I saw what works in the class so I reinforced the use of those techniques or dynamics that work. At the same time I took very seriously what did not work and tried to implement different strategies to reverse the weaknesses into strengths using recommendations from the consultants and the students." The resourceful secret agent MacGyver, the title character from the hit 1980s television series, represents the third pattern we identified among male instructors. Just as MacGyver could solve almost any problem with duct tape, a paperclip, and his handy Swiss army knife, this kind of instructor is willing to work with student feedback and consider issues raised by consultants.

SGID feedback from an information systems and quantitative sciences class informed the instructor of a classroom dynamic he hadn't noticed before. Students commented that "it disrupts the class when the same student shows up 30–45 minutes late every class period. That student then asks questions about topics which were covered in detail before his very late arrival" (personal communication, October 16, 2007). The instructor obviously was familiar with the student's tardiness but did not recognize how it disturbed the other students. He met with the chronically late arriver the next day and resolved the problem. Perhaps this is why his students also volunteered that this MacGyver-style instructor "cooperates with students" and "is open to questions and to making sure that we keep learning new things" (personal communication, October 16, 2007).

A graduate student from computer science, Fred, transformed from Mr. Inconceivable into MacGyver in a process that was recognizable only over time. Classroom observations and SGIDs with his introductory class clearly indicated that his traditional lecture-based format was not engaging his students or giving them opportunities to program and code. Fred struggled to accept these problems as he reexamined his teaching goals. Slowly he began to incorporate in-class problem solving and student-led discussion, and to invite students to show their techniques on the board. A student who took a class with him one semester and another class the next semester remarked about the change: "I have seen significant improvement in his teaching methods" (personal communication, March 20, 2006). The faculty developers he worked with counted his MacGyver-like transition as a highlight of the year.

Instructors who fit into the MacGyver pattern wrote comments on our survey like these:

> I became aware of some improvements I could do in the semester itself, so that the learning process could be enhanced. I also could see that there were areas I could do much better, in terms of idiosyncrasies and mannerisms, and overall pedagogy.
>
> The constructive nature of the feedback helped to focus my attention on making my teaching as good as possible (rather than focusing on how bad my teaching may be now).
>
> Becoming aware of areas of improvement helped me address the issues which I could work on to make the classes more worthwhile.
>
> My attitude towards students and teaching has changed significantly. Before the SGID, I was not conscious of student-centered learning and engaging students actively. After the SGID, every time I get into the classroom, I ask myself, "Will this aspect of my teaching benefit students or not?" [personal communication, November 21, 2008]

As these comments reveal, MacGyvers are eager to improve their classroom experiences quickly and thoughtfully.

Responding to the Patterns

Knowing these patterns can help faculty developers prepare themselves to meet the individual needs of each instructor and respond wisely to the faculty reaction to the feedback and consultation process. Finding the right combination of empathy, time, and resources is ultimately the key to an effective collaborative consultation model (Brinko, 1997) and what we have termed *relational perseverance*—that is, the motivation to invest appropriately in an individual faculty member. Relational perseverance is needed to effect change and represents the partnership between faculty developer and instructor as they negotiate negative feedback.

Empathy

One of our Medeas, Erin, described the significance of the consultation process by saying that the "discussion was particularly helpful because it [the feedback] was a painful experience." In describing the process of working through the student comments and understanding the years of missed connections with her students, Erin said that she was "raw and fragile" and appreciated how the faculty developer "attended to her emotions" (personal communication, October 8, 2008). Using empathy to identify with and demonstrate understanding of situations and feelings after reading the negative comments from students can be crucial to the relationship between the faculty developer and the instructor. Simple but powerful phrases such as, "If I'm hearing you correctly," "It sounds as though you're saying," "Do you mean . . . " and "I sense that you're feeling . . . " can aid communication and give the instructor freedom to explore his or her emotions. Even though most faculty developers use empathic skills in their consultation practices, it does not hurt to review the skills needed to demonstrate active listening while working with a faculty member, particularly one who has received negative feedback and may be processing difficult feelings.

Time

We observed Jeff, a Mr. Inconceivable–style instructor, multiple times over the course of three semesters. After several semesters of argumentative feedback sessions with Jeff, we had the privilege of observing an a-ha moment as he finally opened up and revealed his fear of judgment from students and his departmental colleagues. He stopped arguing and started asking questions such as, "How do I make my students care?" No doubt the time invested in building a trusting relationship with him contributed to Jeff's epiphany. Similarly, Yolanda, a Medea turned Bionic Woman, communicated her desire for more consultation time and follow-up from the faculty developer. Although she made tremendous strides in her teaching, she lost some of her newfound confidence and momentum over time and expressed a need to extend her relationship with her consultant (personal communication, September 26, 2008). All faculty developers undoubtedly know instructors who repeatedly return yet make seemingly few changes to their teaching. Because time is a precious commodity for any faculty developer, perhaps we can all find solace knowing that our investments can pay off.

Resources

Gloria, an accounting instructor and Bionic Woman, came to a workshop offered through our teaching and learning center. During the session, she asked many questions and took voracious notes. A few weeks later, she popped in to our center, excited to share her success in implementing directed reading strategies she had learned. Likewise, we gave Donald, one of the Mr. Inconceivables profiled here, scholarly articles and current active-learning literature, and eventually he began successfully incorporating ideas from what he perceived to be credible sources. It behooves faculty developers to familiarize themselves with classic teaching and learning literature as well as current SoTL research and make these resources readily available to our instructors. This will not only help us in our day-to-day practice but also solidify our profession as academically respectable.

Relational Perseverance

To meet the individual needs of instructors, faculty developers must find the best formula combining empathy, time, and resources. Perhaps Scarletts and Medeas, who take criticism personally, will benefit from a greater level of empathy, while Mr. Inconceivables and Neros may respond well to more resources and time. In a nutshell, simply *hang in there* to find what works to build the best relationship, to wait out the skepticism or indifference, and to offer the best resources for that individual. Persevering and hopefully finding that magical combination of empathy, resources, and time, we have discovered, can help instructors process the feedback in a way meaningful to them. Then maybe a one-time Medea can transition into a Bionic Woman, like Erin or Yolanda; or a Mr. Inconceivable can become a MacGyver, like Donald or Fred.

What's Gender Got to Do with It?

Although we found many commonalities among the various response patterns, we also identified some underlying differences along gender lines. Gender differences on the survey questions about the SGID process were not statistically significant, but the content analysis of their open-text responses revealed language-use differences that might speak to the ways these instructors navigated their feedback. In male comments, for instance, we repeatedly saw references to honesty and candidness ("I believe my students were being honest in trying to help me," "I liked them for their honesty," and "I appreciated their willingness to give candid feedback"), whereas female responses uses more emotive language ("I was happy they tried to be constructive," "It was insightful but slightly disappointing," and "I felt somewhat exasperated"). Another difference was the verb tense used. Male instructors consistently used the past tense when describing changes made to their teaching, while female instructors favored the present tense. For example, males gave comments such as, "I increased the time I spent explaining points," while females wrote remarks such as, "I give better directions, slow down, and give more feedback on assignments." If the past tense represents finished action and the present a continuous and dynamic state, this seemingly innocuous tense difference may reveal deeper beliefs about change.

Internal Versus External

Other responses from our female respondents suggested a more personal and internalized approach to the feedback and change process. Consider the instructors who wrote, "I tried to soften my approach," "Saying I had a four-year-old seems to endear females toward me," or "I really took the feedback to heart." Conversely, among male respondents, the reactions were generally externalized—for example, "slides were criticized and completely reworked," and "I was interested in trying some of the ideas given," or "it has been three years and [he] does not remember" if he made any postconsultation changes. Regardless of whether the feedback received was positive or negative in nature, the female instructors seemed to process it internally, to see it as a memorable reflection on themselves as individuals, whereas the male instructors often viewed feedback as a series of helpful hints or instructions that that they could pick and choose from to improve their teaching. This pattern reflects that identified by Roberts and Nolen-Hoeksema (1989), who found that women responded to performance-related feedback "in a way that indicated that they, more readily than the men, considered the external information, whether positive or negative, to have self-evaluative meaning" (p. 741). For instance, although both Scarletts and Neros appear to respond to feedback with apathy, the major difference was in the end result. Some Scarletts shut down and quit, deciding to leave teaching altogether, as Lauren did; whereas Neros could remain unaffected and unconcerned, pursuing the same career regardless of the negative feedback, as Mark did.

Holistic Versus Specific

Another distinguishing difference between male and female responses was the implicit attitude toward embracing and implementing the feedback. Male respondents exhibited a tendency to make class-specific changes. For instance, in response to the question, "What changes, if any, did you make to your class or your teaching in response to the SGID process?" one male instructor wrote, "I eliminated an extra-credit scenario that many students perceived as being unfair. They were likely a few other minor adjustments that I can't identify presently." Another wrote, "I worked out a system of regular feedback to find out what topics were clearly understood." By contrast, female instructors leaned toward changing their teaching across courses. One female responded to the same question, "I have used more active learning and other class activities"; another wrote, "For valid suggestions about the course's foundation, I was able to change things in future classes." Both the Bionic Women and the MacGyvers reacted to their consultations with energetic action to make positive changes, but the genders differed in the extent to which the instructor incorporated feedback and made changes in overall teaching style.

Being aware of these subtle gender differences (internalization versus externalization of feedback, holistic versus specific approaches to reflective teaching) can prime the faculty developers' expectations of their clients and can help them tailor their consultations to the individual, creating a productive relationship that will foster the positive professional growth of the instructor in need.

Value to Faculty Development

So how does this research benefit other faculty developers? An overarching theme of all the survey and interview responses was the importance of the consultant–instructor relationship, whether working through difficult feedback, offering helpful resources, brainstorming new approaches, or just listening. The patterns we have identified may be recognizable to any faculty developer, but being more aware of them can help consultants prepare a toolkit of strategies for each individual instructor and build a stronger relationship. Just knowing that one might have to be patient and wait out a Mr. Inconceivable or a Nero, listen to the complaints of a Scarlett, or wipe the tears of a Medea can encourage the faculty developer to persevere. Recognizing gender patterns can help the consultant antici-pate the approach an instructor may bring to the consultation. Will she be looking for long-term inspiration? Will he desire an effective, immedi-ate solution to a problem he currently faces in his class? With the proper combination of empathy, time, and resources, a Medea may be a Bionic Woman in waiting, and a Mr. Inconceivable can evolve into a MacGyver.

REFERENCES

Andersen, K., & Miller, E. D. (1997). Gender and student evaluations of teach-ing. *PS: Political Science and Politics*, 30(2), 216–219.

Bachen, C., McLoughlin, M., & Garcia, S. (1999). Assessing the role of gender in college students' evaluations of faculty. *Communication Education*, 48(3), 193–210.

Basow, S. A. (2000). Best and worst professors: Gender patterns in students' choices. *Sex Roles*, 43(5/6), 407–417.

Brinko, K. T. (1997). The interactions of teaching improvement. In K. T. Brinko & R. J. Menges (Eds.), *Practically speaking: A sourcebook for instructional consultants in higher education* (pp. 3–8). Stillwater, OK: New Forums Press.

Centra, J. A., & Gaubatz, N. B. (2000). Is there gender bias in student evalua-tions of teaching? *Journal of Higher Education*, 71(1), 17–33.

Diamond, N. (2002). Small group instructional diagnosis: Tapping student per-ceptions of teaching. In K. H. Gillespie, L. R. Hilsen, & E. C. Wadsworth (Eds.), *A guide to faculty development: Practical advice, examples, and resources* (pp. 83–91). Bolton, MA: Anker.

Franklin, J., & Theall, M. (1994, April). *Student ratings of instruction and sex differences revisited.* Paper presented at the 75th annual meeting of the American Educational Research Association, New Orleans.

Kearney, P., & Plax, T. G. (1992). Student resistance to control. In V. P. Richmond & J. C. McCroskey (Eds.), *Power in the classroom: Communication, control, and concern* (pp. 85–100). Hillsdale, NJ: Erlbaum.

Laube, H., Massoni, K., Sprague, J., & Ferber, A. (2007). The impact of gender on the evaluation of teaching: What we know and what we can do. *NWSA Journal*, 17(3), 87–104.

Meyers, S. A. (2003). Strategies to prevent and reduce conflict in college class-rooms. *College Teaching*, 51(3), 94–98.

Meyers, S. A., Bender, J., Hill, E. K., & Thomas, S. Y. (2006). How do faculty experience and respond to classroom conflict? *International Journal of Teaching and Learning in Higher Education, 18*(3), 180–187.

Nasser, F., & Fresko, B. (2002). Faculty views of student evaluation of college teaching. *Assessment and Evaluation in Higher Education, 27*(2), 187–198.

Piccinin, S. (1999). How individual consultation affects teaching. In C. Knapper & S. Piccinin (Eds.), *New directions for teaching and learning: No. 79. Using consultants to improve teaching* (pp. 71–84). San Francisco: Jossey-Bass.

Piccinin, S., Cristi, C., & McCoy, M. (1999). The impact of individual consultation on student ratings of teaching. *International Journal for Academic Development, 4*(2), 75–88.

Pogue, L., & AhYun, K. (2006). The effect of teacher nonverbal immediacy and credibility on student motivation and affective learning. *Communication Education, 55*(3), 331–344.

Roberts, T., & Nolen-Hoeksema, N. (1989). Sex differences in reactions to evaluative feedback. *Sex Roles, 21*(11/12), 725–747.

Schmelkin, L. P., Spencer, K. J., & Gellman, E. S. (1997). Faculty perspectives on course and teacher evaluations. *Research in Higher Education, 38*(5), 575–592.

Sprague, J., & Massoni, K. (2005). Student evaluations and gendered expectations: What we can't count can hurt us. *Sex Roles, 53*(11/12), 779–793.

Theall, M. (2005, April). *Valid faculty evaluation data: Are there any? An interactive symposium exploring issues in evaluation and student ratings.* Paper presented at the 85th annual meeting of the American Educational Research Association, Montreal.

Theall, M., & Franklin, J. (2001). Looking for bias in all the wrong places: A search for truth or a witch hunt in student ratings of instruction? In M. Theall, P. C. Abrami, & L. A. Mets (Eds.), *New directions for institutional research: No. 109. The student ratings debate: Are they valid? How can we best use them?* (pp. 45–56). San Francisco: Jossey-Bass.

9

CONVERSATIONS ABOUT ASSESSMENT AND LEARNING

EDUCATIONAL DEVELOPMENT SCHOLARSHIP
THAT MAKES A DIFFERENCE

Sue Fostaty Young, Susan Wilcox, Queen's University

To facilitate deeper understanding of teachers' assessment practices, we undertook an educational development inquiry with college and university faculty. Our conversations with instructors about their assessment practices highlighted the complex relationship between teachers' beliefs about teaching, their institutional contexts, and their experiences of teaching. The project gave us valuable opportunities to examine our interactions with faculty and enabled us to identify approaches to educational development that help postsecondary faculty understand and improve their practice.

Assessment can be a very positive force for student learning. As teachers create tasks through which to gather and interpret information about student learning, they shape students' approaches to course material (Biggs, 2003). The project we describe in this chapter had two broad purposes: first, to explore the connection between postsecondary teachers' assessment practices and their intentions for student learning by examining influences on the choices teachers make when they conduct assessment; and second, to learn about assessment in a way that offered immediate benefits to the teachers we were learning from and helped us acquire more effective strategies for educational development concerning assessment practices. Our ultimate goal is to promote development of assessment beliefs and practices that will best support student learning in higher education.

Underlying this initiative is our vision of educational development as scholarship uniting research and practice. We are particularly interested in promoting collaborative self-study with teachers as a means of understanding and improving teaching and learning. Self-study is a mode of scholarly inquiry in which teachers examine their beliefs and actions for the purpose of improving their practice (Louie, Drevdahl, Purdy, & Stackman, 2003; Whitehead, 1993). For example, Richards and Barksdale-Ladd (1997) used cases describing educational problems to unearth subconsciously held professional beliefs that influenced teachers' decision-making processes. Self-study inquiry can promote transformational educational development (Wilcox, Watson, & Paterson, 2004) and as such is entirely suited to the purposes of this particular project. In practical terms, this meant we were committed to reflecting on our own educational development practices while at the same time helping faculty participants take a self-reflective approach to their teaching.

Background

Conceptions of teaching are presented in the literature as idiosyncratic, largely unarticulated composites of assumptions, knowledge, and beliefs about learning, and how to facilitate it, that teachers amass through past and ongoing experience (for example, Biggs, 1999; Entwistle, Skinner, Entwistle, & Orr, 2000). Teachers' implicit theories have a stronger influence on their practice than their cognitive reasoning does (Kember, 1997; Pratt, 1992; Samuelowicz & Bain, 1992, 2002). Kane, Sandretto, and Heath (2002) conducted a comprehensive critical analysis of existing studies on academics' teaching beliefs and practices and concluded that there is a real need for research interventions "that enable university academics to make explicit their own theories-in-use and to interrogate these in light of espoused theories and intentions" (p. 200). In educational development terms, teachers' practice is unlikely to develop unless their conceptions of teaching also develop (Akerlind, 2004; Ho, Watkins, & Kelly, 2001).

Therefore, we need to engage faculty members in meaningful interactions that help them develop and then act on sophisticated conceptions of teaching (Wilcox, 2000) with the ultimate aim of supporting and eliciting the type of learning outcomes and ends expected through higher education. We anticipated that guiding teachers through an exploration of beliefs and practices might facilitate their understanding of the motivations for their actions. We accept Schön's assertion (1987) that when teachers reflect on their actions, they may be able to uncover previously unarticulated assumptions that informed those actions. When we can make explicit the assumptions that shape conceptions of teaching, those assumptions become more susceptible to change (Mezirow, 2000).

Pratt (1992) identified assessment as the aspect of teaching that, more than any other, reveals an individual's dominant beliefs about teaching and learning. Assessment is also recognized to be the single most important factor influencing students' approaches to learning (Biggs, 2003; Boud, 1990; Ramsden, 1992). Students interpret a teacher's system of values through what and how she or he chooses to assess (Boud, 1990; Gass, 2004), thus the critical need for assessment practices to be aligned with intentions for learning (Biggs, 2003; Gibbs & Simpson, n.d.). Brookfield (1995) urged teachers to "take a long, hard look at your evaluative criteria and indicators" (p. 112). For all these reasons, we were keen to explore the impact of teachers' conceptions of teaching and learning on their assessment practices.

Wilson (1990) contended that any effort to understand assessment practices that does not also attempt to locate those practices in an educational context is "doomed to failure" (p. 227); because teachers' assessment beliefs and practices may be constrained by institutional expectations and conditions. Class size and student ability are two conditions commonly assumed to affect assessment practices, but other factors come to mind as well. For example, in some institutions course learning outcomes are fixed, but the choices of text(s), delivery method(s), learning activities, and method(s) of assessment are up to the teacher. In this case, teachers are expected to make instructional decisions that will support the stated learning outcomes, but it is uncertain how and whether they make this connection. In other settings, most aspects of course design and implementation are up to the individual instructor. In theory, teachers in such settings are free to conduct assessment in ways they feel will best document achievement of intended student learning outcomes, but is this the case? We felt compelled to explore aspects of institutional context as an area of influence regarding teachers' assessment choices.

Recognizing the impact of assessment on student learning and appreciating the intimate relationship among teachers' beliefs about teaching, their institutional contexts, and their assessment choices, we concluded that a collaborative self-study of teachers' assessment beliefs and practices would be an especially fruitful approach to educational development scholarship.

Approach

We invited four teachers to participate in an examination of assessment beliefs and practices with the two of us. We chose four because it allowed us to delve intensely into conversation with them about particular practices. Having two educational developers involved in this small project enabled productive conversation with a colleague about the process and findings.

We were interested in how these teachers' conceptions of teaching and learning related to their assessment practices and how institutional contexts influenced their conceptions of teaching and learning and shaped their assessment practices. We hoped this critical inquiry into practice would be of immediate benefit to the teachers involved and would help us devise ways of working effectively with teachers to help them reflect on their assessment beliefs and practices and make wise assessment choices.

Participants

The authors and project leaders are experienced educational developers with a disciplinary background in adult and higher education. We are skilled consultants regarding postsecondary assessment practices but have had few opportunities to reflect on assessment issues in collaboration with teachers.

Two college and two university faculty members accepted our invitation to explore assessment with us. We knew the university teachers at our own institution to be thoughtful and successful teachers who took their teaching seriously; the college teachers were recommended to us for similar reasons by the academic vice president at a neighboring institution. (The province of Ontario's colleges of applied arts and technology focus on career preparation through certificate, diploma, and apprenticeship programs, although some programs lead to a degree.) Participating faculty (three women, one man) came from disparate disciplines: one college teacher taught public relations, consumer behavior, and marketing, and the second taught accounting. One university professor taught politics while the second taught microbiology. All were experienced instructors with fifteen to thirty years in the classroom. As with most postsecondary teachers, they did not have much formal preparation for teaching. Although one college instructor had completed a Teacher of Adults certificate, the others had learned through occasional participation in teaching development workshops, interactions with a senior mentor, consultation with educational development specialists, or informal discussion with colleagues. Each participant completed a written questionnaire and met twice with one of us for conversations about assessment practices.

Questionnaire

We designed and administered a questionnaire based on items available on standard teaching questionnaires. Included, for example, were items from the Assessment Experience Questionnaire (Gibbs & Simpson, 2003) and from our university's new faculty questionnaire, which asks respondents whether particular statements about teaching reflect their own views (based on Kember & Kwan, 2000). In their responses, participants identified relevant material to discuss during our conversations.

Conversations

We reviewed the completed questionnaires and identified some initial topics for the one-on-one conversations. Our conversations always began with participants' comments on or questions about the project. We then asked if they wanted to address any one issue first. Together, we then went through the questionnaire to areas that either we had identified for elaboration or the instructor wanted to talk about. We took notes during the conversation. At the close of the first meeting, we asked participants to bring an artifact from their teaching and assessment practice to our second meeting. We left selection of items up to the participants, hoping they would choose something significant and evocative to facilitate a rich discussion.

Luce-Kapler (2006) proposed the side-shadow interview as a useful technique for exploring the nature of a process such as writing or teaching. The technique helps the writer or teacher engaged in decision making see "the path of decision nestled among alternative pathways." During side-shadow interviews, an interested "other" reviews an individual's "text" with him or her using both prepared questions and conversational discovery. The interviewer asks the interviewee to talk about the choices made in the text. We experimented with this technique during our second meeting with teacher participants. The artifact supplied by each teacher served as the "text" under discussion. We audiotaped and later transcribed these conversations.

Postintervention Analysis

After our meetings with the teachers, we reviewed the records of our conversations and their responses to the initial questionnaire. None of the participants accepted our offer of a copy of the transcript of our tape-recorded conversations for their review. But to ensure accuracy, along with a letter of thanks we sent a synopsis of each conversation to the participants and asked for their feedback. Every participant verified that we had accurately captured what was said. In reviewing the records, our goal was to identify (1) themes and insights about influences on these teachers' assessment practices and (2) how our future interventions with teachers might improve postsecondary assessment practices. Faculty participants did not contribute directly to this aspect of the project. We did share a final copy of this manuscript with them and once again asked them to advise us if we had misrepresented them, or the process, in any way. All were satisfied with project outcomes as we had described them.

Outcomes

Here we focus on communicating the value of this "inquiry" approach to educational development by describing some of what we learned while working with the participating instructors. We do not mean to suggest that our findings about these teachers' particular approaches to assessment are especially significant. We do wish to convey something of the flavor of our conversations so that others who wish to engage in this form of developmental scholarship will know what to expect from the process.

Questionnaires

Responses to the initial questionnaires furnished us with some helpful information about the participants. For example, we learned that one teacher with thirty years' experience was not very confident in his skills as a teacher (rating himself as 3 on a scale of 1 to 10, where 10 is very confident), while the other three teachers were very confident (9 on the scale) in their teaching skills. Interestingly, all rated the caliber of their students quite highly, ranging from 7 to 10 on a scale of 1 to 10 where 10 is excellent. We learned that these teachers described themselves as more focused on "helping students learn" than on "measuring students' learning." We were encouraged to find that all the participants were well able to describe both their strengths and their weaknesses and to describe how their students probably viewed them. They reported that they used or had used quite a range of assessment strategies, including essay assignments, open-book essay exams, objective tests/exams/quizzes, take-home exams, oral presentations, group project reports, class attendance and participation, and lab reports. Their assessment challenges included "giving useful feedback," "assigning fair grades," "correcting students' style," "avoiding favoritism or bias," "finding enough time for grading," and "giving marks to a poorly presented paper"—in other words, nothing unusual.

Conversations

Our subsequent conversations helped us understand how individual teachers think about assessment in specific contexts. One participant simply described his methods of assessment—the oral presentations, participation, journals, and exams he used. The other three readily detailed the assessment strategies they had put in place in one or more of their courses. Their strategies incorporated such things as performance criteria, communication of requirements to students, the mixture of assessment methods, grading policies, and mechanisms for providing feedback. These participants explained how their assessment approaches fitted the learning outcomes they valued. For example, having maintained strong ties to their respective work fields, both college instructors designed assessment tasks that reflected the skill set demanded by prospective employers. Valuing critical thinking and analytic research skills, the politics teacher developed assignments that targeted those skills. The fourth participant also connected his rather rudimentary notion of assessment with valued learning outcomes, indicating that his students gained a lot of skills doing the tasks he assigned.

All four faculty were intentional about their assessment strategies, even if their approach was not particularly sophisticated. Their decisions were clearly based on their understanding of what students needed to learn in their course. The two university faculty members seemed to rely heavily on personal beliefs about the content and learning processes that were most desirable for their students to demonstrate, while the college faculty members used graduate employment criteria to guide the content and format of their assessment tools.

When discussing assessment challenges, the college instructors seemed particularly concerned that their grading practices be manageable, reasonable, and fair. Grades should reflect the students' level of competence in a particular field, as measured through tests and assignments. At the same time, these teachers indicated that the students should be expected to demonstrate competence only in areas that had been taught, and that they must know up-front what is expected of them. These faculty also expressed interest in finding ways to assess that were feasible given their workload.

The two university instructors were more interested in discussing grading practices that encouraged student engagement and promoted learning. They seemed to assume that most students would meet the basic course requirements and attain a good grade. Their challenge was finding assessment strategies to motivate students to do the kind of work that resulted in real learning.

In discussing the reasons behind their assessment approach, all the participants talked about the quality of their students' learning and identified ways in which their assessment strategies influenced learning. Some participants recounted how they modified their approach in order to improve learning by introducing rubrics and authentic assessment tasks to replace tests. Still, their level of awareness of the practices was not especially high. For example, one teacher explained that his assessment approach differed between two of his courses because one course was more student-oriented while the other was more teacher-focused. But he could not articulate why he approached the two courses so differently.

All four participants said they considered class size in selecting assessment methods, but they did not necessarily abandon worthwhile assessment strategies simply because class size made the strategies harder to implement. Rather, they were more likely to include a complementary assessment strategy (for example, rubrics, group work, self- or peer-assessment) that enabled them to assess a larger class effectively.

Participants were invited to talk about how institutional grading policies influenced their assessment practices. One college teacher insisted that grading policies had no impact at all. Yet she interpreted the college's policy that "student work must be consistently outstanding to earn an A" to mean that only three or four students in each of her sections could achieve an A, and she graded in a way that reflected this thinking. The other college instructor commented disparagingly on a recent change to an institutional grading policy: a pass is now 50 percent where it used to be 60 percent. In her view, this change lowered students' motivation because "many just want to pass." However, she stated that course learning outcomes and her knowledge of the job requirements in the field most influenced her approach to assessment, not the college's policies.

One of the university instructors did not know whether his institution had any official grading policies. He described a departmental culture in which faculty did not discuss teaching, so he did not know how his colleagues approached assessment. He did know that his graduate students had to maintain an A average to receive funding, and so he graded to avoid putting their funding at risk. Rather than addressing institutional grading policies, the other university instructor chose to comment on the reaction of her departmental colleagues to the grades she gave. Her colleagues complained that her grades were too high, while she contended that the grades accurately reflect the quality of her students' learning. In her department, the official grading policy appeared to be irrelevant, and grading practices were considered a professional prerogative that nonetheless colleagues could challenge. For both these university faculty, the informal assessment and evaluation culture of their respective departments significantly influenced their assessment practices and their reflection on their assessment practices.

Exhibit 9.1. Factors Affecting Assessment Choices

Educator identity (authenticity)
• Who am I and what do I value?

Educator role (influence)
• How can I best help students learn?
• What part do I play in their learning?

Educator limits (finding balance)
• How much am I prepared to do?

Prior assessment experiences of educator (knowledge)
• What have I "learned" about assessment through experience?

Assessment skills of educator (ability)
• What do I know how to do?

Ecology of assessment (context)
• How does my approach to assessment fit within the assessment climate or culture in my unit or institution?
• What is the relationship between my own values and practices and the values and practices of my colleagues?
• Is it necessary to achieve integration?

Educator's assumption about students (expectations)
• Who are my students?

Intended learning outcomes (broad and specific goals)
• What do my students need to learn?

When we met a second time with the participants, we were able to delve further into the various factors that influenced these instructors' assessment practices. We were able to identify eight interrelated factors shaping their decisions about how best to conduct assessment (see Exhibit 9.1).

Discussion

Faculty members who participated with us in this critically self-reflective process described purposeful approaches to assessment in their courses. Their beliefs about quality learning and valuable learning outcomes had a more overt affect on their assessment practices than did institutional contexts. In addition, through the collaborative process of inquiry we used, we were able to identify several ways to improve educational development practices.

Influences on teachers' assessment practices

THE IMPACT OF TEACHERS' BELIEFS ON ASSESSMENT PRACTICES. Our participants were reflective instructors who cared about student learning, and their assessment practices supported their commitment to student learning. They expected their assessment activities to help students achieve the outcomes—that is, assessment was primarily *for* learning, not *of* learning.

Although their practices did fit their conceptions of teaching and beliefs about the purposes of assessment, it would be more accurate to say that teachers' practices reflected beliefs to the extent that their skills enabled them to do so. It was important to them to act in accordance with their beliefs, and they appeared to do so within the scope of their abilities. We sometimes suggested new assessment strategies that they had not yet tried, but if an idea did not support their beliefs they did not accept it.

Generally speaking, these faculty articulated sound rationales for their assessment approaches. Even the most tentative one said that he knew when something was "right" to do, even though he could not always explain why his choice was the right one. Like the other three, he looked to students for guidance—that is, he paid attention to student responses in considering the legitimacy and efficacy of an approach.

The fact that the teachers were mostly well aware of their intentions enabled them to be purposeful. In our experience as educational developers, many teachers are not so purposeful in their approach to assessment; rather, assessment is something they do because they have to. We observed that participants' intentionality was not a function of their specific underlying conceptions of teaching. Rather, it was the participants' level of awareness of their deeply held beliefs, values, and intentions that allowed them to be purposeful in their approach.

The college instructors' identity as disciplinary professionals with considerable prior experience in the workplace had a significant impact on their assessment practices. Although they taught full-time and described themselves as educators, they had a very strong connection to the workplace where they had once been and would be sending their graduates. This meant that they saw their role as preparing their students for work and viewed their previous work experience as a real asset in determining what to teach.

THE IMPACT OF INSTITUTIONAL CONTEXTS ON ASSESSMENT PRACTICES. We learned that institutional expectations and conditions influenced these teachers in a variety of ways, and the lens of teachers' conceptions mediated the impact of conditions on practice.

Class size proved to be a significant influence by restricting what was possible, although our participants responded differently to increasing class size. One of the university instructors, for example, stated adamantly that, no matter the size of her classes, she would always include extensive writing assignments because they enabled the kind of learning she valued, even though they increased her work load. The other university teacher commented that he had less confidence in his ability to grade effectively when he did not know his students, as was the case in very large classes. In his view, his assessment skills were the limiting factor. One college faculty member had changed from individual to group assignments to reduce the grading workload but realized that group work increased student learning. This teacher had also introduced multiple-choice questions but restricted them to testing factual knowledge. The other college teacher explained that her motivation for introducing rubrics was to save herself from writing extensive feedback to her many students, but she also learned that rubrics enhanced learning. Notably, none of the faculty claimed that small classes were necessary to ensure quality assessment.

Institutional policies about grading and assessment did have an impact on the teachers, though not in particularly significant ways. Mostly the faculty acted independently. They were responsible for most teaching and learning decisions and could choose to influence policies through their departments, if they wished. Most interesting to us was the teachers' blindness to how institutional policies might influence *them*, because they were so enmeshed in the environment. When institutional contexts and personal beliefs conjoined, it was difficult to tease out the direction of the impact. Participants were likely to remark on those policies they did not agree with and would then explain how they managed to act in ways that reflected their own beliefs or how they might persuade colleagues to change the policy.

Institutional contexts did seem related to the participants' conceptions of teaching. The two college instructors leaned toward student- and learning-centered conceptions, while the two university teachers leaned toward a teacher and content focus. Both college instructors noted how important it was that students develop and demonstrate skills that make them successful in the workplace, whereas the university teachers expressed interest in assessing the quality of their students' critical thinking. One college teacher did show interest in developing her students' criticality, but her learning outcomes did not reflect that goal. Conversely, the university instructor who gave assignments to develop workplace skills felt like the "odd one out" in her department.

The climate for collegial interaction around teaching had a significant impact on the participants. The university faculty highlighted negative aspects of institutional climate, while the college faculty described a more supportive climate. The latter described regular opportunities to get together with departmental colleagues to discuss approaches to teaching and assessment. The university teachers described situations with no collegial interaction or with very uncomfortable, even antagonistic, interaction.

They ventured outside their academic units to find colleagues with whom to discuss teaching and assessment.

At the outset of this project, we had wondered about the impact of preset learning outcomes on teaching. Might they affect a teacher's sense of ownership of the course and commitment to it? In fact, we learned that, because of their experience at the institution, the college instructors had shaped the learning outcomes in the courses they taught. Outcomes were not distributed from "on high" but were negotiated among the faculty who taught the course or related courses. The teachers explicitly tied their assessment practices to course learning outcomes and valued preset learning outcomes to guide their approaches to assessment.

Working with Teachers to Understand and Improve Assessment Practices

We hoped that this initiative would afford us the opportunity to encourage postsecondary faculty to adopt a critically self-reflective approach to assessment. In many ways, it did. Our asking teachers to give rationales for their assessment practices meant that critical self-reflection was inherent to their participation. We sometimes elicited quick responses indicating that reflection regularly permeated their practice. To other questions, notably those about collaborative approaches to criterion setting and the effects of negative language in rubric descriptors on learning, the response was, "That's an interesting question; I never thought to ask that before."

We identified some specific questions that were effective in inviting participants to explore their approach (see Exhibit 9.2) and found some general approaches that worked well in our interactions with these instructors (see Exhibit 9.3). The last two approaches of the five listed in Exhibit 9.3 recall Entwistle and Walker's study (2002), in which they guided university instructors to attend to previously ignored aspects of their practice. This shift in teachers' strategic alertness expanded their awareness of their practice and frequently led them to develop more sophisticated conceptions of teaching and learning. We found that our own attempts to guide teachers' attention in similar ways gave them the chance to view their practice through an alternative lens.

What didn't work? First, we found that paying too much attention to the assessment practices of their colleagues or the response of their colleagues to their own assessment practices seemed to provoke anxiety and discomfort and led some to justify their approach. Considering colleagues' approaches had only one positive outcome: helping the instructors articulate the uniqueness of their approach. Second, we found it challenging to use the

---

Exhibit 9.2. Effective Questions to Ask Teachers in Exploring Their Assessment Practices

- Have you ever done/tried this . . . ?
  Is there something you would like to try?
- What do you anticipate would be the result if you did this . . . ?
- How do you imagine your approach might change if . . .
  . . . There were no institutional requirements or policies?
  . . . Class sizes were smaller (or larger)?
  . . . You had no one to answer to?
- I noticed. . . . Did you notice that as well?
  How did or do you make sense of that?
- Would you tell me more about . . . (for example: the odd student, the difficult scenario, or the curious situation) that you mentioned earlier?
- My perception is that you do that . . . for this reason. . . . Am I correct?

Exhibit 9.3. Effective Strategies for Interacting with Teachers Regarding Assessment Practices

- Tie suggested or possible approaches to assessment to learning outcomes that are valued by the instructor—that is, explaining how a particular (alternative) approach might also support a specific goal the instructor has for students.
- Invite further reflection on how students have responded to their assessment practices, especially in terms of whether the students have achieved valued learning outcomes. Assume teachers are interested in furthering student learning.
- Acknowledge at the outset their successes as teachers.
- Introduce an alternative perspective by indicating, "In my experience . . . " because most teachers value experience. Done sensitively, this approach honors all teachers' experiences but also invites teachers to reflect critically on their experience.
- Notice details and consider underlying intentions concerning the teachers' assessment practices. Assume that instructors had or have good reasons for the particular choices they make, but do not assume approaches are cast in stone.

side-shadow interview technique effectively in this context. Because many faculty already believe that it is professionally risky to give a third party access to their teaching tools, methods, strategies, and decisions, our participants seemed to interpret our "what if" and "why not" as challenging, almost adversarial. So we quickly decided to focus instead on such questions as, "What else have you tried and abandoned?" or "What other methods have you heard about and liked but haven't yet had a chance to try?"

We had also hoped that the project would help us improve our own practices as educational developers. Certainly the way we facilitated conversations with the participants fostered our own critical self-reflection. Rather than sticking to a set list of questions, we used any tactic that seemed reasonable to help the instructors to explain how they undertook assessment tasks and why they approached the tasks as they did. This, we think, was crucial. So much of educational development is normative and interventionist without sufficient attention paid to faculty's current understandings of teaching and their own practice. In this project, we engaged in in-depth conversation, open-ended dialogue that is not typical of many educational development interactions. Because we focused on helping ourselves better understand each teacher's approach, rather than helping the teacher better understand assessment, the instructors were quite willing to share and explain. Our questions tended toward those that requested further information, though we did not shy away from sharing our own experiences and ideas if we thought it would stimulate further reflection and a deeper response. This type of dialogue did indeed encourage reflection, and the issues raised by the teachers challenged us to really listen. In turn, our deep listening seemed to help the teachers address—and in some cases resolve—challenging assessment issues on their own. Inviting them to discuss artifacts from their assessment practice stimulated concrete, fruitful discussion about particular practices. In addition, our checking with participants about the validity of our assumptions as to the meaning of particular artifacts (or of particular questionnaire responses) was sometimes affirming (when we got it right) and at other times a well-deserved prompt to loosen our own tightly held views about what matters. Participants' stories of teaching included statements we did not readily agree with and thus challenged us to see the faculty in all their personal and professional complexity. In a traditional educational development context, we might actually feel compelled to voice our disagreement and perhaps become directive, but in this sharing-and-listening scenario, we felt no such compulsion. Perhaps this factor also increased the participants' openness. We heard the best stories after we'd spent some time and established trust with the teller.

Conclusion

Because we selected the four participants on the basis of their reputation as reflective and effective teachers, we were not surprised that they all focused on their students' learning when they designed and carried out assessment. They also responded to the particulars of their teaching situations, observant of class dynamics and fully prepared to adapt their practices to suit their students' learning needs. Their teaching beliefs had more of an impact on their assessment practices than did institutional context. However, the insidious pervasiveness of institutional context seemed to blind instructors to ways in which it might shape beliefs and practices.

Our conversations highlighted the complex relationship between teachers' beliefs about teaching and their experiences of teaching. Teachers' beliefs are immediately affected by their experiences in the classroom with particular students, which in turn are shaped by their beliefs. Conceptions of teaching, which guide practice, arise through the back-and-forth interplay of experience and beliefs. For example, a beginning teacher who believed in the importance of feedback gave her student lots of it. When a student remarked on how helpful that feedback was to his learning, the instructor vowed to make time to offer all her students extensive feedback on their work. Her experience would have been very different if her first few students had never remarked on the feedback she gave them. Clearly, in working with teachers we need to address both their teaching experiences and their teaching beliefs, and tease apart the relationship between the two (Akerlind, 2003). In this way, conceptions can become more sophisticated, and faculty can learn to appreciate the practical implications of their conceptions.

Although our participants articulated rationales for how they conducted assessment, they reported being less successful in improving student learning by explaining their assessment strategies to their classes. We intend a follow-up project to investigate how closely tying assessment to learning outcomes using a formal framework, such as the ICE approach (Fostaty Young & Wilson, 2000), may affect the faculty's teaching and their students' learning.

We found genuine value in working with successful teachers. Talking with those who excel at what they do put into words—teachers' words—what good practice is and made the tacit explicit. The participants told us they learned through this project, and three of them want to pursue their search for an assessment framework to share with students that would support their learning. We too learned a great deal. The project gave us valuable opportunities to examine our interactions with faculty and determine the practices and questions most successful in helping faculty understand, improve, and align their practice. Rather than intervening, we simply asked questions. We have modified our practice accordingly to respond to the real needs of instructors wanting to improve their assessment practices.

REFERENCES

Akerlind, G. S. (2003). Growing and developing as a university teacher—Variation in meaning. *Studies in Higher Education, 28*(4), 375–390.

Akerlind, G. S. (2004). A new dimension to understanding university teaching. *Teaching in Higher Education, 9*(3), 363–375.

Biggs, J. B. (1999). What the student does: Teaching for enhanced learning. *Higher Education Research and Development, 18*(1), 57–75.

Biggs, J. B. (2003, April). *Aligning teaching and assessing to course objectives.* Paper presented at the International Conference on Teaching and Learning in Higher Education: New Trends and Innovations, University of Aveiro, Portugal.

Boud, D. (1990). Assessment and the promotion of academic values. *Studies in Higher Education, 15*(1), 101–111.

Brookfield, S. (1995). *Becoming a critically reflective teacher.* San Francisco: Jossey-Bass.

Entwistle, N., Skinner, D., Entwistle, D., & Orr, S. (2000). Conceptions and beliefs about "good teaching": An integration of contrasting research. *Higher Education Research and Development, 19*(1), 5–25.

Entwistle, N., & Walker, P. (2002). Strategic alertness and expanded awareness in sophisticated conceptions of teaching. In N. Hativa & P. Goodyear (Eds.), *Teacher thinking, beliefs, and knowledge in higher education* (pp. 15–40). Dordrecht, Netherlands: Kluwer.

Fostaty Young, S., & Wilson, R. (2000). *Assessment and learning: The ICE approach.* Winnipeg, Manitoba: Portage and Main Press.

Gass, L. (2004). *McGraw-Hill lecture.* Kingston, Ontario: Queen's University.

Gibbs, G., & Simpson, C. (2003, September). *Measuring the response of students to assessment: The Assessment Experience Questionnaire.* Paper presented at the International Improving Student Learning Symposium, Hinckley, UK.

Gibbs, G., & Simpson, C. (n.d.). *Does your assessment support your students' learning?* Centre for Higher Education Practice, Open University. Retrieved November 30, 2008, from http://isis.ku.dk/kurser/blob .aspx?feltid=157744

Ho, A., Watkins, D., & Kelly, M. (2001). The conceptual change approach to improving teaching and learning: An evaluation of a Hong Kong staff development programme. *Higher Education, 42,* 143–169.

Kane, R., Sandretto, S., & Heath, C. (2002). Telling half the story: A critical review of research on the teaching beliefs and practices of university academics. *Review of Educational Research, 72*(2), 177–228.

Kember, D. (1997). A reconceptualisation of the research into university academics' conceptions of teaching. *Learning and Instruction, 7*(3), 255–275.

Kember, D., & Kwan, K. (2000). Lecturers' approaches to teaching and their relationship to conceptions of good teaching. *Instructional Science, 28*(5), 469–490.

Louie, B. Y., Drevdahl, D. J., Purdy, J. M., & Stackman, R. W. (2003). Advancing the scholarship of teaching through self-study. *Journal of Higher Education, 74*(2), 150–171.

Luce-Kapler, R. (2006). The side-shadow interview: Illuminating process. *International Journal of Qualitative Methods, 5*(1). Retrieved November 30, 2008, from www.ualberta.ca/~iiqm/backissues/5_1/html/luce-kapler.htm

Mezirow, J. (2000). Learning to think like an adult: Core concepts of transformation theory. In J. Mezirow & Associates, *Learning as transformation: Critical perspectives on a theory in progress* (pp. 3–33). San Francisco: Jossey-Bass.

Pratt, D. D. (1992). Conceptions of teaching. *Adult Education Quarterly, 42*(4), 203–220.

Ramsden, P. (1992). *Learning to teach in higher education.* New York: Routledge.

Richards, J. C., & Barksdale-Ladd, M. A. (1997, April). *Creating and sharing teaching cases: A practical method of collaborative self-study.* Paper presented at the 78th annual meeting of the American Educational Research Association, Chicago.

Samuelowicz, K., & Bain, J. D. (1992). Conceptions of teaching held by academic teachers. *Higher Education, 24*(1), 93–111.

Samuelowicz, K., & Bain, J. D. (2002). Identifying academics' orientations to assessment practice. *Higher Education, 43*(2), 173–201.

Schön, D. A. (1987). *Educating the reflective practitioner.* San Francisco: Jossey-Bass.

Whitehead, J. (1993). *The growth of educational knowledge: Creating your own living educational theories.* Bournemouth, UK: Hyde.

Wilcox, S. (2000). *Promoting educational development: From models to modeling.* Unpublished manuscript, Queen's University, Kingston, Ontario.

Wilcox, S., Watson, J., & Paterson, M. (2004). Self-study in professional practice. In J. J. Loughran, M. L. Hamilton, V. K. LaBoskey, & T. Russell (Eds.), *International handbook of self-study of teaching and teacher education practices* (pp. 273–312). Dordrecht, Netherlands: Kluwer.

Wilson, R. J. (1990). Classroom processes in evaluating student achievement. *Alberta Journal of Educational Research, 36*(1), 4–17.

UNDERSTANDING STUDENTS AND THEIR LEARNING

10

DYSFUNCTIONAL ILLUSIONS OF RIGOR

LESSONS FROM THE SCHOLARSHIP OF TEACHING AND LEARNING

Craig E. Nelson, Indiana University

My initial teaching practices were based on nine "dysfunctional illusions of rigor." Overcoming them required revision of my ideas on the value of "hard" courses, the effectiveness of traditional methods, grade inflation, what students should be able to do initially, the fairness of traditional approaches, the importance of fixed deadlines, the importance of content coverage, the accessibility of critical thinking, and the appropriate bases for revising courses and curricula. I present the initial illusions and some more realistic views. These more realistic views are framed in terms of key research findings and some readily accessible models for improved practices.

> *The important point that should not be lost is that all profession-als—including . . . faculty members and students affairs staff—are loaded down with assumptions, expectations, customs, routines, and personal preferences that make it difficult to see and do things differently.*
>
> —George Kuh

I could have not made the journey encapsulated here without major help, much of which came from faculty developers. From IU, I especially thank Tom Schwen, Samuel Thompson, and Jennifer Robinson. So many others from other institutions have given me help at various meetings that I am unable thank them individually. Hence I dedicate this chapter to all faculty developers. I hope that you find it useful.

After I became a faculty member, I slowly realized that much of my teaching was less successful than I had hoped. I began attending teaching workshops, searching for changes that would increase students' success without lowering academic expectations. My progress was impeded by a series of misconceptions about teaching and learning that I used at least implicitly to justify my existing approaches. I now think of these misconceptions as "dysfunctional illusions of rigor." Such illusions may support traditional teaching even after faculty understand more effective practices and the data that support their use.

Can We Reduce or Eliminate Fs—Even in Tough Classes?

Let us begin by confronting three basic illusions of rigor that are commonly held in the academy.

Some Key Findings

Treisman (1992; Fullilove & Treisman, 1990) found that about 60 percent of the African Americans enrolled in calculus at the University of California at Berkeley made a D or F or withdrew. He surveyed faculty from multiple departments for solutions. They overwhelmingly suggested that something was wrong with the African American students: ability, preparation, social shock, employed excessively, and so on. Treisman showed that these hypotheses were largely not applicable. Most spectacularly, the African Americans with the *highest* math entry scores were the most likely to do poorly. The groups of students who were doing best spontaneously formed study groups, consulted with older peers, and obtained old exams and homework from older friends. Students who were not doing as well tended to do as the instructor suggested—study two hours out of class for every hour in class—but did it by themselves with little social support. Treisman invited the African Americans into *honors* homework sections and required that they do group work. They attended the regular large lectures sections and took the regular exams. The D, F, or W rate went from 60 percent to 4 percent. There were no deficits that were not made irrelevant by appropriate pedagogy.

Hake's meta-analysis for introductory physics (1998) also changed my thinking. Standardized pretests and posttests of conceptual understanding had been used in a variety of introductory courses. For each course, Hake calculated the *average normalized gain,* $<g>$, as the ratio of the actual average gain in class understanding (posttest mean minus pretest mean) to the maximum possible average gain for that class (100 minus the pretest mean). Traditional lectures produced an average normalized gain of 23 percent. Various forms of structured student-student interaction ("interactive engagement") produced an average gain of 48 percent. No traditionally taught class came near the mean for interactive engagement. There was comparatively little difference in gain between the worst and best of the standard lecture courses. Effort spent on improving lectures was a waste of time in comparison with that spent on transforming the pedagogy.

Many additional studies have shown similarly large changes in achievement, and often also in equity and retention. To cite three examples: using writing out of class and group work in class to teach calculus with no Fs (Angelo & Cross, 1993), teaching economics with active learning and finding no Fs over three years against several control sections (Nelson, 1996), and reducing low grades with active learning for the chemistry students with the lowest mathematics SAT scores (Jacobs, 2000). Froyd (2007) discussed several additional examples. A meta-analysis for science and related fields (Springer, Stanne, & Donovan, 1999) found that the average effect of small-group learning would move a student from the 50th percentile to the 70th. Handelsman et al. (2004) supplied a synthesis.

Readily Available Models for Easy Changes

The persistence of traditional teaching methods is not due to a lack of alternatives. Several books furnish easily adaptable examples (for example, Barkley, Cross, & Howell Major, 2004; Bonwell & Eison, 1991; Cooper, Robinson, & Ball, 2003; Johnson, Johnson, & Smith, 2006; Millis & Cottell, 1997). The Science Education Resource Center (2009) has featured thirty-five methods, usually with links and other resources. Nelson (2008) listed several important links.

Four key components of many effective interactive pedagogies are extensive structuring of the learning tasks by the teacher, strongly interactive student-student learning, effective immediate debriefing or other assessments that furnish prompt feedback to the teacher on the actual learning, and subsequent instructional modifications.

Thus far, I have summarized several key findings and some alternative pedagogical models. These illuminate three dysfunctional illusions that I once held strongly.

Dysfunctional illusion of rigor 1. Hard courses weed out weak students. When students fail it is primarily due to inability, weak preparation, or lack of effort.

This was the way I had viewed my own education. When I did poorly, I blamed my own lack of effort, not flaws in the pedagogy.

More realistic view. When students fail it is often due to inappropriate pedagogy. Substantial improvements were produced (see above) even in classes traditionally regarded as *necessarily* difficult, among them calculus, physics, chemistry, and economics. This is not to say that students have no responsibility for their own work. Rather, we have grossly underemphasized the faculty members' responsibilities.

Dysfunctional illusion of rigor 2. Traditional methods of instruction offer effective ways of teaching content to undergraduates. Modes that pamper students teach less.

I certainly believed this enthusiastically. Hadn't the lecture method worked for me? Wasn't it the approach embraced by all of my undergraduate science professors and by most of those I had in other fields? Wasn't it the main method used by my colleagues?

More realistic view. In a paper that partially foreshadowed this one, "Living with Myths: Undergraduate Education in America," Terenzini and Pascarella (1994) stated, "The evidence we reviewed is clear" that the lecture mode "is not ineffective" (p. 29). Remember that in introductory physics, classes taught with traditional lectures usually learn about 23 percent of what they collectively missed on the pretest (Hake, 1998). Lectures do indeed teach something. Terenzini and Pascarella (1994) continued: "But the evidence is equally clear that these conventional methods are *not* as effective as some other far less frequently used methods" (p. 29). The comparison, still from physics, is that alternative methods teach on average twice as much as traditional lectures (Hake, 1998).

Dysfunctional illusion of rigor 3. Massive grade inflation is a corruption of standards. Unusually high average grades are the result of faculty giving unjustified grades.

This follows from the preceding illusions. If low grades were mainly a consequence of students' inadequacies, then massive improvements would be quite unlikely unless standards were lowered. This was a view I advocated well after I began teaching.

More realistic view. When Treisman massively improved the achievement of African Americans, he produced substantially improved grades. Similar results are clear in several of the studies cited above. Thus, we need to distinguish between *bad grade inflation* resulting from unjustifiably high grades and *good grade inflation* from more effective pedagogy and consequently improved achievement. We need a lot more of the good kind of grade inflation. It is the faculty member's job to document good grade inflation. It is the administration's job to reward good grade inflation and punish bad grade inflation.

Producing Brighter and Harder-Working Students in a Flash

In this section, we examine four more widespread illusions of rigor that are somewhat more "advanced."

Some Key Findings

In the previous section I focused on studies that have produced numerically powerful results. Equally important and impressive results have come from narrative traditions. Rose (1990) offered stunning examples of the barriers to students from "America's underclass" that result from faculty implicitly or explicitly assuming that the students have already mastered an array of disciplinary conventions before they arrive at college. (I regard Chapters Seven and Eight as essential reading for faculty.) Colomb (1986) found that one of the hardest tasks in learning to write for college (and work) was learning to avoid all of the perfectly reasonable things that one might say or write that are not allowed by the conventions of the discipline.

In biology, remarks on memories evoked by the colors of the chemicals used are out of bounds, as are comments indicating empathy for the lettuce or fruit flies that one is grinding up. Conversely, in humanities it is rarely appropriate to speculate on how different a visual piece would seem if we had, like many birds, four rather than three pairs of contrasted primary color responses. In either case, it may also seem digressive to wonder about any environmental racism involved in the extraction of the minerals that were used to produce the chemicals or pigments—even though exactly such considerations might be central to some courses in other departments.

Models for Change

Streepey (in Nelson, 1996) taught her classes how to write essay questions. She had them compare various B answers she had written for a question and then construct ideal answers individually and in groups. In one hour, she converted an average English section to a high-achieving one. Similarly, Walvoord and Anderson (1998) had students use rubrics to rate alternative examples prior to using those rubrics in actual writing.

These studies seemed to me to clearly support fundamental changes. But, I still was initially loath to use class time to teach students how to read and write appropriately.

Ultimately, I found that four additional illusions had blocked my progress.

Dysfunctional illusion of rigor 4. Students should come to us knowing how to read, write, and do essay and multiple-choice questions.

I was especially appalled when I saw that students did not know how to do multiple-choice questions in my introductory biology course. How, I wondered, could they have possibly have graduated from high school and made it into Indiana University without knowing how to do multiple-choice questions? It took me some time to see that university level exams included a much greater emphasis on conceptual understanding, applications, and synthesis than was likely to have been possible early in high school when students typically take biology. I was similarly incredulous when I saw that about 90 percent of the students in my first-year seminars could not easily answer an essay question that required them to summarize the author's argument. This was true even when they were directed to read the two pages on which the argument occurred while working on the question. It became evident that students were used to saying what the text was about but not used to being able to accurately summarize the arguments made in the book. Clearly, they needed to learn to summarize the arguments before they were going to be able to learn to evaluate them.

More realistic view. Each of us needs to teach our students how to read pertinent materials and evaluate arguments and evidence. We need to teach this interactively in class, not just explain them. Because each discipline has its own conventions for how to read a book, how to write papers, what makes a great essay question answer, and more, we each have to do this repeatedly in different courses. I suspect that most students who are ready to start college without such help learned these skills in multiple AP courses.

Dysfunctional illusion of rigor 5. Traditional methods of instruction are unbiased and equally fair to a range of diverse students of good ability.

When I attended my first workshops on cultural and other biases in college teaching, I was shocked at the idea that courses such as calculus, physics, and biology were thought to be anything but nearly fully objective in both content and pedagogy.

More realistic view. Traditional methods of instruction favor students who have had multiple AP courses and have otherwise had the exceptional preparation for college offered by elite high schools. In addition, many or most such students come from well-off families, families that also have high expectations for academic success.

Rose (1990) convinced me that unintended discrimination is inherent in any assumption that students should come to us knowing how to read the way we want them to read, how to write the way we want them to write, and generally how to do the various tasks required to excel in our courses properly. Treisman's work (see above) convinced me that even well-prepared students (high math SATs) are often disadvantaged by high school experiences that lead them to work alone. My own high school math teacher taught us that checking your homework with another student is cheating. It was a shock to find Treisman describing years later my solitary approaches to studying. It was an even greater shock to find him suggesting that if faculty didn't like the usual levels achieved by less-privileged students, they needed to build the social support required for learning.

Dysfunctional illusion of rigor 6. It is essential that students hand in papers on time and take exams on time. Giving them flexibility and a second chance is pampering the students.

More realistic view. Giving limited time flexibility on some assignments and a limited number of repeats on exams can be a way of fostering increased achievement and increasing fairness.

After I began to understand how standard classroom practices discriminated against students from less-privileged backgrounds, I asked myself what I was assuming when I gave an exam only once to a freshman biology class. It seemed that I was assuming that the student knew what it would feel like to have mastered the content at the university A level, that she had a realistic idea of how long this would take, and that she had control over her own time.

I hadn't understood that she might not have full control of her own time if, for example, she were a single parent with two children who caught the flu in the week before the exam, or if she had a real job and was ordered to take extra shifts to make up for someone who had the flu. Thus, the idea that students should be able to manage time equally is another idea that favors privileged students, in the sense that it assumes things that are most likely to be true of traditional age students with limited other responsibilities.

I reluctantly decided that I should give each exam twice. Initially, so as to not to cut into coverage, I offered the second try in the evening at a time possible for everyone who wanted to take the exam. Students kept the better of the two grades. Performance improved markedly. I ultimately saw that studying twice for exams (which not every student did) taught on average more content than another lecture would have. I then started giving both exams in class time. Once this approach to exams proved successful, I adopted it in all courses (Nelson, 1996, in press-a).

I then asked myself whether I should continue to insist on rigid deadlines for other assignments. I ended up separating deadlines into two groups. Some were essential for my classes to function well. Preparation for discussion had to be done on time or the discussion would not work. I could allow limited flexibility on some other deadlines. Would it really matter if some lab reports were a bit late? On these, limited time flexibility might be appropriate. Perhaps lab reports would improve if students were allowed as many late days total as there were lab reports, with a penalty if the total were exceeded.

I have no evidence to support these practices beyond the fact that they worked for me and the feeling that they will obviously improve learning. I have found that many other faculty are fairly sure that they would also improve grades in their courses—and that like me, they initially are reluctant to sacrifice coverage or are worried that flexibility might lower standards. I suspect they will find that flexibility improves learning. Part of the change may be in students' attitudes. Students remarked that I had made it unusually clear that I really cared whether they learned and said that they consequently were trying harder.

Dysfunctional illusion of rigor 7. If we cover more content, the students will learn more content.

As evidence of my strong initial adherence to this view, I initially regretted each class period given over to an exam as a period in which I could not cover more of the important and fascinating biology. So much would have had to be left uncovered even if there were no exams.

More realistic view. The best courses are those that most successfully achieve the outcomes we see as most important. Initially, I was most strongly focused on content, especially on conceptual mastery.

The studies already discussed show that learning, student retention, and equity can be strongly increased by adopting active learning, by actively teaching students how to read and write within the framework of the course, and probably by allowing more flexibility on exams and deadlines. As I began to understand much of this, I realized with some dismay that I really was going to have to cover noticeably *less* material in class.

However, I stumbled on an approach that partially softened this blow, especially for courses for advanced majors. I transferred part of the coverage to work outside of class time. I knew that even advanced majors tended to learn relatively little from reading assignments. I decided to try using more detailed study guides. These guides would be of a set of essay questions from which any exam questions over that reading would be drawn in whole or part, thus ensuring that the students paid attention.

I first set out to write all reasonable essay questions over one chapter. My goal was to list each question that I might have written after just assigning the students to read the chapter. I reached about fifty questions and was not yet done with the chapter. It was suddenly clear to me why As on my exams typically had previously started at 70 percent when I included several questions over the readings. There was entirely too much material for the students to be expected to learn, and I had not been providing much guidance as to what was important. More appallingly, I realized that I had not decided what I most wanted to achieve by assigning the chapter. Making those decisions required substantial effort but deepened my understanding of my objectives. After the first few chapters, these tasks became easier.

Soon I was giving the students a set of about twenty essay questions over each chapter well before the exam. Often I told them that some parts of the text could be skimmed, skipped, or read optionally. Most important, I often gave questions that asked for more careful analysis, synthesis, and critical thinking generally than I had been able to use previously. Even so, grades quickly rose: A's began at 90 percent. *Thus I found that by using guided reading I could foster out-of-class learning to teach some key aspects of the content more effectively than when I had lectured on it.* The fault lay not with my students but rather with my pedagogy. The new approach specified deeper and clearer learning objectives, gave substantial help in seeing how to reach them, and limited coverage both in lecture and by skipping parts of the text.

Even more realistic view. What I had come to gradually was an outcomes-based course design. Traditionally, we have chosen the most important content and covered it, hoping that outcomes such as critical thinking would automatically result from learning the content. An alternative approach starts by selecting the outcomes that one most wishes to foster and then choosing the pedagogies, and finally the content that seems most likely to achieve these outcomes. The American Association of Colleges and Universities (www.aacu.org) has strongly advocated and effectively illustrated such intentional approaches to effective education. Key books now aid faculty in understanding and designing courses with these approaches (Bean, 1996; Diamond, 2008; Fink, 2003; Grunert O'Brien, Millis, & Cohen, 2008; Mentkowski & Associates, 1999; Wiggins & McTighe, 2000).

Switching from a Content-Centered Course to One Focused on Major Outcomes: Confronting a Major Illusion

The course I taught initially was evolution for senior majors. On the first exam, I asked what I thought was a give-away question, one requiring quite modest rearrangement of the content. Virtually all of the students failed the question. One woman asked for a clue as she left the exam, saying essentially: "I thought about using this block of information, but it only had three parts, and about using this other block, but it only had four parts—but the question asked for five parts and I just couldn't think of anything that had five parts." I was stunned. Any five of the seven she listed could have sufficed! It was clear from such comments many of the students were working hard. I had somehow not prepared them for the exam. The A's started at 70. And they continued to start at 70 on subsequent exams so dependably over the next few years that I announced this new standard in my syllabi. I justified this standard to myself as teaching for critical thinking and as letting A students see further challenges.

Some Key Findings

Perry (1970) found that many first-year students thought knowledge was truth acquired from authority and memorized. It was not in their power, they thought, to think further. Perry termed this approach, with its contrast between either really true or really false, *dualism*. This explained for me the student's comment about nothing having five parts. In areas where authority apparently had no clear answers, especially when authorities disagreed, a quite different standard prevailed: many students thought that in such areas an opinion was made valid simply by the act of affirming it, with no expectations of justification by evidence or other criteria. Perry termed this approach, with its emphasis on multiple but unjustified truths, *multiplicity*. Even as seniors, few students actually seemed to understand how to reason within disciplines; even fewer could justify stances that transcended single disciplines and took account of consequences, tradeoffs, and alternative approaches.

Faculty have assumed that a major part of higher education was reasoning within and across disciplines and thinking about complex real-world situations. But they usually have given little help to the students in moving to these approaches. Rather, many have presumed, as I did initially, that if we taught the content clearly, then critical thinking and other outcomes would arise more or less by induction. Perry's study helped to explain why my students were not learning to think critically from the ways I had been teaching the content.

Readily Available Models for Pedagogical Changes

Several books that follow up on Perry's scheme include a major section on how to apply it or modifications of it to help students become more sophisticated (for example, Belenky, Clinchy, Goldberger, & Tarule,

1986; King & Kitchner, 1994). Some books have had such applications as their major focus (Baxter Magolda, 2000, 2001; Baxter Magolda & King, 2000, 2004; Mentkowski & Associates, 1999). Many articles have had similar emphases. As examples: Kloss (1994) presented a quick overview, and Finster (1991) applied Perry to general chemistry, thus showing how to use it in basic introductory science. Nelson discussed applications across the curriculum (1999) and, specifically, to evolution (2007) and environmental literacy (in press-b).

Dysfunctional illusion of rigor 8. A good, clear argument in plain English can be understood by any bright student who applies herself.

When I began teaching, I assumed that this was true. I had no real understanding of student difficulties and how to address them.

More realistic view. In brief, many students, even if quite bright, will be unable to understand our examples of critical thinking and of contextually constrained conclusions without much more support than is usually offered. It is clear that even very bright and relatively well-prepared students often have major problems; remember that the core difficulties here were first delineated by studying undergraduates at Harvard (Perry, 1970).

Rose (1990), and the other cases cited above, has clearly shown how a number of factors make our "clear" arguments inaccessible to many or even most of our students, including many of the most talented. These factors include our vocabulary and our conventions for how to read, what it is acceptable to write, how to answer exam questions, and so on. As noted above, the remedy for these problems, once recognized, is to use active learning to teach our students to understand these expectations and how to meet them.

The pedagogical problems raised by the studies that began with Perry are deeper and more recalcitrant. Perry's focus (1970) was intellectual and ethical development. Development means that students usually must master one form of thinking before they can really understand a more complex one. When I began teaching, I merged several levels without providing any signals or help to the students.

The more recalcitrant aspects of the problem of fostering complex critical thinking were captured initially by Perry's choice of "intellectual and ethical." Belenky et al. (1986) focused on the switch from reliance on others to make decisions to development of one's own voice. Baxter Magolda and King (2000) enlarged the objectives further: *Teaching to Promote Intellectual and Personal Maturity: Incorporating Students' Worldviews and Identities into the Learning Process.* In 2004 they encapsulated the goal as fostering "self-authorship," a term Baxter Magolda had also used in 2000. Mentkowski and Associates (1999) stated the larger context as integrating learning, development, and performance. They presented both a synthesis of relevant literature and an exceptionally well-developed model of how to foster student change.

The essence is that to successfully foster critical thinking we must not only change the students' cognitive frameworks but also help them adapt their ethical frameworks, their sense of agency and self, and how they view others. In many cases, core difficulties in advancing in critical thinking flow from these other dimensions of concurrent change. Hence the need to broaden pedagogies, as advocated and illustrated by Baxter Magolda and King (2000, 2004), Mentkowski and Associates (1999), and others. Explicitness, attention to the level of argument, and use of active learning together go a long way.

Switching from Idiosyncratic Practices to Scholarly Pedagogy and Curricular Design: Confronting the Central Illusion

The previous sections argue that the extent and quality of learning can be greatly improved using insights from the pedagogical literature. But few faculty have had any introduction to taking such a scholarly approach. This is changing. For example, twenty-nine programs at Indiana University now offer discipline-based, graduate courses in teaching for Ph.D. students (www.iub.edu/~teaching/allabout/prepare/pedagogy.shtml).

Dysfunctional illusion of rigor 9. Without further study, faculty know enough to revise their courses and departments know enough to revise their curricula. Course and curricular revision are primarily about deciding what content to cover in what courses.

When I started teaching, I was not aware of any helpful pedagogical research. Indeed, some senior members of my departments said that good teachers were born, not trained; they explicitly discouraged asking for help from faculty in science education. Most of the curricular revisions I have been privy to over the last forty years assumed that appropriate teaching and curriculum really could be figured out by one or a few faculty members with little or no systematic perusal of evidence or of examples from elsewhere.

More realistic view. Teaching and curricula revision should be informed by pedagogical and curricular research and by an examination of best practices elsewhere.

Before initiating a new disciplinary research project, one would need to know the already existing research base. Similarly, for both teaching and curricular revision one should know current best practices at least nationally and either adopt those practices or be able to argue, with evidence, for doing something else. Further, it is important to assess the extent to which one's attempts are achieving what one intends.

Current best practices for pedagogy within a discipline can be ascertained by scanning the appropriate pedagogical journals (see *Periodicals Related to College Teaching* at www.indiana.edu/~sotl/) or by checking meeting abstracts (for example, those of the International Society for the Scholarship of Teaching & Learning at www.issotl.org/conferences.html). Searches for current best practices in curricula might start with the Association of American Colleges and Universities (http://aacu.org/). The success of one's teaching can be examined with, for example, classroom assessment techniques (Angelo & Cross, 1993) or course portfolios (Hutchings, 1998).

Conclusion

I first wrote about some of these ideas in 1996. I reached three important conclusions.

- There is no doubt that we know how to make a massive difference in overall student achievement, including gains in comprehension, application, synthesis, retention, and enthusiasm.

- These nontraditional approaches usually produce large gains by the groups of students who have been hardest to reach with standard pedagogy. Clearly, if no one is making an F, then no one from the hard-to-reach groups can be making an F either.

- The evidence that these alternative pedagogies are more effective and equitable is so strong that it seems to me that the burden of proof has shifted. Anyone using a relatively unmodified traditional pedagogy might well be required to show that it is at least as effective in producing student learning as it would be if enriched with a generous admixture of nontraditional approaches.

These conclusions still hold. I realized even then that I had been quite regrettably slow to grasp these ideas myself and even slower to make appropriate changes in my pedagogies. I now see that key problems for me lay in a series of dysfunctional illusions that tended, conveniently, to support my existing practices and make them resistant to change. I have presented some examples here hoping that they may help others find and master some of their own illusions and more seriously consider revised practices.

REFERENCES

Angelo, T. A., & Cross, K. P. (1993). *Classroom assessment techniques: A handbook for college teachers* (2nd ed.). San Francisco: Jossey Bass.

Barkley, E., Cross, K. P., & Howell Major, C. (2004). *Collaborative learning techniques: A handbook for college faculty*. San Francisco: Jossey-Bass.

Baxter Magolda, M. B. (2000). *Creating contexts for learning and self-authorship: Constructive-developmental pedagogy*. Nashville, TN: Vanderbilt University Press.

Baxter Magolda, M. B. (2001). *Making their own way: Narratives for transforming higher education to promote self-development*. Sterling, VA: Stylus.

Baxter Magolda, M. B., & King, P. M. (Eds.). (2000). *Teaching to promote intellectual and personal maturity: Incorporating students' worldviews and identities into the learning process*. San Francisco: Jossey-Bass.

Baxter Magolda, M. B., & King, P. M. (Eds.). (2004). *Learning partnerships: Theory and models of practice to educate for self-authorship*. Sterling, VA: Stylus.

Bean, J. (1996). *Engaging ideas: The professor's guide to integrating writing, critical thinking, and active learning in the classroom*. San Francisco: Jossey-Bass.

Belenky, M., Clinchy, B., Goldberger, N., & Tarule, J. (1986). *Women's ways of knowing: The development of self, voice, and mind*. New York: Basic Books.

Bonwell, C. C., & Eison, J. A. (1991). *Active learning: Creating excitement in the classroom* (ASHE-ERIC Higher Education Report No. 1). Washington, DC: George Washington University, School of Education and Human Development.

Colomb, G. G. (1986). *Disciplinary secrets and the apprentice writer*. Institute for Critical Thinking. Upper Montclair, NJ: Montclair State College.

Cooper, J. L., Robinson, P., & Ball, D. (Eds.). (2003). *Small group instruction in higher education: Lessons from the past, visions of the future*. Stillwater, OK: New Forums Press.

Diamond, R. M. (2008). *Designing and assessing courses and curricula* (3rd ed.). San Francisco: Jossey-Bass.

Fink, L. D. (2003). *Creating significant learning experiences: An integrated approach to designing college courses*. San Francisco: Jossey-Bass.

Finster, D. C. (1991). Developmental instruction: Part II. Application of the Perry model to general chemistry. *Journal of Chemical Education, 68*(9), 753–756.

Froyd, J. E. (2007). *Evidence for the efficacy of student-active learning pedagogies*. Retrieved December 8, 2008, from www.pkal.org/documents/BibliographyofSALPedagogies.cfm

Fullilove, R. E., & Treisman, P. U. (1990). Mathematics achievement among African American undergraduates at the University of California, Berkeley: An evaluation of the Mathematics Workshop Program. *Journal of Negro Education, 59*(3), 463–478.

Grunert O'Brien, J., Millis, B. J., & Cohen, M. W. (2008). *The course syllabus: A learning-centered approach* (2nd ed.). San Francisco: Jossey-Bass.

Hake, R. R. (1998). Interactive engagement vs. traditional methods: A six-thousand-student survey of mechanics test data for introductory physics courses. *American Journal of Physics, 66*(1), 64–74.

Handelsman, J., Ebert-May, D., Beichner, R., Bruns, P., Chang, A., DeHaan, R., et al. (2004). Scientific teaching. *Science, 304*(5670), 521–522.

Hutchings, P. (Ed.). (1998). *The course portfolio: How faculty can examine their teaching to advance practice and improve student learning.* Sterling, VA: Stylus.

Jacobs, D. C. (2000). *An alternative approach to general chemistry: Addressing the needs of at-risk students with cooperative learning strategies.* Retrieved December 8, 2008, from http://cms.carnegiefoundation.org/collections/castl_he/djacobs/index2.html

Johnson, D., Johnson, R., & Smith, K. (2006). *Active learning: Cooperation in the college classroom* (3rd ed.). Edina, MN: Interaction Books.

King, P. M., & Kitchner, K. S. (1994). *Developing reflexive judgment: Understanding and promoting intellectual growth and critical thinking in adolescents and adults.* San Francisco: Jossey-Bass.

Kloss, R. J. (1994). A nudge is best: Helping students through the Perry scheme of intellectual development. *College Teaching, 42*(4), 151–158.

Kuh, G. D. (1998). Lessons from the mountains. *About Campus, 3*(2), 16–21.

Mentkowski, M., & Associates. (1999). *Learning that lasts: Integrating learning, development, and performance in college and beyond.* San Francisco: Jossey-Bass.

Millis, B. J., & Cottell, P. G. (1997). *Cooperative learning for higher education faculty.* Phoenix, AZ: American Council on Education and Oryx Press.

Nelson, C. E. (1996). Student diversity requires different approaches to college teaching, even in math and science. *American Behavioral Scientist, 40*(2), 165–175.

Nelson, C. E. (1999). On the persistence of unicorns: The tradeoff between content and critical thinking revisited. In B. A. Pescosolido & R. Aminzade (Eds.), *The social worlds of higher education: Handbook for teach-ing in a new century* (pp. 168–184). Thousand Oaks, CA: Pine Forge Press.

Nelson, C. E. (2007). Teaching evolution effectively: A central dilemma and alternative strategies. *McGill Journal of Education, 42*(2), 265–283.

Nelson, C. E. (2008). Teaching evolution (and all of biology) more effectively: Strategies for engagement, critical reasoning, and confronting misconceptions. *Integrative and Comparative Biology, 48*(2), 213–225.

Nelson, C. E. (in press-a). Effective education for environmental literacy. In H. L. Reynolds, E. Brondizio, D. Karpa-Wilson, B. L. Gross, & J. Meta Robinson (Eds.), *Teaching environmental literacy in higher education: Multidisciplinary approaches to campus-wide integrated learning.* Bloomington: Indiana University Press.

Nelson, C. E. (in press-b). Want brighter, harder working students? Change pedagogies! Examples from biology. In B. J. Millis (Ed.), *Cooperative learning in higher education: Across the disciplines, across the academy.* Sterling, VA: Stylus.

Perry, W. G. (1970). *Forms of intellectual and ethical development in the college years: A scheme.* New York: Holt, Rinehart, & Winston.

Rose, M. (1990). *Lives on the boundary: A moving account of the struggles and achievements of America's educationally unprepared.* New York: Penguin.

Science Education Resource Center. (2009). *Teaching methods.* Retrieved December 8, 2008, from http://serc.carleton.edu/sp/library/pedagogies .html

Springer, L., Stanne, M. E., & Donovan, S. S. (1999). Effects of small-group learning on undergraduates in science, mathematics, engineering, and technology: A meta-analysis. *Review of Educational Research, 69*(1), 21–51.

Terenzini, P. T., & Pascarella, E. T. (1994). Living with myths: Undergraduate education in America. *Change, 26*(1), 28–32.

Treisman, U. (1992). Studying students studying calculus: A look at the lives of minority mathematics students in college. *College Mathematics Journal, 23*(5), 362–372.

Walvoord, B. E., & Anderson, V. J. (1998). *Effective grading: A tool for learning and assessment.* San Francisco: Jossey-Bass.

Wiggins, G., & McTighe, J. (2000). *Understanding by design.* Alexandria, VA: Association for Supervision and Curriculum Development.

11

CLASS SIZE

IS LESS MORE FOR SIGNIFICANT LEARNING?

John Zubizarreta, Columbia College

Mixed as it might be, educational research suggests that engaged students are more effectively stimulated and fulfilled in the small class. Of course, students can thrive in large classes if discipline, course level, teacher characteristics, goals, methods, assessment strategies, and outcomes work together to inspire and produce significant learning. The small class environment does not by itself necessarily ensure higher level learning, but studies indicate that if faculty and institutions want to promote and support the active learning pedagogies, mentoring, reflection, feedback, and personal relationships that result in deep and lasting learning, then less is more.

A quick browsing of brochures, handbooks, websites, and other available marketing literature for academic programs designed for higher-level learning reveals that one of the most commonly touted advantages of such courses of study is the prevalence of small classes. Advocates of accelerated, enriched, developmental, or differentiated learning rally around the ubiquitous claim that class size is tied to more engaged teaching and enhanced learning opportunities, the kinds of special academic experiences that come from classroom environments that encourage and support closer relationships among students and between professors and students. Smaller classes, especially those taught by challenging, enthusiastic, and skillful instructors, are essential to higher-level education because they allow individualized, constructivist approaches such as active learning, collaborative and cooperative groups, problem- or inquiry-based pedagogies, experiential learning, discussion-centered curricula, and alternative assessment strategies.

Faculty believe intuitively in the power of small classes. We argue for the advantages of smaller enrollments every semester when institutional pressures for efficiency weigh on us, grounding our arguments in the intellectual mentoring and intimate academic culture made possible by fewer numbers in our courses. In other words, many faculty reason that smaller classes are essential to active engagement, close mentoring, and significant learning.

Aside from faculty, student, and sympathetic administrators' shared anecdotes that affirm the benefits of small classes, what evidence exists that students, ranging from the exceptional to the struggling, learn more or more deeply in courses with limited enrollment? Is smaller necessarily better? Is less really more?

The Debate on Class Size

A review of major investigations and meta-analyses of the correlation between class size and student learning uncovers that, even though the results of such inquiries are mixed, the research, according to Chism (1998), indicates that programs "that use immediate recall of factual information as the measure of success find large classes slightly more effective or at least equally effective" (see the Comparative Measures of Student Learning in Large and Small Classes section). However, as Chism observes, courses of study that privilege "problem-solving, critical thinking, long-term retention, and attitude toward the discipline find small classes more successful" (see the Comparative Measures of Student Learning in Large and Small Classes section). For courses mindfully designed for significant learning, represented by the latter goals and outcomes listed by Chism, the argument for smaller classes can and should be made. Honors programs, for example, commonly argue for small classes, intentionally rallying around active learning pedagogies such as collaborative and cooperative learning; experiential learning; inquiry- and field-based explorations; learning and living communities; and integrative, interdisciplinary curricula that promote the kind of deep, lasting learning described by Chism (see the National Collegiate Honors Council's website for information on honors teaching and learning: www.nchchonors.org). Developmental educators too have long advocated for small classes to create a positive learning environment that students requiring remediation need if they are to be academically successful. Boylan and Saxon (1999), for instance, share thirty years of developmental education research on the National Association for Developmental Education website (www.nade.net). In their study, Boylan and Saxon (1999) emphasize the importance of "small units of instruction" in "mastery learning" as the key to providing remedial students with optimal learning opportunities. To be fair, higher education organizations such as

NCHC and NADE recognize that significant learning can happen in classes of all sizes when pedagogies are adjusted to the learning environment, but they readily concur with Chism's observations about the fit between small classes and their respective missions to promote deep learning for their diverse student populations. They are not alone in their conclusions.

Where do we find data supporting the importance of class size in producing higher-level learning? Much of the research undergirding the argument for small classes has been focused for decades on K–12. The organization called Reduce Class Size Now (www.reduceclasssizenow.org), with connections to the National Education Association (www.nea.org) and other agencies dedicated to primary education, illustrates the pervasiveness of the issue. Such sources look pointedly at the earliest years of school, but some of the information is applicable to higher education, and some of the studies do mention the value of small classes in college-level work.

The K–12 Debate

Finn (1997) asserts that the "debate about class size is not new" (p. 3), traceable even further back than the Babylonian Talmud, fifteen to twenty centuries ago. He adds that the longevity of the issue demonstrates the time-honored "desirability of limiting the number of students working with one teacher" (1997, p. 3). In more modern times, the Health and Education Research Operative Services (HEROS) website (2003) offers an overview of the class size debate, citing, among others, the work of Howard Blake in the mid-1950s, who concluded that "small classes were better" after adjusting his research data for "scientific acceptability." The HEROS site also refers to subsequent studies by Educational Research Service (ERS; www.ers.org), whose findings were more mixed, showing "some support for the hypothesis that smaller classes are related to higher achievement" (2003, 7) but hedging with the caveat that the advantage is more prominent among certain students in selected elementary school disciplines. The HEROS summary of the ERS study adds that because the difference in achievement does not appear significant until class enrollments drop below twenty, with fifteen being the ideal number, reducing class size may be an untenable option that by itself does not guarantee higher student achievement, though it does seem to result in "better teacher morale and job satisfaction" (2003, 11). Such qualified conclusions characterize the controversial literature on class size.

A reasonable starting point in the unsettled deliberations about class size is the set of landmark meta-analyses of Glass and Smith (1978, 1979) and Smith and Glass (1979), whose studies launched a furious exchange on the topic, concluding unequivocally, according to Ellis (1984, 7), that "a positive correlation can be drawn between smaller classes" and "student achievement, classroom processes, and teacher and student attitudes." Detractors emerged almost immediately; for instance, Hess (1979) and Simpson (1980) countered Glass and Smith's findings with charges that biased data collection, statistical errors, and disregarded variables affected the study. McIntyre and Marion (1989) added that the research on class size is "contradictory and inconclusive" (p. 1) and does not support the financial implications of reduced course enrollments. Financial implications, undoubtedly, appear as a constant concern in the discourse.

In contrast to negative views, many published studies support the thesis that smaller classes promote greater student achievement and faculty engagement. One notable outcome of such studies is that small classes, although surely benefiting students, actually have an even more affirming influence on teachers, whose morale and investment in pedagogical innovation increase, creating in turn a potentially better environment for learning. Finn (1997), Dillon and Kokkelenberg (2002), HEROS (2003), and the educational commentator Bracey (1995), among others, do a good job surveying the history of research literature on class size and underscoring the preponderance of evidence that small classes enhance learning, achievement, and attitudes. All of them mention the massive STAR Class Size Project, a large-scale, comprehensive analysis conducted over several years in Tennessee (www.heros-inc.org/star.htm). The project resulted in a number of conclusions that have grounded the plethora of arguments for small classes since the mid-1980s STAR study. As Dillon and Kokkelenberg (2002) state, the project provided "clear evidence that smaller class sizes improve student performance" (p. 5). However, they hint at some of the same limitations explicitly stated in Finn's report (1997)—most prominently, that the greater gains were made by minority students and other disadvantaged populations of learners and that small classes are most beneficial in primary grades. Such studies have been replicated in Canada, Australia, Britain, the United States, and elsewhere. In the United States, at least "about half the states," according to Finn, have implemented "small-class initiatives for some or all of their school districts" (1997, p. 6), involving sweeping legislation and huge budget allocations.

Class Size at the College and University Level

The confounding contradictions in the research about class size in elementary schools carry over into examinations of the issue in higher education. Among the voices expressing reservations, Williams, Cook,

Quinn, and Jensen (1985) assert that data from a large project that observed student achievement in university classes ranging in enrollment from thirteen to more than a thousand indicate that the importance of class numbers in college is overstated. In their ambitious, research-based study of how colleges affect student learning and overall development, Pascarella and Terenzini (1991) are also guarded in their view of the advantages of small classes. They emphasize a crucial theme later elaborated by McKeachie (1994): small classes, per se, do not necessarily result in more or deeper learning. The key is matching size to teaching practices that take the most advantage of the mentoring potential and opportunity for significant, active, higher-level learning inherent in the well-designed smaller class context. Pascarella and Terenzini put the matter this way: "Class size is not a particularly important factor when the goal of instruction is the acquisition of subject matter knowledge and academic skills. . . . It is probably the case, however, that smaller classes are somewhat more effective than larger ones when the goals of instruction are motivational, attitudinal, or higher-level cognitive processes" (1991, p. 87).

The conclusions about the value of small classes in higher education are made more compelling by adding to the mix the influence of matching innovative, active, creative pedagogies to significant learning and higher-level outcomes (Fink, 2003). McKeachie (1994) best articulates the twist: "If one takes [the] more basic outcomes of retention, problem solving, and attitude differentiation as criteria of learning, the weight of the evidence favors small classes. . . . In general, large classes are simply not as effective as small classes for retention of knowledge, critical thinking, and attitude changes" (pp. 198–201). When he adds that "meta-analyses of research on class size in classes ranging in level from elementary schools to universities. . . tend to support small classes" (p. 198), he is not discounting the effectiveness of large classes in appropriate contexts. In fact, his point is that when the small class model is matched judiciously with particular groups of students and with teachers whose pedagogies synchronize with small class course goals, outcomes, and assessment strategies, the result is the kind of powerful, deep learning that forms the core of enhanced higher-level curricula. In other words, writes McKeachie, "Size and method are almost inextricably intertwined" (p. 197).

A number of other studies of class size at the college and university level pick up McKeachie's message. Chism (1998) says that for simple knowledge transmission, class size is irrelevant, but if discussion, application, and other active learning methodologies are prized, smaller is better.

On the importance of participatory discussion as an anchor pedagogical strategy in successful small classes, McKeachie notes, "Because active thinking is so important to learning and retention of learning, constraints upon oral participation are likely not only to induce passivity but also to be educationally harmful" (1994, p. 199). Chism (1998) too advocates small classes when the methods used rely on discussion, problem solving, critical thinking, reflection, and writing—that is, the kinds of exercises that should predominate in courses designed to go beyond simply dispensing knowledge.

Measuring up to his own title, Follman (1994) studies the "Conundrum of Class Size at the College Level," offering a number of contradictory explorations of the subject. Yet he reveals one significant conclusion within the history of competing studies: "Students in small classes of 15 or fewer did engage in greater use of the higher order thinking processes" (1994, Illustrative, Representative Studies section, 2). His discovery reinforces the importance of small classes in achieving the goals and educational outcomes of enriched curricula and programming for higher-level learning. However, one cautionary remark in Follman's study bears mentioning: "Ancillary but perhaps more important findings were that talk in college classrooms seldom encouraged higher order thinking, and also that most discourse was conducted at the lowest cognitive level" (1994, Illustrative, Representative Studies section, 2). Rather than discrediting small classes, this comment should motivate teachers and students to work diligently and creatively to ensure rigor, challenge, risk, and innovation in not only small classes but classes of all sizes. Again, size and method are intertwined, and one of the other themes emerging from research on class size is that faculty development must inform the design of both small and large classes. Often, shifting from a large, lecture-hall class to a small-class, seminar model requires that faculty rethink teaching and learning philosophies, methodologies, materials, and assessment. Certainly, the same is true of shifting the other way, from small to large classes. Either way, appropriate faculty development is the common denominator for success.

Cuseo (2007) wrote one of the most thorough and critically astute reviews of the literature on class size in higher education. With a mass of seminal, empirical research data, he argues persuasively for the value of small classes for achieving deep learning. He attributes deep learning to teaching strategies grounded in close mentoring, active-learning methodologies, sophisticated discussion, reflective practice, ample feedback, and frequent writing practice. Synthesizing scores of research studies, Cuseo (pp. 2–9) outlines eight consequences of large classes—all negative—to underscore the critical value of small classes, especially for first-year courses, in achieving significant learning goals and outcomes:

1. Large class size increases faculty reliance on the *lecture* method of instruction.

2. Large classes reduce students' level of *active involvement* in the learning process.

3. Large class size reduces the frequency and quality of instructor *interaction* with and *feedback* to students.

4. Large-class settings reduce students' *depth of thinking* inside the classroom.

5. Large class size limits the breadth and depth of *course objectives, course assignments,* and course-related *learning outside the classroom.*

6. Students' academic *achievement (learning)* and academic *performance (grades)* are lowered in courses with large class size.

7. Students report *less course satisfaction* in large-size classes.

8. Students give *lower overall ratings (evaluations)* for course instruction delivered in large classes.

Ultimately, after carefully exploring much of the vast research on each of the items on his list, Cuseo (2007) declares: "Viewed collectively, the foregoing research findings and policy statements make a relatively strong case that 15 or fewer students represents an optimal class size. It may be that when class size becomes this small, a qualitative shift take [sic] place in the behavior of students and/or the instructor that can result in a sharp jump or spike in positive educational outcomes" (p. 12).

Light's examination (2001) of students' perceptions and experiences in college also draws on the chief insights of McKeachie (1994), Belenky, Clinchy, Goldberger, and Tarule (1986), Brookfield (1987), Meyers (1986), Meyers and Jones (1993), and others who recognize the value of small classes in building strong, critically reflective learning communities and productive environments for greater achievement. Summarizing one of his major findings, Light notes, "Student after student brings up the importance of class size in his or her academic development. Not surprisingly, small-group tutorials, small seminars, and one-to-one supervision are, for many, their capstone experience" (p. 9). Later in his volume, he adds that his extensive project "sends a clear message—that most of the time smaller is better, with stronger student engagement" (p. 45).

In Light's later descriptions (2001) of what constitutes transformative small-class experiences, he implies that they emerge from the powerful teaching methods listed earlier—the innovative, active, creative pedagogies that are more possible in small classes and essential to tapping the full potential of an intimate classroom. Reduced numbers alone do not create the magic reported by Light's student subjects. Implicit in their appreciative assessments of their rich learning is the students' acknowledgment of the wise choices, innovation, care, and pedagogical skill of an engaged, well-trained teacher in a small seminar or individual mentoring relationship. The "connected classroom" defined by Belenky et al. (1986), the "reflective classroom" mentioned by both Brookfield (1987) and Meyers (1986), the "silence" and active-learning environment envisioned by Meyers and Jones (1993)—all of these are spaces for the kind of applied, integrative, higher-order learning that is admittedly achievable in larger classrooms with proper approaches but more easily activated in smaller, more interactive classes.

Small Classes, Student Ratings, and Grades

Another interesting feature of the literature on small classes is the correlation between student ratings and class size. Generally, student rating data show that students have a higher level of satisfaction in small classes compared to large classes. Cashin (1988), Centra (1977, 2003), Feldman (1984), McKeachie (1994), Seldin (1984), and others agree, although most researchers caution that the association between high ratings and either small or large class size should not be overly emphasized in faculty evaluation. Seldin (1984), for instance, says, "In general, slightly higher ratings are awarded to professors who teach courses that have fewer than fifteen students. . . . [But] it is only prudent. . . to avoid placing heavy weight on comparison of the ratings of professors teaching courses differing greatly in such characteristics" (p. 135).

Cashin (1988) adds that "there is a tendency for smaller classes to receive higher ratings," but the assertion rests on a "weak inverse association" (p. 3).

Centra (1977), on the other hand, factors the crucial dimension of learning into the research on student ratings of small classes. That is, he studies the degree to which student ratings correlate with actual student learning outcomes, contributing to what Cuseo (2007) calls "a substantial body of research indicating that students' course evaluations correlate positively with actual *learning*. . . . In other words, there is evidence that students tend to rate most highly those courses in which they learn the most" (pp. 9–10). The contention seems well supported by Dillon and Kokkelenberg's study (2002) within the limited context of a single, large, highly selective institution. The authors examine the cumulative probability

of grades and grade point averages received in more than 360,000 undergraduate samples from 1996 to 2001. Overwhelmingly, their data reveal
that "the null hypothesis that class size does not matter can be rejected"
(p. 10). As class size increases beyond twenty, grade performance drops
sharply until the size is forty, when results level off and decline more slowly
all the way to beyond four hundred in a class. Dillon and Kokkelenberg
conclude, "Again, the message is that large classes have a high [sic] probability of lower grades than small classes" (p. 12), an ostensible causal relation that does not bode well for underrepresented, at-risk, and women
students, who generally perform worse as class size increases.

Still, looking at the equation of grades, student ratings, class size, and
learning from another side (as the authentic assessment and learning-
outcomes movements in education have taught us) grades may not necessarily correlate with learning, just as student ratings may not. In fact, Dillon
and Kokkelenberg (2002) admit that, despite their discovery of "a link
between grades and class size," they hesitate to "conclude that students
learn more in smaller classes" even though they firmly submit that "class
size has a negative relationship to grades" (pp. 14–15). But if we assume the
best in our faculty and our students, perhaps higher grades—especially in
well-designed courses for higher-level learning—at least indirectly measure
not grade inflation but rather actual learning. In one of the most detailed
studies of the issue, Franklin, Theall, and Ludlow (1991) conclude that
grade inflation is not the reason for higher grades in small classes; instead,
genuine learning and appreciation for good teaching may be. In scrutinizing
student ratings results from more than thirteen thousand course sections
over a six-year span at a large, urban, private university, the authors write:

> Class size emerged as the single most powerful predictor of grades and
> ratings for single-course sections, courses, and instructors. The rela-
> tively strong inverse correlations between class size and grades in each
> level of analysis may be the result of differences in grading standards,
> methods, or philosophy for small sections versus large sections; or a
> selection bias placing more experienced/higher-achieving students (and,
> hence, more satisfied) in small, elective, or upper level courses. Similarly,
> the pattern of inverse associations found between class size and overall
> instructor ratings at each level of analysis suggest [sic] that the student's
> lack of satisfaction with the instructor is matched by a lack of achieve-
> ment in larger sections compared with smaller ones. (p. 4)

Hence, if we reframe the connection between high ratings and small
classes as a sign of real learning and effective teaching, instead of bias, then
Centra's comment (2003) makes good sense: "Small classes with fewer

than 15 students get higher evaluations than do larger classes, but if students learn more in smaller classes because they allow for more personal attention, then class size is not truly biasing the evaluations" (p. 498). Also convincing is Cohen's powerful evidence (1981) of the correlation between ratings and learning as demonstrated in common examinations across multiple sections of various classes. In short, if we are willing to allow the possibility, if not probability, that good teaching results in deep, meaningful, lasting learning, then the results of such studies further corroborate the position that higher grades and higher ratings feedback constitute additional evidence of the importance of class size in promoting, supporting, and rewarding both effective teaching and enhanced learning.

Benefits of Small Classes and Small Class Strategies

The research on the impact of class size on learning leaves us with a compelling lesson. McKeachie (1994) cites several major studies that suggest "the ablest students are most favorably affected by being taught in small classes" (pp. 198–201). His assertion is one on which honors programs and other accelerated academic courses of study depend for the appropriate resources needed to fulfill their goals. But we also know from Boylan and Saxon's research (1999) on the learning styles, potential, and success of students at developmental and other levels of academic ability that small class strategies, even when applied in a large lecture hall, can enhance the learning of all students. Many scholars (for example, Carbone, 1998; Gibbs & Jenkins, 1992; Heppner, 2007; Michaelsen, Knight, & Fink, 2002; Millis & Cottell, 1998; Nilson, 2007; Stanley & Porter, 2002) provide guidance for using interactive, small-group tactics in large classes to improve students' learning. But such methodologies are most naturally suited to the classroom with reduced numbers and more opportunities for both instructors and students to take advantage of the relational power of teaching and learning.

Other extensive research studies posit that small classes also help strengthen faculty morale while improving students' experiences in the classroom. For instance, Connor and Day (1988, as cited in Delaware State Education Association, 2007) report these positive outcomes of smaller class size in grade schools (though most of the items on their list can apply to higher education as well):

For students
- More individual attention
- Increased time on task

- Increased opportunities to participate
- Improved self-image
- Greater interest and improved attitude toward learning
- Improved attendance

For teachers
- More job satisfaction
- Increased enthusiasm for teaching
- More activities initiated by the teacher, especially enrichment activities; teachers cover more material with students
- Improved class management and curriculum; lessons proceed more smoothly
- Less time spent on discipline
- Better able to assess and monitor student performance

Such benefits of smaller classes stem largely, as stated earlier, from the relational dimension of teaching and learning. As Palmer (1998) reminds us, "Good teachers possess a capacity for connectedness. They are able to weave a complex web of connections among themselves, their subjects, and their students so that students can learn to weave a world for themselves" (p. 11). Knowing students' names, their ambitions, their fears, their triumphs, and their strengths and weaknesses establishes a connection that unlocks potential and real achievement. The small class furnishes ideal ground for such academic growth and transformative relationships.

Small Classes: Less Is More

Earlier, we noted that financial considerations are often the block to widespread adoption of small classes as a model for richer, more active learning in all our institutions, small and large, private and public alike. But reorienting our thinking about the cost of small classes is a shift worth careful consideration. We should recognize that small classes have the considerable impact of giving both faculty and students opportunities to reap the benefits of collaboration, mentoring, active learning, and community building. We should also acknowledge that when institutions multiply the number of larger classes as a presumed handy solution to financial pressures, they miss seeing the high cost of ratcheting up infrastructure needs such as academic skills labs, first-year experiences, peer mentoring programs, supplemental instruction, and other ventures designed to offset the potentially deleterious effects of large classes on recruitment and retention. In addition, faculty developers can help faculty move large classes away from passive lecture and low-level knowledge acquisition by infusing active, small-group pedagogies. But the cost of such training and retooling is not insignificant. The question is whether small classes and other small-group or individual experiences are merely a financial drain or really an investment with payoffs for faculty, students, programs, and institutions. The business analogy is anathema to educators—rightly so, but sometimes the economic argument is the one that wins the day with institutional leadership and external constituents.

A long history of research, mixed as it might be, suggests that properly engaged students would be more effectively stimulated and fulfilled in the small class. The argument, however, has several provisions. Good students can also thrive in large classes when the variables of discipline, course level, teacher characteristics, goals, methods, assessment, and outcomes work together to inspire and produce significant learning. For example, the work of Mazur (1997) and Miller, Groccia, and Miller (2001) on interactive, peer instruction in large classes offers convincing models of how to activate small-group pedagogies in large classroom settings. Not every student wants or needs a small class environment. Not every course needs to be situated in a small class. Not every discipline requires small classes for all its offerings. Not every instructor is suited for or has the pedagogical skill to succeed in the small class. Yet when the pieces all come together, size makes a difference, and the research on class size, despite a lack of unanimity, lends sufficient credence to faculty intuition that smaller classes, or alternatively small-class methodologies adapted to large-class environments, substantially enhance learning.

As we reflect on the value of small classes in fostering significant, higher-level learning, we must always remember that real student achievement depends on many course components: appropriate pedagogy aligned with the preparation level and learning preferences of students, the expectations and outcomes of the course, class size, and many other important elements of a well-designed course. The role of faculty development in helping instructors design a powerful, productive learning environment in any size class cannot be emphasized enough. Versatile, responsive, engaged instructors can work wonders in small or large classes when they synchronize goals, methods, materials, assessment, and outcomes with size, level, and student learning styles. But if we pay attention to the compelling body of research on the benefits of smaller classes in producing deep, lasting learning, then matching a well-trained teacher with a small class of eager students yields a winning combination.

REFERENCES

Belenky, M. F., Clinchy, B. M., Goldberger, N. R., & Tarule, J. M. (1986). *Women's ways of knowing: The development of self, voice, and mind.* New York: Basic Books.

Boylan, H. R., & Saxon, D. P. (1999). *What works in remediation: Lessons from 30 years of research.* Retrieved January 6, 2009, from www.ncde.appstate.edu/reserve_reading/what_works.htm

Bracey, G. W. (1995). Research oozes into practice: The case of class size. *Phi Delta Kappan, 77*(1), 89–90.

Brookfield, S. D. (1987). *Developing critical thinkers: Challenging adults to explore alternative ways of thinking and acting.* San Francisco: Jossey-Bass.

Carbone, E. (1998). *Teaching large classes: Tools and strategies* (Survival skills for scholars, Vol. 19). Thousand Oaks, CA: Sage.

Cashin, W. E. (1988). *Student ratings of teaching: A summary of the research* (IDEA Paper No. 20). Retrieved January 6, 2009, from www.theideacenter.org/sites/default/files/Idea_Paper_20.pdf

Centra, J. A. (1977). Student ratings of instruction and their relationship to student learning. *American Educational Research Journal, 14*(1), 17–24.

Centra, J. A. (2003). Will teachers receive higher student evaluations by giving higher grades and less course work? *Research in Higher Education, 44*(5), 495–518.

Chism, N.V.N. (1998). *Overview: Class size research in higher education.* Retrieved January 6, 2009, from http://web.archive.org/web/20051016190456/ftad.osu.edu/Publications/Class_Size.html

Cohen, P. A. (1981). Student ratings of instruction and student achievement: A meta-analysis of multisection validity studies. *Review of Educational Research, 51*(3), 281–309.

Cuseo, J. (2007). The empirical case against large class size: Adverse effects on the teaching, learning, and retention of first-year students. *Journal of Faculty Development, 21*(1), 1–22.

Delaware State Education Association. (2007). *Class size reduction and student achievement.* Retrieved January 6, 2009, from www.dsea.org/PoliticalAction/ClassSize.aspx

Dillon, M., & Kokkelenberg, E. C. (2002, June). *The effects of class size on student achievement in higher education: Applying an earnings function.* Paper presented at the 42nd annual meeting of the AIR Forum, Toronto, Ontario.

Ellis, T. I. (1984). *Class size* (ERIC Document Reproduction Service No. ED259454). Retrieved January 6, 2009, from www.ericdigests.org/pre-922/size.htm

Feldman, K. A. (1984). Class size and college students' evaluations of teachers and courses: A closer look. *Research in Higher Education, 21*(1), 45–116.

Fink, L. D. (2003). *Creating significant learning experiences: An integrated approach to designing college courses.* San Francisco: Jossey-Bass.

Finn, J. D. (1997). *Class size: What does research tell us?* (ERIC Document Reproduction Service No. ED461693). Retrieved January 6, 2009, from www.eric.ed.gov/ERICDocs/data/ericdocs2sql/content_storage_01/0000019b/80/19/c8/e5.pdf

Follman, J. (1994). The conundrum of class size at the college level. *College Quarterly, 2*(1). Retrieved January 6, 2009, from www.senecac.on.ca/quarterly/1994-vol02-num01-fall/follman.html

Franklin, J. L., Theall, M., & Ludlow, L. (1991, April). *Grade inflation and student ratings: A closer look.* Paper presented at 72nd annual meeting of the American Educational Research Association, Chicago.

Gibbs, G., & Jenkins, A. (1992). *Teaching large classes in higher education: How to maintain quality with reduced resources.* London: Kogan Page.

Glass, G. V., & Smith, M. L. (1978). *Meta-analysis of research on the relationship of class size and achievement: The class size and instruction project.* San Francisco: Far West Laboratory for Educational Research and Development.

Glass, G. V., & Smith, M. L. (1979). Meta-analysis of research on the relationship of class size and achievement. *Educational Evaluation and Policy Analysis, 1*(1), 2–16.

Health and Education Research Operative Services (HEROS). (2003). *Class size research.* Retrieved January 6, 2009, from www.heros-inc.org/classsizeresearch.htm

Heppner, F. (2007). *Teaching the large college class: A guidebook for instructors with multitudes.* San Francisco: Jossey-Bass.

Hess, F. (1979). *Class size revisited: Glass and Smith in perspective.* (ERIC Document Reproduction Service No. ED172402)

Light, R. J. (2001). *Making the most of college: Students speak their minds.* Cambridge, MA: Harvard University Press.

Mazur, E. (1997). *Peer instruction: A user's manual.* Upper Saddle River, NJ: Prentice Hall.

McIntyre, W. G., & Marion, S. F. (1989). *The relationship of class size to student achievement: What the research says* (ERIC Document Reproduction Service No. ED323643). Retrieved January 6, 2009, from www.eric.ed.gov/ERICDocs/data/ericdocs2sql/content_storage_01/0000019b/80/22/56/c8.pdf

McKeachie, W. J. (1994). *Teaching tips: Strategies, research, and theory for college and university teachers.* Lexington, MA: Heath.

Meyers, C. (1986). *Teaching students to think critically: A guide for faculty in all disciplines*. San Francisco: Jossey-Bass.

Meyers, C., & Jones, T. B. (1993). *Promoting active learning: Strategies for the college classroom*. San Francisco: Jossey-Bass.

Michaelsen, L. K., Knight, A. B., & Fink, L. D. (2002). *Team-based learning: A transformative use of small groups in college teaching*. Sterling, VA: Stylus.

Miller, J. E., Groccia, J. E., & Miller, M. S. (2001). *Student-assisted teaching: A guide to faculty–student teamwork*. Bolton, MA: Anker.

Millis, B. J., & Cottell, P. G. (1998). *Cooperative learning for higher education faculty*. Phoenix, AZ: American Council on Education and Oryx Press.

Nilson, L. B. (2007). *Teaching at its best: A research-based resource for college instructors* (2nd ed.). San Francisco: Jossey-Bass.

Palmer, P. J. (1998). *The courage to teach: Exploring the inner landscape of a teacher's life*. San Francisco: Jossey-Bass.

Pascarella, E. T., & Terenzini, P. T. (1991). *How college affects students: Findings and insights from twenty years of research*. San Francisco: Jossey-Bass.

Seldin, P. (1984). *Changing practices in faculty evaluation: A critical assessment and recommendations for improvement*. San Francisco: Jossey-Bass.

Simpson, S. N. (1980). Comment on "Meta-analysis of research on class size and achievement." *Educational Evaluation and Policy Analysis, 2*(3), 81–83.

Smith, M. L., & Glass, G. V. (1979). *Relationship of class-size to classroom processes, teacher satisfaction and pupil affect: A meta-analysis*. San Francisco: Far West Laboratory for Educational Research and Development.

Stanley, C. A., & Porter, M. E. (Eds.). (2002). *Engaging large classes: Strategies and techniques for college faculty*. Bolton, MA: Anker.

Williams, D. D., Cook, P. F., Quinn, B., & Jensen, R. P. (1985). University class size: Is smaller better? *Research in Higher Education, 23*(3), 307–318.

12

WEAVING PROMISING PRACTICES FOR INCLUSIVE EXCELLENCE INTO THE HIGHER EDUCATION CLASSROOM

María del Carmen Salazar, University of Denver

Amanda Stone Norton, Texas Woman's University

Franklin A. Tuitt, University of Denver

Higher education is faced with an increasingly diverse student body and historic opportunities to foster inclusive excellence, meaning a purposeful embodiment of inclusive practices toward multiple student identity groups. Although the benefits of inclusive excellence are well established, college faculty often cite barriers to promoting it in classrooms, and this creates an opening for faculty developers to support them in weaving promising practices for inclusive excellence into their teaching. This chapter highlights the practices of inclusive faculty and the methods faculty developers can use to promote inclusive excellence along five dimensions: (1) intrapersonal awareness, (2) interpersonal awareness, (3) curricular transformation, (4) inclusive pedagogy, and (5) inclusive learning environments.

Institutions of higher education have become increasingly diverse in the past thirty years (Gandara & Maxwell-Jolly, 1999), during which time research has established the benefits of diversity in higher education (Baez, 2004; Chang, Jones, & Hakuta, 2003). Nonetheless, not much has changed in terms of overall approaches to students (Gandara & Maxwell-Jolly, 1999). Diversity efforts continue to be fragmented, with an evident disconnect between diversity and educational excellence (Milem, Chang, & Antonio, 2005).

Initiatives fostering inclusive excellence are particularly critical for reinforcing the academic resiliency of students who have been historically marginalized in educational systems, notably students of color, gays, lesbians, bisexuals, transgendered, women, and students with disabilities. Inclusive excellence means a purposeful deployment of inclusive practices toward multiple student identity groups (Milem, Chang, & Antonio, 2005). The benefits of inclusive excellence include increased student academic, diversity, and civic outcomes. Improved academic outcomes are evidenced in higher educational aspirations, motivation, and self-confidence, heightened creativity and innovation, and stronger critical-thinking and problem-solving skills (Milem, 2003). Furthermore, inclusive excellence positively affects diversity outcomes such as experiences with diversity, cultural awareness, and commitment to issues of equity (Milem, 2003). Finally, inclusive excellence leads to a higher level of civic engagement and a more informed citizenry (Milem, 2003).

The focus on inclusive excellence in the higher education classroom is a recent phenomenon in response to changing demographics. As a result, limited research exists on inclusive classroom practices in higher education. Much of the theoretical foundation for inclusive excellence derives from three decades of K–12 educational research illuminating inclusive pedagogies and techniques to create a multicultural curriculum (Cochran-Smith, Davis, & Fries, 2004). Even though significant differences exist between K–12 and college students—for example, student development, educational policies and testing, and institutional contexts—we believe that the K–12 literature can inform higher education because we have successfully applied techniques tested in K–12 in our own college classrooms.

Inclusive excellence is vital because faculty and students do not leave their values, cultures, genders, and ethnicities at the door when they enter to teach and learn (Chesler, Lewis, & Crowfoot, 2005). Rather, they bring all of those identities with them into the learning experience. However, many educational experiences in the classroom are based on the white, heterosexual, male culture, often leaving students of color, women, and members of gay, lesbian, and bisexual communities isolated in their learning (Chism, 1994; Maher & Tetreault, 2003). Faculty are often unaware of their bias in favor of the dominant culture (Chism, 1994), and in many instances their adherence to the dominant culture creates a barrier to learning (Gurin, Dey, Hurtado, & Gurin, 2003).

Although many institutions promote inclusive excellence, faculty members often cite barriers to implementing inclusive practices. In our faculty development experience, instructors cite barriers such as their own perceived lack of competence in diversity related aspects of curriculum and pedagogy, the lack of resources and time, and their fear of the unknown. Instructors also blame the persistence of homogeneous classrooms in which students are unaware of their own identity and may resist instructor attempts to diversify the curriculum, as well as their lack of skills for managing classroom conflict. They also see classroom size and layout as inhibitors to authentic classroom dialogue. Finally, they fear that students from diverse identity groups may experience cultural and social isolation, and tokenization and requests to speak as native informants (hooks, 1994) or objects of research and study. Furthermore, because they are encouraged to be color-blind in the classroom (Rosenberg, 2004), faculty are concerned about being labeled as radicals if they promote inclusive excellence (Shor & Freire, 2003). Finally, they have little support and training in implementing inclusive excellence (Kumashiro, 2006).

Five Dimensions of Inclusive Excellence

These concerns and others underscore the need for faculty developers to build faculty confidence and skills in incorporating inclusive practices. In response, we have developed a framework for inclusive excellence that has five dimensions: (1) intrapersonal awareness, (2) interpersonal awareness, (3) curriculum transformation, (4) inclusive pedagogy, and (5) inclusive learning environments. The following sections describe promising practices of inclusive faculty along the five dimensions, summarized in Table 12.1. In addition, we propose methods that faculty developers can use to facilitate faculty learning and adoption of such practices.

Intrapersonal Awareness

Inclusive faculty members are reflective practitioners. Self-reflexivity (Kumashiro, 2006) is a critical component of learning about and embracing difference (Banks, 2004), and it requires personal awareness of one's own worldview. This awareness grows when faculty critically examine their ideas, assumptions, and values; articulate where and how their worldview has developed (Elenes, 2006); and share their own background and experiences with students. It is also fostered when they expand their knowledge of other cultures. According to Geneva Gay: "Ignorance of people different from ourselves often breeds negative attitudes, anxiety, fears, and the seductive temptation to turn others into images of ourselves. . . . [The] inability to make distinctions among ethnicity, culture, and individuality increases the risk that teachers will impose their notions

Table 12.1. Practices for Inclusive Excellence

Intrapersonal Awareness
- Actively commit oneself to the process of self-actualization
- Increase personal awareness of one's own worldview
- Critically examine own ideas, assumptions, and values, and how those beliefs have an impact on one's pedagogies
- Articulate where and how worldview has developed
- Share own background and experiences with students
- Expand knowledge of the *other* through readings about diverse cultures and identity groups, and immersing oneself in diversity
- Develop awareness of how their beliefs, cultures, and privileges influence curriculum and pedagogies
- Invite students to provide feedback on the instructor's facilitation of discussions and academic assessment

Interpersonal Awareness
- Create opportunities for interpersonal dialogue where multiple perspectives are honored
- Invite students to share cultural experiences with faculty and peers
- Validate students' experiences by engaging in empathetic listening and asking questions openly and constructively
- Assist students in identifying differences and similarities in opinions
- Be aware of nonverbal communication
- Engage students in creating classroom norms reflective of diversity, and revisit norms often
- Facilitate dialogue between students using a coconstructed framework of classroom norms
- Promote an academic perspective during critical discussions
- Develop and practice conflict resolution skills
- Recognize both overt and covert forms of conflict
- Foster opportunities for group work

Curricular Transformation
- Integrate multiple identity groups into the curriculum through inclusion of cultural histories, local histories, and contributions
- Use culturally accurate curriculum, books, and teaching tools
- Incorporate multiculturalism throughout course content
- Reflect critically on whom the curriculum includes or excludes
- Review curriculum for hidden forms of oppression and make appropriate changes
- Include local histories

Inclusive Pedagogy
- Recognize students' personal experiences as worthy knowledge
- Elicit and build on students' funds of knowledge
- Invite students to share their knowledge in multiple ways
- Collaborate with students as coconstructors of knowledge

- Establish critical dialogues with students
- Incorporate noncompetitive, collaborative assignments and group work
- Facilitate large and small group discussions
- Use formative assessments such as journal writing and portfolios
- Include assignments such as life history interviews, personal stories of survival, and autobiographical writing that will diversify and personalize learning
- Engage students in debate, student-led discussion, read-alouds, and experiential learning activities
- Foster student choice

Inclusive Learning Environment
- Build opportunities for authentic interactions among students
- Demonstrate caring through attitude, expectations, and behavior
- Demonstrate pride in student achievement
- Engage in supportive outreach efforts
- Demonstrate respect through inclusion of multiple identity groups
- Pronounce students' names correctly
- Learn about students' backgrounds, social identities, and learning styles
- Identify and build on students' interests
- Meet with students outside of scheduled class time
- Provide constructive feedback
- Avoid actions that promote tokenism
- Consistently challenge racist and prejudicial remarks

on ethnically different students, insult their cultural heritages, or ignore them entirely in the instructional process" (2000, p. 23).

Inclusive faculty expand their knowledge of other cultures through reading about diverse cultures and identity groups (Cochran-Smith, 2003; Kumashiro, 2006) and immersing themselves in diverse cultures (Causey, Thomas, & Armento, 1999).

In addition, faculty enhance their intrapersonal awareness when they learn how their beliefs, cultures, and privileges affect their curricular options and pedagogical decisions (Banks, 2004; Chesler, Lewis, & Crowfoot, 2005; Gloria & Castellanos, 2006; Sfeir-Younis, 1993; Weinstein, Tomlinson-Clarke, & Curran, 2004). Inclusive faculty members reflect on their curriculum and pedagogies and the powers and privileges they reinforce (Rendón, 2004). Rendón suggests three questions to guide this reflective process: (1) To what extent does the curriculum privilege majority and minority students? (2) Who is excluded and included in the curriculum? and (3) What are the politics of knowledge in the classroom?

Faculty developers can play a key role in helping faculty develop intrapersonal awareness. First, they can give instructors opportunities to examine their personal identities and privileges. Through this examination, faculty can recognize that their own worldview is not universal and can begin to encourage students to share their worldviews. To the extent instructors view the classroom as value-free, this can be a difficult process, particularly in the hard sciences, where there is often a "right" answer. However, even in disciplines such as math and science, a student's worldview often mediates his or her understanding of concepts and ability to apply new knowledge (Civil, 2002; Clark Orey & Rosa, 2006; Diez Palomar, Simic, & Varley, 2007; Gutstein, 2006; Noblit, Hwang, Seiler, & Elmesky, 2007). For example, mathematical discourse is often viewed as a universal language, yet one's interpretation of the concepts can vary according to one's problem-solving strategies and the presence or absence of culturally relevant referents. In addition, religious beliefs and cultural understandings can call scientific knowledge into question. Although much of the research on the impact of culture on math and science knowledge has been done in K–12 contexts, faculty developers can find in it concrete, discipline-specific examples of how a student's worldview affects understanding of concepts and can ask instructors to make connections to their own classes.

In addition, faculty developers can suggest resources to help faculty expand their knowledge of their students' diverse experiences and guide them in adjusting their curriculum and pedagogies accordingly, starting with one course. These resources can lead faculty to redefine what it means to teach and learn on the basis of diverse student experiences. Equally important, faculty developers can provide ongoing, structured opportunities for reflection through dialogic interactions between faculty. These experiences help faculty view the development of intrapersonal awareness as a dynamic process that evolves continuously throughout one's teaching career.

Interpersonal Awareness

Inclusive faculty recognize the importance of developing interpersonal awareness in their classrooms. It motivates them to furnish opportunities for classroom dialogue where multiple perspectives are honored and students are invited to share their cultural experiences, thereby validating those experiences (Cochran-Smith, 2003; Gay, 2000; hooks, 1994). Of course, just the act of saying something out loud does not automatically guarantee that students will deem their experiences "validated"; faculty must also respond by engaging in empathic listening, asking questions openly and constructively, helping students identify differences and similarities in ideas, and attending to nonverbal behavior (Billson & Tiberius, 1994). Inviting students to share their experiences can help faculty build relationships with and among their students.

Inclusive faculty also ensure that students agree to classroom norms for communication, including those that honor diversity (Diouf, 1998; Elenes, 2006; Sfeir-Younis, 1993; Stone Norton, 2008). Diouf (1998) recommends that faculty and students cocreate these norms at the beginning of the course and revisit them throughout the term. Stone Norton (2008) puts forward eight group norms that can create an inclusive learning environment:

1. Everyone has the right to be heard.
2. Be respectful while still being critical.
3. No name calling.
4. One person speaks at a time.
5. Maintain confidentiality.
6. Hold yourself and each other to high standards of excellence at all times.
7. Have the humility to recognize that you do not know everything and that everyone can stand to improve.
8. Recognize that everyone will start from different bases of knowledge.

Group work is another highly effective tool for facilitating inclusive interpersonal interactions (Rosser, 1998). Felder and Brent (1996) reported that students of color who participated in group work exhibited greater academic achievements than those who did not. However, even though group work can facilitate dialogue between students, any conflict that erupts must be channeled appropriately, lest it damage interpersonal connections.

Rather than minimizing conflict, inclusive faculty foster academic disagreement (Osei-Kofi, Richards, & Smith, 2004), which allows more ideas to enter the sphere of learning. In fact, they embrace conflict in several ways: by preparing ahead for conflict resolution (Chesler et al., 2005; Stone Norton, 2008); by encouraging (if not demanding) students to respect and appreciate those who disagree with them (Elenes, 2006); by acknowledging the value of learning through a crisis (Kumashiro, 2003); by recognizing and engaging both overt and covert forms of conflict (Sfeir-Younis, 1993); and by physically reorganizing the classroom to deal with negative intergroup dynamics, such as rearranging desks or assigning seats (Chesler et al., 2005). Another conflict-mediating technique is encouraging students to keep an academic perspective during critical discussions, by reminding them to "learn to discuss the philosophies at an abstract and not personal level" (Elenes, 2006, p. 251; Stone Norton, 2008). Instructors must recognize however, that this can be difficult for students who have been marginalized in our society. Their experiences are often painful and hard to discuss on an abstract level. In response, Stone Norton (2008) suggests having students identify the characteristics of good and bad discussions by answering three questions: What is a good discussion? What is a bad discussion? When and how does a discussion turn into a fight? Instructors should also invite their classes to give them feedback on their discussion facilitation (Billson & Tiberius, 1994; Chickering & Gamson, 1994).

Faculty developers can support faculty in developing their interpersonal awareness in a number of ways. First, they can create opportunities for dialogue on issues of equity (Causey, Thomas, & Armento, 1999). Of course, they must also participate in the dialogue (Tuitt, 2003; Lawrence, 1997), model empathic listening, ask questions openly and constructively, identify differences and similarities in ideas, and attend to nonverbal behavior. Second, they can present examples of multiple perspectives across disciplines to illuminate diverse student experiences and world-views, such as varying approaches to disease and wellness. Third, they can engage instructors in coconstruction of classroom norms for discussions that are responsive of diversity. Fourth, they can recommend strategies to facilitate group work and manage academic disagreement, personalization of discussions, and overt and covert forms of conflict.

Curriculum Transformation

Inclusive faculty transform learning through curriculum content changes (Tuitt, 2003), integrating into the curriculum multiple identity groups (not just black and white) in the form of cultural histories and contributions (Banks, 2007; Chesler et al., 2005; Knight, Dixon, Norton, & Bentley, 2006; Ladson-Billings, 2006; Osei-Kofi et al., 2004) and using culturally accurate curriculum, books, and teaching tools (Banks, 2007; Gay, 2000; Yosso, 2002). They go beyond superficial multiculturalism (Rios, Trent, & Castañeda, 2003) that molds, distorts, and devalues the lived experiences of communities of color by incorporating multiculturalism throughout a course, not just in one lesson or at the end (Stone Norton, 2008; Tuitt, 2003). Furthermore, they review the curriculum for hidden forms of oppression such as stereotyping, inaccurate generalizations, and historical omissions and make appropriate changes (Cochran-Smith, 2003; Gay, 2000; Ladson-Billings, 2006). They also recognize students' personal experiences as worthy knowledge (Elenes, 2006; González, 2001; Matusov & Smith, 2007; Yosso, 2006) and introduce local histories into the syllabi (Danigelis, 1998).

Faculty developers can facilitate curriculum transformation by helping faculty find curricular resources that integrate multiple identity groups and multiple perspectives, such as culturally accurate curriculum models, books, and websites (Tuitt, 2003). For faculty in the physical sciences, they can give examples of culturally responsive pedagogy, social justice endeavors, and advocacy for equity in areas such as science, technology, engineering, and mathematics (Ares, 2008; Johnson, 2005; Mertens & Hopson, 2006). Faculty developers can coach instructors to use an inclusive lens when examining course syllabi and finding spaces where the curriculum can be improved through a multicultural lens and local histories. Finally, they can help instructors identify overt and subtle forms of oppression in curricular materials.

Inclusive Pedagogy

A large body of research supports the notion that promising curricular and pedagogical practices that benefit historically marginalized students also benefit all students (Anderson, 2002; Mahendra, Bayles, Tomoeda, & Kim, 2005). Inclusive faculty use pedagogy that builds on students' funds of knowledge and supplements the cultural practices and information that students need to succeed academically and socially (Moll, Amanti, Neff, & Gonzalez, 2001; Tuitt, 2003). They rely on teaching methods that enhance the engagement, motivation, and learning of historically marginalized groups—methods that usually invite the whole student into the learning process (Tuitt, 2003). Inclusive pedagogy positions instructors and students as coconstructors of knowledge. It also encourages faculty from the dominant culture to invest time and energy in establishing critical dialogue with underrepresented students and giving them a sense of who they are as individuals when they enter the classroom (Vella, 2002).

Inclusive pedagogy encompasses a variety of specific assignments and in-class activities. It embraces noncompetitive collaborative assignments (Umbach & Wawrzynski, 2005), large and small group discussions (Chesler et al., 2005), journal writing (Chesler et al., 2005), debates (Danigelis, 1998), portfolios (Chism, 1994), student-led discussions (Frankel, 1993; Moya-Raggio, 1993), life history interviews of those from a different culture, autobiographical writing (Delpit, 2006), and experiential learning activities (Kolb, 1994). It endorses giving students choice in assignments (Chism, 1994), sharing personal stories (Cochran-Smith, 2003; Gay, 2000), and reading aloud in class (hooks, 1994).

Of course, faculty developers consider training faculty in new, effective methods such as these to be part of their job. They can teach faculty how to elicit and build on students' background knowledge by using diagrams, graphic organizers, and other visual representations. They can model ways to facilitate small and large group discussions and engage students in coconstruction of knowledge, moving from teacher-centered approaches to student-centered approaches. Furthermore, they can encourage instructors to incorporate new practices that are responsive to diverse identity groups and advise them on how to implement these practices.

Inclusive Learning Environment

Inclusive faculty use curriculum and pedagogies to transform learning environments into ones where "all perspectives are welcome" (Elenes, 2006, p. 249) and where "everybody believes that they can contribute to discourse" (p. 257). This includes caring for and respecting students, building professional relationships with them, and ensuring safe learning environments.

Inclusive faculty truly care about their students (Brookfield, 2006; Cranton & Carusetta, 2004). As Geneva Gay (2000) explains, "Caring is one of the major pillars of culturally responsive pedagogy for ethnically diverse students. It is manifested in the form of teacher attitudes, expectations, and behaviors about students' human value, intellectual capability, and performance responsibilities" (p. 45). Instructors demonstrate caring when they empower students to succeed both academically and personally (Delpit, 2006), hold high academic expectations for all students (Garrison-Wade & Lewis, 2006; Gilmore, Smith, & Kairaiuak, 2004), show pride in their achievements, and engage in sustained supportive outreach (Stone Norton, 2008).

In their research, Garrison-Wade and Lewis (2006) characterize a respectful instructor as one who is friendly and helpful and who does not embarrass the students. "Too often teachers forget that respect is important," they caution. "Once respect is lost, it is nearly impossible to regain" (p. 154). According to Nicolet (2007), "Respect and dignity must be operationalized nouns because the authentic endeavor of giving and receiving respect and dignity is what makes a learning community work effectively" (p. 218). In Simmons' terms: "Respect is given by acknowledging your humanity, as well as theirs. Respect comes by seeing all of your students' cultures, races, and ethnic characteristics not as 'minority,' but as parts of the norm/mainstream. Respecting who they are means respecting their differences in gender, race, socioeconomic status, religion, ability, sexual preference, country of origin, native language, and age. Respecting who they are means they will respect you" (2006, pp. 49–50).

Faculty create an inclusive learning environment by building relationships with students and empowering them to participate in the learning process. To build relationships with students, they must remember and correctly pronounce their names (Stone Norton, 2008); learn about their backgrounds, social identities, and learning styles (Chesler et al., 2005; Weinstein et al., 2004); recognize them as holistic individuals (Tuitt, 2003); and identify their passions to use as motivators (hooks, 1994). Additionally, inclusive faculty mentor students (Gloria & Castellanos, 2006) and meet with them outside of class (Stone Norton, 2008; Umbach & Wawrzynski, 2005).

Instructors make safe environments when they "empower students by legitimizing their 'voice' and visibility" (Gay, 2000, p. 49)—that is, they build students' self-esteem through constructive feedback and encourage them to share their opinions. Wlodkowski & Ginsberg (1995) identify seven characteristics of constructive feedback: (1) based on agreed standards, (2) specific and constructive, (3) prompt, (4) frequent, (5) positive, (6) personal, and (7) informational rather than controlling. This feedback should include telling students in front of their peers when an answer is correct and in private when it is incorrect, using examples to help them identify their mistakes (Stone Norton, 2008).

Other teaching behaviors that foster safe learning environments include reiterating questions in multiple ways, furnishing alternative methods for asking questions, and treating all students equally (Stone Norton, 2008). Equitable treatment encompasses avoiding tokenism (Gurin et al., 2003) and addressing students' racist and prejudicial remarks immediately (Billson & Tiberius, 1994; Gloria & Castellanos, 2006; Tuitt, 2003). According to Gurin et al. (2003): "The worst consequence of the lack of diversity arises when a minority student is a token in a classroom. In such situations, the solo or token minority individual is often given undue attention, visibility, and distinctiveness, which can lead to greater stereotyping by majority group members" (p. 35).

Inclusive faculty avoid tokenism by asking open-ended questions to the entire class, by setting up the class norm that individuals speak only for themselves, and by asking students to share personal experiences only when they have previously shared those experiences with the class on their own accord (Stone Norton, 2008). Because they firmly believe that racism and prejudice are not welcome in the classroom, they interrupt racist and prejudicial remarks immediately (Tuitt, 2003; Vacarr, 2003). In addition, they pose questions about such comments to the entire class for discussion and cite research that disproves racist claims (Stone Norton, 2008).

Faculty developers are vital in helping faculty create inclusive learning environments because instructors may not be aware of their actions that undermine such environments and make students feel tokenized. To help faculty adjust their practices, faculty developers can offer student accounts of learning environments characterized by caring, respect, professional relationships, and safety, as well as student accounts of unresponsive and unsafe environments. They can also suggest and encourage ways to develop and maintain inclusive learning environments, such as recognizing student progress, correctly pronouncing students' names; avoiding tokenism, accommodating different learning styles, engaging students through their interests, providing constructive feedback, and interrupting expressions of racism and prejudice.

Institutional Challenges to Inclusive Excellence

No matter how committed they are to promoting inclusive excellence, faculty developers may face challenges in institutional cultures that prioritize research and scholarship over teaching. In such settings, tenure and promotion committees may not consider inclusive teaching in their decisions, and norms may discourage challenging instructors' teaching practices. Furthermore, faculty in the physical sciences may regard their disciplines as neutral and value-free, thereby exempting them from inclusive practices. Even faculty developers may be unaware of their own non-inclusive values, attitudes, and behaviors, in which case institutions must ensure their developers receive training in the practices of inclusive excellence.

Despite these challenges, faculty developers are in a position to significantly influence institutional change by fostering inclusive excellence. They can create opportunities for faculty to become reflective practitioners who redefine the meaning of excellence and take action to promote inclusive practices. And through their work with faculty, they can reach hundreds if not thousands of students and possibly other faculty who recognize the positive results of inclusive excellence.

Williams, Berger, and McClendon (2005) contend that, even though individuals foster inclusive excellence, it is equally important that an institutional framework exist to encourage large-scale organizational change, such as a sustained and substantive effort to infuse inclusive excellence across university practices—from promotion and tenure to organizational structure and leadership, targeted resources, and accountability mechanisms. Specifically, leaders in higher education must move from rhetoric to action by involving the entire campus community in the work of infusing diversity and excellence (Milem, Chang,

& Antonio, 2005). In the absence of such efforts, faculty developers may find themselves engaged in a process of transformation focused on one faculty member at a time. Ultimately, inclusive excellence is fostered by individual efforts and university commitment to transformational change.

Conclusion

Higher education faculty and students are caught in a cycle that reinforces inequity. As Tatum (2003) puts it: "We cannot be blamed for learning what we were taught. Yet as adults, we have a responsibility to try to identify and interrupt the cycle of oppression. . . . We have a responsibility to seek out more accurate information and to adjust our behavior accordingly" (p. 141).

We maintain that faculty developers are vital to interrupting the cycle of inequity. They can be catalysts for faculty to weave inclusive excellence into their practices. After all, the tools for inclusive excellence benefit students and faculty alike, and students from dominant cultures also benefit academically from practices suggested for diverse students. Faculty developers should familiarize themselves with the range of promising practices and infuse them in programs that enhance the overall effectiveness of teaching. In particular, they should keep in mind that instructors who teach inclusively will increase student success overall.

REFERENCES

Anderson, J. (2002). Race in American higher education: Historical perspectives on current conditions. In W. Smith, P. Altbach, & K. Lomotey (Eds.), *Racial crisis in American higher education: The continuing challenges for the twenty-first century* (pp. 3–22). Albany: SUNY Press.

Ares, N. (2008). Cultural practices in networked classroom learning environments. *International Journal of Computer-Supported Collaborative Learning, 3*(3), 301–326.

Baez, B. (2004). The study of diversity: The "knowledge of difference" and the limits of science. *Journal of Higher Education, 75*(3), 285–307.

Banks, J. A. (2004). Multicultural education: Historical developments, dimensions, and practice. In J. A. Banks & C. A. McGee Banks (Eds.), *Handbook of research on multicultural education* (pp. 3–29). San Francisco: Jossey-Bass.

Banks, J. A. (2007). *Educating citizens in a multicultural society* (2nd ed.). New York: Teachers College Press.

Billson, J. M., & Tiberius, R. G. (1994). Effective social arrangements for teaching and learning. In K. A. Feldman & M. B. Paulsen (Eds.), *Teaching and learning in the college classroom* (pp. 561–576). Boston: Pearson.

Brookfield, S. D. (2006). Authenticity and power. In P. Cranton (Ed.), *New directions for adult and continuing education: No. 111. Authenticity in teaching* (pp. 5–16). San Francisco: Jossey-Bass.

Causey, V. E., Thomas, C. D., & Armento, B. J. (1999). Cultural diversity is basically a foreign term to me: The challenges of diversity for pre-service teacher education. *Teaching and Teacher Education, 16*(1), 33–45.

Chang, M. J., Jones, J., & Hakuta, K. (2003). *Compelling interest: Examining the evidence on racial dynamics in colleges and universities.* Stanford, CA: Stanford University Press.

Chesler, M., Lewis, A., & Crowfoot, J. (2005). *Challenging racism in higher education: Promoting justice.* Oxford, UK: Rowman & Littlefield.

Chickering, A. W., & Gamson, Z. F. (1994). Seven principles for good practice in undergraduate education. In K. A. Feldman & M. B. Paulsen (Eds.), *Teaching and learning in the college classroom* (pp. 543–549). Boston: Pearson.

Chism, N.V.N. (1994). Taking student diversity into account. In K. A. Feldman & M. B. Paulsen (Eds.), *Teaching and learning in the college classroom* (pp. 185–191). Boston: Pearson.

Civil, M. (2002). Culture and mathematics: A community approach. *Journal of Intercultural Studies, 23*(2), 133–148.

Clark Orey, D., & Rosa, M. (2006). Ethnomathematics: Cultural assertions and challenges towards pedagogical action. *Journal of Mathematics and Culture, 1*(1), 57–78.

Cochran-Smith, M. (2003). Blind vision: Unlearning racism in teacher education. In A. Howell & F. Tuitt (Eds.), *Race and higher education: Rethinking pedagogy in diverse college classrooms* (pp. 97–127). Cambridge, MA: Harvard Educational Review.

Cochran-Smith, M., Davis, D., & Fries, K. (2004). Multicultural teacher education: Research, practice, and policy. In J. A. Banks & C. A. McGee Banks (Eds.), *Handbook of research on multicultural education* (pp. 931–975). San Francisco: Jossey-Bass.

Cranton, P., & Carusetta, E. (2004). Perspectives on authenticity in teaching. *Adult Education Quarterly, 55*(1), 5–22.

Danigelis, N. L. (1998). Theory and classroom applications. In H. Ball, S. D. Berkowitz, & M. Mzamane (Eds.), *Multicultural education in colleges and universities: A transdisciplinary approach* (pp. 105–114). Mahwah, NJ: Erlbaum.

Delpit, L. (2006). *Other people's children: Cultural conflict in the classroom.* New York: New Press.

Diez Palomar, J., Simic, K., & Varley, M. (2007). Math is everywhere: Connecting math to students' lives. *Journal of Mathematics and Culture, 1*(2), 20–36.

Diouf, M. (1998). Teaching the conflicts: Race and ethnic relations. In H. Ball, S. D. Berkowitz, & M. Mzamane (Eds.), *Multicultural education in colleges and universities* (pp. 67–75). Mahwah, NJ: Erlbaum.

Elenes, C. A. (2006). Transformando fronteras. In D. D. Bernal, C. A. Elenes, F. E. Godinez, & S. Villenas (Eds.), *Chicana/Latina education in everyday life: Feminista perspectives on pedagogy and epistemology* (pp. 245–259). Albany: SUNY Press.

Felder, R. M., & Brent, R. (1996). Navigating the bumpy road to student-centered instruction. *College Teaching, 44*(2), 43–47.

Frankel, L. (1993). A circle of learners: Teaching about gender, race, and class. In D. Schoem, L. Frankel, X. Zuniga, & E. A. Lewis (Eds.), *Multicultural teaching in the university* (pp. 95–109). Westport, CT: Praeger.

Gandara, P., & Maxwell-Jolly, J. (1999). *Priming the pump: Strategies for increasing the achievement of underrepresented minority undergraduates.* New York: College Board.

Garrison-Wade, D. F., & Lewis, C. W. (2006). Tips for school principals and teachers: Helping black students achieve. In J. Landsman & C. W. Lewis (Eds.), *White teachers/diverse classrooms: A guide to building inclusive schools, promoting high expectations, and eliminating racism* (pp. 150–161). Sterling, VA: Stylus.

Gay, G. (2000). *Culturally responsive teaching: Theory, research, and practice.* New York: Teachers College Press.

Gilmore, P., Smith, D. M., & Kairaiuak, A. L. (2004). Resisting diversity: An Alaskan case of institutional struggle. In M. Fine, L. Weis, L. P. Pruitt, & A. Burns (Eds.), *Off white: Readings on power, privilege, and resistance* (2nd ed., pp. 273–283). New York: Routledge.

Gloria, A. M., & Castellanos, J. (2006). Sustaining Latina/o doctoral students: A psychosociocultural approach for faculty. In J. Castellanos, A. M. Gloria, & M. Kamimura (Eds.), *The Latina/o pathway to the Ph.D.* (pp. 169–187). Sterling, VA: Stylus.

González, F. E. (2001). Haciendo que hacer—Cultivating a mestiza worldview and academic achievement: Bringing cultural knowledge into educational research, policy, and practice. *International Journal of Qualitative Studies in Education, 14*(5), 641–656.

Gurin, P., Dey, E. L., Hurtado, S., & Gurin, G. (2003). Diversity and higher education: Theory and impact on educational outcomes. In A. Howell & F. Tuitt (Eds.), *Race and higher education: Rethinking pedagogy in diverse college classrooms* (pp. 9–42). Cambridge, MA: Harvard Educational Review.

Gutstein, E. (2006). *Reading and writing the world with mathematics: Toward a pedagogy for social justice.* New York: Routledge.

hooks, b. (1994). *Teaching to transgress: Education as the practice of freedom.* New York: Routledge.

Johnson, E. (2005). The use of contextually relevant evaluation practices with programs designed to increase participation of minorities in science, technology, engineering, and mathematics (STEM) education. In S. Hood, R. Hopson, & H. Frierson (Eds.), *The role of culture and cultural context: A mandate for inclusion, the discovery of truth, and the understanding of evaluation theory and practice* (pp. 217–235). Charlotte, NC: Information Age.

Knight, M. G., Dixon, I. R., Norton, N.E.L., & Bentley, C. C. (2006). Critical literacies as feminist affirmations and interventions: Contextualizing Latina youth's constructions of their college-bound identities. In D. D. Bernal, C. A. Elenes, F. E. Godinez, & S. Villenas (Eds.), *Chicana/ Latina education in everyday life: Feminista perspectives on pedagogy and epistemology* (pp. 39–58). Albany: SUNY Press.

Kolb, D. A. (1994). Learning styles and disciplinary differences. In K. A. Feldman & M. B. Paulsen (Eds.), *Teaching and learning in the college classroom* (pp. 127–138). Boston: Pearson.

Kumashiro, K. K. (2003). Against repetition: Addressing resistance to antioppressive change in the practices of learning, teaching, supervising, and researching. In A. Howell & F. Tuitt (Eds.), *Race and higher education: Rethinking pedagogy in diverse college classrooms* (pp. 45–67). Cambridge, MA: Harvard Educational Review.

Kumashiro, K. K. (2006). Toward a theory of anti-oppressive education. *Review of Educational Research, 70*(1), 25–53.

Ladson-Billings, G. (2006). Yes, but how do we do it? Practicing culturally relevant pedagogy. In J. Landsman & C. W. Lewis (Eds.), *White teachers/ diverse classrooms: A guide to building inclusive schools, promoting high expectations, and eliminating racism* (pp. 29–42). Sterling, VA: Stylus.

Lawrence, S. M. (1997). Beyond race awareness: White racial identity and multicultural teaching. *Journal of Teacher Education, 48*(2), 108–117.

Mahendra, N., Bayles, K., Tomoeda, C., & Kim, E. (2005). Diversity and learner-centered education. *ASHA Leader, 10*(16), 12–14.

Maher, F. A., & Tetreault, M.K.T. (2003). Learning in the dark: How assumptions of whiteness shape classroom knowledge. In A. Howell & F. Tuitt (Eds.), *Race and higher education: Rethinking pedagogy in diverse college classrooms* (pp. 69–95). Cambridge, MA: Harvard Educational Review.

Matusov, E., & Smith, M. P. (2007). Teaching imaginary children: University students' narratives about their Latino practicum children. *Teaching and Teacher Education, 23*(5), 705–729.

Mertens, D. M., & Hopson, R. K. (2006). Advancing evaluation of STEM efforts through attention to diversity and culture. In D. Huffman & F. Lawrenz (Eds.), *New directions for faculty evaluation: No. 109. Critical issues in STEM evaluation* (pp. 35–51). San Francisco: Jossey-Bass.

Milem, J. F. (2003). The educational benefits of diversity: Evidence from multiple sectors. In M. Chang, D. Witt, J. Jones, & K. Hakuta (Eds.), *Compelling interest: Examining the evidence on racial dynamics in higher education* (pp. 126–169). Stanford, CA: Stanford University Press.

Milem, J. F., Chang, M. J., & Antonio, A. L. (2005). *Making diversity work on campus: A research-based perspective.* Washington, DC: Association of American Colleges and Universities.

Moll, L., Amanti, C., Neff, D., & Gonzalez, N. (2001). Funds of knowledge for teaching: Using a qualitative approach to connect homes and classrooms. *Theory into Practice, 31*(2), 132–141.

Moya-Raggio, E. (1993). The Latina: A teaching experience. In D. Schoem, L. Frankel, X. Zuniga, & E. A. Lewis (Eds.), *Multicultural teaching in the university* (pp. 119–132). Westport, CT: Praeger.

Nicolet, J. (2007). Conversations—A necessary step in understanding diversity. In J. Landsman & C. W. Lewis (Eds.), *White teachers/diverse classrooms: A guide to building inclusive schools, promoting high expectations, and eliminating racism* (pp. 203–220). Sterling, VA: Stylus.

Noblit, G., Hwang, S., Seiler, G., & Elmesky, R. (2007). Toward culturally responsive discourses in science education. *Cultural Studies in Science Education, 2*(1), 105–117.

Osei-Kofi, N., Richards, S. L., & Smith, D. G. (2004). Inclusion, reflection, and the politics of knowledge: On working toward the realization of an inclusive classroom environment. In L. I. Rendón, M. García, & D. Person (Eds.), *Transforming the first year of college for students of color* (pp. 55–66). Columbia, SC: National Resource Center for the First-Year Experience and Students in Transition.

Rendón, L. I. (2004). Transforming the first-year experience for students of color: Where do we begin? In L. I. Rendón, M. García, & D. Person (Eds.), *Transforming the first year of college for students of color* (pp. 177–184). Columbia, SC: National Resource Center for the First-Year Experience and Students in Transition.

Rios, F., Trent, A., & Castañeda, L. V. (2003). Social perspective taking: Advancing empathy and advocating justice. *Equity and Excellence in Education, 36*(1), 5–14.

Rosenberg, P. M. (2004). Color blindness in teacher education. In M. Fine, L. Weis, L. P. Pruitt, & A. Burns (Eds.), *Off white: Readings on power, privilege, and resistance* (pp. 257–272). New York: Routledge.

Rosser, S. V. (1998). Group work in science, engineering, and mathematics: Consequences of ignoring gender and race. *College Teaching, 46*(3), 82–89.

Sfeir-Younis, L. F. (1993). Reflections on the teaching of multicultural courses. In D. Schoem, L. Frankel, X. Zuniga, & E. A. Lewis (Eds.), *Multicultural teaching in the university* (pp. 61–75). Westport, CT: Praeger.

Shor, I., & Freire, P. (2003). What are the fears and risks of transformation? In A. Darder, M. Baltodano, & R. D. Torres (Eds.), *The critical pedagogy reader* (pp. 479–496). New York: RoutledgeFalmer.

Simmons, R. W. (2006). The empty desk in the third row: Experiences of an African American male teacher. In J. Landsman & C. W. Lewis (Eds.), *White teachers/diverse classrooms: A guide to building inclusive schools, promoting high expectations, and eliminating racism* (pp. 43–51). Sterling, VA: Stylus.

Stone Norton, A. (2008, November). *Crossing borders: Bringing Latina/o students and teachers to the same side of the river: An inclusive pedagogy.* Paper presented at the 33rd annual meeting of the Association for the Study of Higher Education, Jacksonville, FL.

Tatum, B. D. (2003). Talking about race, learning about racism: The application of racial identity development theory in the classroom. In A. Howell & F. Tuitt (Eds.), *Race and higher education: Rethinking pedagogy in diverse college classrooms* (pp. 139–164). Cambridge, MA: Harvard Educational Review.

Tuitt, F. (2003). Afterword: Realizing more inclusive pedagogy. In A. Howell & F. Tuitt (Eds.), *Race and higher education: Rethinking pedagogy in diverse college classrooms* (pp. 243–268). Cambridge, MA: Harvard Educational Review.

Umbach, P. D., & Wawrzynski, M. R. (2005). Faculty do matter: The role of college faculty in student learning and engagement. *Research in Higher Education, 46*(2), 153–184.

Vacarr, B. (2003). Moving beyond polite correctness: Practicing mindfulness in the diverse classroom. In A. Howell & F. Tuitt (Eds.), *Race and higher education: Rethinking pedagogy in diverse college classrooms* (pp. 129–138). Cambridge, MA: Harvard Educational Review.

Vella, J. (2002). *Learning to listen, learning to teach: The power of dialogue in educating adults* (Rev. ed.). San Francisco: Jossey-Bass.

Weinstein, C. S., Tomlinson-Clarke, S., & Curran, M. (2004). Toward a conception of culturally responsive classroom management. *Journal of Teacher Education, 55*(1), 25–38.

Williams, D. A., Berger, J. B., & McClendon, S. A. (2005). *Towards a model of inclusive excellence and change in postsecondary institutions*. Retrieved February 21, 2009, from www.aacu.org/inclusive_excellence/documents/Williams_et_al.pdf

Wlodkowski, R. J., & Ginsberg, M. B. (1995). *Diversity and motivation: Culturally responsive teaching*. San Francisco: Jossey-Bass.

Yosso, T. J. (2002). Toward a critical race curriculum. *Equity and Excellence in Education, 35*(2), 93–107.

Yosso, T. J. (2006). Whose culture has capital? In A. D. Dixon & C. K. Rousseau (Eds.), *Critical race theory in education: All god's children got a song* (pp. 167–190). New York: Routledge.

13

COMMUNICATION CLIMATE, COMFORT, AND COLD CALLING

AN ANALYSIS OF DISCUSSION-BASED COURSES AT MULTIPLE UNIVERSITIES

Tasha J. Souza, Humboldt State University

Elise J. Dallimore, Northeastern University

Eric Aoki, Colorado State University

Brian C. Pilling, South Jordan, Utah

One of the challenges in discussion facilitation is creating a climate that allows multiple voices to be heard. Although the practice of calling on students whose hands are not raised has been used to engage the entire class in discussions, many believe that cold calling sabotages the communication climate and makes students extremely uncomfortable. This study examines the impact of cold calling on student comfort and communication climate. The results suggest that when instructors choose to cold-call, they must create a supportive communication climate to ensure student comfort. This study challenges the assumption that cold calling makes students uncomfortable.

We would like to thank the reviewers and editors of TIA for their conscientious attention. A special thanks to our mentor and friend Don Wulff, who gave us insightful feedback prior to his untimely passing. This manuscript received the Top Paper Award from the Communication and Instruction Division at the Western States Communication Association convention in Seattle, Washington, in February 2007.

Discussion teaching is a highly effective method to cultivate learning, engage students, and create a positive classroom climate (Brookfield & Preskill, 1999; Christensen, 1991; Dallimore, Hertenstein, & Platt, 2005). It is "a systematic way of constructing a context for learning from the knowledge and experience of students" (Elmore, 1991, p. xiv). It offers pedagogical advantages when the objectives are developing critical thinking, cooperation, sensitivity, and discovery (Christensen, 1991). In addition, it enhances classroom cohesion more than lecture as well as students' sense of acceptance and belonging (Anderson & Nussbaum, 1990). Because discussion can improve students' ability to evaluate the logic of positions that they and others hold (Anderson & Nussbaum, 1990), it develops students' self-awareness and appreciation of diverse perspectives (Brookfield & Preskill, 1999). By fostering "an attitude that all ideas are tentative and are offered for examination" (Leonard, 1991, p. 142) and giving responsibility to the students, it generates an atmosphere of mutual trust and respect.

For decades, instructors and scholars have researched the topic of discussion to identify its strongest uses, and strategies to enhance its effectiveness (Christensen, Garvin, & Sweet, 1991; Christensen & Hansen, 1987). Of the various strategies, "cold calling" has recently captured attention. Dallimore et al. (2005) define the practice as "any instance in which a teacher calls on a student whose hand is not raised" (p. 23). Many instructors assume that cold calling causes severe student discomfort and may therefore create a defensive communication climate. However, Dallimore, Hertenstein, and Platt (2006) found that it can actually enhance student comfort, as well as increase preparation for class and perceived student learning. Students have identified cold calling as a method for enhancing quality participation and discussion effectiveness (Dallimore, Hertenstein, & Platt, 2004). However, research has yet to examine its effect on communication climate. If the practice increases student comfort, it may also help create a positive communication climate. This study examines the impact of cold calling on student comfort and communication climate in discussion-based courses among different student populations and in several types of educational institution.

The Literature on Communication Climate and Cold Calling

One of the challenges in discussion facilitation is creating a communication climate that encourages and allows multiple voices to be heard. Communication climate consists of the negotiated characteristics of the communication context that influence and are influenced by subsequent communication events (Souza, 1999). Because communication is a process, behaviors of "individuals involved in interactions affect each other and eventually serve to create a characteristic communication climate" (Darling & Civikly, 1987, p. 25). The relationship between communication and communication climate is recursive in that communication constructs the communication climate and the communication climate affects communication (Souza, 1999).

If students do not equally participate, the value of discussion is limited, especially for students less inclined to volunteer (Brookfield & Preskill, 1999). Excluding the investigations on cold calling by Dallimore et al. (2004, 2005, 2006, 2008), research examining the effectiveness of strategies to increase student participation during discussion is limited. Fishman (1997) suggests that techniques such as study questions and response logs enhance student participation in classroom discussion. Scollon and Bau (1981) suggest that clearly stated instructor expectations are useful in increasing student participation. Other strategies include requiring students to speak a specific number of times by using poker chips or comment cards for tracking (Davis, 1993), assigning roles in discussions to students (Smith & Smith, 1994), and using online discussions (Arbaugh, 2000; Bump, 1990).

Rosmarin (1987) discusses the experience of students being assigned on short notice to lead each class session's discussion with an analysis of an assigned case. Similarly, Rhodes and Schaible (1992) and Robinson and Schaible (1993) advocate student-led discussion in which the discussion leader is randomly chosen at the beginning of each class. Some specific strategies include asking all students to prepare questions prior to class about their reading, which they may then be asked to share (Frederick, 1987), or soliciting nonvoluntary participation to begin case discussion by calling on students "without previous warning" (Hansen, 1987, p. 134). Dallimore et al. (2004, 2005, 2006) specifically investigate the practice of cold calling to encourage student participation in discussion. Their research (Dallimore et al., 2006) suggests that cold calling (in one discussion-based classroom) increases participation frequency, is associated with increased student preparation, and leads to increased comfort. Other studies indicate that (1) students report that both required (i.e., cold calling) and graded participation increase participation quality and discussion effectiveness (Dallimore et al., 2004), and (2) cold calling leads to increased oral and written communication skill development (Dallimore et al., 2008).

Despite the potential benefits from cold calling, instructors may resist using the practice, contending that cold calling comes at the expense of student comfort (Dallimore et al., 2005). With the notable exception of Dallimore et al. (2006), little investigation of student comfort during discussions has been done. One factor that can have tremendous impact on student comfort is the communication climate.

The Literature on Communication Climate

An examination of the communication climate focuses on the critical role of interaction in creating and sustaining the climate. Communication climate is often compared metaphorically to the weather (Pace & Faules, 1994). A warm climate invites open communication and a cool climate promotes closed or defensive communication. A communication climate is omnipresent and continuously influences people's behaviors and perceptions. As Pace and Faules (1994) state, "a particular communication climate provides guidelines for individual decisions and behavior" (p. 105). However, communication climate is not simply external to individuals; just as people influence weather through deforestation, pollution, depletion of the ozone layer and so on, people's actions, values, and beliefs influence the communication climate (Souza, 1999).

Patel (1970) determined the communication climate using dimensions such as freedom and restriction, and Gibb (1961) included supportiveness and defensiveness. The products of an eight-year study of group interaction, Gibb's dimensions presents six continuums of behaviors that characterize defensive and supportive climates: superiority versus equality, evaluation versus description, neutrality versus empathy, strategy versus spontaneity, control versus a problem orientation, and certainty versus provisionalism. Gibb suggests that people in defensive climates defend themselves and make it difficult to "convey ideas clearly" (p. 148). In this type of climate, communication is characterized by a high level of ambiguity, distortion, and ineffective listening. In contrast, a supportive communication climate has clear messages, few distortions, and effective listening. Gibb contends that communication is more efficient in supportive climates than defensive ones.

Communication climate researchers frequently apply Gibb's framework to analyze the communication climate in a variety of contexts. For example, Rozema (1986) applied it to adolescent communication and suggested that a defensive communication climate hinders sex education in the home. Although Gibb's framework has been highly influential and widely cited, his dimensions emerged in an organizational context and have seen little use in classroom research.

Yet communication plays a primary role in creating a supportive learning environment and establishing relationships (Pierce, 1994). Thus the communication climate can create or disintegrate effective interpersonal relationships between student and instructor and influence learning. For example, Trickett and Moos (1973) found that positive student–teacher interactions resulted in greater course satisfaction and higher student achievement. In addition, research shows that a poor communication climate increases resistance to learning (Rosenfeld, 1983) and reduces commitment to course outcomes (Hill & Northouse, 1978). Conversely, students in supportive communication climates retain significantly more knowledge than those in defensive climates (Hays, 1970).

Because communication climate relates to student learning, retention, relationships, course satisfaction, and achievement, it may also affect students' comfort in classrooms with cold calling. We know a positive climate enhances trust (Gibson & Cohen, 2003), which would seem a necessary ingredient for student comfort with cold calling.

Because research suggests that students are fearful of asking questions (Dillon, 1981; Ortiz, 1988), instructors may assume that students are also fearful of nonvoluntarily answering questions. However, Dallimore et al. (2006) reported that cold calling does not undermine student comfort because it increases student preparation. Might communication climate also play a role in student comfort?

Methodology

Exploratory research suggests that the use of cold calling leads to multiple positive outcomes. However, research has yet to specifically investigate the impact of cold calling in multiple discussion-based courses. Thus, this research represents a study investigating the use of cold calling in multiple classroom contexts. We were particularly interested in the effect of such environments on student comfort and communication climate.

Research Questions

Many instructors fear that cold calling will make their students uncomfortable. So we asked this first research question: How does the use of cold calling affect student comfort? Additionally, because communication climate influences student comfort students may be less apt to participate, and less likely to learn, in a communication climate perceived as defensive. It stands to reason that a major concern of instructors about cold calling is its potentially detrimental effects on the communication climate. Thus we pose the second research question: How does cold calling affect the students' perceptions of the communication climate?

Research Design

This study was a pre-/postsurvey control group design. Four instructors administered the same pre- and postsurvey instrument in nine courses. Six of these courses were experimental groups and enrolled 130 students. Three were control groups and enrolled 62 students. Pedagogical practices were the same across all the instructors involved, except for the use of cold calling in the experimental group classes.

The Instructors, Courses, and Institutions

The research was conducted in nine undergraduate communication courses, both upper and lower division, taught by four instructors (the authors) at four educational institutions. Two of the instructors are male and two are female; three are Euro-American and one is Asian/Mexican American. The courses investigated included four public speaking courses, two gender and communication courses, and one each of cocultural communication, consultation skills, and interpersonal communication courses. The institutions were diverse geographically and institutionally (public and private, rural and urban, small liberal arts to large comprehensive to land grant research). Their student populations varied from economically diverse to largely upper-middle-class and from ethnically diverse to largely homogeneous.

The instructors collaborated to maintain pedagogical consistency across courses. All the courses in the study were primarily discussion-based, with some student presentations, small groups, case studies, and lecture. All of the courses graded participation, ranging from 10 percent to 22 percent of the total grade. In the experimental groups ($N = 6$), the instructors explained the choice, rationale, and advantages of cold calling, although they did not refer to the practice as "cold calling"; nor did they inform the students that this practice was being assessed. Because student experience with cold calling varied, the instructors agreed they would call on a student by name before asking questions and would ask questions from across all levels of Bloom's taxonomy (1956). They also agreed to maintain a supportive communication climate in their classes.

Sample

Of the total number of students enrolled in these courses, 192 completed and returned both pre- and postsurveys and were included in the analysis. To ensure the surveys were anonymous, we used a PIN to pair pre- and postsurvey questionnaires for analysis. (The survey form is available from the first author on request.)

Data

All data are student self-reported measures. We administered the presurvey on the first day of class, before explaining the class structure or participation requirements, and administered the postsurvey during the final week of classes. The presurvey established a baseline of the students' attitudes and behaviors regarding class participation and discussion teaching. The postsurvey questionnaire focused on their views on, comfort with, and behavior during the discussion teaching in the course. Students had about twenty minutes to complete the latter questionnaire after being informed that it was part of a research project on the effectiveness of class discussions as a learning tool. To avoid biasing responses, we did not mention cold call or classroom climate in the questionnaire. In the postsurvey, however, we did ask students if calling on them when their hands weren't raised had an impact on their participation.

The pre- and postsurvey questions (see Tables 13.1 and 13.2) were part of a more extensive questionnaire that asked students to report their level of participation, preparation, and learning in the course relative to others they had taken. The form contained both open-ended questions and close-ended items scored on a seven-point Likert scale. Although all responses were anonymous, we took extra effort to obtain candid responses by assuring students that we would not review the questionnaires until after we submitted final grades.

Data Analysis

In addition to descriptive statistical analysis of the pre- and postsurvey questionnaire data, we conducted a paired sample t test to assess relationships between pre- and postsurvey variables in the control and experimental groups. To analyze the qualitative data, we took a detailed, line-by-line approach, which Strauss and Corbin (1990) characterized as the most detailed and generative type of analysis. We segmented and coded the discourse into thematic "thought" units. We gave one sentence two or three codes if it contained more than one main idea and two or three sentences a single code if the main idea did not change. Our thematic analysis included searching for and developing individual themes, determining theme significance, and grouping relative to others (similar to those used by Peterson et al., 1994).

By noting the emergent themes and patterns (Miles & Huberman, 1994) and clustering data into fourteen themes, we created four broad communication climate categories. A second rater coded the data, and the reliability of these categories was determined by computing a coefficient of agreement. Between coders, Cohen's Kappa intercoder reliability score was 96.8 percent as based on independent coding of 100 percent of the qualitative data.

Results

The results are summarized here as they address the two research questions: How does the use of cold calling affect student comfort? How does cold calling affect the students' perceptions of the communication climate?

Student Comfort and Cold Calling During Discussion

According to the presurvey, respondents moderately enjoyed (5.57) classes in which instructors use discussion, with the control group (5.25) reporting significantly less enjoyment than those in the experimental group (5.72) (t (190) = 2.22, p < .05; see Table 13.1). Respondents reported experiencing some enjoyment (4.82) participating in discussion generally; those in the control group (4.47) reported significantly less enjoyment than those who would be exposed to cold calling (4.88) (t (198) = 2.04, p < .05). Both groups were somewhat comfortable (4.55) participating in discussions generally, with the control group significantly more comfortable than the experimental group. When class participation was graded, respondents were not very comfortable (3.78), with those in the control group significantly less comfortable than the experimental group. Finally, respondents reported that discussion participation in general was a little easier (3.77) than difficult, with the control group reporting significantly more difficulty with discussion participation than the experimental group.

Results from the postsurvey, shown in Table 13.1, indicate that respondents experienced a moderately high level of comfort (5.83) with discussion participation in these specific classes and experienced a moderately higher level of comfort (5.32) in these specific classes as compared to others. No significant differences in comfort were found between groups. However, we did discover a difference in ease during discussions between groups. Those in the control group reported significantly more ease with discussion participation than those in the experimental group, even

Table 13.1. Survey Results: Class Discussion and Enjoyment, Comfort, and Ease

				Anchor Points	
Item	Total	Control	Exp.	1 =	7 =
Results for Presurvey Questions					
Enjoyment in participating in discussion	4.82	4.47	4.98*	Not at all	Very much
Enjoyment in classes with discussion	5.57	5.25	5.72*	Not at all	Very much
Comfort with class discussion	4.55	4.15	3.59*	Uncomfortable	Comfortable
Comfort in classes with graded discussion	3.78	3.44	3.93*	Less comfort	More comfort
Level of ease in participating in discussion	3.77	4.15	3.59*	Easy	Very difficult
Results for Postsurvey Questions					
Comfort participating in this class	5.83	5.92	5.79	Uncomfortable	Comfortable
Comfort participating in this class versus others	5.32	5.52	5.23	Less comfort	More comfort
Ease of participating in this class	3.23	2.83	3.42*	Easy	Very difficult

Presurvey Questions

Enjoyment
- How much do you enjoy participating in class discussion?
- How much do you enjoy class when instructors use discussion in their teaching?

Comfort
- When participation in class discussions is graded, how does this affect your comfort in the course?
- In general, when I participate in class discussions, I feel: (uncomfortable, comfortable)

Ease
- In general, I find participation in class discussion to be: (easy, difficult)

*Indicates significant differences (p < .05) when individual means for control and experimental groups were compared through t tests for independent samples.

though the control group began the semester reporting less ease than the experimental group.

Results from a paired-samples *t* test (see Table 13.2) reveal that respondents felt much more comfortable participating in the classes evaluated for this study (5.83) than they felt about participating in class discussions in general (4.55). Table 13.2 also reports that respondents felt more ease participating in the specific classes in this study (3.23) than about discussion participation in general (3.75). We also used paired-samples *t* tests to assess differences in level of ease in discussion participation within the two groups (experimental and control). We found no significant differ-

---

Table 13.2. Postsurvey Results: Class Discussion and Comfort/Ease Comparison

			Anchor Points	
Item	In General	In This Class	1 =	7 =
Comfort participating in discussion	4.55	5.83*	Uncomfortable	Comfortable
Control group	4.34	5.92*	Uncomfortable	Comfortable
Experimental group	4.64	5.79*	Uncomfortable	Comfortable
Ease in participating in discussion	3.75	3.23*	Easy	Very difficult
Control group	4.15	2.83*	Easy	Very difficult
Experimental group	3.56	3.42*	Easy	Very difficult

Postsurvey Questions

Comfort
- In this class, when I participated in class discussions, I felt: (uncomfortable, comfortable)
- Compared to other courses, when I participated in class discussions in this course, I felt: (uncomfortable, comfortable)
- If you felt *more* comfortable participating in this course than in other courses, why was that true?
- If you felt *less* comfortable participating in this course than in other courses, why was that true?

Ease
- In this class, I found class discussions to be: (easy, very difficult)

*Indicates significant differences (p < .05) when means were compared through a paired-sample *t* test.

ences in the experimental group, suggesting respondents felt similarly about the ease with which they could participate in discussion generally (3.56) and the ease with which they actually participated in the classes used for data collection (3.42). However, we did identify a significant difference in the control group, indicating that these respondents felt discussion participation in general (4.15) was significantly more difficult than participating in the classes used for this study (2.83).

Eighty-five percent of the experimental group and 87 percent of the control group reported being more comfortable in the course under investigation than in other courses. Therefore, only 15 percent of respondents in the experimental groups (N = 20 of 130) felt less comfortable in the cold-calling courses than in others; 12 percent of control group respondents (N = 7 of 62) felt less comfortable in control classes. When asked why they were more or less comfortable, respondents cited communication climate characteristics, though they were not specifically asked about them in the survey. The themes related to communication climate are described in the following section. However, responses not referencing communication climate related largely to three themes: the teacher, the nature of the course, and student preparation and comprehension.

Although no respondents mentioned the instructor as a reason for being less comfortable, twenty-one stated that they were more comfortable in the given class than in others because of the instructor. They explained that instructors helped them feel comfortable by being flexible and creating an encouraging, supportive, and respectful environment. For example, one experimental group respondent described being more comfortable "[b]ecause the [instructor] was willing to change things to make students more comfortable." A control group respondent noted, "The teacher created an environment that leaves everyone feeling comfortable in their own opinion. There is no judgment presented by the teacher on wrong and right opinions."

Twenty respondents stated that the nature of the course content was the reason for more or less comfort in the given class. Fourteen respondents who were more comfortable in the given course than in others stated it was because it was a "speech" or a "communication" course. Other respondents mentioned course design as affecting their comfort. For example, a respondent suggested, "This class was designed for participation in class discussion." The six respondents less comfortable in the given class claimed it was due to the difficulty of the course content or design. One respondent claimed, "I felt less comfortable because the concepts were very challenging." Another maintained, "The subject matter was sometimes really difficult to discuss."

Student preparation and comprehension were mentioned by fourteen respondents. Six claimed they were more comfortable because they were better prepared. To illustrate, one respondent wrote, "I got used to talking in this course because I was prepared so I'd know what I was talking about." Although no one attributed less comfort to poor preparation, four respondents blamed their comprehension level. As one stated, "When I felt uncomfortable, it was not that I was unprepared, but that I didn't fully comprehend the subject matter." Conversely, four respondents felt *more* comfortable as a result of their solid comprehension.

Impact of Cold Calling on Communication Climate

We identified fourteen themes identified from the data related to communication climate and grouped them into four categories: (1) climate of confirmation, (2) climate of engagement, (3) climate of familiarity, and (4) climate of freedom (listed in order of frequency from most to least). When asked why they were less comfortable in the given class, respondents gave reasons related to two of four communication climate themes.

Climate of confirmation. Forty-two respondents alluded to a communication climate of confirmation as the reason they were more comfortable. In a communication climate of confirmation, the negotiated characteristics of the communication context recognize another person's worth (Cissna & Seiburg, 1995). We distilled four indicators of this type of climate: accepting communication, nonjudgmental communication, personal communication, and respectful communication. For instance, one respondent reported, "The atmosphere was very open and I felt I could express my opinion without being judged" (experimental group respondent: coded nonjudgmental). Here are further examples of each indicator (comments came from respondents in courses from all four instructors):

Exhibit 13.1. Student Comfort: Climate of Confirmation

N = 42, 69% experimental, 31% control

Accepting
- "I felt like my contributions were valued and discussed. I could get my questions answered." (Experimental group respondent)
- "I felt that my opinion was important." (Control group respondent)

Nonjudgmental
- "It was expected that everyone would participate and therefore I felt less scrutinized by peers." (Experimental group respondent)

(Continued)

Exhibit 13.1. (*Continued*)

- "The teacher created an environment that leaves everyone feeling comfortable in their own opinion. There is no judgment presented by the teacher on wrong and right opinions." (Control group respondent)

Personal
- "The people were just connected, it was comfortable getting to know everyone." (Experimental group respondent)

Respectful
- "The instructor set a tone that made you want to respect others." (Experimental group respondent)

In fact, the most common theme among the more comfortable respondents was a climate of confirmation, and the most common theme among the less comfortable ones was a climate of disconfirmation. Nine of the twenty-five less comfortable respondents described a communication climate of disconfirmation, with characteristics such as judgment, intimidation, and lack of acceptance. As one experimental group respondent claimed, "There are a lot of opinionated people in this class that [sic] I feel judge others." Another remarked, "I felt that some people didn't like what I had to say because of my background."

Climate of engagement. Thirty-three respondents gave communication climate of engagement as the reason for being more comfortable. This type of climate is one in which the negotiated characteristics of the communication context promote involvement and engagement. We identified

---

Exhibit 13.2. Student Comfort: Climate of Engagement

N = 33, 82% experimental, 18% control

Expectation of engagement or participation
- "[I felt more comfortable] because everyone was expected to and did participate rather than a few select people." (Experimental group respondent)

Equal student involvement
- "Because I felt that a lot of people participated in this class, so it made it more comfortable to speak up as well." (Experimental group respondent)
- "Other students were participating also, so I felt more comfortable participating myself." (Control group respondent)

Personal engagement
- "As I started participating more, I felt more confident." (Experimental group respondent)

three themes related to a climate of engagement: expectation of engagement or participation, equal student involvement (participation), and personal engagement (individual participation). Exhibit 13.2 offers examples of each indicator. Comments came from respondents in courses from all four instructors. Less comfortable respondents did not mention engagement or lack of it in the given course.

Climate of freedom. Twenty-six respondents cited a communication climate of freedom as the reason for their greater comfort. In this kind of climate, the negotiated characteristics of the communication context are not confined to restrictive rules; nor do they seem to be under the control or power of another person or persons. We found three indicators of a communication climate of freedom: open communication, unrestricted communication, and discussion-based communication. We consider these to be indicators because they offer students the freedom to communicate about various topics in various ways. Exhibit 13.3 offers examples of each indicator. Comments came from students in courses from all four instructors. Four respondents, however, felt less comfortable in the given class. One experimental group respondent asserted, "I didn't like feeling forced to talk for 25 percent of my grade; too much pressure." No one gave cold calling, which might be seen as controlling, as a reason for discomfort.

Climate of familiarity. Fifteen respondents attributed their greater comfort to a communication climate of familiarity—that is, one in which the negotiated characteristics of the communication context are known and familiar. Respondents claimed that knowing their fellow students, the instructor, and the environment enhanced their comfort. Comments came from students in courses from all four instructors (see Exhibit 13.4 for sample comments). Neither familiarity nor the lack of it was mentioned by less comfortable respondents.

Exhibit 13.3. Student Comfort: Climate of Freedom

N = 26, 61% experimental, 39% control

Open communication
"The class was a much more open and friendly environment, therefore it was easier to give input." (Experimental group respondent)

Unrestricted communication
"I just wanted to be heard and get my opinion out there and maybe introduce a different view for others to consider." (Control group respondent)

Discussion-based communication
"I felt like the atmosphere was more open to discussion and the class was set up to participate in easily." (Control group respondent)

Discussion

We set out to examine the practice of cold calling more precisely by exploring its relationship to comfort and climate. This study is the first to relate communication climate to cold calling and examine the effects of cold calling in multiple classrooms at multiple institutions.

Comfort May Not Decrease with Cold Calling

Our results present a strong argument against the common belief that cold calling decreases student comfort in the discussion classroom. Similar significant differences were found in the results for both the experimental and control groups when those groups were analyzed through two separate paired-samples *t* tests, indicating that factors other than cold calling increased their comfort participating in discussions. The experimental group results—with respect to increasing student comfort—are especially relevant because an increase in student comfort with discussion runs counter to common beliefs regarding the effects of cold calling.

The presurvey data provided an interesting baseline assessment. Although the experimental group liked discussions generally, neither group enjoyed participating in them. However, both groups asserted some level of comfort with discussion participation. The control group began the semester reporting significantly more comfort than the experimental group. However, the control group reported significantly less comfort than the experimental group when such participation was graded. This finding suggests respondents are moderately comfortable speaking in class but less so when their contributions are graded.

Although levels of enjoyment and comfort differed, and both groups claimed a moderate level of comfort during discussion generally, the post-surveys revealed that both groups reported a moderately high level of comfort with discussion in these specific classes. Regardless of cold-calling use, both groups' comfort increased, and there were no significant differences found in comfort level. Further, both groups reported much more comfort participating in the classes evaluated than participating in other classes. Finally, not one respondent mentioned cold calling as a

---

Exhibit 13.4. Student Comfort: Climate of Familiarity

N = 15, 73% experimental, 27% control

- "I felt more comfortable in this class because . . . I got to know and trust my classmates." (Experimental group respondent)
- "Got to know the people in my class and I was comfortable with them." (Control group respondent)

reason for their discomfort. These results suggest that comfort is neither decreased nor increased by cold calling (at least not among these students and instructors). Rather the increase in student comfort was related to other classroom variables.

Cold Calling Can Make Discussions More Difficult for Students

Although both groups experienced increased comfort, they differed in their reported level of ease with discussion participation. They both reported that discussion participation was somewhat easier than difficult in these specific classes, but the control group reported significantly more ease with discussion participation than those in the experimental group. It makes sense that students would find a discussion with cold calling more difficult, given the need to prepare and respond to questions nonvoluntarily. But despite this finding, both were equally comfortable. Student comfort is an important element of a supportive communication climate—and therefore critical to effective discussion—but we suggest that difficulty (as opposed to "ease") of discussion participation can be desirable. Discussion strategies that raise difficulty can challenge students positively, both intellectually and communicatively, because they usually give students more practice in constructing, articulating, defending, and critiquing arguments.

Student Participation, Not Preparation, Is More Important for Student Comfort

Eighty-six percent of the students in both groups claimed more comfort in the course under study than in other courses. When asked why, they referred to the communication climate, the teacher, the nature of the course, and student preparation and comprehension, in order of frequency. Previous research by Dallimore et al. (2006) suggests that "when students are well prepared, they may be more comfortable participating, and the more they participate, the more comfortable they may become with it" (p. 18). Only five respondents from the experimental group claimed increased preparation was the reason for their greater comfort. Respondents did, however, claim that their (and their peers') increased participation was a significant reason for greater comfort.

Communication Climate Is the Most Important Factor for Student Comfort

What is clear from this research is the importance of communication climate for student comfort in discussion-based classrooms. An overwhelming majority of students (78 percent) who reported increased comfort described some aspect of communication climate as the reason they were more comfortable; 48 percent of those reporting less comfort relative to other courses identified communication climate as a factor. The difference in percentages suggests (1) elements of a supportive communication climate had the greatest influence on increased student comfort (relative to other factors reported), and (2) elements of a defensive communication climate were rarely cited as a reason for decreased comfort, with more than 52 percent attributing to other factors such as course content and their lack of comprehension. Both the experimental and control groups reported that they were more comfortable because the communication climate was confirming, engaged, free, and familiar.

This study confirms the importance of a communication climate that recognizes another's worth, similar to "empathy" as suggested by Gibb (1961). Our unique contributions to the communication climate research are the characteristics of engagement, freedom, and familiarity. From this study, we deem such qualities, which are not present in Gibb's framework, as central to classroom interaction. Regardless of the use of cold calling, students are comfortable during discussion when all students are engaged, have the freedom to express a variety of viewpoints, and are familiar with the instructor, the students, and the environment. Counter to widespread suspicions, the experimental group did not perceive the communication climate as restrictive in the classroom with cold calling.

Cold Calling Can Increase Overall Student Engagement

Qualitative responses from the experimental (two-thirds) and control groups (one-third) were consistent with the overall N. Roughly one-third of the responses for each of the climate categories came from respondents in the control group, with one notable exception. Of the comments on a climate of engagement, 82 percent were from the experimental group. Although we expected both groups to participate, more respondents commented on student engagement in the cold-calling classroom. This finding suggests greater engagement in classes with cold calling.

Practical Applications and Pedagogical Implications

From these findings, we see four major pedagogical implications for the practice of cold calling. Instructors should consider several facets of classroom climate, including some not in Gibb's framework (1961).

Create a Climate of Confirmation in the Classroom

Students must anticipate they will not be ridiculed or shamed before they take the risk of participating. Before speaking up comfortably either voluntarily or nonvoluntarily, they need to feel they will be affirmed and valued as individuals. Similar to Gibb's climate characteristics (1961) of empathy and equality, the communication climate of confirmation is accepting and nonjudgmental. We maintain that effective communication should be a relationship-building process rather than merely a means for transferring information and ideas (Robertson, 2002). Instructors must recognize the importance of affirming students before considering cold calling, because students could easily see it as punitive or threatening in a climate of disconfirmation.

Create a Climate of Engagement

Students are comfortable during discussions when participation is expected, when all students are engaged and personally contribute, and cold calling makes this happen. Now that several studies demonstrate that the practice need not sacrifice student comfort, instructors can feel confident in using it and other strategies to increase student engagement, such as grading participation and using multiple active-learning strategies.

Create a Climate of Freedom

The climate of freedom is similar to Gibb's (1961) notion of "spontaneity," which refers to messages that are open, honest, and free from ulterior motives. Respondents described this climate as characterized by openness, lack of confining rules, and an emphasis on discussion. These distinctions are appropriate for the classroom context. Students feel more comfortable participating when no rules restrict how to communicate and what to say. They described the allowance of multiple opinions and humor in a relaxed environment as the key to their comfort. Having a climate of freedom creates opportunities for them to "share the teaching task with one another and their instructor" (Christensen, 1991, p. 99). This freedom encourages students to share power over and responsibility for the learning experience of the class (Christensen, 1991).

Create a Climate of Familiarity in the Classroom

Individuals feel more comfortable with self-disclosure or speaking in public when the audience and setting are known. Students too feel more comfortable participating in discussion when familiar with the instructor, other students, and class setting. This familiarity develops through interaction. Its value extends the literature on the importance of establishing clear and explicit expectations for students (Davis, 1993).

Limitations of the Study and Future Research

Our contributions must be understood alongside the limitations of our research. First, although our sample is impressive at the individual level (192 surveys, with nearly sixteen hundred words in our text database), it included nine classes and four instructors at the classroom level. The fact that all four instructors work diligently to create and maintain a supportive communication climate and have been recognized for effective teaching likely affected the results. Future research should examine a variety of instructors with differing styles to further investigate student comfort and positive communication climate in the discussion-based classroom. Although this study suggests what *does* work when using nonvoluntary participation, it is equally important to know what does *not* work as well.

This study was based on students' anonymous self-reports. However, some variables, such as frequency of student contributions, grades, and attendance, could be measured directly though observation, video recording, and course outcome data. We would welcome extensions of our research that capture the complexity of the classroom context by using ethnographic approaches and student interviews. Future research also should examine the generalizability of the conclusions, perhaps to graduate students or to courses in other disciplines.

Although we worked to be consistent in the manner and frequency of our use of cold calling, the question remains: Did we cold-call in precisely the same manner? Another important next step in cold-calling research is to turn the lens on the instructor to assess the nature of the cold call and address the effects of various types of cold calls.

In addition, the specific behaviors and characteristics of the instructor and students merit investigation. What role does teacher immediacy play in perceptions of cold calling? Do the student perceptions and expectations of instructors vary according to instructor characteristics, such as ethnicity, sex, gender, and social class? How do student characteristics affect their reactions to cold calling? What does the use of cold calling say to students about power in the classroom? What impact do cold calling and communication climate have on student confidence about participation, participation quality and quantity, and learning?

Despite these limitations, our research has several implications for practice. When instructors use discussion as a pedagogical tool, they must consider the communication climate. When they choose to cold-call, they must create a supportive communication climate. Students must feel valued, respected, and not judged; they must be engaged personally and as a group during discussions and must feel that communication is open and unrestricted. Further, students must feel a sense of familiarity with the environment, instructor, and other students. In addition to underscoring the need for a supportive communication climate, our research challenges the assumption that cold calling makes students uncomfortable. Can it? Of course. But when the instructor is thoughtful about creating a supportive communication climate, cold calling can serve to engage a wider range of students and incorporate greater diversity of perspective in the discussion.

REFERENCES

Anderson, J., & Nussbaum, J. (1990). Interaction skill in instruction settings. In J. A. Daly, G. W. Friedrich, & A. L. Vangelisti (Eds.), *Teaching communication: Theory, research, and methods* (pp. 301–316). Hillsdale, NJ: Erlbaum.

Arbaugh, J. B. (2000). The virtual classroom versus physical classroom: An exploratory study of class discussion patterns and student learning in an asynchronous internet-based MBA course. *Journal of Management Education, 24*(2), 213–233.

Bloom, B. S. (1956). *Taxonomy of educational objectives: The classification of educational goals, by a committee of college and university examiners. Handbook 1: Cognitive domain.* New York: Longman.

Brookfield, S., & Preskill, S. (1999). *Discussion as a way of teaching: Tools and techniques for democratic classrooms.* San Francisco: Jossey-Bass.

Bump, J. (1990). Radical changes in class discussion using networked computers. *Computers and the Humanities, 24*(1–2), 49–65.

Christensen, C. R. (1991). Every student teaches and every teacher learns: The reciprocal gift of discussion teaching. In C. R. Christensen, D. A. Garvin, & A. Sweet (Eds.), *Education for judgment: The artistry of discussion leadership* (pp. 137–152). Boston: Harvard Business School Press.

Christensen, C. R., Garvin, D. A., & Sweet, A. (Eds.). (1991). *Education for judgment: The artistry of discussion leadership.* Boston: Harvard Business School Press.

Christensen, C. R., & Hansen, A. J. (Eds.). (1987). *Teaching and the case method: Text, cases, and readings.* Boston: Harvard Business School Press.

Cissna, K. N., & Seiburg, E. (1995). Patterns of interactional confirmation and disconfirmation. In J. Stewart (Ed.), *Bridges not walls: A book about interpersonal communication* (6th ed., pp. 292–301). New York: McGraw-Hill.

Dallimore, E. J., Hertenstein, J. H., & Platt, M. B. (2004). Quality participation and discussion effectiveness: Student generated strategies. *Communication Education, 53*(1), 103–115.

Dallimore, E. J., Hertenstein, J. H., & Platt, M. B. (2005). Faculty-generated strategies for "cold-calling" use: A comparative analysis with student recommendations. *Journal on Excellence in College Teaching, 16*(1), 23–62.

Dallimore, E. J., Hertenstein, J. H., & Platt, M. B. (2006). Nonvoluntary class participation in graduate discussion courses: Effects of grading and cold-calling. *Journal of Management Education, 30*(2), 354–377.

Dallimore, E. J., Hertenstein, J. H., & Platt, M. B. (2008). Using discussion pedagogy to enhance oral and written communication skills. *College Teaching, 56*(3), 163–172.

Darling, A. L., & Civikly, J. M. (1987). The effect of teacher humor on student perceptions of classroom communicative climate. *Journal of Classroom Interaction, 22*(1), 24–30.

Davis, B. G. (1993). *Tools for teaching.* San Francisco: Jossey-Bass.

Dillon, J. T. (1981). Duration of response to teacher questions and statements. *Contemporary Educational Psychology, 6*(1), 1–11.

Elmore, R. F. (1991). Foreword. In C. R. Christensen, D. A. Garvin, & A. Sweet (Eds.), *Education for judgment: The artistry of discussion leadership* (pp. ix–xix). Boston: Harvard Business School Press.

Fishman, S. M. (1997). Student writing in philosophy: A sketch of five techniques. In M. D. Sorcinelli & P. Elbow (Eds.), *New directions for teaching and learning: No. 69. Writing to learn: Strategies for assigning and responding to writing* (pp. 53–66). San Francisco: Jossey-Bass.

Frederick, P. (1987). The dreaded discussion: Ten ways to start. In C. R. Christensen & A. J. Hansen (Eds.), *Teaching and the case method: Text, cases, and readings* (pp. 211–216). Boston: Harvard Business School Press.

Gibb, J. (1961). Defensive communication. *Journal of Communication, 11*, 332–337.

Gibson, C. B., & Cohen, S. G. (2003). *Virtual teams that work: Creating conditions for virtual collaboration effectiveness.* San Francisco: Jossey-Bass.

Hansen, D. J. (1987). Background information on a graduate school of business administration. In C. R. Christensen & A. J. Hansen (Eds.), *Teaching and the case method: Text, cases, and readings* (pp. 133–134). Boston: Harvard Business School Press.

Hays, E. R. (1970). An ego-threatening classroom communication: A factor analysis of student perceptions. *Speech Teacher, 19*(1), 43–48.

Hill, S. K., & Northouse, P. G. (1978). A research design for studying communication climate within an organization. *Journal of Business Communication, 15*(2), 37–44.

Leonard, H. B. (1991). With open ears: Listening and the art of discussion teaching. In C. R. Christensen, D. A. Garvin, & A. Sweet (Eds.), *Education for judgment: The artistry of discussion leadership* (pp. 137–152). Boston: Harvard Business School Press.

Miles, M. B., & Huberman, A. M. (1994). *Qualitative data analysis.* Thousand Oaks, CA: Sage.

Ortiz, J. (1988, March). *Creating conditions for student questions.* Paper presented at the National Seminar on Successful College Teaching, Orlando, FL.

Pace, R. W., & Faules, D. F. (1994). *Organizational communication* (3rd ed.). Englewood Cliffs, NJ: Prentice Hall.

Patel, I. J. (1970). *Communication in the classroom.* Baroda, India: Centre of Advanced Study in Education.

Peterson, T. R., Witte, K., Enkerlin-Hoeflich, E., Espericueta, L., Flora, J. T., Florey, N., et al. (1994). Using informant directed interviews to discover risk orientation: How formative evaluations based in interpretive analysis can improve persuasive safety campaigns. *Journal of Applied Communication, 22*(3), 199–215.

Pierce, C. (1994). Importance of classroom climate for at-risk learners. *Journal of Educational Research, 88*(1), 37–42.

Rhodes, G., & Schaible, R. (1992). Talking students/listening teachers: The student-led discussion. *Issues and Inquiry in College Learning and Teaching, 16,* 44–61.

Robertson, E. (2002). *Using leadership to improve communication climate model: A strategy for engaging leaders in organizational communication.* London: Melcrum.

Robinson, B. D., & Schaible, R. (1993). Women and men teaching "Men, Women, and Work."*Teaching Sociology, 21*(4), 363–370.

Rosenfeld, L. B. (1983). Communication climate and coping mechanisms in the college classroom. *Communication Education, 32*(2), 167–174.

Rosmarin, A. (1987). The art of leading a discussion. In C. R. Christensen & A. J. Hansen (Eds.), *Teaching and the case method: Text, cases, and readings* (pp. 235–240). Boston: Harvard Business School Press.

Rozema, H. J. (1986). Defensive communication climate as a barrier to sex education in the home. *Family Relations, 35*(4), 531–537.

Scollon, S., & Bau, K. (1981, April). *Professional development seminar: A model for making higher education more culturally sensitive*. Paper presented at the Conference of the National Association for Asian and Pacific American Education, Honolulu, HI.

Smith, L. J., & Smith, D. L. (1994, April). The discussion process: A simulation. *Journal of Reading, 37*(7), 582–584.

Souza, T. J. (1999, November). *The social construction of communication climate: An analysis of at-risk students in an alternative high school*. Paper presented at the National Communication Association Convention, Chicago.

Strauss, A. L., & Corbin, J. (1990). *Basics of qualitative research*. London: Sage.

Trickett, E. J., & Moos, R. H. (1973). Social environment of junior high and high school classrooms. *Journal of Educational Psychology, 65*(1), 93–102.

14

THEORETICAL FRAMEWORKS
FOR ACADEMIC DISHONESTY

A COMPARATIVE REVIEW

Michele DiPietro, Carnegie Mellon University

Academic dishonesty has so far been understood using theoretical frameworks derived from criminology literature. These frameworks contribute pieces of the puzzle and even enjoy some empirical support, but conceptualizing students as delinquents is problematic and ultimately ineffective. This chapter reviews the current frameworks, including their theoretical underpinnings, empirical support, and strategies they suggest, and goes on to analyze their limitations and suggest alternative frameworks.

Since the landmark study of Bowers (1964), where 75 percent of five thousand students at ninety-nine colleges and universities admitted to cheating at least once, the figures have not changed much. More recent estimates range from 70 percent to 80 percent, with a peak of 95 percent of students admitting to cheating (Brown & Emmett, 2001; McCabe & Trevino, 1993; Stern & Havlicek, 1986; Whitley, 1998). Faculty, educational developers, student affairs professionals, and higher education researchers have all devoted effort, resources, and programs to reduce cheating, but given these figures, the return on investment of such initiatives is disheartening.

This chapter explores possible reasons for this disconnect. To understand the limitations of current approaches, it is helpful for faculty developers to understand the theoretical frameworks that have been used to explain academic dishonesty and their origination. This chapter is divided into three sections. The first section reviews the theoretical frameworks scholars currently use to conceptualize academic integrity and the research supporting them, as well as their fundamental limitations. The second section proposes alternative ways to think about cheating, and the last section addresses the implications for educational development.

Current Frameworks

In my review of the literature on cheating and academic integrity, five theoretical frameworks are the most common: (1) deterrence theory, (2) rational choice theory, (3) neutralization theory, (4) planned behavior theory, and (5) situational ethics. Before I describe them, some caveats are in order.

First, as in every field that investigates stigmatized behavior, research subjects will understate their participation in such behaviors or deny them altogether. Although it is possible to employ research techniques that reduce such positive response bias, it is generally not possible to eliminate it altogether. Second, studies of cheating may not be directly comparable. The researcher can avoid positive response bias by not asking about cheating directly. Some studies ask about cheating behaviors observed in peers, while others ask about hypothetical scenarios ("Given this situation, would you engage in this behavior?"). Still others set up experimental situations where the researchers themselves can observe cheating. Diversity of methods yields diversity of results, creating a problem for comparability across research studies. I have relied heavily on Whitley's meta-analysis (1998) of 107 studies of the correlates of cheating and effect size measures for each correlate to obviate the problem of comparing studies conducted using different methods. The results of his meta-analysis are more compelling than the results of each individual study. I use his estimates as measures of support of the theoretical frameworks I consider.

Finally, and most important, the theoretical perspectives that have informed research on academic dishonesty thus far all share a common bias: they are all derived from theories of criminal behavior. Although some people may philosophically disagree with conceptualizing students as delinquents, this bias also creates a pragmatic problem. Criminal theories are theories of deviant behavior, designed to explain why a few individuals deviate from behavior that the rest of the population observes as normative and ethical. When more than 70 percent of students admit to having cheated, it is not clear who is deviant and who is in the norm anymore, and these theories lose much of their descriptive and predictive power.

Deterrence Theory

The deterrence theory posits that cheating is a function of the severity of the consequences (Zimring & Hawkins, 1973). If we want to curtail a certain behavior, we should punish it with consequences severe enough to discourage students, including failing the assignment, failing the course, academic probation, or even expulsion. Research on the correlates of cheating behaviors partly supports the deterrence theory in that students' self-perception of their ability to cheat has a medium positive effect on cheating (Whitley, 1998). In other words, if students think they are able to engage in their behavior without consequences, they are likely to do so. Here and throughout this chapter, the strength of an effect (small, medium, and large) is calculated according to the rules for the d statistic, a measure of effect size based on the standardized mean difference between cheaters and noncheaters on a given variable (Cohen, 1988).

The approach suggested by deterrence theory has some practical problems. Professors can dole out punishment with consequences only at the assignment and course level; therefore centralized academic review boards must lead in increasing the severity of the consequences. However, instructors are reluctant to report cases to their academic review board because of the extra effort involved (Schneider, 1999). Research also shows that the effectiveness and intensity of deterrents varies among cultures. For instance, Western students asked to list deterrents to cheating are very likely to mention expulsion as the ultimate deterrent. In Japan, students asked the same question are more likely than American students to focus on public humiliation—for example, making cheaters use only red ink pens to write for the rest of the year (Burns, Davis, & Hoshino, 1998). Therefore, responses to academic dishonesty are not universal but should be tailored to the particular culture of the institution.

Rational Choice Theory

The rational choice theory treats dishonest actions as the result of decisions that rational agents make (Cornish & Clarke, 1986). The eventual course of action is chosen after weighing the advantages and disadvantages of all possible alternatives. Therefore, deciding to cheat results from a cost-benefit analysis. The factors involved in the decision might include the effort involved in cheating rather than studying the material, the expected improvement in the grade due to cheating, the stakes involved in the assignment, and so on. Of course, the severity of the possible consequences also factors in, making the strategies suggested by deterrence theory, as well as its limitations, relevant to rational choice theory as well. Rational choice theory finds further support in the research on the correlates of cheating. The risk of being caught has a medium negative effect on cheating, the fear of punishment has a small negative effect, and the importance of the outcome has a medium positive effect (Whitley, 1998).

Neutralization Theory

Other frameworks conceptualize students as moral beings as well as rational ones. Cost-benefit considerations aside, surely the effect of engaging in morally wrong acts should have psychological consequences on those who do so. In fact, earlier research on academic dishonesty focused on the so-called self-esteem cycle (Aronson & Mettee, 1968; Ward, 1986). Cheaters were believed to start out with low-self esteem. They didn't think they would do well on the task, and they were not invested in maintaining a positive image with the instructor, because they didn't think he or she believed in their abilities. When they engaged in cheating, the knowledge of their morally wrong behavior further lowered their self-esteem, precipitating future iterations of this vicious cycle. This cycle unravels in view of the finding that, even though it is true that reported past cheating has a large positive effect on future cheating, it is *not* true that cheaters have low self-esteem (Whitley, 1998).

Neutralization theory (Sykes & Matza, 1957), on the other hand, hypothesizes that students are able to engage in morally wrong acts without damage to their self-concept if they can rationalize those acts and think of them as morally neutral rather than wrong. Research on the correlates of cheating has found that neutralization techniques have a medium to large positive effect on cheating, thus lending support to this theory (Whitley, 1998). Out of the classic neutralization techniques used by delinquents, Storch, Storch, and Clark (2002) have identified four neutralization techniques used by college students:

1. Some cheaters might deny responsibility, saying they did nothing wrong or they didn't mean to and were influenced by circumstances beyond their control.

2. Others might deny consequences, claiming that cheating is no big deal or that it is a "victimless crime."

3. Still others might blame the authorities, saying it's the professor's fault if they have to cheat because the tests are always unfair, or professors too probably cheated as students.

4. Some might invoke a more compelling value system or higher loyalties that supersede academic rules, such as the value of helping friends pass the course.

This framework posits that efforts to prevent cheating should focus on deneutralizing it, perhaps emphasizing the consequences of various kinds of academic dishonesty (such as fabrication or falsification of data) to the scientific and intellectual community or stressing personal responsibility and agency.

Planned Behavior Theory

Planned behavior theory posits that cheating happens as a result of the opportunity as well as the intention to cheat (Ajzen, 1969). Therefore, efforts to prevent cheating should also act on both situational and behavioral factors. Instructors who reduce opportunities to cheat by being more vigilant during exams may only create frustrated cheaters who still have every intention to cheat at the next available opportunity. Proponents of planned behavior theory would focus their efforts both on prevention and on educating people about the value of academic integrity. Research on the correlates of cheating support both sides of the planned behavior theory. On the opportunity side, empty seats between students and multiple forms of the same test during exams have a medium and small negative effect on cheating, respectively. Conversely, letting students sit in the back of the room and letting them sit next to their friends have a small and medium positive effect on cheating, respectively. On the intention side, perception of a moral obligation to avoid cheating has a medium negative effect (Whitley, 1998).

Situational Ethics

Some people have raised the question of whether students cheat in response to extraordinary circumstances, where breaking the usual rules of ethical behavior is possibly justified. Consider the hypothetical situation of a student who needs to decide whether to help his foreign-born girlfriend cheat on an exam. He knows that she is on academic probation and that if she fails this test she will be expelled from the university, lose her student visa, and be deported back to her country, where her family will force her into an arranged marriage. He has a tough dilemma, and it is not clear which choice will lead to the best outcome. Situational ethics posits that such unique situations should be decided on the basis of a unique set of considerations that don't normally apply to other situations (Fletcher, 1966).

However, the situational ethics framework does not have empirical support. The high incidence of reported cheating suggests that students don't cheat in response to extreme—and therefore rare—circumstances, where breaches of academic integrity would possibly be understandable. In fact, reported past cheating has a large positive effect on cheating (Whitley, 1998). The premise that students use one set of ethical rules for most aspects of their life but suspend them in a few situations such as cheating is also undermined by findings; in their study of business students from six universities who worked a part-time or full-time job in the past five years, Nonis and Swift (2001) found a moderate to strong correlation between the frequency of academic dishonesty and the frequency of workplace dishonesty. The workplace dishonesty behaviors they considered included using office supplies for personal use, leaving early when the boss was absent, calling in sick when well, padding an expense report, or taking credit for someone else's work. Similar results hold for other populations, such as engineering students (Carpenter, Harding, & Finelli, 2006).

Limitations of Current Approaches and Need for New Ones

The conceptual frameworks discussed so far and the empirical support they enjoy add to our understanding of cheating in higher education. Yet these theories have not given us tools to counteract cheating effectively. As mentioned previously, the reason these frameworks inevitably fall short is that they are actually theories of criminal behavior, with a less-than-perfect fit to academic situations.

That students do not conceptualize cheating as a criminal act is apparent from the research on perceptions of what constitutes cheating. Although most people agree on a few clear-cut situations (stealing a paper from a friend, fabricating research results, buying a paper from the Internet and submitting it as your own), gray areas and disagreement in perception exist not only between faculty and students but also among groups of faculty and groups of students. Different groups attribute varying degrees of seriousness to certain actions, such as submitting the same paper for two classes, referencing an article without having read it, paraphrasing words without attribution, or collaborating inappropriately (Higbee & Thomas, 2002).

Cross-cultural research highlights even more discrepancies in perceptions of the seriousness of certain behaviors. In a study involving 885 students from the United States, Russia, the Netherlands, and Israel, Magnus, Polterovich, Danilov, and Savvateev (2002) presented a scenario in which "Student C reports to the departmental office that student A, while taking an exam, copied answers from student B's paper with the consent of student B" (p. 126). The researchers asked the students to rate the behavior of all three characters. As expected, the ratings for student A (the cheater) ranged from slightly negative to negative, those for student B (the friend) ranged from negative to slightly positive, and those for student C (the whistleblower) ranged from neutral to very negative. Neutralization techniques can explain the positive ratings for student B and negative ratings for student C, where the former was rewarded for being a good friend and the latter was punished for not exhibiting solidarity. Interestingly, the U.S. average for student C was the only neutral rating; all other countries rated him negatively.

The high variability of judgment across students and instructors together with the high prevalence of cheating exposes the limitations of the current approaches to academic dishonesty and the need for alternative modes of conceptualizing cheating. We turn now to discussion of some possibilities.

Cheating as Ignorance or Confusion About Instructor's Expectations

Certain behaviors that instructors classify as cheating can actually stem from unarticulated expectations, especially those behaviors regarding plagiarism and collaboration. Misconceptions about plagiarism abound; for instance, many students think it is acceptable to quote without attribution if they do not use the actual language (Wilhoit, 1994). Collaboration policies have incredible variability across courses, from no collaboration allowed to collaboration encouraged, to rules such as the "Gilligan's Island collaboration policy" common in computer science departments (for an example, see Rutgers University, 2009). If this is the problem, instructors can easily obviate it by articulating and clarifying their expectations, policies, and the rationale behind them.

Cheating as Learned Behavior

By not explaining the value of academic integrity and not enforcing consequences for cheating, perhaps the environment in which students have been educated so far reinforces cheating and actually socializes them to do it. Given the prevalence of cheating, it is apparent that students do indeed grow up in a culture of cheating. Research on the correlates of cheating supports the learned behavior hypothesis because cheating norms on campus have a medium-to-large positive effect on the behavior (Whitley, 1998). If we subscribe to the learned behavior theory, then reducing cheating requires changing the campus culture.

The most effective known mechanism for changing the culture is introducing honor codes, which have a medium-to-large effect in reducing cheating (McCabe & Trevino, 1993; McCabe, Trevino, & Butterfield,

1999; Whitley, 1998). Pure honor codes have four defining features (Melendez, 1985):

1. A written pledge to academic integrity that each student signs
2. Significant student involvement in academic review boards in charge of academic integrity violations
3. Unproctored exams
4. A clause that obliges students to report violations they learn about or observe

Modified honor codes involve some subset of the four elements, and predictably they are less effective than pure honor codes but better than no code at all (McCabe & Pavela, 2000). Though the most controversial, the reporting clause seems to be the most effective (McCabe, Trevino, & Butterfield, 2001).

Cheating as a Coping Strategy in a Stressful Environment

We need to acknowledge that students, especially millennials, are under tremendous pressure to achieve (Howe & Strauss, 2000). This pressure comes from parental expectations, the rising cost of tuition, societal emphasis on grades, and a tighter job market. In the face of such pressure, cheating might be a way for a student to keep head above water in spite of the best intentions. Research on the correlates of cheating lends support to this hypothesis. In fact, achievement motivation has a small positive effect on cheating, while external pressure to achieve high grades, perceived workload, and perceived competition all have a medium positive effect on cheating (Whitley, 1998).

Cheating as Professional Development

Unfortunately, some recent public scandals have demonstrated that people can cheat their way to the top and profit, while many others suffers as a result. Some students might make sense of events such as the Enron and other corporate and political scandals by deciding that cheating skills are essential for professional success, and that higher education is the perfect setting in which to develop and hone them. Almost twenty years ago, Moffatt (1990) warned that the university is "a place where cheating comes almost as natural as breathing, where it's an academic skill almost as important as reading, writing, and math" (p. 2). Sadly, the literature supports this speculation. Business undergraduates have long been documented as cheating at a higher rate than other students (Bowers, 1964), but recent research documents that even MBA students do the same (McCabe, Butterfield, & Trevino, 2006). Ghoshal (2005) has argued that "by propagating ideologically inspired amoral theories, business schools have actively freed their students from any sense of moral responsibility" (p. 76).

Cheating as a Developmental Stage

Might cheating be just a stage that most students naturally outgrow once they become professionals and see a more direct link between actions and their consequences? During my workshops on academic integrity, several instructors invariably come forth and volunteer their "confessions of a reformed cheater." Research on the correlates of cheating lends some support to the developmental hypothesis. Students' age has a moderate negative effect on cheating, as does marital status; married students tend to cheat less. Number of hours per week employed has a small negative effect on cheating, financial support from parents has a small positive effect, and living off campus as opposed to on campus has a small negative effect (Whitley, 1998). All these variables taken together point to the fact that the more maturity, independence, and responsibility students develop, the less they cheat.

This developmental hypothesis also implies a developmental strategy: helping students reach a higher level of maturity sooner by giving them more responsibility for their own lives.

Cheating as a Game

Game theory (von Neumann & Morgenstern, 1944) is a mathematical formalization of strategic situations among two or more players who have at their disposal a set of strategies, or moves, that they can use toward the goal of maximizing their individual payoff. Each individual move has a payoff that is dependent on the other player's move. In this vein, a student has several moves available during an exam—for example, attempt to solve the problem on his own, look over another student's test, or reach for his cheat sheet. The game is sequential in that each student move triggers the proctor's moves. For example, if the student looks over another student's test and the proctor sees him doing so, the proctor can ignore it, give a warning, or fail the student for the exam. If given a warning, the student can heed it or ignore it and try again. If the student is eventually failed for cheating, he can still do nothing or plead, cry, appeal the decision to the academic review board, and so on. Depending on the value the student associates with each possible outcome, and also depending on the probability the student ascribes to the proctor's moves, the student can find the optimal path through this game. The game reaches equilibrium if the players, in trying to maximize their payoff, arrive at a sequence of moves from which neither derives an advantage by deviating. The current high level of cheating, which has been fairly stable for forty years, can be interpreted as an aggregate equilibrium between students and instructors' current strategies.

The game theory approach is similar to the rational choice theory, but it has two main differences. In game theory, the instructor is also a player, with a set of strategies to use and the option of suddenly changing strategy or even affecting the payoffs. The payoffs can be modeled to incorporate a number of variables. For instance, Magnus et al. (2002) suggest that the social cost of going against the grain of the cheating culture on campus could be incorporated in the payoff function. The second difference is that game theory makes no ethical or moral claims on the situation and thus is likely closer to many students' thinking.

Despite the promise of the game-theory approach, scholars have not yet applied it to student cheating, so I have been unable to locate an empirical analysis of cheating through this theoretical lens.

Implications for Educational Development

In many institutions, educational developers lead the campus community in conversation about academic integrity. We have opportunities in several areas. First, we can push for efficient and transparent processes for our academic review boards. In time, this effort would encourage more instructors to pursue breaches of academic integrity. Second, we can give faculty more effective countermeasures to cheating. When instructors discuss cheating prevention, they often focus on decreasing the opportunities to cheat, especially in the wake of new technologies that promote cheating, such as calculators and phones that can store documents and give access to the Internet. Instead, we can remind faculty to act on the intention side, encouraging them to think of interventions to reduce students' inclination to cheat, such as educating students about the far-reaching consequences of academic dishonesty. Using the game theory approach, we can ask instructors to think about how they are increasing or decreasing the payoffs for certain courses of action with the messages they explicitly or implicitly communicate in their courses. Third, partnering with student affairs and health services professionals, we can work to equip students with better coping strategies to deal with stress, such as time management skills, holistic wellness programs, and the like. Fourth, we can prompt the administration to review overload policies. We know increased workload leads to more cheating, so we should be thinking about how many credits or units per semester we allow students to take. Finally, we can engage the campus community in conversations about honor codes. Apart from personality variables, which we can't control, honor codes reduce cheating more than all the situational factors. Yet their adoption has been very slow. Our signature skill set—listening actively, bringing in various constituencies, reconciling conflicting viewpoints, and gradually building consensus—can surely help here.

As we support our faculty in the scholarship of teaching and learning, we can help our colleagues document and disseminate classroom interventions that work in preventing cheating. More broadly and importantly, as we continue to promote creation of learning experiences that meaningfully engage students and call for authentic assessments, we help transform the educational system in ways that make cheating inefficient and undesirable. Undoubtedly, cheating is a daunting problem to solve, but educational development has a lot to offer and can effect significant change.

REFERENCES

Ajzen, I. (1969). The prediction of behavior intentions in a choice situation. *Journal of Experimental Psychology, 5*(4), 400–416.

Aronson, E., & Mettee, D. (1968). Dishonest behavior as a function of differential levels of induced self-esteem. *Journal of Personality and Social Psychology, 9*(2), 121–127.

Bowers, W. J. (1964). *Student dishonesty and its control in college.* New York: Columbia University, Bureau of Applied Social Research.

Brown, B., & Emmett, D. (2001). Explaining the variations in the level of academic dishonesty in studies of college students: Some new evidence. *College Student Journal, 35*(4), 529–538.

Burns, S., Davis, S., & Hoshino, J. (1998). Academic dishonesty: A delineation of cross-cultural patterns. *College Student Journal, 32*(4), 590–596.

Carpenter, D., Harding, T., & Finelli, C. (2006). The implications of academic dishonesty in undergraduate engineering on professional ethical behavior. *Proceedings of the 2006 World Environmental and Water Resources Congress.* Red Hook, NY: Curran Associates.

Cohen, J. (1988). *Statistical power analysis for the behavioral sciences* (2nd ed.). Hillsdale, NJ: Erlbaum.

Cornish, D., & Clarke, R. (1986). *The reasoning criminal: Rational choice perspectives on offending.* New York: Springer-Verlag.

Fletcher, J. (1966). *Situational ethics*. Philadelphia: Westminster Press.

Ghoshal, S. (2005). Bad management theories are destroying good management practice. *Academy of Management Learning and Education, 4*(1), 75–91.

Higbee, J., & Thomas, P. (2002). Student and faculty perceptions of behaviors that constitute cheating. *NASPA Journal, 40*(1), 39–52.

Howe, N., & Strauss, W. (2000). *Millennials rising: The next great generation.* New York: Vintage.

Magnus, J., Polterovich, V., Danilov, D., & Savvateev, A. (2002). Tolerance of cheating: An analysis across countries. *Journal of Economic Education, 33*(2), 125–135.

McCabe, D., Butterfield, K., & Trevino, L. (2006). Academic dishonesty in graduate business programs: Prevalence, causes, and proposed action. *Academy of Management Learning and Education, 5*(3), 294–305.

McCabe, D., & Pavela, G. (2000). Some good news about academic integrity. *Change, 32*(5), 32–38.

McCabe, D., & Trevino, L. (1993). Academic dishonesty: Honor codes and other contextual influences. *Journal of Higher Education, 64*, 522–538.

McCabe, D., Trevino, L., & Butterfield, K. (1999). Academic integrity in honor code and non-honor code environments: A qualitative investigation. *Journal of Higher Education, 70*(2), 211–234.

McCabe, D., Trevino, L., & Butterfield, K. (2001). Dishonesty in academic environments: The influence of peer reporting requirements. *Journal of Higher Education, 72*(1), 2–45.

Melendez, B. (1985). *Honor code study*. Cambridge, MA: Harvard University Press.

Moffatt, M. (1990). *Undergraduate cheating*. Unpublished manuscript, Rutgers University, New Brunswick, New Jersey. (ERIC Document Reproduction Service No. ED334921)

Nonis, S., & Swift, C. (2001). An examination of the relationship between academic dishonesty and workplace dishonesty: A multicampus investigation. *Journal of Education for Business, 77*(2), 69–77.

Rutgers University. (2009). *198:415 compilers, spring 2009: Academic integrity.* Retrieved March 2, 2009, from http://remus.rutgers.edu/cs415/academicInteg.html

Schneider, A. (1999, January 22). Why professors don't do more to stop students who cheat. *Chronicle of Higher Education*, pp. A8–A10.

Stern, E., & Havlicek, L. (1986). Academic misconduct: Results of faculty and undergraduate student surveys. *Journal of Allied Health, 15*(2), 129–142.

Storch, J., Storch, E., & Clark, P. (2002). Academic dishonesty and neutralization theory: A comparison of intercollegiate athletes and nonathletes. *Journal of College Student Development, 43*(6), 921–930.

Sykes, G. M., & Matza, D. (1957). Techniques of neutralization: A theory of delinquency. *American Sociological Review, 22*(6), 664–670.

von Neumann, J., & Morgenstern, O. (1944). *Theory of games and economic behavior.* Princeton, NJ: Princeton University Press.

Ward, D. (1986). Self-esteem and dishonest behavior revisited. *Journal of Social Psychology, 126*(6), 709–713.

Whitley, B. (1998). Factors associated with cheating among college students: A review. *Research in Higher Education, 39*(3), 235–274.

Wilhoit, S. (1994). Helping students avoid plagiarism. *College Teaching, 42*(4), 161–164.

Zimring, F. E., & Hawkins, G. J. (1973). *Deterrence: The legal threat in crime control.* Chicago: University of Chicago Press.

ENHANCING OUR PROGRAMMING

15

ENGAGING FACULTY IN CONVERSATIONS ABOUT TEACHING THROUGH A RESEARCH PROPOSAL WORKSHOP

Susanna Calkins, Denise Drane, Northwestern University

Faculty who consider themselves primarily researchers can be difficult to engage in faculty development activities. However, as agencies such as the National Science Foundation now require educational activities in research grants, proposal writing may represent a new avenue for engaging research faculty in their teaching. In this chapter, we outline an innovative workshop on writing the pedagogical component of a grant proposal that was developed for faculty at Northwestern University. During the workshop, while learning how to structure an education plan for their grant, faculty engaged in a lively discussion about formulating learning objectives and aligning them with pedagogical methods and activities, assessments, and evaluation strategies.

Because teaching and research are often viewed as distinct academic practices in higher education (Brew & Boud, 1995; Colbeck, 1998; Wolverton, 1998), many faculty developers may find it difficult to reach beyond the "converted"—faculty who value teaching and learning—to reel in the "unconverted," faculty who view themselves primarily as researchers (Brew, 2003; Light, 2003). Over the last few years, funding agencies such as the National Science Foundation (NSF) and the National Institutes of Health (NIH) have begun to require educational activities in research grant proposals and evaluation of those activities. Yet although many funding agencies and institutions offer extensive tutorials and workshops devoted to grant writing generally, there are few readily available resources that faculty can turn to for assistance in developing the educational components of the grant.

Although handbooks and manuals devoted to grant writing abound, some of which may touch on writing the pedagogical component of a grant (Frankel & Wallen, 2000), little information is readily available on the Internet or even in scholarly databases. Indeed, a great deal of the Web-based information focuses on common grant writing tips (start early, follow instructions, pay attention to deadlines, and so on) that, though undoubtedly useful in their own right, will do little to help faculty struggling to put together the pedagogical component of a grant. Bordage and Dawson (2003), for example, offer eight steps and twenty-eight questions that are designed to help a researcher in the health sciences construct a strong study and viable proposal, but they do not explicitly advise how to structure the evaluation, let alone a pedagogical component.

In response to these new grant requirements and the lack of available resources, the Searle Center for Teaching Excellence at Northwestern University has received many requests from faculty to help them develop the pedagogical components of their grants. Demand for this service has increased over the past five years, a trend that has opened the door to rich discussion on teaching and learning with faculty who otherwise would not request a consultation about teaching.

Recognizing grant writing assistance as an alternative means of engaging faculty in faculty development, and to meet the demand, we developed a faculty workshop focused on designing the pedagogical component of a grant proposal. Much has been written in faculty development literature about engaging faculty in significant discussions about their teaching and learning as it relates to a specific learning context (Gillespie, Hilsen, & Wadsworth, 2002; Sorcinelli, Austin, Eddy, & Beach, 2006) and through the Scholarship of Teaching and Learning. But it seems that no one has addressed the topic through grant writing. We saw this as a novel and innovative way to bring new faculty through our doors and to enthuse the "unconverted" about their teaching. A workshop on issues on writing pedagogical components of grants may represent a new means of engaging research faculty in meaningful conversation about teaching and learning.

The Design and Activities of the Workshop

Northwestern enrolls about fifteen thousand students, half of whom are undergraduates, and employs approximately twenty-five hundred full-time faculty, with close to two-thirds drawn from the medical school. Research and scholarly publications weigh heavily in promotion and tenure decisions, and in many fields grant getting is considered essential for continued employment.

The workshop was one of eight faculty development workshops offered monthly by the Searle Center throughout the academic year. Like the other workshops in the series, it was two hours long; was facilitated by two center staff members; was open to faculty, staff, and postdocs across the university; and featured both interactive presentations and hands-on activities. Unlike other faculty workshops, however, its content did not focus directly on instructor–student interactions, such as engaging students in large class settings, using clickers in class, or facilitating discussion.

We offered the workshop twice in the same calendar year, but in two separate academic years. The workshop was well attended and received positive evaluations from faculty (discussed more fully below). Combining both workshops, we had twenty-seven participants (fourteen men, thirteen women) who drew from a range of disciplines and units across campus. Fourteen faculty members came from medicine and engineering; six faculty came from social sciences, music, and humanities; four staff members came from various administrative units, and three were graduate students (two from engineering and one from the humanities). A handful (seven participants) had attended other workshops or sessions offered by our center, but most had not attended a session before or at least had not in the four years since we started keeping individual participation records.

Workshop Goals and Objectives

We designed the workshop to furnish participants with (1) detailed information on how to structure an educational plan and evaluation within a grant proposal, (2) tips on avoiding common mistakes in educational grant writing, and (3) information on additional grant-writing resources at our university and elsewhere. In terms of our workshop objectives, we wanted our participants to be able to examine and revise the objectives, rationale, and methods described in a grant proposal and gauge their overall alignment, clarity, and precision. We also wanted them to design an evaluation plan that was aligned constructively with the educational objectives of the grant (which refer to the specific and concrete aims that are meant to be achieved by the grant) and that in turn used appropriate quantitative and qualitative research methods (Light, Cox, & Calkins, 2009).

Description and Structure of Workshop

Both offerings of the workshop, titled "Developing an Effective Pedagogical Component for Your Grant Proposal," followed the same facilitator plan, as displayed in Table 15.1. We opened the session by asking participants to share their reasons for attending the workshop and their experience in writing the pedagogical sections of a grant. We found that our participants' experience with grant writing varied considerably. Some had never pursued a grant at all, while others had written grants before, although not necessarily with an educational component; nor were they necessarily funded. Although "getting funding" was commonly expressed as an important reason for attending the workshop, the seriousness of this pursuit seemed to vary considerably among our participants. Some faculty, particularly those in engineering and science fields, were actively planning to submit, or had already submitted, a proposal with a pedagogical component, viewing it as essential to their research and position at the university. Other participants were simply gathering information for future grant opportunities.

Table 15.1. Grant Writing Workshop Plan

Session	Activity	Description
I. 20 min.	Introductions and icebreaker	In small groups, participants discuss: *What brought you to the workshop today? What experiences have you had writing the pedagogical sections of a grant?*
	Overview	Facilitators outline workshop's purpose, learning goals, structure, and activities.
II. 30 min.	Developing the pedagogical section of your grant	Facilitators focus on aligning project objectives, methods, and assessment in proposal.
	Case study	In small groups, participants clarify pedagogical objectives and activities drawn from a real proposal. Small groups share their suggestions for improvement with large group.
III. 60 min.	Key aspects of evaluation	Facilitator identifies common evaluation myths and describes a common evaluation structure.
	Case study exercise	In small groups, participants identify formative and summative assessments in different cases.
	Broader impact statement	Faculty expert or facilitator explains the components of the broader impact statement and identifies relevant resources.
IV. 10 min.	Final thoughts	How Searle Center staff can help Workshop evaluation

We then explained the general structure of the workshop, which consisted mainly of our interactive presentations and two case-study activities during which the participants would work together in small groups. In the first case study, we asked our participants to analyze the pedagogical section of a grant proposal, focusing their critique on learning objectives and pedagogical activities. In the second case study, we homed in on the evaluation plan, asking our participants to generate formative and summative assessments for specific educational activities. We concluded the workshop by discussing the "broader impact" section of proposals and educational activities that could be used to demonstrate the far-reaching benefits of research programs. In the first workshop offering, we also asked a faculty member with expertise in writing about broader impacts to give advice on the process.

Aligning Objectives and Activities

Before we began the first case study, we explained the notion of alignment to our participants—that is, the fit among the funding agency goals, project goals, project objectives, project methods and activities, and project assessment and evaluation, as shown in Figure 15.1. Just as alignment is crucial in designing a course (Biggs, 2003; Light et al., 2009), so too is the alignment of educational objectives, educational activities, and evaluation.

The overall goals of the funding agency and the project lay outside the scope of our workshop, but we did spend a few minutes clarifying the difference between goals and objectives. Goals, we explained, tend to be large statements of what the grant seeker hopes to accomplish; they create the

Figure 15.1. Aligning the Pedagogical Component of a Grant Proposal

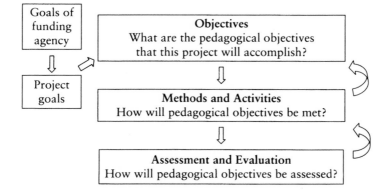

setting for the proposal and must match the goals of the funding organization. They are not necessarily measurable. Objectives, on the other hand,
are operational, measurable, and specific as to the outcomes that the grant
seeker intends to accomplish (Light et al., 2009). We asked our participants
to consider several sample goals and objectives, such as those for an imag-
ined grant on doctoral training in the biosciences (Table 15.2).

The First Case Study: Educational Objectives and Activities

We asked our participants to read over and comment on the case study in
small groups of three and four, an activity known to facilitate active learning and critical reflection (Bligh, 2000; Light et al., 2009). The case study
had been modified from the educational component of a real—but heavily
disguised—proposal for a major science foundation grant written by a faculty member (see Exhibit 15.1 for a condensed version of the case study).

In their small groups, participants considered whether the educational
objectives identified in the grant were clear and whether the rationale
clearly stated the significance of the problem. They further examined the
proposed activities for their alignment with the proposed objectives.
Lastly, we asked them how the proposal could be improved.

Our participants identified a number of crucial problems: lack of definition of the problem to be addressed, lack of specificity in the rationale
for addressing the problem and the stated objectives, lack of alignment
between objectives and activities, and lack of support for methods.

**Table 15.2. Sample Goals and Objectives: "Doctoral Training
Program in the Biosciences"**

Goal 1: To increase the number of students from underrepresented groups
admitted to doctoral programs in the biosciences at the university

Objective 1.1   Revise current admissions criteria

Objective 1.2   Conduct a workshop on revised admissions criteria for admis-
                   sion committees at the university

Goal 2: To increase the number of students from underrepresented groups
retained in doctoral programs in the biosciences at our university

Objective 2.1   Implement a mentoring program in which faculty serve as
                   mentors for doctoral students

Objective 2.2   Implement a peer-led collaborative learning program for doc-
                   toral students enrolled in the biosciences

They also viewed the language as imprecise and even misleading in parts. For example, several participants suggested that an expression such as "raising public awareness" lacks clarity and is virtually meaningless. Others suggested that a reviewer would stop reading when the grant seeker stated he wished to "continue the university's successful practice" because it wouldn't be necessary to fund successful practices.

Exhibit 15.1. Clarifying Pedagogical Objectives and Activities: A Case Study

3. Education and training. The *education objective* of the proposed program is to train future Ph.D.s to become leaders in research and industrial development in related fields who will help raise public awareness about environmental issues, and who will act as liaisons to the public to explain these issues.

3-1. Leaders on research and industrial development. We will continue the university's successful practice of integrating multidisciplinary research and application, using internships, international collaboration, teamwork, and mentoring. We will introduce a new concept of *Academic Task Squads* in Ph.D. training. Each academic squad will comprise several teams, made up of members from different engineering disciplines, who will each work on a relevant engineering problem involving theory, experiment, and product design. Each multidisciplinary academic squad will develop one line of products. To ensure our success, we will:

1. Create and modify new and existing courses to ensure a multidisciplinary multiscale engineering curriculum that effectively includes new knowledge.
2. Create teams with at least three members possessing the required expertise for the problem, with at least one member from outside the university.
3. Obtain summer internships for graduate students in our Engineering Fellows (EF) program working in industrial or government labs. Through such experience, our EFs will better appreciate the significance of their work and acquire the skills to be leaders in research and development. Each student working with his or her advising committee will develop an improvement plan, which will include (1) presenting research in the weekly EF seminars; (2) maintaining regular contact with his or her industrial advisor/mentor; and (3) designing a website that offers a means to exchange and search for research information.

3-2. Public liaisons. Even though this environmental issue is important, the public has been slow to act. Our Engineering Fellows, as scientists trained to explore such environmental issues, will also raise the awareness of the general public, by visiting local schools. This will attract high school students and teachers to work in our labs, which in the long run will help society welcome environmental reforms in the future.

Despite the many problems identified with the proposal, participants did identify ways to enhance the work. They recommended that the faculty member provide more specifics (What kinds of courses would be created or modified? What are the nature and scope of the problem being addressed? How specifically can the program raise public awareness?), strengthen the rationale by more fully describing the problem and its importance (Why is it necessary for future Ph.D.s to become leaders in research and industrial development and to raise public awareness about environmental issues?), furnish a rationale for the educational activities used to achieve the educational objectives, and formulate measurable objectives and a plan with a defined timeline (identify expectations and guidelines for academic squad leaders within six months; complete preliminary product line within one year). Several participants also suggested that the faculty member scale back expectations a bit and make the overall goals and objectives more manageable. Almost everyone agreed, too, that the writing should be more concise and omit jargon.

The Second Case Study: Developing an Evaluation Plan

The second part of our workshop focused on evaluation. Before turning to the second case study, we identified some common myths about evaluation. First, many proposal writers assume there is one standard evaluation format. We receive many calls from faculty, often within a few days of the grant deadline, asking if we can send them a paragraph about evaluation that they can then insert into their proposals. As we explain, every project has its own objectives and the evaluation must be aligned with those objectives, so no single magic, one-size-fits-all paragraph about evaluation will work; each project requires a uniquely tailored evaluation plan. Second, because many faculty assume that evaluation costs very little, they consistently underestimate the budget allotment. We try to disabuse them of this notion; reviewers may not take seriously proposals that do not allot sufficient resources for conducting the evaluation. We suggest allocating it 5–10 percent of the total budget. Third, many faculty dismiss the evaluation as just a "hoop jumping" exercise that does not have any practical value.

In framing the second case study, we described a simple evaluation structure in which each objective and the activities designed to achieve it are assessed in terms of process (formative assessment) and outcomes (summative assessment). Assessing process—that is, implementation of the educational activity—might include examining the overall integrity of the program (the number of sessions attended by participants, group size in a small-group learning program) using administrative data, observations (of participants, classrooms), or feedback from key participants (surveys, focus groups, interviews, reflective journals). Assessing outcomes (impact) would look at products (materials created, courses delivered, curricula developed, evidence of research activity) or student outcomes. Such outcomes might emphasize learning as measured in multiple ways (course grades and retention; learning inventories; purpose-built instruments, think-aloud protocols), or they might also focus on attitudes, motivation, or other behaviors or skills.

We asked our participants to focus on one of four cases. Each case had a goal, an objective, and an educational activity designed to achieve the objective. We asked participants to identify two or three formative and summative ways in which they could assess the process (implementation) and the outcomes (impact) of the program. To save space, we describe only three of the four cases in Table 15.3.

Initial Assessment of Workshop Outcomes

Our initial assessment of workshop outcomes, conducted immediately after the session concluded, indicated that our participants were very satisfied with the workshop and felt they had taken away something useful. We had our participants complete a questionnaire at the end of the workshop, asking them what they had found most valuable and what they expected to use in their grant writing. Although only fifteen completed the survey, fourteen of them (92 percent) indicated that, in terms of overall helpfulness, the workshop rated a 4 or a 5 on a 1-to-5 scale. More significantly, they identified a range of components that they found valuable, including the evaluation framework, practical examples, the explanation of goals and objectives, and various evaluation resources. We have already consulted individually with several participants on their grants, and we anticipate more of these consultations as the major funding agency deadlines grow closer.

We plan to conduct a more formal follow-up survey to gauge the effectiveness of our workshop in helping our participants write successful pedagogical components of their grants. We will also track their submissions and funding outcomes. But in an initial follow-up study, conducted eleven months after the first incarnation and five months after the second, we found that at least ten participants were working on or had submitted a grant since they participated in the workshop—most of these major NSF, NIH, or comparable large grants—with at least three being funded so far. Three participants indicated they had attended the workshop as part of their job of helping faculty secure grants. When asked about what

Table 15.3. Evaluation Case-Study-Based Activity and Participant Response

Case Study	1	2	3
Specific aim	To maximize opportunities for successful Ph.D. completion and competition for training grant awards		To prepare students to transition into competitive postdoctoral research positions and to successfully participate in academic research, administrative, and leadership positions beyond graduation
Objective	To enhance students' research skills	To provide students with a mentor to guide their professional development	To give students experience in presenting and publishing their research
Activity	Create research skills course that allows students to write proposals and present research findings	Create a mentoring program where students meet monthly with faculty mentor from their department	Require students to present research at meetings and submit work to be peer reviewed
Example of formative assessment (implementation)	• Track participant numbers • Track level and quality of participation	• Compare group with mentors with those without mentors • Track participation of mentors • Determine number and overall quality of mentoring meetings • Surveys and focus groups to identify what students gained from being mentored	• Observe students to gauge understanding and misconceptions • Interview subset of students (ex. random sample 10%)
Example of summative assessment (impact)	• Count number of proposals submitted by students • Track papers given by students • Use questionnaires (e.g., self-efficacy standard measures to gauge attitudes)	• Program retention • Time to graduation • Grades • Classes taken by students	• Student presentation • Pre- and postsurvey

aspects of the workshop they felt had helped them, most indicated that they found it helpful simply to get a better grasp of pedagogical language, and the structure associated with the evaluation component of educational-related grants.

Critical Reflections

With so few resources available on the Web or in scholarly databases, faculty are hard pressed to find out how to structure the educational component of a grant on their own. Yet even though many universities offer their faculty support in the grant-writing process, we have not seen much evidence that other institutions offer the type of workshop we did. Given the high interest generated from a similar workshop we conducted at the last Professional Organizational Development Network conference, we believe that this workshop is easily transferable to other campuses and should prove just as useful elsewhere. It has given us an innovative way to reach faculty with whom we do not otherwise connect and to engage them in conversation about teaching and learning, including formulating educational goals and learning objectives, articulating rationales for the pedagogical methods and activities chosen to achieve the objectives, and ensuring alignment among the objectives, the pedagogy, and assessment techniques. We have also been able to acquaint faculty with our other teaching-relevant programs and sessions.

For these reasons, we want to share what we have learned from doing this innovative pilot program to help other faculty developers:

1. *Faculty working on grants related to teaching and learning have not necessarily thought much about teaching and learning.* As we suspected when we first decided to put the workshop together, it strongly appealed to faculty wanting help with the pedagogical component of their grant. But we were surprised by how little these same faculty had reflected on teaching and learning. This workshop promised, to borrow a phrase, the start of a wonderful friendship with "unconverted" research-focused faculty who have never set foot through our doors. Indeed, the great majority of the participants had either never attended a workshop or not attended one in the last four years.

2. *Faculty have widely varying experience with and knowledge of evaluation.* Although we designed the case-based activities to help the participants think about different methodologies for evaluation, we spent more time than we anticipated explicating qualitative, quantitative, and mixed methods. We also explained how multiple

data sources can be used for triangulation, particularly because some faculty mistakenly think that funding agencies consider only quantitative assessments as valid. In addition, we spent more time than expected responding to faculty concerns about validity, specifically how to do valid assessments with small sample sizes that may be unable to produce statistically significant results.

3. *The language of assessment needs to be clearly articulated.* Some of our participants were confused about the meaning and goals of formative and summative assessment. We found that using "process assessment" for formative assessment and "outcome assessment" for summative assessment helped them understand the difference.

4. *"Broader impact" requires more time.* A two-hour workshop allowed too little time to address the broader impacts of the participants' proposed research. We provide a handout about what the broader impact entails, but the questions and discussion surrounding the topic suggested that it could be its own workshop.

5. *The workshop crosses disciplines.* Although many of the workshop examples and terms came from NSF and NIH grants, faculty from the social sciences and humanities reported they were able to draw out the principles and still found the workshop helpful. Because we strive to open dialogue about teaching to faculty from all disciplines, we were gratified when participants told us how much they had learned from talking to colleagues in other disciplines.

Ultimately, the changing expectations for major grants have given us a new and novel opportunity to attract and converse with faculty who do not typically focus on their teaching. The workshop offered an innovative way for us to reach faculty whom we do not usually encounter on our campus, and it gave us a way to encourage a dialogue about teaching and learning that transcends disciplines.

REFERENCES

Biggs, J. B. (2003). *Teaching for quality learning at university.* London: SRHE/ Open University Press.

Bligh, D. (2000). *What's the use of lectures?* San Francisco: Jossey-Bass.

Bordage, G., & Dawson, B. (2003). Experimental study design and grant writing in eight steps and 28 questions. *Medical Education, 37*(4), 376–385.

Brew, A. (2003). Teaching and research: New relationships and their implications for inquiry-based teaching and learning in higher education. *Higher Education Research and Development, 22*(1), 3–18.

Brew, A., & Boud, D. (1995). Teaching and research: Establishing the vital link with learning. *Higher Education, 29*(3), 261–273.

Colbeck, C. L. (1998). Merging in a seamless blend: How faculty integrate teaching and research. *Journal of Higher Education, 69*(6), 647–671.

Frankel, J. R., & Wallen, N. E. (2000). *How to design and evaluate research in education* (4th ed.). New York: McGraw-Hill.

Gillespie, K. H., Hilsen, L. R., & Wadsworth, E. C. (Eds.). (2002). *A guide to faculty development: Practical advice, examples, and resources.* Bolton, MA: Anker.

Light, G. (2003). Realizing academic development: Embedding research practice in the practice of teaching. In H. Eggins & R. MacDonald (Eds.), *The scholarship of academic development* (pp. 152–162). London: SRHE/ Open University Press.

Light, G., Cox, R., & Calkins, S. (2009). *Learning and teaching in higher education: The reflective professional.* Thousand Oaks, CA: Sage.

Sorcinelli, M. D., Austin, A. E., Eddy, P. L., & Beach, A. L. (2006). *Creating the future of faculty development: Learning from the past, understanding the present.* Bolton, MA: Anker.

Wolverton, M. (1998). Treading the tenure-track tightrope: Finding balance between research excellence and quality teaching. *Innovative Higher Education, 23*(1), 61–79.

16

DEVELOPING AND RENEWING DEPARTMENT CHAIR LEADERSHIP

THE ROLE OF A TEACHING CENTER IN ADMINISTRATIVE TRAINING

Mary C. Wright, Constance E. Cook, University of Michigan, Ann Arbor

Chris O'Neal, University of California, Irvine

Most faculty development centers offer limited resources for leadership development, and most existing programs focus on training the new chair. The key questions we address are: What role do teaching centers play in administrative professional development? How can we develop programs that assist new chairs with their immediate questions, while also promoting continued growth in institutional leadership? We present one model at the University of Michigan, initiated by the provost and organized by the Center for Research on Learning and Teaching, which involves an extensive needs assessment process, a developmentally oriented leadership training program, and an evaluation.

Department chairs play a key role in faculty development. They are well-positioned to help individual faculty develop their teaching, research, and service capacities; facilitate departmental effectiveness; and work with upper-level administrators to carry out the university's mission (Cuban, 1999; Feldman & Paulsen, 1999; Hecht, 2000; Hecht, Higgerson, Gmelch, & Tucker, 1999; Lucas, 1990; Rice & Austin, 1990; Sorcinelli, Austin, Eddy, & Beach, 2006; Walvoord et al., 2000). The benefits are also reciprocal: department heads who feel that they are effective faculty developers are more likely to stay longer in the position (Seagren, Creswell, & Wheeler, 1993).

However, many challenges exist for chairs in their roles as faculty developers. Given the intensity of the workload and frequently the short tenure of the position, many chairs often just do not have time to focus on pedagogical issues. Many of them report that in spite of their intention to improve the quality of teaching in a department or build a "culture of teaching," they are unsuccessful at doing so (Lucas, 1989; Wright, 2008). Therefore they often perceive themselves as being more supportive of faculty than do the faculty themselves (Whitt, 1991). Clearly, institutions need to ensure that this key administrative role is functioning most effectively.

In 1986, Lucas documented that little chair training was taking place in higher education, with a few notable exceptions (for instance, American Council on Education, University of Tennessee, Michigan State University, and Kansas State University). Unfortunately, both our benchmarking (described later) and the literature confirm that little has changed (Lucas, 2002). Furthermore, existing programs focus primarily on new-chair audiences, especially on managerial skills to help academic leaders with the immediate faculty–chair role transition.

The paucity of ongoing chair training raises several questions. First, is there an unmet need for programming inclusive of more experienced chairs? If so, are there key differences in the training needs of new and experienced department heads? How can instructional developers encourage continued growth and leadership potential in chairs? Finally, what are effective and efficient ways of organizing this programming, and who should be facilitating it?

In this chapter, we present a model for a developmentally oriented chair training program organized by the Center for Research on Learning and Teaching (CRLT) at the University of Michigan. The University of Michigan is a large research university, with nineteen schools and colleges. Every year, approximately thirty faculty become new chairs, and because of these recurring transitions the provost invited CRLT to design a new program. Its success stems not only from the design we describe here but also from her support and participation.

Because faculty developers have not prioritized training for department leaders (Sorcinelli et al., 2006), we begin with a discussion about how teaching centers can facilitate (and benefit from) such initiatives. We then present a model for development of a leadership program, beginning with a needs assessment that identifies the difference in perspective among new and experienced chairs, faculty, and deans. Drawing on our needs assessment findings, we describe a model for a developmental program that not only assists new chairs with their immediate ("hit the ground running") questions but also promotes their continued growth in institutional leadership skills. Finally, we describe the evaluation process and findings that CRLT used to judge the effectiveness of the program. This three-part model focuses on how faculty developers can facilitate the transition from faculty to chair, as well as ongoing administrative leadership skill development.

The Role of Teaching Centers in Chair Training

As with any university program, the first question we had to address was, Who will initiate the program? The Offices of the Provost and Human Resources (HR) are the most common locations for chair training programs. Although the University of Michigan provost's office initiated the program development process, we felt it was strategic to locate the program in CRLT, the university's teaching center—a departure from most other chair training programs. (A notable exception is Michigan State University, where the Office of Faculty and Organizational Development, which reports to the head of HR, runs the New Administrator Orientation.) Perhaps faculty development centers have not prioritized training for department leaders because they have not been given the opportunity (Sorcinelli et al., 2006).

Hecht (2000) argues that faculty developers can play a key role in supporting department chairs during their individual development from managers to leaders. Indeed, for other institutions considering an administrative leadership program, we note that this institutional location yields several organizational benefits.

First, teaching centers are usually part of the provost's office, thereby connected to the administration's current initiatives and familiar with the key issues facing the university. Because of its organizational location, a center can focus a training program on topics of special interest to the provost, and it can make connections to relevant university speakers.

Second, teaching centers routinely plan programs for various groups of faculty, so they are adept at interacting well with faculty and handling logistics. Instructional consultants know how to plan engaging programs that incorporate active learning strategies. They also know how to conduct programming that brings together faculty from many units to discuss interdisciplinary topics.

Third, and especially important for a developmentally oriented administrative leadership program, center staff members often play an interstitial role themselves. They work closely with individual faculty by providing new faculty orientations, consulting with them about their pedagogy and course design, serving their needs in center programs and workshops, and reviewing their grant applications. They also collaborate with decanal offices by helping to design curricular reform, facilitating retreats and meetings, and strategizing ways to evaluate and reward good teaching.

The advantages extend to the center as well. As Lucas (2002) notes, "Staff in faculty development centers can significantly increase their effectiveness in higher education by gaining access to academic departments and teaching chairs to promote faculty development" (pp. 158–159). Department chairs are often the missing link in the outreach and work of a center. The training serves to connect chairs with the center; chairs meet center staff and are therefore more likely to call on them for their own programming or curricular evaluation and redesign in the future. Likewise, through informal discussions during the programs, center staff members can learn about departmental needs and offer services responsively. They may also be able to weave some teaching and learning topics into the programs for administrators.

Needs Assessment Design and Findings

Other research has documented key elements of chair training programs (for example, Lucas, 1986), but a thorough needs assessment was the key to understanding what University of Michigan chairs and deans sought in a local initiative. The needs assessment was especially important because two previous attempts to establish a chair training program had proven to be unsuccessful and were discontinued after only one year. Our assessment had three stages: (1) a benchmarking study of peer institutions, (2) interviews with successful chairs, and (3) a focused survey of new chairs, experienced chairs, faculty and deans, which asked them to rank topics for a program. (This study was approved by the University of Michigan Institutional Review Board.)

Benchmarking

CRLT began by researching what the university's peer institutions were doing for chair or leadership development. A Web search, performed in 2006 and again in 2008, for "department chair training or orientation programs" discovered several training programs at community colleges across the nation, as well as a host of programs not affiliated with educational associations (for example, the Department Leadership Programs offered by the American Council on Education and the Council of

Graduate Departments of Psychology leadership training). However, we found very few department chair preparation programs at large universities.

Because in many cases internal programs such as chair training may not be advertised on the Web, we also surveyed colleagues at peer universities via email to determine if their institutions offered chair training programs. This informal survey of eighteen Big Ten and Ivy League Universities confirmed that most institutions had no centralized training program for new chairs. Notable exceptions are Cornell, Michigan State, Minnesota, Ohio State, Penn State, the University of Chicago, and Wisconsin. However, all of these programs focused primarily on new administrators.

According to our Web search and informal survey, most Big Ten and Ivy Plus institutions offer some form of support for new chairs, though this support often takes the form of written resources only (for instance, extensive resource websites for chairs at Princeton University), or it is restricted to certain units. Although more localized programs do have some advantages, a universitywide program would best encourage networking across departments and between new and experienced administrators.

Interviews with Experienced Chairs

Next, one of the authors conducted interviews with fifteen experienced chairs to identify the issues of particular concern to them and to obtain advice about an orientation and training for new chairs. The interviewees, six women and five faculty of color, represented the humanities, social sciences, sciences, quantitatively oriented fields, and professional schools. They were recommended by University of Michigan associate deans as effective departmental heads.

The new chairs universally responded with enthusiasm for a program. They talked about how the absence of an orientation had led them to seek advice from books and articles before assuming their administrative roles. However, even experienced administrators saw benefits to a training program. They endorsed the opportunity to network with their peers across disciplinary boundaries, as well as to share ways to address common issues and challenges.

In addition, chairs reacted to a list of potential topics drawn from the literature on department chair tasks, such as responsibilities related to departmental governance, faculty, budgeting, office management, curriculum, student issues, facilities management, data management, and communication with external constituencies (Hecht et al., 1999; Lucas, 1986). Out of this list, they recommended integrating several topics into the training: working with the department's key administrator, setting a vision and developing a strategic plan, working with the dean, and understanding the university. However, beyond these instrumental tasks, chairs also advised that the program prioritize collegial interaction, or topics such as effective communications, department climate, mentoring faculty, tenure and promotion, and conflict resolution. For example, one head noted that when he started his new role he thought it was about managing the budget, but he quickly learned that the job was about managing people.

Surveys

The next step in the needs assessment was to survey new chairs (defined as those who started the chair position in the current calendar year), experienced chairs, faculty of various ranks, and deans. (Key administrators, the senior staff person in academic departments, also received surveys, but these results are not presented here.) We purposively selected survey recipients from university lists of each population to get a broad spectrum of disciplines and perspectives. Table 16.1 displays the response rates. Respondents were asked to select the seven most important orientation and training topics from a list of fourteen: communicating with colleagues and running meetings; evaluating and improving teaching; managing budgets; managing conflict and dysfunctional dynamics; managing the workload; mentoring faculty; understanding the organization of the university; handling searches, hiring, and position requests; setting a vision and developing a strategic plan; space planning; managing tenure and promotion issues; understanding the university's financial picture; working with the dean; and working with a key administrator.

Interestingly, experienced administrators reported needs that differed from those of the new chairs. The new chairs' requests for programming were primarily instrumental, focusing especially on such organizational issues as managing budgets and academic hiring processes (see Table 16.2).

Table 16.1. Response Rates for Needs Assessment Survey

Survey Population	Survey Numbers and Response Rate
New chairs	8 out of 11 responded (73%)
Experienced chairs	25/38 (66%)
Faculty	35/125 (28%)
Deans	10/20 (50%)

After these top two priorities, these new administrators showed much less consensus. In contrast, experienced chairs prioritized more affectively oriented training: conflict management and interpersonal dynamics, and then tenure and promotion (human capital management). They also agreed with new chairs, though less strongly, on the importance of fiscal management (65 percent compared to 100 percent). In summary, our results confirm Hecht's comment: "While new chairs are particularly concerned about task mastery, the truth is that the attitudinal adjustments are the ones most important for chairs to make if they are to become effective leaders" (2000, p. 30). She notes that some of these key adjustments include the chair's thinking about managing human relationships, time, and articulation of purpose.

In addition to surveying new and experienced chairs, we also asked faculty and deans to rank topics. Table 16.3 shows the congruence between rankings of faculty and chairs (highlighted in light gray) and deans and chairs (highlighted in dark gray). The priorities of experienced chairs significantly overlapped with those of both deans and faculty. For example, deans and experienced department heads shared tenure and promotion, as well as conflict management, as top priorities. Likewise, experienced chairs and faculty shared tenure and promotion and budget management as key priorities. This finding suggests that experienced chairs have learned to be effective liaisons between higher-level administration and faculty. The literature has identified this "conduit" role (Lucas, 1986, p. 112)—communication between deans and faculty—as being particularly important for successful chairs (Murray & Stauffacher, 2001; Walvoord et al., 2000).

In contrast, new chairs' rankings overlapped some of those of faculty (managing budgets) and experienced chairs (managing budgets and conflict management), but there was no alignment with deans' priorities. In other

---

**Table 16.2. Comparison of New and Experienced Chairs'
Ranking of Topics**

Experienced Chairs	New Chairs
1. Managing conflicts and dysfunctional dynamics (77%)	1. Managing budgets (100%)
2. Managing budgets (65%)	2. Searches, hiring and position requests (71%)
3. Tenure and promotion (62%)	3. University organization; working with the dean; understanding university finances; managing conflicts; managing workload (tie at 57% each)

Table 16.3. Comparison of Ranking of Topics by Deans, New Chairs, Experienced Chairs, and Faculty

| | Chairs | | |
Deans	Experienced Chairs	New Chairs	Faculty
1. Mentoring faculty (100%)	1. Managing conflicts and dysfunctional dynamics (77%)	1. Managing budgets (100%)	1. Tenure and promotion (71%)
2. Tenure and promotion (89%)	2. Managing budgets (65%)	2. Searches, hiring, and position requests (71%)	2. Managing budgets (68%)
3. Managing conflicts and dysfunctional dynamics (89%)	3. Tenure and promotion (62%)	3. (Tie at 57% each): • University organization • Working with the dean • Understanding university's finances • Managing conflicts • Managing workload	3. Mentoring faculty (65%)

Note: Overlap of deans' and chairs' rankings is highlighted in dark gray, while overlap of faculty and chairs' rankings is highlighted in light gray.

words, new chairs were not yet able to straddle the perspectives of both faculty and experienced chairs, perhaps because they still had one foot in the faculty role and the other in their new administrative responsibilities (Hecht, 2006).

Overall, these rankings indicate the need for a developmentally oriented chair training program. A comparison of new and experienced chairs shows key differences in needs relative to seeking immediate, instrumentally oriented programming, in comparison to development around retention and management of human resources. Also, the survey findings document the progression of training needs, from the faculty–chair role transition to the move through higher administrative ranks.

Program Development and Structure

Given the need for chair professional development, how did the University of Michigan create a developmentally oriented program? In this section, we describe many aspects of the program-development process. The primary objectives of the program meetings were to encourage networking across administrative levels and the university and to engage administrators in topics that they indicated were important to their own professional development.

The needs assessment pointed to two requirements of the new program. First, new chairs had specific immediate training needs, which should be addressed in order to develop self-efficacy in their position. Second, experienced chairs also had training needs, but they sought programming around managing departmental dynamics. Therefore, CRLT developed two programs: an orientation for new chairs and an ongoing Campus Leadership Program for administrators of all experience levels. (An orientation for new associate deans was also developed, but this program is not described here.)

New Chair Orientation

A one-and-a-half-day program at the beginning of the academic year focused on getting new chairs up and running in their position. The first day, an evening program, began with welcoming remarks from the provost and ended with an interactive theater sketch on mentoring faculty.

The second day opened with a Q&A session with the university's president. Next, the provost spoke about administrative roles in higher education, such as the stewardship responsibility of the chairs and the interface between the central administration and the university's schools and colleges. Another interactive theater sketch triggered discussions about productive staff relationships. During lunch, very brief presentations addressed an assortment of topics: faculty searches and offers; faculty, staff, and student worklife assistance programs; ways to work with the campus's lecturer and teaching assistant unions; and legal issues. A panel of deans focusing on what makes for a successful chair led into small-group case-study discussions about a faculty member who wants to spend all of his time on research, and faculty dissensus about the rationale for a new hire. The busy day ended with a session on budgeting.

At the event, new chairs were invited to the Campus Leadership Program (to be described), where they could interact with more experienced chairs and administrators. In addition, there was a final lunch, late in the academic year, for the new chairs to check in about their first year in the role.

Campus Leadership Program

All chairs and associate deans were invited to participate in an ongoing leadership development program consisting of six meetings during the academic year. The provost or vice provosts attended most sessions as well. These sessions aimed to encourage horizontal and vertical networking, as well as engage administrators in topics that they indicated were important to their own professional development (see Table 16.4).

Program Evaluation

To refine the program, we included an evaluation in the program development process. We used attendance and participant self-reports of the programs' utility, as measured through a survey, to assess the New Chair Orientation and the Campus Leadership Program. Our first measure, attendance, identified that the topics resonated with our campus administrators. Most new chairs and associate deans, and a plurality of experienced chairs, attended at least one event (see Table 16.5). A significant proportion of these administrators also attended multiple events.

For individual sessions, attendance data indicate that the role-specific orientation sessions were effectively targeted. A majority (21/30) of new chairs and almost half (28/68) of associate chairs attended the orientation programs geared to their roles (see Table 16.6). The session Dealing with Difficult People was by far the best-attended; it seemed to resonate with administrators at all levels. Sessions on conducting searches and department meetings, as well as a final new-chair gathering, were the least attended, likely because of competing events at the university.

CRLT also surveyed the participants to identify the program's strengths and to gather suggestions for next year. The survey (two rounds) went to all chairs (new and experienced) and associate deans who attended at least one of the Campus Leadership Programs. Fourteen new chairs (a 56 percent response rate), nineteen experienced chairs (a 37 percent response rate), and

Table 16.4. Campus Leadership Program

Month	Topic
October	Assessment of faculty performance
November	Conducting searches and running faculty meetings (interactive theater)
December	Accreditation
January	Dealing with difficult people (workshop by Gunsalus, 2006)
February	Methods for evaluating and improving teaching
March	Developing and carrying out a vision for the department

eight associate deans (a 19 percent response rate) completed the survey. The questions were: (1) Which event(s) did you find the most useful, and why? (2) Do you have suggestions for changes for next year's Provost's Campus Leadership Programs? and (3) The provost initiated these Campus Leadership Programs; is there any message you want us to give her about them?

We found the key findings very gratifying. First, certain sessions evoked praise. The new chairs found the fall orientation to be a particularly helpful source of information, and everyone appreciated Dealing with Difficult People. Combined with the attendance data, these findings suggest that these topics should be continued in any future programming. Second, all the chairs and associate deans highly evaluated the orientation and roundtables as important networking resources, enabling them to meet colleagues and share strategies around common challenges. Because this reflected one of

Table 16.5. Attendance at New Chair Orientation and Campus Leadership Program

	Number Attending at Least One Event	Number Attending at Least Two Events
New chairs (30 total)	25 (85% of all new chairs)	20 (66%)
Experienced chairs (121)	51 (42%)	21 (17%)
Associate deans (68)	43 (63%)	29 (43%)

Table 16.6. Attendance by Program

Topic	Attendance
New chair orientation	21
Assessment of faculty performance	43
Conducting searches and running faculty meetings (interactive theater)	14
Accreditation	28
Dealing with difficult people (Gunsalus, 2006)	60
Methods for evaluating and improving teaching	29
Developing and carrying out a vision for the department	38
Final reception for new chairs	11
Associate dean orientations	28

CRLT's objectives for these events, we were gratified by the reaction. Third, almost every respondent described the programs as valuable and thanked the provost for offering them. Because chair training was her initiative, she was highly visible at many of the meetings. We hoped to have her take credit for the initiative, and we appreciated that respondents did so.

The suggestions for improvement helped us with program refinement. First, we found that these busy administrators preferred programs that were specific and practical, in contrast to theoretical and abstract topics. Second, we learned that the associate deans wanted much of the same training as what the chairs received, so in the program's second year we invited both groups to the same orientation and monthly programs. This format enhanced opportunities for networking, and the chairs were pleased that the associate deans had a chance to hear about the special challenges faced by department chairs.

Conclusion

This chapter has described a three-step model for teaching centers to construct a developmentally oriented administrative leadership program: (1) a needs assessment, (2) program implementation, and (3) useful evaluation. This model fills a gap in programming for ongoing leadership support. For other institutions that wish to initiate a developmentally oriented leadership program, we have four suggestions.

First, think strategically about how to build a sustainable program that will be attractive to a diverse group of chairs. To develop programs that speak to the realities of your campus and to those in different administrative stages, a thorough needs assessment is essential. Likewise, collect evaluation data during and after the program to demonstrate the value of continuation and glean useful suggestions for improvement.

Second, plan carefully about how to attract attendees, considering the busy lives of academic administrators. It is important to limit the time commitment required for the programs and to get complete buy-in from upper-level administration. Busy department heads will not make time for professional development unless upper-level administration has given its imprimatur. We believe it critical that our provost recommended the programs to the deans (to then recommend to chairs) and was visible at the events.

Third, integrate networking opportunities among administrators, vertically and horizontally. This practice encourages formation of informal support groups that further encourage professional growth across the administrative spectrum.

Finally, consider the important role that your center has to play in organizing a chair training program. A teaching center can facilitate high-quality professional development for administrators while also increasing campus receptivity to instructional improvement. Specifically, it can help chairs understand and execute their important role as "faculty developers" in their department, helping faculty balance their teaching with their other university responsibilities.

REFERENCES

Cuban, L. (1999). *How scholars trumped teachers: Change without reform in university curriculum, teaching, and research, 1890–1990.* New York: Teachers College Press.

Feldman, K. A., & Paulsen, M. B. (1999). Faculty motivation: The role of a supportive teaching culture. In M. Theall (Ed.), *New directions for teaching and learning: No. 78. Motivation from within: Approaches for encouraging faculty and students to excel* (pp. 71–78). San Francisco: Jossey-Bass.

Gunsalus, T. (2006). *The college administrator's survival guide.* Cambridge, MA: Harvard University Press.

Hecht, I.W.D. (2000). Transitions and transformations: The making of department chairs. In D. Lieberman & C. M. Wehlburg (Eds.), *To improve the academy: Vol. 19. Resources for faculty, instructional, and organizational development* (pp. 17–31). Bolton, MA: Anker.

Hecht, I.W.D. (2006). Becoming a department chair: To be or not to be. *Effective Practices for Academic Leaders, 1*(3), 1–16.

Hecht, I.W.D., Higgerson, M. L., Gmelch, W. H., & Tucker, A. (1999). *The department chair as academic leader.* Phoenix, AZ: American Council on Education and Oryx Press.

Lucas, A. F. (1986). Academic department chair training: The why and how of it. In M. Svinicki (Ed.), *To improve the academy: Vol. 5. Resources for student, faculty, and institutional development* (pp. 111–119). Stillwater, OK: New Forums Press.

Lucas, A. F. (1989). Motivating faculty to improve the quality of teaching. In E. C. Galambos (Ed.), *New directions for teaching and learning: No. 37. Improving teacher education* (pp. 5–16). San Francisco: Jossey-Bass.

Lucas, A. F. (1990). The department chair as change agent. In P. Seldin & Associates, *How administrators can improve teaching: Moving from talk to action in higher education* (pp. 63–88). San Francisco: Jossey-Bass.

Lucas, A. F. (2002). Increase your effectiveness in the organization: Work with department chairs. In K. H. Gillespie, L. R. Hilsen, & E. C. Wadsworth

(Eds.), *A guide to faculty development: Practical advice, examples, and resources* (pp. 157–166). Bolton, MA: Anker.

Murray, J. W., & Stauffacher, K. B. (2001). Departmental chair effectiveness: What skills and behaviors do deans, chairs, and faculty in research universities perceive as important? *Arkansas Educational Research and Policy Studies Journal, 1*(1), 62–75.

Rice, R. E., & Austin, A. E. (1990). Organizational impacts on faculty morale and motivation to teach. In P. Seldin & Associates, *How administrators can improve teaching: Moving from talk to action in higher education* (pp. 23–44). San Francisco: Jossey-Bass.

Seagren, A. L., Creswell, J. W., & Wheeler, D. W. (1993). *The department chair: New roles, responsibilities and challenges* (ASHE-ERIC Higher Education Report No. 1). Washington, DC: George Washington University, School of Education and Human Development.

Sorcinelli, M. D., Austin, A. E., Eddy, P. L., & Beach, A. L. (2006). *Creating the future of faculty development: Learning from the past, understanding the present.* Bolton, MA: Anker.

Walvoord, B. E., Carey, A. K., Smith, H. L., Soled, S. W., Way, P. K., & Zorn, D. (2000). *Academic departments: How they work, how they change* (ASHE-ERIC Higher Education Report, 27[8]). San Francisco: Jossey-Bass.

Whitt, E. J. (1991). Hit the ground running: Experiences of new faculty in a school of education. *Review of Higher Education, 14*(2), 177–197.

Wright, M. C. (2008). *Always at odds? Creating alignment between administrative and faculty values.* Albany: SUNY Press.

17

R$_X$ FOR ACADEMIC MEDICINE

BUILDING A COMPREHENSIVE FACULTY
DEVELOPMENT PROGRAM

Megan M. Palmer, Mary E. Dankoski, Randy R. Brutkiewicz,
Lia S. Logio, Stephen P. Bogdewic, Indiana University
School of Medicine

Faculty in academic medical centers are under tremendous stress and
report low satisfaction. The need for faculty development in medical
schools is great, yet it remains largely unmet across the United States. To
ensure ongoing success in academic medicine, medical schools must insti-
tute comprehensive faculty development programs. In this chapter, we
describe the development of an office for faculty affairs and professional
development at the Indiana University School of Medicine, including key
collaborations, budget trends and infrastructure development, strategic
planning, ongoing assessment planning, goal setting, and early patterns
of participation.

Academic medical centers are complex institutions that must maintain
multiple missions: to conduct research that advances discoveries in health
and healthcare delivery, to educate the next generation of physicians and
other health care providers, and to provide direct patient care, often to
medically underserved and underinsured citizens, while also merging the
business aspects of the health care industry with the university system and
culture. Faculty members are at the heart of this complexity, and institutions need a cadre of engaged, productive, and vital faculty members to
achieve these important agendas. Research shows, however, that faculty in
academic medical centers are facing high stress and low satisfaction.

Schindler et al. (2006) surveyed more than three thousand faculty at
four U.S. medical schools and found that 20 percent had significant symp-
toms of depression and that depression was particularly prevalent among

young faculty. In addition, the faculty's perception of financial instability was associated with higher levels of work strain, depression, and anxiety, which affected their mental health and job satisfaction. Another study of medical school faculty showed that 40 percent believed their career was not progressing satisfactorily, and 42 percent were "seriously considering leaving academic medicine in the next five years" (Lowenstein, Fernandez, & Crane, 2007, p. 3). The challenges in balancing work and family, poor recognition of teaching and clinical service for promotion, few opportunities for faculty development, and lack of input and feedback all predicted serious intent to leave. This intent was most common among faculty in clinical departments.

It is not surprising that academic clinicians are expressing dissatisfaction. More than ever before, thanks to major reductions in federal and state support, academic medical centers are relying on clinical revenue to fund operating costs. In the 1960s, only 6 percent on average of operating expenses in medical schools were due to clinical sources; this number reached 50 percent in the 1990s (AAMC, 2006). To generate this needed revenue, the Indiana University School of Medicine (IUSM) and medical schools across the country have hired an increasingly large number of faculty whose primary obligation is clinical work and, within their practice, student instruction. Subsequently, as the number of clinical faculty has risen, the number of tenure track M.D. faculty has declined (Bunton & Mallon, 2007).

This significant change has had an impact on how academic medical centers have organized faculty recruitment, reward and promotion systems, productivity standards, and faculty work in general. Although some centers have made attempts to help clinical faculty pursue their academic career goals, such as creating promotion systems for nontenure-track faculty, many academic clinicians carry a heavy clinical load, which interferes with their ability to pursue these goals. In one study of faculty in a clinical department, 45 percent identified the high clinical workload and 42 percent cited lack of time to achieve academic goals as disincentives for staying in academic medicine (Kelly, Cronin, & Dunnick, 2007). Clinical faculty also tend to be promoted in academic rank at a much slower rate than faculty who are primarily researchers. Compared to faculty members whose primary role was research, clinicians who spent 50 percent or more of their effort in patient care faced odds of achieving an advanced rank that were 69 percent to 85 percent lower (Thomas et al., 2004). Not surprisingly, the clinical faculty in this study were also far less satisfied with their progress toward promotion.

Though more likely to advance in rank, research faculty also face significant challenges in today's academic medicine. The number of tenure-eligible basic science faculty has also declined nationally, though less dramatically than have tenure-track clinicians (Bunton & Mallon, 2007). Funding from the National Institutes of Health (NIH) has grown increasingly more competitive, with the probability of a proposal being funded dropping from 32 percent in 1999 to as low as 10–12 percent for some institutes today (NIH, 2008b). At the same time, the age at which faculty members become independently funded is rising steadily, especially for physician-scientists (NIH, 2008a). This increased competition for funding has occurred while medical school budgets become more constrained. Thus research faculty, like their clinical colleagues, are experiencing more pressure to generate financial support for their salary during a time when researchers face greater competition for grants and high expectations of scholarship to achieve tenure and advance academically.

Despite many medical school deans being aware of the low morale of their faculty (Souba & Day, 2006) and faculty development being capable of improving the deteriorating situation, a 2000 survey of seventy-six medical schools revealed that only 20 percent had an office devoted to faculty development, with none offering a comprehensive faculty development program (Emans, Teperow Goldberg, Milstein, & Dobriner, 2008). Many schools and national organizations have begun to see this as problematic and are calling for change. For example, in November 2007 participants in the American Medical Association's medical schools interim meeting concluded that change was needed in several areas of medical education, including making faculty development an expectation and providing financial and other incentives for participating in teaching and educational planning at all levels (American Medical Association, 2007). Darrell Kirch, M.D., the president and CEO of the Association of American Medical Colleges (AAMC), maintains that faculty vitality is of utmost importance to sustaining the national resource that is the American medical school. Indeed, the AAMC recently launched a large national program called Faculty Forward to conduct faculty needs assessments and interventions at medical schools that choose to enroll in the program (Kirch, 2008). Some schools are already conducting such assessments and offering faculty development programs (Bland, Seaquist, Pacala, Center, & Finstad, 2002; Pololi & Frankel, 2005). The IUSM is one such school that has taken proactive, strategic action to address many institutional needs through sustaining faculty vitality. This chapter outlines the development of the IUSM's Office for Faculty Affairs and Professional Development (OFAPD) and the partnerships and strategic planning that have been critical in creating a comprehensive and successful effort, even in our early building days.

Forming a Faculty Development Office

On June 1, 2005, professional development became an "executive level function" at the IUSM for the first time. Prior to this date, the core functions of faculty affairs and academic administration (oversight of recruitment, promotion and tenure, posttenure reviews, faculty governance, and so on) were administered by a .50 FTE associate dean for faculty affairs, two staff members serving as director and assistant director of academic administration (2.0 FTE), and a .50 FTE administrative assistant. In addition to the typical functions of faculty and academic affairs, some faculty development initiatives were developed with this limited infrastructure: the Teacher-Learner Advocacy Committee (begun in 2002); a new-faculty orientation; a yearlong new-faculty development program called Leadership in Academic Medicine Program (LAMP, begun in 2003); promotion and tenure workshops; individual coaching for faculty and department chairs; and periodic faculty development workshops, such as leadership workshops for women faculty.

Program Development

Table 17.1 outlines the development of the OFAPD from June 2005 until May 2009.

Needs Assessment

In the course of the OFAPD's development, all the authors joined its professional staff. To enhance our effectiveness as faculty developers, we conducted a needs assessment and reviewed a variety of sources to inform our work. We sought answers to two questions: (1) How satisfied are the faculty overall? (2) What do faculty need most to sustain their academic vitality? The needs assessment included a faculty survey of vitality, interviews with department chairs, chair review 360 degree surveys, and faculty focus groups. Beyond the needs assessment, we also hired a consultant to research and write a report on our faculty's development needs and recommendations, reviewed the AAMC national survey on the value of faculty affairs and faculty development efforts in U.S. medical schools, reviewed findings from a national survey of offices of faculty affairs and faculty development in academic medical centers to determine the scope of services offered, and collaborated with the IUPUI Office for Professional Development. The results were used to draft and later refine a strategic plan for OFAPD.

Before fully implementing the strategic plan, we worked to ensure that we adopted appropriate measures to determine the effectiveness of faculty

Table 17.1. Development of OFAPD from June 2005 to Current Academic Year

Year	Infrastructure and Collaborations	Budget*	New Programs+
2005–06	• Professional development becomes an executive function • Associate dean title changed to executive associate dean for faculty affairs and professional development, and scope of office was expanded to include advancement of women, diversity affairs, faculty development, and academic administration	$94,692	• Schoolwide committee formed: Faculty Development Coordinating Committee • Leading Change in Academic Medicine (LCAM) for mid-career faculty • Strategic planning process began
2006–07	• Two assistant deans at .20 FTE each • Collaboration with Indiana University–Purdue University Indianapolis (IUPUI) Center for Teaching and Learning (.20 FTE of director's effort dedicated)	$552,727	• Office of Multicultural Affairs conceived and planned • Developed strategic plan for diversity • Schoolwide committee formed: IUSM Women's Advisory Council • Women in Medicine and Science Leadership Workshop • Schoolwide faculty development seminar on scientific writing from reader's perspective • Standards of Excellence for Promotion and Tenure revised • Began cosponsoring the Faculty Enrichment and Education Development (FEED) series with Department of Medicine • Assessment of faculty vitality begins (survey, focus groups, chair interviews) • Hosted Annual Diversity Week

2007–08	$894,599	
• Executive associate dean effort increased to .75 FTE • One assistant dean's effort increased to .40 FTE (other remained at .20 FTE) • Additional assistant dean added at .25 FTE • Addition of 1.0 FTE program manager • Addition of 1.0 FTE director of Office of Multicultural Affairs • Added two 1.0 FTE administrative assistants • Collaboration with Center for Urban and Multicultural Education (educational research center)		• Website launched • Online promotion and tenure modules developed • Executive briefing communication system developed • Research faculty development series launched • Stepping Stones of Women in Leadership series launched • History of Women at IUSM project completed • Schoolwide plenary on emotional intelligence • Department chair 360 degree evaluations administered • Organizational development services implemented for two divisions • Standard peer review and observation of teaching forms developed • Cosponsored schoolwide faculty development seminar on teaching • Academy of Teaching Scholars Program conceived and planned • Lunch and Learn workshops developed by Office of Multicultural Affairs • Partnered with Faces of Faith program • Hosted Aesculapian Society meeting

(*Continued*)

Table 17.1. (*Continued*)

Year	Infrastructure and Collaborations	Budget*	New Programs+
2008–09 (current year)	• Director of Center for Teaching and Learning becomes assistant dean of faculty affairs and professional development with .55 FTE dedicated to School of Medicine • Associate dean for diversity recruited at .91 FTE • Web and instructional technologist specialist at .50 FTE • Collaboration with Medical Education and Curricular Affairs • Secured $50,000 funding from IU president's office to develop pilot leadership program for faculty of color	$1,083,826	• State of the Faculty Report produced • Speaker's Bureau catalogue developed by Faculty Development Coordinating Committee • Tier One of Academy of Teaching Scholars launched • Schoolwide mentoring task force instituted • Search committee training offered • Online modules regarding observation and peer review of teaching developed • White paper on the tenure system produced • Hosted two Aesculapian Society meetings • Reorganized schoolwide Diversity Council • Held Office of Multicultural Affairs open house reception • Biennial faculty vitality survey conducted

Notes: Full budget, including all faculty and staff salary and fringe, program costs, hospitality, and supplies and expenses.

+ Programs from previous year continue into the next year unless otherwise noted. Only new programs are listed each year.

development. The results of the needs assessment yielded the foundational information to prepare a strategic plan for the office. A full version of the plan is available at http://faculty.medicine.iu.edu/docs/stratPlan.pdf. In the following sections, we describe our approach to faculty development, including our main areas of focus and samples of our programming.

Vision

In a time when faculty in academic medical centers are facing increased stress and report low satisfaction, we determined it essential to offer strategic programs for faculty development, the advancement of women, diversity affairs, and academic administration. In organizing an office and obtaining resources, we articulated these core values: (1) faculty are the single greatest resource of the institution, (2) talent is a strategic resource and has no limits, (3) faculty and institutional vitality are interdependent, (4) leadership development is not optional because leadership ensures the ability to initiate and sustain functional relationships and achieve shared goals, and (5) investment in faculty development is crucial to retaining productive, well-balanced faculty and to accomplishing the mission of the school. From these values, we formulated this vision for OFAPD: to develop a vibrant, diverse community where each member has the optimal capability to make meaningful contributions to his or her career goals and the institution's mission.

We then developed the mission, which is to:

- Establish and sustain a culture that promotes faculty vitality and diversity.

- Plan and implement faculty development activities that ensure effective and successful recruitment, appointment, retention, and promotion of faculty.

- Train and educate visionary, innovative leaders who are capable of promoting the school's mission and capitalizing on emerging challenges.

- Implement a life cycle of learning experiences that enable faculty to achieve their highest ambitions as educators, investigators, and clinicians.

- Communicate current faculty development opportunities to the medical school community.

- Ensure consistency with the school's strategic plan and core beliefs, and ensure optimal use of limited resources by coordinating school and university wide faculty development offerings.

- Expand participation in national and international groups that assist or promote faculty affairs, leadership, and professional development.

Approach to Faculty Development

The still common view in academic medical centers of faculty development as improving poor teachers is out of date. With faculty salaries and support now making up well over two-thirds of most academic expenses, we forward a new, comprehensive model. Helping faculty reach their full professional potential, aligned with the organization's goals, is essential to attain the gains in faculty productivity required today (Morahan, Gold, & Bickel, 2002).

Comprehensive professional development is also increasingly necessary in recruiting and retaining the most highly skilled faculty, in particular women and faculty of color. As industry has found, employees migrate to organizations that offer the greatest professional and career development opportunities. The comprehensive model for faculty and professional development shown in Figure 17.1 includes the traditional domains of teaching, research, and service but also encompasses personal, professional, and organizational development and leadership. OFAPD works to address these areas for all faculty as well as furnish additional development opportunities in each area that are directed specifically to women and faculty of color.

Using this new model, Table 17.2 classifies existing and new programs by each component of the model and by faculty career stage. Bolded items are new initiatives for the 2008–09 academic year. The programs

---

Figure 17.1. Comprehensive Model for Professional Development

Table 17.2. Sample of OFAPD Programs by Component of Professional Development Model and Career Stage

	Research	Service	Teaching	Personal and Professional Development	Organizational Development and Leadership
Junior	Grant and scientific writing workshops K30 Clinical Investigator Training Enhancement (CITE) Program **Internal grant peer review program** Translational research skills for new investigators	IUSM Continuing Medical Education (CME)	Faculty Enrichment and Education Development (FEED) Series **Innovations in Medical Education conference** **Academy of Teaching Scholars** Observations of teaching	New faculty orientation LAMP Promotion and tenure workshops Personal and career coaching AAMC Early-Career Women Faculty Professional Development Seminar	Developmental instruments (e.g., 360 degree, MBTI) Organizational diagnosis and cultural analysis (e.g., climate surveys) **Program for support staff to provide structured feedback to faculty**
Midcareer	Mentor development program Grant and scientific writing workshops	IUSM CME activities	Annual education retreat **Academy of Teaching Scholars**	AAMC Midcareer Women Faculty Professional Development Seminar Career coaching	Indiana Healthcare Leadership Academy (IHLA)
Senior	Grant and scientific writing workshops		**Academy of Teaching Scholars**	Leadership consultations Career coaching	IHLA **Executive leadership workshop for senior women faculty**

listed represented only a sample of the many faculty and professional development programs available.

Response

To assess the reach of our efforts, we collect data on the faculty who participate in faculty development workshops and cohort-based programs. In the future, we also will be able to report the number of faculty who consult with a member of the OFAPD for the purposes of mentoring, goal setting, observations of teaching, and the like.

Patterns of Participation

The number of unique contacts in Table 17.3 represents the number of faculty we served within the time period, removing any duplication. That is, whether a faculty member attended one event or ten events, he or she is only counted once for the purpose of unique contacts. In contrast, the total number of contacts does duplicate faculty members. It represents a cumulative number of attendees at events over the twelve-month period. During this growth period, we experienced a 73 percent increase in both the number of faculty members we served and the number of event attendees. In the 2007–08 academic year, approximately 35 percent of all faculty in the school participated in at least one faculty development activity associated with our office.

The increase in participation is obvious, and given the growth in offerings it is not at all unexpected. We anticipate this growth continuing at this substantial pace for at least one more year, after which we will set participation goals for future years. To set these goals, we will consider not only the current level of participation but also the percentage of faculty we would ideally want, in a twelve-month period, to engage in faculty development. No doubt 100 percent is a false ceiling.

A common concern or criticism of faculty development is that it focuses only on the needs of more junior faculty. In contrast, the OFAPD's strategic plan reaches out to faculty at all career stages and therefore at

Table 17.3. Number of Contacts with OFAPD

	2006–07	2007–08
Number of contacts	449	779 (+73%)
Number of unique contacts	312	540 (+73%)

all ranks. To evaluate how effectively we engage faculty across ranks, we look at unique contacts by rank. As depicted in Figure 17.2, participation has grown across the ranks during the last two years. In 2007–08, these contacts represent about 35 percent of all assistant professors, 24 percent of associate professors, and 22 percent of full professors. Table 17.4 enumerates the events and contacts by career stage and topical area.

Also of interest is the degree to which we serve women and faculty of color. Given that the OFAPD's focus includes the advancement of women and multicultural affairs, we would anticipate that the percentage of women and faculty of color who participate in faculty development would be greater than their peers. Indeed, the unique contact data in Table 17.5 show this gender difference. In 2007–08 about 40 percent of all women faculty participated in some type of faculty development activity, compared to 17 percent of men. This follows trends presented in

Figure 17.2. Number of Unique Contacts by Rank

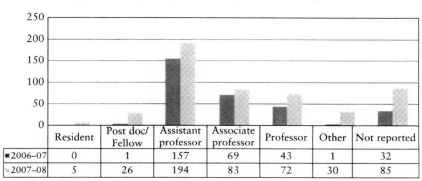

	Resident	Post doc/ Fellow	Assistant professor	Associate professor	Professor	Other	Not reported
■ 2006–07	0	1	157	69	43	1	32
▪ 2007–08	5	26	194	83	72	30	85

Table 17.4. Number of Events and Contacts by Career Stage and Topical Area

	Research (No. of Events and No. of Contacts)	Teaching (No. of Events and No. of Contacts)	Personal and Professional Development (No. of Events and No. of Contacts)	Organizational Development and Leadership (No. of Events and No. of Contacts)
Entry-level	5; 60	7; 120	20; 374	2; 17
Midcareer	5; 8	7; 67	20; 117	5; 22
Senior	2; 2	7; 49	20; 67	4; 25

other research (Chism & Szabo, 1996). But we hope to increase the percentage of male participants in the future.

Table 17.6 displays the number of unique contacts by race. In 2007–08 about one-third of all Asian and Asian American faculty participated in faculty development, compared to 25 percent of white faculty and 27 percent of underrepresented faculty (African American, Latino/Latina, and Native American). The participation of faculty from underrepresented groups is slightly higher than of white faculty. However, given the current culture of the school and the location of diversity affairs in the OFAPD, we believe we should increase the development efforts targeted to faculty from underrepresented groups and similarly increase faculty participation from these groups.

Ongoing Assessment

Since the very first faculty development offerings, the OFAPD has gathered data about satisfaction and application of learning from seminar and workshop participants. Like most centers, we can report a very high level of satisfaction from participants, as well as qualitative feedback that what participants learned was meaningful and applicable to their current work. For example, faculty who participated in a two-day session on scientific

Table 17.5. Number of Unique Contacts by Gender

	2006–07	2007–08
Women	184	302
Men	127	216
Not reported	1	22

Table 17.6. Number of Unique Contacts by Race

	2006–07	2007–08
Asian and Asian American	48	96
Caucasian	207	293
African American, Hispanic, and Native American	12	21
Not reported	45	130

writing shared comments such as, "I am already using the information presented when reviewing abstracts for presentations at an upcoming conference" and "I will immediately use what I learned to write a paper I intend to submit soon." Further, after a session on negotiations and compromise, a faculty member in LAMP remarked, "I will look for opportunities to compromise in my everyday practice—to listen better to other points of view."

Give the OFAPD's data-driven strategic planning effort, we collected baseline data on faculty satisfaction, department chairs' views of unmet faculty development needs, and overall faculty vitality. These assessment data will allow us to evaluate our successes, areas for growth, and missed opportunities, while also informing the dean and medical school faculty about the return on the investment in faculty development. Therefore, we developed intended outcomes for all four of the OFAPD's major areas—faculty development, diversity affairs, advancement of women, and academic affairs—and for these outcomes devised effectiveness indicators, success criteria, data collection and analysis procedures, and finally, strategies for using the findings. Following good assessment practice, we sought several assessment methods to measure the effectiveness of each area. Further, these measures will allow us to determine the success of our efforts at all levels—reaction, learning, behavior, and results, as defined by Kirkpatrick (1994). Table 17.7 displays the intended outcomes and our planned methods to measure effectiveness.

Protocol and sampling for focus groups and the design of case studies will vary slightly each year, but over time these data collection methods will provide a valid picture of the influence of faculty development on faculty success. For example, in 2007 only associate professors participated in the focus groups. Once we combine the results from the 2007 groups with the faculty of color focus groups being conducted in 2009 and those of other subgroups, we will obtain a more complete picture of the climate and identify the needs and experiences of these important subpopulations.

We will use our data not only to assess but also to refine or redirect the OFAPD efforts. This flexibility makes our strategic plan a living document that may require adjustment according to new assessment data. Further, the OFAPD will share its assessment findings with the community as a whole. For example, we recently disseminated an executive briefing of results from the vitality survey, chair interviews, and focus groups. This ensures that the feedback loop is complete and also serves to positively influence the community by making our work and research about our work transparent.

Table 17.7. Measuring Effectiveness

	Participation Data	Workshop Evaluations	Vitality Survey	Focus Groups	Exit Interviews	Case Studies	Faculty Annual Reviews	Chair 360s
Faculty Development	X	X	X	X	X	X	X	X
1. Community is aware of faculty development opportunities.								
2. Faculty development is integrated in many ways and at many levels across the school.								
3. Participation in and commitment to development increases among faculty.								
4. Success and competence in teaching, research, service, and leadership is increased.								
Diversity Affairs								
1. A prominent and visible role of our diverse culture is present.	X	X	X	X	X	X	X	X
2. Recruitment, retention, and advancement of graduate and medical students, postdoctoral fellows and house staff, and faculty from diverse backgrounds are increased.								
3. Opportunities for leadership of underrepresented minorities (including at senior levels) at the IUSM are increased.								
4. Cultural competence of faculty, staff, and learners is increased.								
5. Community partnerships are developed and enhanced.								
Advancement of Women	X	X	X	X	X		X	X
1. Recruitment, retention, and advancement of women faculty is increased to reach the goal of having 50% women in all faculty ranks and positions of leadership.								
2. Maintain 50% women students matriculating and graduating.								
3. A climate of inclusiveness and equity is present.								
4. Flexible faculty policies are in place.								
Academic Affairs								
1. All faculty will report a defined area of excellence in their annual faculty review.					X			
2. All faculty will have a professional development plan, as reported in their annual faculty review.							X	

Future Growth

Although OFAPD has grown over the past several years, some areas of faculty development still need attention. For example, from triangulating findings from the vitality survey, chair interviews, and focus groups, we identified the need for more leadership development; enhanced mentoring; increased recognition of faculty contributions to the teaching, research, and service missions; and better alignment of personal and organizational values across the entire system. In response, we recently assembled a task force to look into developing a schoolwide mentoring program and a plan to examine the exemplary leadership and mentoring practices in some departments to guide our wider efforts. A second faculty vitality survey is under way to discern any improvements since OFAPD's founding as well as additional needs.

We also face a new challenge in that medical education at Indiana University will expand to include clinical education (years three and four) at the eight regional centers around the state. Currently, faculty teach only the first two years of the curriculum, all in the classroom setting. This change will require expanding faculty development, particularly in the area of clinical teaching, across the state. We intend to seriously consider how to use technology to serve our faculty.

Conclusion

Fortunately, medical schools across the United States are initiating or enhancing efforts to support their faculty, and IUSM is prepared to be a national leader in this area. Teaching and faculty development centers that now serve the broader university faculty can also fill the void, and expanding their services to the medical school may give them access to additional resources. When both the broader university and the medical school centers share the same campus, they are likely to find collaboration mutually beneficial, as we did joining forces with the center on our host campus. Although the demands, daily life, and role of faculty in medicine may differ from faculty in other fields, much of the development work is the same. For instance, a writing skills workshop will serve not only medical faculty but those across the disciplines as well. Therefore, these units should coordinate certain programs, intentionally deciding where to share offerings, where to specialize, and where to duplicate efforts. Such collaborations can help meet the largely unmet faculty development needs in academic medicine, while bridging what is often a great divide between schools of medicine and other disciplines and allowing each to support the growth and development of the other.

REFERENCES

American Medical Association. (2007, November). *Proceedings of the AMA Section on Medical Schools (AMA-SMS) Interim Meeting, USA*. Retrieved March 12, 2009, from www.ama-assn.org/ama1/pub/upload/mm/44/i07highlights.pdf

Association of American Medical Colleges. (2006). *AAMC data book*. Washington, DC: Author.

Bland, C. J., Seaquist, E., Pacala, J. T., Center, B. A., & Finstad, D. (2002). One school's strategy to assess and improve the vitality of its faculty. *Academic Medicine, 77*(5), 368–376.

Bunton, S. A., & Mallon, W. T. (2007). The continued evolution of faculty appointment and tenure policies at U.S. medical schools. *Academic Medicine, 82*(3), 281–289.

Chism, N.V.N., & Szabo, B. (1996). Who uses faculty development services? In L. Richlin & D. DeZure (Eds.), *To improve the academy: Vol. 15. Resources for faculty, instructional, and organizational development* (pp. 115–128). Stillwater, OK: New Forums Press.

Emans, S. J., Teperow Goldberg, C. E., Milstein, M. E., & Dobriner, J. (2008). Creating a faculty development office in an academic pediatric hospital: Challenges and successes. *Pediatrics, 121*(2), 390–401.

Kelly, A. M., Cronin, P., & Dunnick, N. R. (2007). Junior faculty satisfaction in a large academic radiology department. *Academic Radiology, 14*(4), 445–454.

Kirch, D. (2008, August). *Is your academic medical center a great place to work? Lessons in building faculty vitality*. Paper presented at the AAMC Group on Faculty Affairs Conference, Pittsburgh, PA.

Kirkpatrick, D. L. (1994). *Evaluating training programs: The four levels*. San Francisco: Berrett-Koehler.

Lowenstein, S. R., Fernandez, G., & Crane, L. A. (2007). Medical school faculty discontent: Prevalence and predictors of intent to leave academic careers. *BMC Medical Education, 7*(1), 37.

Morahan, P. S., Gold, J. S., & Bickel, J. (2002). Status of faculty affairs and faculty development offices in U.S. medical schools. *Academic Medicine, 77*(5), 398–401.

National Institutes of Health. (2008a). *New and early-stage investigator policies*. Retrieved March 13, 2009, from http://grants.nih.gov/grants/new_investigators/index.htm

National Institutes of Health. (2008b). *Research project success rates by type and activity for 2008*. Retrieved March 13, 2009, from http://report.nih.gov/award/success/Success_ByActivity.cfm

Pololi, L. H., & Frankel, R. M. (2005). Humanizing medical education through faculty development: Linking self-awareness and teaching skills. *Medical Education, 39*(2), 154–162.

Schindler, B. A., Novack, D. H., Cohen, D. G., Yager, J., Wang, D., Shaheen, N. J., et al. (2006). The impact of the changing health care environment on the health and well-being of faculty at four medical schools. *Academic Medicine, 81*(1), 27–34.

Souba, W. W., & Day, D. V. (2006). Leadership values in academic medicine. *Academic Medicine, 81*(1), 20–26.

Thomas, P. A., Diener-West, M., Canto, M. I., Martin, D. R., Post, W. S., & Streiff, M. B. (2004). Results of an academic promotion and career path survey of faculty at the Johns Hopkins University School of Medicine. *Academic Medicine, 79*(3), 258–264.

18

THE CASE FOR EXCELLENCE IN DIVERSITY

LESSONS FROM AN ASSESSMENT OF AN EARLY CAREER FACULTY PROGRAM

Dorothe J. Bach, University of Virginia

Mary Deane Sorcinelli, University of Massachusetts Amherst

Many colleges and universities have come to understand the added educational value of having a more diverse faculty, and some have created specific programs to enhance recruitment, development, and retention of underrepresented faculty. How do these programs help underrepresented faculty start a successful career? How can they help a diverse faculty build thriving, long-term careers in academia? This chapter addresses these questions by sharing the findings and lessons learned from an internal and external assessment of the Excellence in Diversity Fellows Program at the University of Virginia.

Research on new faculty has been conducted across a variety of disciplines and institutional types, using a range of methodological approaches. Findings consistently indicate that many new faculty members, especially women and those of color, encounter roadblocks that can negatively affect their productivity and career advancement: getting oriented to

The authors thank Esther Kingston-Mann and Christine Stanley for their expertise as members of the external review team. They also wish to acknowledge the EDF Advisory Committee members, Marva Barnett, Gertrude Fraser, Sherwood Frey, and José Fuentes, for their leadership and vision. Finally, the authors thank Brian Baldi, Marva Barnett, Deandra Little, Erin McGlothlin, Michael Palmer, Judith Reagan, and Jung Yun for their comments on various drafts of this paper, and Xiaohui Wang for her help with analyzing our dataset.

a new departmental and institutional culture, excelling at research and teaching, navigating the tenure track, building substantive professional networks, and balancing work and life (Boice, 1991; Fink, 1984; Menges, 1999; Olsen & Crawford, 1998; Olsen & Sorcinelli, 1992; Reynolds, 1992; Rice, Sorcinelli, & Austin, 2000; Solem & Foote, 2004; Sorcinelli, 1988; Tierney & Bensimon, 1996; Yun & Sorcinelli, 2008).

Newcomers who also are underrepresented faculty may face additional challenges. The literature suggests that nonmajority faculty encounter added stresses such as isolation, lack of mentors, marginalization of identity-based scholarship and ethnic epistemologies, narrow definitions of merit in tenure and promotion, "cultural taxation" in teaching such as having to teach nontraditional courses or deal with higher student scrutiny because of their diversity, heavier student advising and service obligations, and conflict between cultural and institutional values (Boice, 1993a, 1993b; Maher & Thompson Tetreault, 2007; Moody, 2004; Stanley, 2006).

Like many institutions of higher education, the University of Virginia actively recruits underrepresented faculty with the goals of increasing diversity, invigorating the intellectual climate, and enhancing the educational experience of students. The institution has been aware, however, that the success of new and diverse faculty depends largely on the level of support they receive from the university. To better support these new hires, the Teaching Resource Center (TRC) designed and piloted an Excellence in Diversity Fellows Program (EDF) with funding from the provost and the deans of the Colleges of Arts and Sciences, Engineering, and Medicine. This chapter describes what the coauthors, who also served as the EDF program coordinator and the leader of an external review team, learned from a multilayered assessment of the three-year pilot phase of this program (2003–2006). It also identifies action steps the university has taken throughout 2006–2008 in response to the assessment's recommendations.

Background of the Excellence in Diversity Fellows Program

The EDF program assists new and diverse faculty in navigating the challenges of being pretenure, reaching their potential as teachers and researchers, and building thriving, long-term careers at the university. These are the goals of the program:

- Offering new, diverse faculty early and direct insights into how to succeed in the academic world, including engaging them in defining their teaching and research agendas.

- Promoting a peer-level support network and serious intellectual discourse among a diverse group of faculty members.

- Initiating and supporting productive interactions between Fellows and the senior faculty (senior consultants) who serve as knowledgeable, generous mentors, thus deepening and broadening connections to colleagues and to the institution.

- Fostering improved communication among junior and senior faculty members and academic administrators.

- Establishing and maintaining an environment in which junior faculty—particularly those from diverse backgrounds—develop a sense of belonging to a community, not only within individual academic units but also to the university as a whole.

To realize these goals, the EDF program offers a yearlong fellowship to a group of eight to fifteen first-year, tenure-track faculty who are interested in connecting to a diverse peer network. The fellowship includes an opening daylong retreat; a match with one or two senior colleagues who serve as teaching coaches, research counsels, and university confidants; and concrete professional assistance through ongoing professional development workshops, panel discussions, and meetings grounded in the concerns of the Fellows (Bach, Barnett, Fuentes & Frey, 2005; University of Virginia, 2007).

An Internal Assessment

There are only a small number of faculty development programs for new, underrepresented faculty, and little evaluation data on their effectiveness (Alire, 2002; Kosoko-Lasaki, Sonnino, & Voytko, 2006; Phillips, 2002; Piercy et al., 2005). Careful assessment of the three-year EDF program pilot, therefore, was important for identifying the initiative's early successes and areas of concern, determining and communicating the long-term direction of the program, and sustaining faculty and administrative support.

As a first step, the TRC conducted a self-study of the program. From the outset of the three-year pilot phase, the EDF program coordinator collected consistent and ongoing feedback from participants. Qualitative assessment data from years one through three included evaluations of each professional development session, a brief midyear questionnaire, and a substantial final report submitted by each Fellow and his or her senior consultant(s). The report also asked for quantitative, "global" rating items on two central questions: How would you rate the impact of this program on your sense of connection to the university community? How would you rate the impact of this program on giving you insights into how to succeed in the academic world?

Overall, the self-study found high satisfaction with the EDF program. The Fellows reported that they valued the strong connections they built with a diverse peer group, appreciated the support of a senior consultant from outside their department, and found the program activities beneficial overall. One Fellow summed up the experience: "The EDF reinforced my sense of being welcomed and valued; it broadened my awareness of the university outside my own and related disciplines; and it put faces to the names of high-up people in the administration."

At the same time, the self-study uncovered declines from year one to year three in Fellows' ratings on the two central questions of program impact: "sense of connection to the university" declined from 4.71 to 3.96, and "insights into academic career success" declined from 4.43 to 3.75 (see Table 18.1). The TRC and the EDF Program Advisory Committee were not entirely sure how to interpret these declines. Were they due to a programmatic change made in response to pressures from constituencies in and outside of the university? After a successful first year, the campus administration had asked that the EDF program be opened to all incoming faculty. As a result, the number of Fellows doubled in years two and three and the percentage of faculty from diverse groups declined. Interestingly, it was some of the majority Fellows in years two and three who suggested a lack of fit with the program. They were more likely to report that they already had insights into academic career success and "knew the ropes" in terms of getting

Table 18.1. EDF Fellows' Ratings on the Overall Program Impact 2003–2006

Year	Number of Returned Reports/Number of Fellows	Overall Program Impact on Sense of Connection to the University Community	Overall Program Impact on Giving Insight into How to Succeed in Academe
2003–04	8/8	4.75	4.13
2004–05	13/14	4.38	3.54
2005–06	13/15	4.04	3.77

Note: Five-point scale: 5 = very significant, 4 = significant, 3 = moderate, 2 = not very significant, 1 = none.

started, finding mentors, and building a professional network. Conversely, nontraditional faculty in years two and three wanted a program that provided more support for discussing concerns specific to minority faculty.

An External Review

To better understand the findings of the self-study and permit a more comprehensive view of program outcomes, the EDF Advisory Committee invited an external review team to the university in fall 2006. In selecting outside reviewers, the Advisory Committee looked for experienced faculty developers with a demonstrated commitment to supporting women faculty and faculty of color. The three reviewers chosen held tenured faculty appointments, were or had been directors of teaching centers, and were well regarded nationally as experienced professionals with expertise in teaching, learning, and faculty development. All three had conducted research on and built multiculturalism into faculty development programs and demonstrated a strong commitment to fostering inclusive campus communities.

The team addressed three broad questions:

1. Is the EDF program achieving its current goals and objectives? How could it better achieve goals and objectives?

2. To what extent does the EDF program meet the needs of participating faculty from underrepresented groups? the needs of participating faculty from majority groups? How could the program better meet all participants' needs?

3. In what ways does the EDF program serve the larger university community? Is the program well aligned with wider university goals? What improvements would benefit both the program and the university?

Methodology

The review team used two primary sources of information on the EDF program. First, before visiting the University of Virginia, the team reviewed written documents: EDF brochures, website, workshop agendas, mentoring plans, and all program evaluations. They also reviewed the self-study that outlined the history, context, activities, and resources of the EDF program. Second, the review team spent two and a half days conducting interviews and focus groups with various constituencies to learn about the program's perceived strengths, areas for improvement, and future directions.

Over the course of the campus visit, twelve individual interviews or focus groups were held with a wide range (N = 65) of faculty members, staff, and academic leaders, including faculty in early-, mid-, and late-career stages, instructors in a number of disciplines, and administrators in various institutional roles. The review team met with three focus groups of EDF Fellows from years one, two, and three; two focus groups of EDF senior faculty mentors; four members of the EDF Program Advisory Committee; and a focus group of department chairs and deans. They also interviewed the vice provost for faculty advancement, the vice provost for academic programs, the vice president and provost, and the vice president and chief officer for diversity and equity. The team guided the interview and focus group discussions in a semistructured way, asking participants to share to what extent and how the EDF program had met their own and institutional needs.

Findings: Program Strengths

The external review team concluded that the EDF program was highly regarded among campus participants. Data suggested four key reasons for the EDF program's success, which are described below.

EDF Develops a Peer Network

Collegial networks may not be as accessible to nontraditional new faculty as they are to those from majority groups. The EDF program directly addresses this concern by offering a structure through which new and diverse faculty meet regularly with each other. In meetings, workshops, and panel discussions, they share strategies for how to start their research and teaching, find mentors, navigate departmental politics, balance work and family, and deal with the unique stresses particular to underrepresented faculty. According to one participant, "Most valuable has been the opportunity for peer group discussion in which all of us, women and academics of color, discovered common concerns, shared strategies, and learned from each other."

EDF Cultivates Senior Faculty Consultants

Fellows often mentioned the involvement of senior faculty as a key feature of the EDF program. Senior consultants are selected with two criteria in mind. First, because there are often only a few women and minorities at advanced career levels, senior consultants are recruited not on the basis of shared identities but rather on their specific skill sets or experience.

This selection strategy recognizes that successful mentoring depends on a set of behaviors and practices rather than on gender or cultural identity (Harley, 2005). Second, senior consultants are always selected from outside of the Fellow's department so that they can provide the kind of guidance and feedback that newcomers might be reluctant to seek from departmental colleagues. One new faculty member stated: "My mentor was great. Because he was outside of my department, he was able to help me with some specific issues that would have been awkward to talk about with my departmental colleagues."

EDF Engages Senior Administrators

Early-career faculty need to know the expectations of their institution in order to have access to the resources that will help them succeed and achieve tenure. Fellows cited annual sessions with university leaders as particularly helpful to them in these matters. One Fellow noted, "Meetings with the campus administrators were especially informative and helpful. The meetings also seemed to signal a good-faith effort on the part of administration to retain minority/underrepresented faculty." Participants also appreciated the opportunity to engage with the EDF program's Advisory Committee, whose diverse members have a long-standing commitment to the program.

EDF Offers Resources and Support

During the campus interviews, numerous people expressed strong affirmations of respect and appreciation for the efforts of the administrative units involved in the EDF program, most notably the Teaching Resource Center. Faculty members and academic leaders agreed that development of the EDF program through the TRC was important, substantive, and well executed. In particular, Fellows cited the fall retreat and peer-focused meetings among Fellows as especially well planned and instructive. Fellows also perceived the TRC staff to be welcoming, highly professional, and faculty-focused: "We've all benefited from the ongoing support and resources from the amazingly dedicated professionals/scholars at the TRC."

Findings: Issues of Concern, Recommendations, Action Steps

There was considerable alignment between the internal self-study report and the findings of the external review team. Bringing in national experts to review the program, however, created a forum for the TRC, the EDF Advisory Committee, Fellows, consultants, and administrators to more deeply explore issues of concern. The external review team's written report also provided specific recommendations to address the assessment's findings, enabling the university to build concrete, data-based action steps. In addition, the EDF program coordinator and lead reviewer developed an ongoing, online mentoring partnership during implementation of the committee's recommendations.

The next section describes four key issues of concern, recommendations arising from the assessments, and action steps taken by various stakeholders to improve both the EDF program and support for all new faculty programs at the university.

Size of the EDF Program

Issue of concern. The review team specifically asked all participants, especially Fellows and senior consultants, for feedback on the decision to open up the program to all new faculty. The responses to this question were mixed, offering no clear consensus. For example, although some clearly saw the potential advantages to extending the program so that all new faculty could benefit from the mentoring, workshops, and social gatherings, others expressed concern that the scaled-up program was not meeting the particular needs of faculty from underrepresented groups. Furthermore, some feared that doubling the cohort of Fellows was directly tied to the decline in the sense of mutual support and camaraderie that was possible in a small group setting.

Recommendations. The review team encouraged administrators to take several immediate steps: to move quickly to explore other campus programs that might serve as successful models for scaling up the EDF program and offering it to all new faculty; to compare the advantages of such models with the advantage of maintaining the EDF program at a size that is recognized as particularly successful for learning communities (eight to twelve faculty); and to consider whether there were elements of the program that could be scaled up and offered to all new faculty (for example, meeting with administrators, tenure preparation seminars) and elements that should be experienced in a small learning community that addresses the specific career development needs of underrepresented faculty.

Action steps. Concerns about the program's scale were quickly addressed. In spring 2007, the Office of the Vice Provost for Faculty Advancement scaled up a number of the highly rated EDF program events so that they were available to all new faculty. These included a new faculty tour of the Lawn, a Q&A session with the provost's senior administrators on promotion and tenure procedures and policies, a life-work balance workshop, a workshop on negotiation skills, and an end-of-the-year social for new faculty. In addition, during the same semester the TRC partnered with the vice president for research and graduate studies and the vice provost for faculty advancement to offer the successful EDF grant-writing workshops to all faculty.

As a result, the EDF program was able to refocus on its original goal: to help attract, develop, and retain a diverse faculty. In fall 2007, the program offered fellowships to a smaller cohort of eight to twelve faculty, thus cultivating the intimacy crucial for fostering deep conversation and meaningful relationships. The key to accomplishing this goal was a confirmation, both internally and externally, that the ability to help new and diverse faculty build substantive peer and senior faculty networks was central to the program's success.

Focus of the EDF Program

Issue of concern. During the external review, focus groups debated the meaning of "excellence in diversity." They also debated whether the EDF program should focus on the broad professional development needs of new and diverse faculty, on diversity issues, or both. Most Fellows wanted it all: more formal and timely help in adapting to their new academic and cultural environment in Charlottesville; more one-on-one support for writing for publication and grant writing; more focus on the tenure process and how to prepare the tenure packet; more assistance with teaching skills (as well as more reward for teaching well); and more emphasis on diversity and uniqueness—be it race, gender, motherhood, and the like, and discussion of the links between their research agendas and diversity.

Recommendations. The review team suggested that the EDF program and the broader academic community needed to clarify the focus of the program. Some key questions were raised: Was the primary goal of the program to provide professional development opportunities for new faculty from underrepresented groups? Was it to emphasize diversity issues related to the research, teaching, and service of new and diverse faculty members? Should issues of diversity be infused into all programming or highlighted as stand-alone topics?

Action steps. Once a variety of offices on campus began to expand faculty development opportunities to all new faculty, the TRC and EDF Advisory Committee were empowered to sharpen the mission of the EDF program and tailor its events more specifically to meet the needs of new faculty with an interest in *both* professional development *and* diversity. To be sure, the program still remains open to all incoming assistant professors, but the TRC more specifically communicates its focus on diversity. For example, the

TRC fine-tuned the EDF application form to better identify diverse faculty and faculty committed to diversity who would benefit from and contribute to this unique network. They also revised the EDF website and brochure to further clarify the emphasis on diversity and inform the broader academic community of the program's focus within the teaching and professional development mission of the Teaching Resource Center.

Conversations among the TRC staff and review team suggested that it was generally more productive to infuse issues of diversity into all EDF programming rather than highlight diversity as a stand-alone topic. For example, the opening retreat now features a "uniqueness exercise" that encourages Fellows to share personal stories and raise diversity concerns. The Fellows also wanted to link discussions of their research to diversity. As a result, the EDF year newly includes a series of peer conversations in which Fellows share their often interdisciplinary and culturally diverse scholarship and collectively develop strategies for effectively communicating their work to senior colleagues. In fall 2008, the EDF partnered with the TRC's successful Professors as Writers Program (http://trc.virginia.edu/Programs/PAW/PAW.htm) to encourage peer-writing groups among the Fellows.

The program also continues to sponsor at least one or two sessions every year that directly respond to diversity issues raised by the EDF cohort. In 2007–08, the program arranged a specifically tailored, highly rated panel discussion, Teaching While Female: Negotiating Gender in the Classroom, as well as a workshop called Solo Faculty: Work Stresses and How to Deal with Them. These events were open to all cohorts of EDF Fellows and fostered peer connections and mentoring (for complete list of program activities see http://trc.virginia.edu/Programs/EDF/EDF.htm.)

Finally, the TRC also sharpened its focus on helping new faculty develop a level of comfort in the classroom by offering faculty multiple entry points to explore how best to teach diverse students and design effective courses. For example, in 2007–08, half of the current EDF Fellows requested individual teaching consultations, and six former Fellows applied for the university Teaching Fellows Program, a campuswide program that supports course design projects through one-year Fellowships. As part of its standard programming, the TRC also offered workshops and consultations on teaching and learning in the diverse classroom to all new faculty.

Mentoring in the EDF Program

Issue of concern. Fellows and senior consultants alike suggested that their mentoring partnerships might be strengthened with more explicit guidelines. Some Fellows felt that their senior consultants did not provide enough research support, give guidance about the tenure process, or help with political or relationship tensions in the new faculty members' departments. Other Fellows suggested more contact—in and out of meetings—with past EDF Fellows so that these "near-peers" could furnish additional mentoring on issues faced by women and faculty of color.

Recommendations. The review team suggested that the EDF program would be well served to explore other mentoring initiatives that have broadened the notion of who can mentor—peers, near-peers, recently tenured faculty, and administrators as well as senior consultants (Sorcinelli & Yun, 2007; Yun & Sorcinelli, 2008). In addition, the program should be more explicit about "naming" the variety of mentoring networks that have already been developed (for instance, the peer mentoring among the Fellows, mentoring by senior consultants and administrators, and so on). Finally, they recommended intentionally connecting current Fellows with earlier EDF cohorts as a way to broaden the network of underrepresented faculty on campus.

Action steps. The TRC initially decided to retain its "traditional model" of mentoring between a new faculty and senior consultant for two reasons. First, overall the matches have been highly successful. Second, as a matter of policy, the TRC avoids asking early-career faculty to give time to activities that do not directly help them gain tenure. However, in 2007–08, the Advisory Committee made two changes. First, they matched a new Fellow with a junior colleague whose personal and research interests were especially closely aligned—and their relationship flourished. Also, the program now highlights the fact that it offers not only a senior consultant mentoring network but also peer and near-peer networks of current and former EDF Fellows. A panel discussion, Planning Ahead to the Tenure Review, was reorganized in 2007 to draw on the experience of former Fellows who have gone through third-year and tenure reviews. This event is now open to all EDF cohorts and has become a highly rated forum for exchange (the event also complements a campuswide session with senior administrators on promotion and tenure). In light of these positive experiences, the EDF program will continue to expand its reliance on a broader range of mentoring partnerships while continuing to derive the considerable benefits of having senior colleagues serve as mentors.

Recognition and Reward for Involvement in the EDF Program

Issue of concern. Participants of both the internal and external assessments expressed concern about how participation in the program was valued by the university at large. Some Fellows reported that their chairs thought the program was remedial and "for poor teachers" or "only focused on teaching." Relatedly, some of the senior consultants reported that although they were honored to be selected as mentors, the mentoring role was purely voluntary; in general it was not acknowledged or rewarded in annual faculty reports or symbolically in academic departments (recognition by department chairs).

Recommendation. There was widespread agreement that the university should recognize and reward both participation in the EDF program and mentoring by senior consultants. This may require that the program build more connections with department chairs and school and college deans. Application materials and descriptions of the program should emphasize that it is a rich professional development opportunity for new and underrepresented faculty. Chairs should be encouraged to match the EDF stipend to recognize and reward newcomers who are proactively developing their career. Senior consultants might be recognized in annual faculty reviews and by modest remuneration. Finally, Fellows and consultants could be encouraged to share the goals and outcomes of the program in departmental meetings and the director of TRC, or members of the Advisory Committee, might be asked to speak about the program at a dean's or provost's council.

Action steps. From the beginning, the EDF program was promoted as an award for new faculty members; now revised promotional materials and a webpage more explicitly advertise the program as an award. In addition, individual schools such as the Schools of Education, Engineering, and Medicine now recognize Fellows on their websites and in their newsletters. To further highlight the award character of the program, the provost inaugurated an annual reception in honor of the Fellows to which former Fellows, senior consultants, chairs, and deans are invited. At this end-of-year celebration, three or four Fellows speak about the value of the program and the program coordinator invites department chairs to encourage the incoming cohort of new faculty to apply for the fellowship.

Finally, since 1990 the TRC has taken a lead in establishing sustained formal mentoring programs through the university Teaching Fellows Program and the EDF program, and it was well positioned to advocate for faculty who give generously of their time to mentor a pretenure colleague. The advocacy of the director of the center as well as the review committee's conversations with the senior leadership both contributed to the creation of an all-campus mentoring award. In 2007, the campus launched an Excellence in Faculty Mentoring Award (http://trc.virginia. edu/Awards/Faculty/FMA.htm), with a $5,000 prize.

Discussion and Conclusion

Overall, the internal and external assessments confirmed that the EDF program "is highly regarded among campus participants." Both reviews found that the program fostered strong mentoring and peer-support networks, access to faculty development resources, and direct interaction with senior administrators. Findings confirmed the importance of the "learning community" size of the program, while offering new insights to help guide campus efforts to better realize the program's original mission and focus and recognize the faculty members engaged in its activities. Additionally, the reviews offered an additional impetus to make more faculty development available to all new faculty members.

The program's outcomes for the two years following the multifaceted assessment suggest that efforts to refocus the program have been successful. Between 2005–06 and 2007–08, the global ratings of the impact of the program showed statistically significant increases. The Fellows' sense of connections rose 0.82 points on a five-point scale, and ratings of the program's impact on Fellows insights into how to succeed in the academic world rose 0.93 points (see Table 18.2 and Figure 18.1.)

These outcomes are particularly noteworthy given expanding departmental mentoring initiatives and additional programs for all early-career faculty. We attribute the continuing high levels of participation and perceived impact of EDF to the program's ability to build strong and sustained peer-support networks and to support the professional development needs of underrepresented faculty and faculty interested in diversity through specifically tailored program activities.

Table 18.2. EDF Fellows' Ratings on the Overall Program Impact 2006–2008

Year	Number of Returned Reports/Number of Fellows	Overall Program Impact on Sense of Connection to the University Community	Overall Program Impact on Giving Insight into How to Succeed in Academe
2006–07	13/14	4.54/5	4.15/5
2007–08	11/12	4.82/5	4.60/5

Notes: Five-point scale: 5 = very significant, 4 = significant, 3 = moderate, 2 = not very significant, 1 = none.
We excluded one set of ratings from a Fellow who attended fewer than one-third of the meetings.

Figure 18.1. Overall Program Ratings by Year

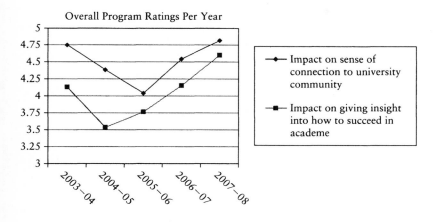

The results of the assessment also have important implications for developing and evaluating programs to support new and early-career faculty, especially those from underrepresented groups. The findings remind us, once again, that all new and early-career faculty benefit from programs that promote access to orientation, mentoring, grants, fellowships, and other resources to develop as teachers and scholars. Organizational factors can also promote the success of new faculty, especially the support of department chairs, senior colleagues, and other academic leaders with responsibilities for faculty development.

Second, the literature indicates that researchers and practitioners are still struggling to determine which faculty development models and practices best support women and faculty of color (Sorcinelli & Yun, 2006). Our results suggest that flexibility and attention to campus context is the key in determining best programs and practices. Some universities benefit from developing special opportunities for new and underrepresented faculty to participate in focused peer and mentoring networks such as the University of Virginia's EDF program or Purdue University's mentoring program for women faculty (Washburn, 2007). Other programs, such as the University of Massachusetts Amherst's Mutual Mentoring Initiative (Yun & Sorcinelli, 2008), are designed to encourage all new faculty, especially women and those of color, to build the professional networks that best support their career development. In all of these cases, however, it is clear that peers, near-peers, senior colleagues, and chairs need not be the same race or gender as the new faculty or even be from the same department as the new faculty as long as their definitions of mentoring align.

Finally, the benefits of continuous assessment cannot be overstated. An internal assessment can yield an ongoing database of a program's strengths and challenges, as well as elicit continuous feedback from participating faculty members. At the same time, an outside review by national experts can add value by bringing the voices of junior faculty, senior colleagues, and senior administrators into dialogue with one another, across identities such as gender, race, and ethnicity, and a variety of departmental and college contexts. It can bring conflicting interests to light and engage a much larger community in finding creative solutions. It can encourage multiple stakeholders to imagine the "ideal" features of a faculty development program and work together as institutional partners to establish and maintain an environment in which all new faculty can find professional success and personal well-being in the academic community.

REFERENCES

Alire, C. A. (2002). The new beginnings program: A retention program for junior faculty of color. In T. Y. Neely & K. H. Lee-Smeltzer (Eds.), *Diversity now: People, collections, and services in academic libraries* (pp. 21–30). Binghamton, NY: Haworth.

Bach, D. J., Barnett, M. A., Fuentes, J. D., & Frey, S. C. (2005). Promoting intellectual community and professional growth for a diverse faculty. In S. Chadwick-Blossey & D. R. Robertson (Eds.), *To improve the academy: Vol. 24. Resources for faculty, instructional, and organizational development* (pp. 166–183). Bolton, MA: Anker.

Boice, R. (1991). Quick starters: New faculty who succeed. In M. Theall & J. Franklin (Eds.), *New directions for teaching and learning: No. 48. Effective practices for improving teaching* (pp. 111–121). San Francisco: Jossey-Bass.

Boice, R. (1993a). Early turning points in professorial careers of women and minorities. In R. B. Boice & J. Gainen (Eds.), *New directions for teaching and learning: No. 53. Building a diverse faculty* (pp. 71–80). San Francisco: Jossey-Bass.

Boice, R. (1993b). New faculty involvement for women and minorities. *Research in Higher Education, 34*(3), 291–341.

Fink, L. D. (Ed.). (1984). *New directions for teaching and learning: No. 17. The first year of college teaching.* San Francisco: Jossey-Bass.

Harley, D. A. (2005). In a different voice: An African-American woman's experience in the higher education realm. *Rehabilitation Education, 15*(1), 37–45.

Kosoko-Lasaki, O., Sonnino, R., & Voytko, M. L. (2006). Mentoring for women and underrepresented minority faculty and students: Experience at two institutions of higher education. *Journal of the National Medical Association, 98*(9), 1449–1459.

Maher, F. A., & Thompson Tetreault, M. K. (2007). *Struggling to diversify: Privilege and diversity in the academy.* New York: Routledge.

Menges, R. J. (1999). *Faculty in new jobs: A guide to settling in, becoming established, and building institutional support.* San Francisco: Jossey-Bass.

Moody, J. (2004). *Faculty diversity: Problems and solutions.* New York: RoutledgeFalmer.

Olsen, D., & Crawford, L. A. (1998). A five-year study of junior faculty expectations about their work. *Review of Higher Education, 22*(1), 39–54.

Olsen, D., & Sorcinelli, M. D. (1992). The pretenure years: A longitudinal perspective. In M. D. Sorcinelli & A. E. Austin (Eds.), *New directions for teaching and learning: No. 50. Developing new and junior faculty* (pp. 15–25). San Francisco: Jossey-Bass.

Phillips, R. (2002). Recruiting and retaining a diverse faculty. *Planning for Higher Education, 30*(4), 32–39.

Piercy, F., Giddings, V., Allen, K., Dixon, B., Meszaros, P., & Joest, K. (2005). Improving campus climate to support faculty diversity and retention: A pilot program for new faculty. *Innovative Higher Education, 30*(1), 53–66.

Reynolds, A. (1992). Charting the changes in junior faculty: Relationships among socialization, acculturation, and gender. *Journal of Higher Education, 63*(6), 637–652.

Rice, R. E., Sorcinelli, M. D., & Austin, A. E. (2000). *Heeding new voices: Academic careers for a new generation.* Washington, DC: American Association for Higher Education.

Solem, M. N., & Foote, K. E. (2004). Concerns, attitudes, and abilities of early-career geography faculty. *Annals of the Association of American Geographers, 94*(4), 889–912.

Sorcinelli, M. D. (1988). Satisfactions and concerns of new university teachers. In J. G. Kurfiss (Ed.), *To improve the academy: Vol. 7. Resources for student, faculty, and institutional development* (pp. 121–131). Stillwater, OK: New Forums Press.

Sorcinelli, M. D., & Yun, J. (2006, October). *Building mutual mentoring networks.* Session presented at the 31st annual meeting of the Professional and Organizational Development Network in Higher Education, Portland, OR.

Sorcinelli, M. D., & Yun, J. (2007). From mentor to mentoring network: Mentoring in the new academy. *Change, 39*(6), 58–61.

Stanley, C. A. (Ed.). (2006). *Faculty of color: Teaching in predominantly white colleges and universities*. Bolton, MA: Anker.

Tierney, W. G., & Bensimon, E. M. (1996). *Promotion and tenure: Community and socialization in academe*. Albany: SUNY Press.

University of Virginia, Teaching Resource Center. (2007). *Programs—Excellence in Diversity Fellows*. Retrieved December 1, 2008, from http://trc.virginia .edu/Programs/EDF/EDF.htm

Washburn, M. H. (2007). Mentoring women faculty: An instrumental case study of strategic collaboration. *Mentoring and Tutoring: Partnership in Learning, 15*(1), 57–72.

Yun, J. H., & Sorcinelli, M. D. (2008). When mentoring is the medium: Lessons learned from a faculty development initiative. In L. B. Nilson & J. E. Miller (Eds.), *To improve the academy: Vol. 27. Resources for faculty, instructional, and organizational development* (pp. 365–385). San Francisco: Jossey-Bass.

19

ACCESS TO SUCCESS

A NEW MENTORING MODEL FOR
WOMEN IN ACADEMIA

Amber Dailey-Hebert, Emily Donnelli,
B. Jean Mandernach, Park University

The scarcity of women leaders in academia influences policies, proce-
dures, and expectations and in turn perpetuates a climate that deters
development of future women leaders. Despite research supporting the
need for institutional change to create leadership avenues for women fac-
ulty, little evidence of such change exists. The Presidential Leadership
Program for University Women was developed as a proactive, integrative
mentoring model to link female academics. Crucial to the program's suc-
cess are networking opportunities, peer mentoring in a group setting, and
a culminating "legacy project" designed to improve the campus climate
and services for women.

Several recent studies confirm that institutions of higher education fail to
advance women faculty who are equal in qualification to male counterparts.
This problem is specifically apparent in issues of tenure, promotion, status,
and pay (Hult, Callister, & Sullivan, 2005; Status of Female Leadership,
2002; West & Curtis, 2006). Yet, despite research supporting the need for
institutional change to create leadership avenues for women faculty, little
evidence of such change exists. In the words of the American Association of
University Professors, "The barriers for women in higher education not only
raise questions of basic fairness, but place serious limitations on the success
of educational institutions themselves" (West & Curtis, 2006, p. 4). This
statement underscores the need for research examining best practices and
programs to support women in academic career advancement. Bilimoria
and Piderit (2007) found that "women are not privy to many of the informal networks that involve potential male mentors such as certain clubs and

various sports and other recreational activities" (p. 162). Therefore, it is critical to rethink the traditional model and create a new mentoring model that works for working women in higher education today.

The Center for Excellence in Teaching and Learning (CETL), a centralized faculty development center at Park University, implemented an initiative to address the challenges facing women faculty as they pursue leadership positions: the Presidential Leadership Program for University Women. This women-focused collaborative mentoring program involves an annual cohort of women from varying disciplines, positions, and ranks within the institution who receive resources and opportunities to network with women leaders from the institution and the local area. The centerpiece of the program, a "legacy project," incorporates a peer mentoring component as the participants build on one another's skills, abilities, and talents, engaging in a team effort toward a common goal. The resulting legacy project advances the status of women faculty and contributes to overall development of the university as a "women-friendly" institution (Caplan, 1995). The program is a structure for what research has shown does not happen naturally for women: the informal mentoring, networking, and relationship building women have been challenged to create because of time constraints and other responsibilities. A mentoring model that creates semistructured exchanges and mentoring in a group setting can provide women with the much needed career guidance, networking opportunities, and relationship building required to succeed in their professional careers.

Literature Review

During World War II, Rosie the Riveter became the icon of the advent of women in the workforce. The struggles fought and victories won during the women's movement and the passing of Title IX further signaled the growing professional status and equality of women. More recently, a paradigm shift in the corporate workplace is promoting more flexibility for working women and affirming the value of retaining their female employees through onsite day care, alternative "flex time," extended leaves, and work-share programs (Palmer, 2007). In business, industry, and public service women are increasingly gaining the access, knowledge, skills, and opportunities to assume leadership roles.

Given its role and responsibility to improve society by creating and advancing knowledge, higher education might be expected to lead the way in promoting equality for women. However, this is not the case: "Women tend to take on greater responsibilities for care giving than do men, and the period of most intensive work to establish an academic career coincides with prime childbearing and childrearing years; [this]

may contribute significantly to inequities in faculty status, promotion, tenure, and salary" (Ackelsberg et al., 2004, p. 880). Although more women are earning a terminal degree and entering the labor pool (USDE, 2005), it is astonishing to find that "women hold only 24% of full professor positions in the United States" (West & Curtis, 2006, p. 4). In fact, the proportion of women declines at each step of the promotion and tenure process, thanks to "leaks in the academic pipeline for women" (Ackelsberg et al., 2004). Women who achieve their terminal degree and a tenure-track position in their thirties must balance full-time teaching and committee work with publish-or-perish expectations, while also considering their goals for family, children, and child care (Hamilton, 2002; Toren, 1993). Further exacerbating the problem, women faculty also typically serve on more committees (they are often invited as the "token female" to add representation to the committee) and advise more students—both time-consuming activities that are undervalued in the tenure and promotion process (Hult et al., 2005).

Research has shown the importance, particularly for women, of being mentored in the academic profession (Casto, Caldwell, & Salazar, 2005). Even those who persist through the tenure and promotion process may have difficulty finding mentors or role models in academic leadership positions (Caplan, 1995; Cawyer, Simonds, & Davis, 2002). A scarcity of women leaders in academia often reinforces the very institutional policies, procedures, and expectations that encumber female academics (Cullen & Luna, 1993).

Park University's Center for Excellence in Teaching and Learning (CETL) desired to move from defining the problem of gender disparity to actually solving it. Given limited information and few national models, CETL constructed a program for supporting high-potential women in academia. The goal was to identify successful strategies and models for advancing the status of women at institutions of higher education and create an integrated, generalizable model for advancing and mentoring female faculty. A master's-level institution with both residential and nontraditional students and one of the nation's largest accredited distance and online learning programs, our institution's diversity represents a range of both challenges and opportunities to advance women's leadership through a rich, multilayered mentoring program.

Program Goals

Inspired by the first female president in the institution's history, CETL established the Presidential Leadership Program for University Women in 2007 to furnish an innovative, low-cost approach for professional development to prepare our high-potential women for leadership roles in the institution and beyond. Central to the design of the mentoring program was a desire to modify the traditional dyadic mentoring model (Pololi & Knight, 2005), a design that often results in one-way information sharing and an expert–novice mentor–mentee relationship. In contrast, the program explored a new model, one focused on diverse women collaborating to achieve a shared outcome. Because research highlights both the psychosocial and career development benefits of women mentoring women (Schwiebert, Deck, Bradshaw, Scott, & Harper, 1999), the involvement of a diverse group of women in a nonhierarchical arrangement was critical to our program.

We wanted this program to make available accessible female role models and much needed networking opportunities that could accommodate the demanding lives of women in academia. On reviewing the literature and other successful programs that support the advancement of women in higher education (such as ACE's Office of Women in Higher Education Program initiative), we devised a professional enhancement mentoring program for women that drew on best practices in the literature while also incorporating features we perceived as lacking or deemphasized in other models. Inclusion of faculty from various disciplines and levels, including women in top administrative positions, both fosters collaborative mentoring and allows participants to learn about diverse aspects of the institution. We sought to move beyond the interaction emphasis of so many programs toward a more transformational and action-oriented experience. Not only did we want the program participants to identify critical professional issues at the institution and within the profession, we wanted the program's design to facilitate solutions to those problems.

Thus we incorporated as the culminating experience and centerpiece of the yearlong mentoring program a "legacy project." Uniting the peer-mentoring components, informal and formal networking opportunities with women within and outside the cohort group, guided group collaboration, and issue awareness to encourage the professional development of female faculty, the legacy project is collaboratively designed and incorporates strategic planning and team-building efforts toward a common goal: to improve the advancement of women at our institution. This form of the project is determined by the perspectives and talents of the particular cohort, with the overarching goal of further shaping the university as a "woman-friendly" institution (Caplan, 1995).

Rather than prescribe specific outcomes, we designed the goals of the program to establish a framework for dialogue: (1) define leadership excellence for one's individual academic career, (2) identify barriers to leadership excellence and resources to overcome them, and (3) recommend changes to promote the status of high-potential women at our institution.

Essential elements of the program include:

- *Access and networking with female leaders in academia, business, and government.* Several times a year, the president hosts a formal dinner at her home, to which she invites influential women in a variety of professional fields. Such guest mentors have included congressional representatives, a circuit court judge, the regional president of a nationally renowned bank, small business owners, and members of the institution's board of trustees. In particular, involvement of female trustees has resulted in personal links between the trustees and the faculty, giving both parties invaluable perspectives on faculty and administrative governance. One participant commented: "Having the opportunity to learn from successful role models through the . . . program has contributed to my professional development in so many ways. Most memorable is their sharing of workplace experiences, recounted with wisdom as well as humor, and their reflections on the value of mentorship have been particularly inspiring. What a great program for connecting the academic life to the broader community."

- *Peer mentoring in a group setting.* Both the formal dinners and the informal peer mentoring that resulted from the legacy project work allow natural development of relationships and friendships that extended beyond the traditional forced mentoring relationship of one novice and one veteran faculty member. Peer mentoring in a group setting highlighted each individual's unique gifts and talents, and it allowed the women to share those skills to benefit all women at the institution. A participant commented: "I was surprised by how much I learned from the other women in the program and how well our knowledge, skills, and experiences complemented one another. Even now that the program has concluded, I continue to seek out these women for ideas, guidance, and advice and feel a very special bond with the individuals in our small group that would never have existed otherwise."

- *Semistructured exchange and critical discussion.* Each cohort group is responsible for defining the most appropriate times, dates, methods, and modalities for communicating and engaging with one another—a particular challenge considering that the program involves participants from the institution's flagship campus as well as its nationwide distance learning campuses and its virtual campus. The groups have typically met monthly, communicated via email and online forums, and worked strategically and tirelessly to define their goals for the year and to offer support to one another in the varied and organic mentoring relationships that inevitably result from working on the shared "legacy project." A participant comments: "I found the communication exchange within the . . . program to be a powerful tool in my professional and personal life."

- *Collaborative problem solving toward a shared goal.* Qualitative research has documented the drive shared by women in leadership positions to make a difference and serve others (Madsen, 2008). Therefore, this program incorporates a collaborative problem-solving component in which the participants design, present to the president, and execute a legacy project that will have an impact on all women at the institution. This shared goal unites the participants in a way that other mentoring programs have failed to accomplish. A participant commented, "Working on the legacy project together really made the program about something greater than ourselves. We had the opportunity to make a real impact, to be creative, and to collaborate. For me, this is where the greatest benefit of the program exists."

Program Information

Here are details about the program participants, the required resources, and the legacy project, followed by our formative assessment of this young program.

Participants

Program participants are selected on the basis of their philosophy of helping other women; their ability to exhibit an inclusive and collaborative approach to problem solving; their ability to thrive in roles, disciplines, or departments that are typically male-dominated; and their potential growth to advance within institutions of higher education. Though the pilot cohort was chosen with the assistance of a number of individuals—department chairs, deans, faculty associated with CETL—subsequent participants are chosen via nomination by former program participants, with the goal being to create a new "class" of participants each year. We intend this design to facilitate ongoing involvement of women in the program, even past their first, formal year. For instance, the 2008 participants were welcomed into the program at a kick-off reception with the 2007 pilot class.

Resources Needed

The program was funded through CETL and the Office of the President. To reduce costs and ensure sustainability over time, we capitalized on existing university events and networking dinners sponsored by the Office of the President. Placing a two-hundred-page packet of readings on library reserve or on a website (as opposed to distributing it in hard copy) reduced the cost of program resources. Additionally, the small size of the group—four to six participants per cohort—helped keep costs low. The most significant costs typically result from the legacy project; as discussed later, participants have found creative ways of implementing legacy projects in conjunction with existing university events and initiatives to minimize cost.

Legacy Project

The centerpiece of the program and the culmination of the cohort group's collaboration is the legacy project. This project is collaboratively designed and implemented by the cohort group and is based in the participants' assessment of institutional strengths and areas for improvement related to women's leadership. The only criterion for the legacy project, apart from advancing the university as a "women-friendly" institution (Caplan, 2005), is that it must extend beyond the program participants to reach out to the broader campus community.

The pilot cohort's legacy project is a prime example of the ingeniousness of the program participants in light of limited funding availability. The participants wanted to call attention to the legacy of women's leadership at the institution by highlighting a distinguished alumna. A leader in pediatric medicine and pediatric hospice care, Dr. Doris Howell '44 achieved a successful career as a physician at a time when few females entered or stayed in the profession. Although Dr. Howell had sponsored a leadership award for students at the university, most of the university community was unaware of her connection to the institution. Because the costs of a visit by Dr. Howell would have exceeded the program's budget, the participants worked with other faculty colleagues to determine what resources and initiatives could be garnered to support a celebratory event with Dr. Howell in attendance. Conversations with history faculty resulted in a collaborative event to honor Dr. Howell as part of the university's Women's History Month programming. Drawing on an established budget line, and collaborating with other faculty and the Office of Student Life, the participants met their goal of honoring a distinguished woman in the university's history.

The most recent group's legacy project development process employed an equally fiscally conservative approach. Participants identified a lack of resources on issues faced by women faculty and students. Dialogue within the group led to a project to establish a physical space and donated resources for a "women's center" to be housed in the university's library. The center will be staffed by a student work-study position and will include, among other resources, information related to financial management, child care, women's health, and women's studies as an academic discipline. By collaborating with the university librarian, the student chapter of the American Association of University Women, and a previous program participant who had experience with a women's center at another institution, the participants were able to realize their goals for a legacy project.

The fact that legacy projects involve significant dialogue and negotiation of conflicting ideas about how to best contribute to the institution speaks to the benefits and challenges of bringing diverse women from various positions and levels at the university together. All parties involved benefit from learning about perspectives and experiences from different corners of campus experience.

Assessment of Program Effectiveness

The goal to prepare high-potential females to take leadership roles and advanced positions in the institution and beyond does not lend itself to immediate, measurable milestones of program success. Rather, we recognize that the effectiveness of the program will emerge over time as a paradigm shift with little conscious recognition of the changing roles of female leaders in the academy. Realizing that one cannot, in a short duration, document success in relation to the overarching program goals, we carry out ongoing formative assessment of the effectiveness of the program's design and function using both quantitative and qualitative data.

Eleven program participants (past and current) were asked to complete an online, anonymous survey, requesting that they rate their agreement with various statements on the basis of their experiences in the program, and all of them did so. The seven statements were drawn from the program goals, hallmarks, and design. Results of the survey (see Table 19.1) reveal that the majority of participants believed the program was effective in fostering their leadership potential as women in higher education. It is

Table 19.1. Program Participant Survey Responses

	Strongly Disagree	Disagree	Neutral	Agree	Strongly Agree	Rating Average
I believe participation in this program increased my access to and networking with female leaders in academia, business, and government.	0.0% (0)	0.0% (0)	18.2% (2)	27.3% (3)	54.5% (6)	4.36
Through my involvement, I feel I have increased opportunities to influence policy and procedures at my institution.	0.0% (0)	0.0% (0)	27.3% (3)	45.5% (5)	27.3% (3)	4.00
I believe the peer mentoring in a group setting was a valuable way to enhance my leadership abilities.	0.0% (0)	9.1% (1)	9.1% (1)	36.4% (4)	45.5% (5)	4.18
I believe the Legacy Project was a valuable activity for enhancing my professional activities and for advancing opportunities for all women at Park University.	0.0% (0)	9.1% (1)	9.1% (1)	18.2% (2)	63.6% (7)	4.36
Through my participation in this program, I can better define leadership excellence for my individual faculty career.	0.0% (0)	0.0% (0)	18.2% (2)	36.4% (4)	45.5% (5)	4.27
I am better able to identify challenges to leadership excellence and resources to overcome those challenges.	0.0% (0)	9.1% (1)	9.1% (1)	36.4% (4)	45.5% (5)	4.18
I am now equipped to recommend institutional changes to promote the status of high-potential women at our institution.	0.0% (0)	9.1% (1)	27.3% (3)	27.3% (3)	36.4% (4)	3.91

interesting to note that the two dimensions receiving the least agreement (feeling that they can influence institutional policy, and feeling equipped to recommend institutional changes) deal with the larger institutional impact of the program. Such institutional change and women's confidence in their role in this change are likely products of the paradigm shift that will happen as an increasing number of women gain leadership roles.

In addition to the quantitative data from the survey, participants were allowed an option for open-ended comments. Participant feedback indicated that a highlight of the program is the peer-mentoring component, but that scheduling and location are an ongoing challenge. Specific feedback from the open comments:

> This program is a great networking opportunity, and the advice given by professionals is very valuable. At the institutional level, this program could offer more opportunities to influence women professionally in the university.
>
> The opportunity to dialogue with other women at the university exposed common themes across disciplines and positions.
>
> This was a lovely opportunity. I only wish I lived in the KC/Parkville area so that I could have more fully participated.

Lessons Learned and Recommendations for Other Institutions

The program is a transferable small-scale mentoring program for any institution dedicated to advancing women in higher education. For those interested in coordinating a similar program, we offer these recommendations and suggestions, based on our experience implementing the program.

- *Consider geography.* Although our institution's main residential campus and administrative offices are located on our historic campus, we have a geographically dispersed faculty body and had to consider the involvement of faculty at a distance. For the pilot year of the program, we did not include distance faculty because of the challenges we anticipated. However, in the second year we included faculty who resided in another state, scheduling the formal dinners to coincide with campus visits and incorporating virtual technologies to connect the group.

- *Keep it small.* Because we limited the program to no more than six participants per year, we were not faced with large-scale coordination of multiple participants from multiple geographical locations. Apart from accessibility and cost concerns, our decision to keep the group small was to ensure that each formal networking dinner was able to comfortably host two to three special guest mentors in a reasonable group size to create meaningful dialogue and discussion.

- *Recruit potential supporters to control costs.* Part of our confidence in the transferability of our program model to other institutions lies in its low cost. With an initial budget of $250, recruiting dedicated individuals to support the program was critical to its success. We were fortunate to have the support of our provost and to have our president directly involved; she hosted the formal dinners at her home and covered the cost of the meals. She also drew on her contacts to arrange for outstanding women from the region to participate in the formal dinners as guest mentors. We recommend finding individuals at your institution (provost, vice president, department chair, dean, director, and so on) to help mobilize the initiative and add momentum to the program, highlighting the potential value it can bring to your campus. Connect with local organizations dedicated to advancing women to make contact with influential women leaders in your area. Such highly successful women are typically eager to share their stories and are much more likely to accept an invitation to dinner than to commit to a yearlong mentoring program. If grant or other funding is available, it could be used to support guest speakers, send participants to relevant professional development conferences, or fund legacy initiatives.

- *Consider program justification.* You may encounter faculty who do not find merit in the program and believe that such a program takes a political stance against the many males who also need mentoring opportunities on campus. We recommend doing an evaluation of existing campus resources that support mentoring for all faculty and using that evaluation to prepare a justification for the program. When faced with criticism, we were able to direct faculty to a variety of other sources on campus that promoted mentoring opportunities; we were also able to offer the legacy project as a campuswide resource open to the entire community. Another way to justify the program is to highlight the criteria and process for selection of participants. We have included a nontenured faculty member, a tenured faculty member, a midlevel administrator (department chair, assistant director), and a high-level administrator (dean, director, vice president) in each cohort. Such diversity allows us to say with confidence that the program, even though intended as an honor for its participants, is not exclusive; all women faculty, not just those who have achieved certain positions, have the opportunity to participate.

- *Relinquish some control.* In our pilot program, we took too much of the lead. We preplanned all meetings and dinners, and we coordinated communication among participants regarding the legacy project. As a result of feedback from participants, we changed the program's structure in the second year to allow much greater autonomy and flexibility. Only three formal networking dinners at the president's home were scheduled, and all other meetings pertaining to the legacy project and peer mentoring were managed by the participants themselves. The second cohort seemed to thrive with more flexibility, even meeting more often than the previous year's cohort, thus confirming the value of a more hands-off approach. Yet, to balance that flexibility, we recommend setting a timeframe for the cohort group to submit their legacy project outline. We set the deadline for the Legacy Project proposal submission to CETL and the president by the end of January each year, to allow time for implementation each spring.

- *Consider goals and their assessment.* It is important to be realistic about your program's goals and the manner in which you will assess your program's success. This is not the type of initiative that produces sweeping institutional change in a short timeframe, but rather an initiative that can allow your institution to retain emergent leaders who will, over time, influence their particular corner(s) of the university and, through the combined influence of all classes of participants, work more widespread cultural change. We encourage you to consider outcomes that extend beyond the individual participant, and beyond the cohort's tangible legacy project, toward the intangible paradigm shift in the ways in which you can develop and advance all women.

Conclusion

Equal access to advancement of men and women in higher education is a goal that must be embraced by the faculty development community as part of larger and ongoing efforts to diversify the profession of university teaching. This goal has been admirably and publicly articulated by nine leading university presidents: "There are still significant steps to be taken toward making academic careers compatible with family care giving responsibilities. . . . Our goal . . . is to create conditions in which all faculty are capable of the highest level of academic achievement" (University of California, Berkeley, 2005, paras. 2–3). This goal will be operationalized through the collaborative work of individual faculty and administrators who are dedicated to gender equity and will take shape in varied forms given varied institutional missions and resources. We hope that the program presented herein will inspire faculty developers to mine their institutional resources and uncover key faculty and administrative partnerships that can result in expanded opportunities for female mentoring.

REFERENCES

Ackelsberg, M., Binion, G., Duerst-Lahti, G., Junn, J., Van Assendelft, L., & Yoon, B. S. (2004). Remembering the "life" in academic life: Finding a balance between work and personal responsibilities in the academy. *PS: Political Science and Politics, 37*(4), 879–883.

Bilimoria, D., & Piderit, S. K. (2007). *Handbook on women in business and management.* Northampton, MA: Edward Elgar.

Caplan, P. (1995). *Lifting a ton of feathers: A women's guide to surviving in the academic world.* Toronto, Canada: University of Toronto Press.

Casto, C., Caldwell, C., & Salazar, C. (2005). Creating mentoring relationships between female faculty and students in counselor education: Guidelines for potential mentees and mentors. *Journal of Counseling and Development, 83*(3), 331–336.

Cawyer, C., Simonds, C., & Davis, S. (2002). Mentoring to facilitate socialization: The case of the new faculty member. *International Journal of Qualitative Studies in Education, 15*(2), 225–242.

Cullen, D. L., & Luna, G. (1993). Women mentoring in academe: Addressing the gender gap in higher education. *Gender and Education, 5*(2), 125–137.

Hamilton, K. (2002). Do babies matter when charting an academic career? The academy seems to think so. *Black Issues in Higher Education, 19*(3), 42.

Hult, C., Callister, R., & Sullivan, K. (2005). Is there a global warming toward women in academia? *Liberal Education, 91*(3), 50–57.

Madsen, S. (2008). *On becoming a woman leader: Learning from the experiences of university presidents.* San Francisco: Jossey-Bass.

Palmer, K. (2007, August 26). The new mommy track. *U.S. News & World Report.* Retrieved April 4, 2009, from www.usnews.com/usnews/biztech/articles/070826/3mommy.htm

Pololi, L., & Knight, S. (2005). Mentoring faculty in academic medicine. *Journal of General Internal Medicine, 20*(9), 866–870.

Schwiebert, V., Deck, M., Bradshaw, M., Scott, P., & Harper, M. (1999). Women as mentors. *Journal of Humanistic Counseling, Education and Development, 37*(4), 241.

The status of female leadership: By the numbers (Special report: women in higher education). (2002). *Black Issues in Higher Education, 19*(3).

Toren, N. (1993).The temporal dimension of gender inequality in academia. *Higher Education, 25*(4), 439–455.

University of California, Berkeley. (2005). *Joint statement by the nine presidents on gender equity in higher education.* Retrieved December 1, 2008, from www.berkeley.edu/news/media/releases/2005/12/06_geneq.shtml

U.S. Department of Education (USDE). (2005). *Digest of Education Statistics: Table 246.* Retrieved October 18, 2007, from http://nces.edu.gove/programs/digest/d05_tf.asp

West, M. S., & Curtis, J. W. (2006). *AAUP faculty gender equity indicators 2006.* Retrieved October 18, 2007, from www.aaup.org/NR/rdonlyres/63396944-44BE-4ABA-9815-5792D93856F1/0/AAUPGenderEquityIndicators2006.pdf

20

SURVIVOR ACADEME

ASSESSING REFLECTIVE PRACTICE

Laurel Johnson Black, Terry Ray, Judith Villa,
Indiana University of Pennsylvania

Reflective practice is a goal for many academic professional development programs. What do faculty participants gain from a reflective practice program, and how much reflection do they actually practice? Using interviews and grounded theory, we identified three crucial needs being met by such a program at our university. In addition, we compared participants' comments to the elements of reflection established by Dewey and Rodgers to determine the extent of their reflection. The results call for more assessment to better align the structures of reflective practice programs with participant needs as well as further research on the effects of reflective practice on the participants, their teaching, and their students.

> *The vast majority of men live lives of quiet desperation.*
>
> —Henry David Thoreau (So, too, do
> many professors)

Relatively few professors are well prepared for the many aspects of their job that don't focus on research. Isolated in their teaching and stretched thin by demands to publish research in major journals, earn top teaching evaluations, and share the work of university governance, professors often find little time for reflective, intentional teaching. They hover on the edge of burnout, hoping for inspiration. These are needs deeply felt, for they connect to our sense of self-as-teacher; they are not simply a desire for the most recent technology or a better schedule. Indeed, as Mezirow (1990) states, "No need is more fundamentally human than our need to understand the meaning of our experience. Free, full participation in critical and reflective discourse may be interpreted as a basic human right" (p. 11).

In response to these needs, programs encouraging reflective practice have sprung up at colleges and universities nationwide. At their best, such programs typically offer long-term support and the opportunity to engage in thoughtful research into pedagogical problems. Fullan (1993) argues that practitioners must "engage in continuous corrective analysis and action" (p. 5) and believes that "if people do not venture into uncertainty, no significant change will occur" (p. 25). Thus, institutions that rely on "teaching tips" or that enforce professional development from the top down do not promote significant and meaningful change. Rather, through both small- and large-group focused study and practice over an extended period of time, using local and national expertise, reflective practice programs support and encourage teachers to question their values and assumptions, test their practices, analyze the results, and continue to improve their teaching. With careful planning and the long-term, sustained support of participants, reflective practice programs can lead to widespread cultural change and involve teachers in discussion of theoretical, political, cultural, and ethical issues, not just teaching techniques (Boud, Keogh, & Walker, 1985a, 1985b; Lieberman, 1996; McKinnon & Grunau, 1994; Rodgers, 2002; Szabo, 1996; Schön, 1987).

On paper, reflective practice programs sound good, but do they deliver what they promise? What, in fact, *do* they promise? Reflective practice, according to Wagner (2006), "will help you celebrate your accomplishments, evaluate your skills, use your strengths more efficiently and continue to set and attain goals" (p. 30). But as Korthagen (1993) points out, given our difficulty in "operationalizing and measuring reflection" (pp. 134–135), how we promote it can become problematic as well: "It is remarkable that no generally accepted definition of the concepts reflection and reflective teaching exists, but also that there is no strong evidence for the claim that the emphasis on reflection is effective. And if it is, one may well ask: effective toward what end? The answer to this question is a matter of belief and conviction rather than one of empirical evidence" (p. 137).

Black, Cessna, and Woolcock (2005) argue that programs as complex as reflective practice usually demand multiple measures of assessment and evaluation. In this chapter, we explore the experiences and attitudes of faculty at one research institution who have participated in a reflective practice program. We support Korthagen's desire for empirical data, but the qualitative data generated by our interviews affords a firm jumping-off point for additional, more focused research, and a model for other similar programs.

Assessing Reflective Practice Programs

Public descriptions of reflective practice programs focus on program structure and history; Indiana University of Pennsylvania's (IUP) program brochure, website, and literature are no exception. However, these texts don't describe what participants actually get from their experience in the program or why they're there. At IUP, we wanted to go beyond the almost-always positive surface descriptions of reflective practice programs. We understand why those descriptions exist—funding for sustained professional development is tough to get and keep, and any data that might suggest that a program isn't producing the results it "should" puts it at risk of being discontinued. It is not too hard for most reflective practice groups to connect tangible outcomes—grants received, articles published, new courses designed—to participation in small groups or workshops. We wanted to get at something else, however, something deeper and more visceral. As Fullan (1993) points out, "[Teachers] function in a complex and dynamic environment where cause and effect are not always clear or close in time" (p. 20). Studying teachers' "intuition-in-action" (p. 361), Johansson and Kroksmark (2004) struggled to go beyond simply describing "the-things-that-show-themselves" and tried to understand how intuition blends experience, action, and emotion. When all is said and done and sixty colleagues have dragged their bodies into a Saturday workshop and stayed all day, why did they do it and what did they get out of it? When a group of five people from different departments meets regularly for a year in a cross-disciplinary discussion of critical thinking, how have they been changed? We decided that, as the first step in a more comprehensive exploration, interviews with current and former members of our reflective practice (RP) program could help us better understand what passions, fears, desires, and needs the RP program at IUP fulfills. Additionally and crucially, it could help us begin to assess its effectiveness in supporting reflection.

It may be that other reflective practice programs *are* being assessed, but if so, the researchers are keeping quiet about what they find. This is unfortunate, because discussion of multiple, well-designed accountability and evaluation measures of such programs could further the scholarship of teaching and learning and facilitate a productive allocation of scarce resources.

History and Structure of Reflective Practice at IUP

Indiana University of Pennsylvania is a doctorate-granting research university with approximately twelve thousand students. It has strong roots, however, as a "normal school" with an emphasis on both teaching and preparing teachers. IUP established its RP program in 1994 with approximately twenty members in the founding group. Its purpose has always been to encourage faculty to become more aware of their teaching, be more reflective, and through this process become better teachers. The RP project is headed by five co-directors, each having a specific duty within the group. Participation is voluntary and is open to faculty and teaching assistants from the campus doctoral programs. Participants receive no release time or any other institutional reward. Currently, the program offers faculty small-group activities through Departmental and Cross-Disciplinary Teaching Circles (DTCs and CTCs), each exploring a topic chosen by its members, monthly large-group meetings addressing various teaching issues, and two or more daylong weekend workshops each year. RP members are asked to attend at least half of the group meetings (whether large group or small group) every year. They are also urged to attend one or more of the weekend workshops, which are open to all faculty. RP has grown dramatically over the past decade, some years numbering more than a hundred members; in 2007–08, approximately seventy faculty actively participated. This number represents roughly 11–15 percent of the faculty. Formal recognition for participation is given in an end-of-the-year dinner when active members receive certificates.

What Reflection Is and How One "Does" Reflective Practice

Although many readers are familiar with "reflection," it was important for our research to establish what elements we wished to study. The concept of reflective practice is complex and has been defined and interpreted in a variety of ways since Dewey first named it in 1910. According to Rogers (2001), who surveyed and synthesized a range of definitions for reflection and the theories behind them, there is no clear agreement about what it means to be a reflective practitioner or thinker or learner: "In summary, . . . no fewer than 15 different terms were used to describe the reflective process" (p. 40). In addition, any reflective practice program must be studied as part of a "systems-thinking approach" that takes into account the "interconnectedness of structures" (Sparks & Hirsh, 1997, pp. 6–9). RP is supported, after all, by the very structures that make reflection so difficult to accomplish. Despite these levels of complexity and the range of terminology used among theorists, *some* agreement on the process does exist. In one explanation of the reflective process, Boud, Keogh, and Walker (1985b) posit three stages: "Preparation, engagement in an activity, and the processing of what has been experienced" (p. 9).

Another description is as simple as "What? So what? Now what?" (Barnett & O'Mahony, 2006, p. 502). All versions, however, draw heavily on Dewey's work.

The reflective process starts when practitioners experience what Schön (1987) calls "surprise" when something doesn't work as planned. They analyze the situation and create a new plan of action, test that plan, and reassess their practice. Schön argues that experienced instructors often "correct" practice on the spot, using "reflection-in-action," and reassess their teaching after the fact, which he called "reflection-on-action."

According to Rodgers (2002), who offers a close reading and analysis of Dewey's most relevant scholarship, reflection is a meaning-making, educative process that involves the "intellectual, moral, and emotional growth of the individual, and, consequently, the evolution of a democratic society" (p. 845). Like most scholars of reflection, Rodgers outlines several criteria for determining if reflection is taking place, one of which is that true reflection does not take place in isolation. Dewey (1916) demanded what he called reflection-in-community: "One has to assimilate, imaginatively, something of another's experience in order to tell him intelligently of one's own experience" (pp. 6–7). Those who stress reflection as part of a larger, transformative process see the element of discussion with a larger community as crucial. Zeichner (1996), for example, argues that unless reflective teacher education promotes social justice, it should not be supported; it simply continues to isolate teachers in their own classrooms, where they become "technicians, not professionals" (p. 206).

For Dewey, "educative experience" involved interaction between a person and her environment—between the self and another person, an idea, or whatever else makes up the particular environment. This, in turn, would lead to what Dewey named "intelligent action," another criterion for reflection (Rodgers, 2002). In addition, reflective practitioners would have to be willing to experiment with various actions, paying close attention to the results of every new action they take.

This process is supported by certain attitudes in practitioners that Dewey believed are essential to genuine reflection: wholeheartedness, directness, open-mindedness, responsibility, and readiness. By wholeheartedness, Dewey meant a genuine enthusiasm about one's subject matter as well as curiosity about it. The second characteristic, directness, is freedom from self-absorption and the presence of a reasonable self-awareness. According to Rodgers, this is the difference between "What did I teach today?" and "Where was the learning in today's work?" (p. 860). Open-mindedness, for Dewey, was "hospitality" to new ways of seeing and understanding. This concept included "playfulness," or releasing the mind to play with our ideas rather than clinging to them. Schön (1987) sees testing a hypothesis in a practical situation such as teaching as part of this playfulness.

Rodgers (2002) adds two other characteristics (pp. 962–963). The first, responsibility, means that we must examine the practical applications of our thinking and weigh them carefully. The second is readiness for the critical self-examination and possible changes that may result from deep reflection. To accomplish truly reflective practice as an instructor, then, is to commit to a time-consuming and challenging process of deep thinking and planned and assessed action.

Study Scope and Methodology

We formed a research group to undertake a qualitative study on IUP's RP program to determine its impact on (1) the teaching of past and present members of RP, (2) the students of past and present RP members, and (3) the overall professional life of present and past RP members, as well as to determine what RP activities had the greatest impact on past and present members and any other ways these members perceived RP to have had an impact. We sent a call to all past and present RP members soliciting voluntary participants in the study. Ultimately, twenty-two RP past and present members agreed to participate. Each volunteer completed a short demographic questionnaire and agreed to be interviewed by a member of the research team (see Appendix). All interviews were tape-recorded.

This methodology has its limitations for gathering participants. For one, the interviewees were unavoidably self-selected. As most researchers on reflection point out, the process is jump-started by faculty recognizing that something is awry in their practice. Faculty self-initiate into RP, and the most motivated volunteered for this project. In the future, we hope to interview those who have *not* participated in RP to find out why.

Interview Questions and Analysis

We also decided that at this time we would not ask focused questions about the process of reflection or ask for evidence of reflection. We wanted to begin with general questions and apply criteria for reflection to those answers. Thus, participants had as much time as they needed to respond to these questions:

- What impact, if any, has participation in RP had on your teaching?
- What impact, if any, has participation in RP had on your students?

- What impact, if any, has RP had on your overall professional life?
- Which activities in RP have had the most impact on you? In what ways?
- Are there any other comments you would like to share about RP?

The recorded interviews were transcribed, and we began the qualitative analysis of each transcript using grounded theory. An inductive approach, grounded theory requires researchers to break data into units of information that can then be categorized and subcategorized to define the boundaries of the larger categories. A narrative of sorts is created as categories are compared, contrasted, and sorted repeatedly, and finally central or master categories are selected and used to generate a theoretical model (Strauss & Corbin, 1998). In our study, our research team independently analyzed each transcript, looking for themes. Then we all met to compare perceptions and develop a working consensus. Finally, we looked for the varying prominence of the common themes among all of the interviews. We counted references in a theme according to the number of times an interviewee mentioned it. So if a person made a comment within a particular theme four times during an interview, each time was counted separately. We then tallied the frequency of the overarching themes, as shown in Table 20.1. The total number of comments per theme includes both positive and negative ones.

Table 20.1. RP Themes Ranked by Frequency of References in Interviews

Themes	Frequency
Collegial relationships	58
Changed teaching methods	50
RP effects on students	23
Inspiration	21
Personal growth	21
Overcoming complacency	20
Professional growth	18
Faculty feedback	17
Faculty collaboration	16
Reflection about self as teacher/learner	15

Evidence of Reflection

We also examined the transcripts for evidence of reflection using Rodgers's expanded criteria for reflective practice as touchstones (2002): wholeheartedness, growth, directness, open-mindedness, responsibility, analysis of experience, intelligent action, and inquiry-in-community. We coded the transcripts simply: "yes—clear statement matching criterion"; "no—no statement matching criterion"; or "implied—statements taken together indicate that the criterion has been met, though a direct and supportive statement is not evident." We did not tally the number of yes, no, or implied statements. If, for example, a participant repeatedly expressed a need for developing new skills, we counted them together as evidence of a desire for growth (see Table 20.2).

This portion of the coding was particularly frustrating. We are familiar with the teaching practices and philosophies of our colleagues and knew, for example, that they had taken "intelligent action" in past situations, but we decided that we could work only with what they actually said during the interview. Our interview questions in future research will close this empirical gap.

Findings: The Faculty Needs That RP Met

The themes we discerned in the interviews helped us identify three driving needs that RP was meeting. This information will help us both recruit new participants who have needs and goals consonant with what our

Table 20.2. Frequency of Statements in Interviews Supplying Evidence for Reflection

Criteria for Reflection	Evidence of Reflection		
	Yes	No	Implied
Wholeheartedness	18	3	3
Growth	21	0	1
Directness	16	4	2
Open-mindedness	19	1	2
Responsibility	16	3	3
Analysis of experience	14	1	7
Intelligent action	16	1	5
Inquiry-in-community	22	0	0

Note: Total N of participants = 22.

program can offer and also use our resources more carefully to shape future program offerings.

The Need to Connect

Not surprisingly, the most important participant need met by our RP program was collegiality. In RP, members said they found safety, security, and friendship. Unlike in most educational contexts, they could admit that they were struggling with teaching without getting a "black mark" on their formal or informal record. Because the goal of RP was teaching improvement, talking about their struggles was not an admission of failure but a first step toward becoming a better instructor.

Faye (all names of interviewees have been changed) explained how the safety of her small group allowed her to work deeply on her teaching: "It made me real transparent in some real interesting ways. I could say, 'I did this thing, and God, did it backfire. Have you tried this? How did it work?'" Many participants also mentioned the support, the validation of knowledge and accomplishment, and the sense of being valued that the program afforded.

RP participants also recounted the fun, excitement, passion, connection, and self-esteem they experienced in the program. Though Tony listed his many pedagogical changes and claimed the RP workshops "revolutionized" his teaching, he maintained, "I really value the social stuff more." After a presentation to the large group, he reflected: "People are coming up saying 'That's fantastic,' or 'I really value that' and I think, to me, when I see someone else get up and give a speech, I think, 'Wow, that's another great person doing great stuff, and I try to convey that to them.'"

The Need to Learn

RP members valued continued growth and change in teaching, which is probably why they self-selected into the program. Not surprisingly, the category of "changed teaching methods" ranked almost at the top of the list, and many other categories supported the importance of "good teaching." Excitement and passion about learning drew us into our careers and kept us going to become professors, and most of us expect to stay in the field for a very long time. The fear of stagnation was a driving force in RP participation: overcoming complacency ranked sixth on the list, with twenty references. At IUP, where the teaching load is high and the range of student skills in each class is great, faculty must incorporate a variety of pedagogical techniques to engage, educate, and—some would say—entertain their students. Further, in the cultures of some disciplines, many lower-level courses lack time for exploration and tentativeness. Conflict between disciplinary and student expectations can create a pedagogical tension that must be resolved, perhaps the initiating "surprise" in the process of reflection.

In these interviews faculty make frequent references to "newness," to change, to learning. In lives that are usually defined by the pursuit of knowledge, people eagerly seek structures that support learning. Nancy, for instance, recalled that lecturing to a large class was always the norm. She had been lectured to as a student in the sciences and followed that pattern with her own students in her own large classes. When she at last experienced a small class, she was happily surprised by how her students asked questions and engaged in discussion. Shifting back to a large lecture section, she knew she had to change her teaching to generate student participation: "The students were much more reserved. It just didn't feel right. Reflective practice was the first formal opportunity to reflect on how I taught and what I could do differently."

The Need to Leap Boundaries

The cross-disciplinary nature of RP was also an important draw for many of the participants—a significant subcategory within both "collegiality" and "knowledge gained through RP." Regardless of their discipline, members wanted to know how other disciplines approached teaching problems, even if what they learned was disconcerting. As Louise noted, "There's a tendency to stay where you are and communicate with the people who are in the same area you are in. . . . I've gotten to know people from other areas, to see ideas that are completely different, philosophies that are different."

Another participant, Alice, acknowledged the challenge of moving between disciplines: "I gained an understanding of what it means to be in another discipline. . . . It's disturbing to go out of your zone." This reaction echoed Johansson and Kroksmark's observation: "Teaching actions that harmonize with our own attitude give us a sense of security, especially if they coincide with the hidden attitude (towards the learner, school, knowledge, work methods, etc.) constituting the pedagogical nature of the schools. It is the other way around if the teacher is forced into teaching actions which are not his own" (2004, p. 367).

The interdisciplinary contact that RP encouraged facilitated participants' quest for a new perspective, another angle from which to approach a pedagogical problem. In such a safe environment, they experienced no threat. Rather, moving across disciplines led not only to new friendships among many RP members but also to new knowledge, which enhanced their sense of themselves as learners as well as teachers.

The Degree of Reflection

Of crucial importance to us was to determine whether RP was actually promoting reflection among members. Chism, Lees, and Evenbeck (2002) argue that, as we move from teacher-centered teaching to student-centered learning, we come to realize that we can't focus on technique but must be scholars of teaching and learning: "Instead of relying primarily on 'tips' and workshops that model effective techniques, those involved in the work of faculty development have come to operate on the principle that cultivating intentionality in teaching is at the heart of their work. . . . The concept of faculty development that emerges is based on community activity that depends on constant reflection to assess results and reconceptualize strategies" (pp. 34, 36).

The combination of a high number of references to changes in pedagogy (fifty) and a relatively low number of references to reflection about self (fifteen) might lead readers to believe that participants in RP were not particularly "reflective" by Dewey's and others' formal definitions. We might initially perceive them as merely "tinkering," as one participant put it. For some RP members, the demands of teaching, research, and service at any given time may mean all they feel they can accomplish is tinkering. These numbers, however, are part of a bigger picture.

We saw in our coding that RP participants were attending workshops and meeting with colleagues because they had identified a problem connected to teaching, were making changes as part of a longer process of discussion and learning, and were developing teaching and reflection skills within a community of like-minded colleagues. They were not simply looking for tips; they were seeking tips that supported a *process* of effective, *long-term* change.

Many interviewees recounted how participation in a small group or a workshop changed their teaching *fundamentally*. Nancy referred to a teaching philosophy statement she had revised since her involvement in RP: "I think about what it is I really like about teaching, and I go back and read it all the time." Tony pointed out that although he changed many small things (tinkering and tips) because of RP, more importantly, "I started saying 'I have these core things I believe' and I'm trying to structure the unit so they are aimed toward these things. That has taken me quite a while . . . to revamp the whole course takes a lot of thinking."

Making quick changes based on workshop ideas takes relatively little work; reflection and change are much more difficult. This may account for why collegiality, feedback from colleagues, and support also appeared high on the list.

Assessment: A Missing Link in the Reflective Process

Many RP participants pointed to specific changes, but few were able to say whether these changes were "working"—that is, improving their teaching and their students' learning. Jane declared: "If nothing else, I feel better about what I'm doing, and if I feel better about what I'm doing, then I have every reason to believe I'm doing it more efficiently and trying new things and doing it better. Even if my students don't believe that, I do."

When asked how his participation in RP has had an impact on his students, Paul admitted, "I don't know how I tell that." He continued, "I think overall the impact has been a very positive one, because I think my teaching has improved."

The RP program has sponsored many workshops on assessing student learning. How, then, can we make sense of these statements? Perhaps Paul and Jane were not thinking about student learning outcomes in any conventional use of the term. Attending workshops, thinking about our teaching, drafting teaching philosophy statements, tinkering with courses, and the like make us feel good about ourselves as instructors—more effective, more competent. Participation in RP is not always so much about *student* learning outcomes, at least not on a deep, personal level. The focus may be inward, and the participants' sense of professional self may change. This is a good place to start, but we cannot stop there. Reflective practitioners must also move outward. Feeling good inside does not necessarily equate to effective teaching.

Participants did occasionally reference informal assessment. Ed indicated that after he instituted humor in the form of cartoons to begin each class, one student brought in a cartoon for him to use. Tony said he received some letters saying how much students liked a particular aspect of his teaching. Still, Ed admitted that he didn't "monitor student responses in the classroom all that much," and Tony has many other students who *don't* write him letters. Evidence of *carefully structured assessment* of new course elements and teaching techniques was distinctively lacking in these interviews.

Culture and Community: An Area of Dispute

Dewey strongly argued that changes must move beyond the insulated community of the classroom to the larger culture. Thus the low number of references to changes in the campus culture (ranked twelfth) as a result of the RP program was of interest to the researchers. But our participants did not necessarily agree with Dewey about how widely the net should be cast to create a community of reflection. Anita, one of the long-time RP members in this study, pointed out that initially RP was about being dedicated to teaching and excelling at it, and the small number of faculty who joined the program formed a tightly knit group that was "hell-bent" on improving. In fact, these founders were largely senior faculty: "[We were] looking at those colleagues particularly who are called 'deadwood' and trying to put fire under them and keep fire under us so that we would not lose enthusiasm for our profession." She expressed concern over the larger number of faculty currently involved in RP and their motives—that the larger numbers make a close-knit community difficult to create, and that the newer members might just be going for promotion and could be only "paper participants." Although many program administrators would see increasing numbers as a positive sign of cultural change on campus, it is also possible that more negative aspects of the university teaching structure—the overwhelming need for tenure and the competition for promotion—might be infiltrating, warping, and undermining the structure and goals of reflective practice.

Participants mentioned RP's effects on their students relatively often, but they did not necessarily understand, measure, or appreciate those effects. For example, Nancy bemoaned her students' complaining about her forcing them to take an active role in their learning. In addition, given the structure of most students' programs, these effects might have been highly localized. Faculty in midsized institutions such as IUP or larger ones may not get the opportunity to work closely with the same students over a period of years. Many students take an instructor only once, particularly in large departments; for nonmajors, that professor is likely teaching an introductory level course. So RP's impact on teaching and the student population at IUP is currently very difficult to assess.

However, the knowledge that faculty gained by reflective practice did change a smaller community, especially in the case of the teaching circles. Jane reported that her departmental teaching circle "opened up more communication between my colleagues and myself." Hilda said that her involvement in a cross-disciplinary teaching circle made her question how her own department handles teaching "because there are other ways to think about how to teach and how students learn." The group's protection from administrators' participation and the unwritten confidentiality rules fostered this open sharing. Unfortunately, they also prevented the knowledge gained from going beyond the limits of the group.

The Bottom Line: Is RP Creating Reflective Practitioners?

The findings indicate that, even given the broad interview questions, all the participants clearly demonstrated some level of reflection on their teaching, and many clearly demonstrated it in all categories. In addition, it appears that the combination of safe structures in which faculty can explore their teaching and many opportunities to work across disciplines fosters reflection. However, in the categories of directness, responsibility, analysis of experience, and intelligent action, we saw mixed results. We recorded few mentions of assessing the impact on students of changes to teaching, so the category of "responsibility" had a fairly high number of "no" or "implied" responses. We have no reason to believe that our participants were weak on directness—that is, the ability to analyze the teaching experience from multiple perspectives—but our broad questions did not ask them to do so. In future interviews, we hope to get a clearer picture of where RP members struggle most as they become reflective practitioners and alter the program to address those struggles.

Future Research and Actions

The questions that drove us initially were why faculty participated and whether our RP program actually encouraged and supported their reflective practice. If we further explore RP's impact on participants, we will likely select a smaller number to interview and revisit the most interesting and frustrating elements of the initial interviews. We believe that "made changes in pedagogy" entails some of the assessment that faculty did not articulate in the more general interviews we conducted. Asking targeted questions that break out various elements of teaching—for example, asking about specific kinds of assessment techniques rather than a general question—would likely prompt more detailed answers regarding reflection and practice. We also intend to survey some of the faculty who do *not* participate. What tips the balance for them, making them decide not to take up the invitation, not to go to the workshops, and not to join a small group inside their department? Many scholars observe that institutional structures overwhelmingly support and encourage isolation in the classroom. As Cochran-Smith and Lytle (1996) put it, "Isolation . . . makes for privacy as well as loneliness, autonomy as well as separation" (p. 96). Perhaps some colleagues value their privacy and autonomy so much that the communal nature of reflective practice appears threatening to them. So they will endure loneliness and separation in order to maintain the control they feel they exercise. Perhaps they are introverts who practice reflection on their own, skipping its communal aspects.

Duffy (2008) doubts this, however, arguing that "reflection should not be a lone activity if real learning is to take place" (p. 334). But Duffy's may be too dogmatic an approach to reflective practice. Only by interviewing non-RP colleagues will we begin to understand their reluctance to join the RP program.

We also recognize that, if reflective practice programs want to meet participants' need to learn, workshops cannot simply be repeated. Advanced levels must be offered, or senior participants will find their needs are not being met. Structures to support cross-disciplinary pedagogical exchange must be designed and promoted across campus.

Qualitative research such as ours generates questions, narratives of "how things work" in a particular context that allow comparison and contrast. We hope that the coordinators of other reflective practice programs will begin to look carefully at their members' motivations, concerns, and changes as we have done here. In a culture rapidly embracing a business model, we need a clear understanding of the benefits of spending—and spending wisely—monies and time on reflective practice as part of a larger program of professional development. When we can create the structure that makes reflective practice the norm, hopefully faculty will not simply survive academe but will thrive.

Appendix A. Demographics of Participants in Reflective Practice Study

Name	Gender	Professional Status	College	Years in Reflective Practice	Years at IUP	Years Taught Elsewhere	Age of Participant
Sheila	F	Full prof.	Fine Arts	7–10	20+	4–7	51–57
Carmella	F	Assoc. prof.	Education	4–6	6–10	1–3	44–50
Paul	M	Full prof.	HSS	7–10	15–20	7+	58–64
June	F	Full prof.	HHS	7–10	20+	None	51–57
Jane	F	Asst. prof.	NSM	7–10	11–15	None	38–43
Sarah	F	Assoc. prof.	NSM	4–6	6–10	None	38–43
Gloria	F	Assoc. prof.	Education	7–10	6–10	1–3	51–57
Mia	F	Assoc. prof.	HHS	1–3	6–10	4–7	58–64
Peter	M	Assoc. prof.	Fine Arts	2–6	6–10	None	38–43
Rachael	F	Full prof.	Education	7–10	6–10	None	44–50
Nancy	F	Asst. prof.	NSM	1–3	1–5	None	31–37
Eve	F	Asst. prof.	HHS	4–6	6–10	7+	44–50
Tony	M	Full prof.	HSS	7–10	6–10	None	44–50
Faye	F	Assoc. prof.	HSS	7–10	11–15	7+	44–50
Louise	F	Assoc. prof.	NSM	7–10	11–15	7+	65+
Hilda	F	Full prof.	HHS	7–10	11–15	4–7	51–57
Alice	F	Assoc. prof.	HSS	4–6	1–5	4–7	44–50
Hans	M	Assoc. prof.	HSS	4–6	6–10	None	51–57
Tim	M	Assoc. prof.	HHS	7–10	11–15	7+	51–57
Jacqueline	F	Full prof.	Fine Arts	7–10	11–15	1–3	58–64
Ed	M	Full prof.	NSM	7–10	15–20	1–3	44–50
Anita	F	Full prof.	HSS	7–10	15–20	7+	51–57

Note: All participants' names have been changed. College titles are abbreviated to conserve space. Humanities and Social Sciences is HSS, Health and

REFERENCES

Barnett, B. G., & O'Mahony, G. R. (2006). Developing a culture of reflection: Implications for school improvement. *Reflective Practice, 7*(4), 499–525.

Black, L. J., Cessna, M. A., & Woolcock, J. (2005). The reflective practice project: Faculty production beyond the numbers. In J. E. Groccia & J. E. Miller (Eds.), *On becoming a productive university: Strategies for reducing costs and increasing quality* (pp. 149–157). Bolton, MA: Anker.

Boud, D., Keogh, R., & Walker, D. (1985a). Promoting reflection in learning: A model. In D. Boud, R. Keogh, & D. Walker (Eds.), *Reflection: Turning experience into learning* (pp. 18–40). New York: Nichols.

Boud, D., Keogh, R., & Walker, D. (1985b). What is reflection in learning? In D. Boud, R. Keogh, & D. Walker (Eds.), *Reflection: Turning experience into learning* (pp. 7–17). New York: Nichols.

Chism, N.V.N., Lees, N. D., & Evenbeck, S. (2002). Faculty development for teaching innovation. *Liberal Education, 88*(3), 34–41.

Cochran-Smith, M., & Lytle, S. L. (1996). Communities for teacher research: Fringe or forefront? In M. W. McLaughlin & I. Oberman (Eds.), *Teacher learning: New policies, new practices* (pp. 92–112). New York: Teachers College Press.

Dewey, J. (1916). *Democracy and education.* New York: Free Press.

Duffy, A. (2008). Guided reflection: A discussion of the essential components. *British Journal of Nursing, 17*(5), 334–339.

Fullan, M. (1993). *Change forces: Probing the depths of educational reform.* New York: Falmer.

Johansson, T., & Kroksmark, T. (2004). Teachers' intuition-in-action: How teachers experience action. *Reflective Practice, 5*(3), 357–381.

Korthagen, F. A. (1993). The role of reflection in teachers' professional development. In L. Kremer-Hayon, H. C. Vonk, & R. Fessler (Eds.), *Teacher professional development: A multiple perspective approach* (pp. 133–146). Berwyn, PA: Swets & Zeitlinger.

Lieberman, A. (1996). Practices that support teacher development: Transforming conceptions of professional learning. In M. W. McLaughlin & I. Oberman (Eds.), *Teacher learning: New policies, new practices* (pp. 185–201). New York: Teachers College Press.

McKinnon, A. M., & Grunau, H. (1994). Teacher development through reflection, community, and discourse. In P. P. Grimmett & J. Neufeld (Eds.), *Teacher development and the struggle for authenticity: Professional growth and restructuring in the context of change* (pp. 165–192). New York: Teachers College Press.

Mezirow, J. (1990). How critical reflection triggers transformative learning. In J. Mezirow (Ed.), *Fostering critical reflection in adulthood: A guide to transformative and emancipatory learning* (pp. 1–20). San Francisco: Jossey-Bass.

Rodgers, C. (2002). Defining reflection: Another look at John Dewey and reflective thinking. *Teachers College Record, 104*(4), 842–866.

Rogers, R. (2001). Reflection in higher education: A concept analysis. *Innovative Higher Education, 26*(1), 37–57.

Schön, D. (1987). *Educating the reflective practitioner*. San Francisco: Jossey-Bass.

Sparks, D., & Hirsh, S. (1997). *A new vision for staff development*. Oxford, OH: National Staff Development Council.

Strauss, A., & Corbin, J. (1998). *Basics of qualitative research: Grounded theory procedures and techniques*. Thousand Oaks, CA: Sage.

Szabo, M. (1996). Rethinking restructuring: Building habits of effective inquiry. In M. W. McLaughlin & I. Oberman (Eds.), *Teacher learning: New policies, new practices* (pp. 73–91). New York: Teachers College Press.

Wagner, K. (2006). Benefits of reflective practice. *Leadership, 36*(2), 30–32.

Zeichner, K. (1996). Teachers as reflective practitioners and the democratization of school reform. In K. Zeichner, S. Melnick, & M. L. Gomez (Eds.), *Currents of reform in pre-service teacher education* (pp. 199–214). New York: Teachers College Press.

TRANSFORMING TEACHING CULTURES

DEPARTMENTAL TEACHING FELLOWS AS AGENTS OF CHANGE

Cassandra Volpe Horii, Curry College

The Departmental Teaching Fellows (DTF) program of the Derek Bok Center for Teaching and Learning at Harvard University employs doctoral students as peer teaching mentors. Four years of program assessment data include quantitative work inventories, surveys and self-reports, interviews of faculty and administrators, and a survey of all graduate students recently teaching in arts and sciences. Observed program outcomes include (1) better informal support for teaching, (2) higher quality and quantity of interactions between graduate students and faculty on teaching, and (3) more systematic opportunities for teaching-related professional development. Qualitative assessment data suggest that the DTFs

The DTF program has been supported in part by the Albert W. and Katherine E. Merck Fund. The deans and staff in the Office for Undergraduate Education and the Graduate School of Arts and Sciences have supported the program in material and other ways, for which I am grateful. I acknowledge the DTFs for their vast creativity and dedication, and the departmental faculty and administrators for their generous collaboration and participation. Thanks also to Bok Center staff members Terry Aladjem, Lisa Boes, John Girash, Robin Gottlieb, Barbara Hall, Rebecca Hunter, Eric LeMay, Virginia Maurer, Richard Olivo, Mary Beth Saffo, Ellen Sarkisian, Alexandra Sear, Lee Warren, and James Wilkinson for their enthusiastic sustaining of the program and mentoring of the DTFs. I extend special thanks to Erin Driver-Linn for collaboration in planning and implementing program assessments, for supplying data from the 2006 TF survey, for discussion of the interpretations presented herein, and for mentoring the DTFs. Finally, anonymous reviewers and volume editors are acknowledged for their insightful suggestions about analysis and presentation of data.

occupy several liminal positions that may uniquely position them to facilitate changes in departmental teaching cultures, in some cases overcoming barriers faced by faculty and administrators.

As reported in *The Formation of Scholars: Rethinking Doctoral Education for the Twenty-First Century*, a surprise outcome of the Carnegie Initiative on the Doctorate (CID), a five-year study of Ph.D. programs, was the pervasive importance of "intellectual community" (Walker, Golde, Jones, Bueschel, & Hutchings, 2008). Walker et al.'s focus on intellectual community augments more than a decade of intensive investigation into the development, socialization, and preparation of the next generation of faculty (Austin, 2002; Nyquist & Sprague, 1998). According to Walker et al., the quality of intellectual community in a department "affects . . . how people wrestle with ideas . . . how teaching is valued . . . how [doctoral] students learn to engage with senior colleagues . . . how failure is treated . . . how people work together . . . how independence and creativity are encouraged . . . how the department and its members stay connected to the field" (p. 122). Walker et al. also found in many of the departments they studied "no guarantee (or structure to ensure) that experience actually leads to greater understanding of the complicated dynamics of teaching and learning" (p. 67). Their description of intellectual community extends Feldman and Paulsen's faculty-specific definition of "teaching culture" (1999) to include graduate students. Feldman and Paulsen cite faculty involvement and interaction, professional development opportunities, definitions of scholarship that include teaching, and administrative or central support among the components of a productive teaching culture.

These hallmarks of intellectual community and teaching culture overlap substantially with three observed outcomes of the Departmental Teaching Fellows (DTF) program at Harvard University, in which doctoral students work as peer mentors on teaching in collaboration with department faculty, administrators, and the Derek Bok Center for Teaching and Learning. The program outcomes and the associated aspects of intellectual community are (1) better informal support for teaching that addresses "how teaching is valued" and "how people work together"; (2) higher quality and quantity of interactions between graduate students and faculty on teaching to address "how [doctoral] students learn to engage with senior colleagues"; (3) more systematic opportunities for teaching-related professional development, addressing "how people wrestle with ideas," "how failure is treated," and "how independence and creativity are encouraged" with respect to teaching, as well as the need for "structure" in development of teaching abilities. This chapter presents four years of assessment data supporting the three outcomes and goes on to explore how and why doctoral students may be uniquely positioned in departments to facilitate change in teaching culture.

Program Description

The Derek Bok Center for Teaching and Learning employs nine permanent senior staff members (the majority at half- to three-quarter-time, a few full-time) and several half-time postdoctoral fellows/officers, to serve the teaching development and improvement needs of faculty and graduate students in the forty plus degree-granting departments in the Faculty of Arts and Sciences (FAS). Graduate students in FAS are typically required to serve as teaching fellows (TFs) for between one and four semesters, and many teach additional semesters. (Note that TFs are the same as graduate teaching assistants at many other U.S. institutions; they typically lead discussion sections and labs, and they grade undergraduate student work. Some teach tutorials or seminars, where they have a substantial role in designing the syllabus.) Between eight hundred and eleven hundred TFs teach each semester in FAS. In addition, several hundred section and lab leaders work as "teaching assistants" (TAs) who are not graduate students at Harvard. TAs are usually graduate students at other institutions or have already earned a terminal degree in their field.

Context and History

In 1995, the FAS Faculty Council mandated that all TFs and TAs receive pedagogical training before teaching. Departments were charged with the task of devising and implementing training programs appropriate to their respective disciplines. Implementation of universal TF/TA training remained uneven in the decades following the Faculty Council mandate.

While working to enhance TF/TA training and development in recent years, the Bok Center has also been charged with increasing programs and services for faculty. In an effort to improve training and development for both TF/TAs and faculty without hiring additional permanent staff, the Bok Center began the DTF program in academic year (AY) 2004–05 with two doctoral students, then called Bok Center TFs. As of AY 2008–09, the DTF program has grown to twenty participating departments (see Table 21.1).

With a twenty-year history of employing experienced TFs as "teaching consultants" for hourly pay on a work-as-needed basis at the center, the

Table 21.1. Departments Participating in the DTF Program, by Academic Year

Department	2004–05	2005–06	2006–07	2007–08	2008–09
African and African American Studies			X[a]	X	X
Anthropology[b]		X			
Biostatistics[c]				X	X
Chemistry and Chemical Biology					X
East Asian Languages and Civilizations			X	X	X
Economics[d]			X		
Engineering and Applied Sciences[e]		X	X	X	X
English		X	X	X	X
Government			X	X	X
History	X	X	X	X	X
History of American Civilizations			X[a]	X	X
History of Science	X	X	X	X	X
Literature and Comparative Literature				X	X
Music					X
Philosophy					X
Physics		X	X	X	X
Psychology		X	X	X	X
Religion				X	X
Sociology			X	X	X
Statistics			X	X	X

Department	2004–05	2005–06	2006–07	2007–08	2008–09
Visual and Environmental Studies[f]			X		X
Women, Gender, and Sexuality Studies					X

Notes: [a]Two departments shared a single DTF in AY 2006–07.
[b]Discontinued participation after AY 2005–06 because three departmental subareas did not lend themselves to support from a single DTF.
[c]Harvard School of Public Health (HSPH), not FAS; DTFs participate in training and mentoring at the Bok Center, but the positions are funded and supervised by HSPH.
[d]Discontinued participation after AY 2006–07 because of departmental decision to employ all qualified TFs as section leaders, not as DTF.
[e]Formerly a division within FAS, became a school in 2007; shares costs for DTF positions with FAS because of enrollment of undergraduates in bachelor's degree programs.
[f]Gap in participation in AY 2007–08 for lack of qualified candidates.

DTF program, with salaried appointments and a focus on departments, was both a continuation of and a significant departure from past work. The Bok Center based aspects of the DTF program on similar programs in place at other large, research-intensive universities: the University of Colorado's Lead Graduate Teacher Network (Border, 2005), the University of Michigan's Graduate Student Mentor Programs and Graduate Teaching Consultant (University of Michigan, 2008a, 2008b), and the Ohio State University Graduate Teaching Fellow Program (Rohdieck, 2009). By focusing on departments, the DTF program aimed to address issues of inherent interest to scholars and teachers within their fields (Huber & Morreale, 2002) and to develop pedagogical content knowledge (Ronkowski, 1998) in departments.

Collaboration with Departments

Departmental buy-in is one of the key structural elements of the DTF program. To participate, faculty in the department (as represented by the chair, director of graduate studies, or director of undergraduate studies, plus others), along with administrators who handle TF/TA support, must be involved in several ways.

As part of the departmental half of the application package, faculty are asked to describe goals for the DTF's work during the next AY. Goals may include proposed projects or programs that the DTF will undertake and the rationale behind them (such as creating a new handbook or website on disciplinary teaching, working with faculty to design a syllabus for a new graduate course on disciplinary teaching methods, or supporting a new departmental requirement for TF/TA training). Faculty may also propose standard TA/faculty development methods that the DTF will employ, such as practice teaching, video-based consultations, class observations, and office hours for teaching questions. In addition, departmental goals may modify the plan in various ways, such as accommodating major curriculum changes or groups of TFs/TAs requiring special support, having the DTF serve on departmental committees related to teaching, or raising pedagogical or cultural challenges the department is working to overcome. In the application, the department agrees to engage in the Bok Center's assessment efforts, supply resources for the DTF such as office space and minor material support for projects, and provide ongoing mentoring and guidance.

Each department endorses or nominates one or more graduate students to serve as a DTF through a process aligned with its administrative structure, culture, size, and graduate requirements. Some departments open the process to all interested graduate students and conduct internal interviews to determine which applicant they will endorse; others invite only a selected graduate student to apply; still others nominate several qualified applicants and have the Bok Center interview and select a candidate. The second half of a complete application package consists of the DTF candidate's cover letter and an application form detailing teaching experience, professional development work to date, and references (including academic adviser).

Throughout the AY, the DTFs meet regularly with both departmental and Bok Center mentors. They also communicate formally at the beginning of every semester by sending short memos outlining their unique portfolios of work or progress updates to all parties (faculty mentors, department administrators, Bok Center mentor, DTF program director). These required collaborative structures—faculty/administrative involvement, clear goals, tailored hiring processes, contribution of material and space resources, documentation—are both common across departments participating in the program and individualized for each department.

Hiring and Funding

DTF appointments are structurally and technically considered teaching appointments in FAS. They are equivalent to other TF/TA appointments in time commitment, compensation, and contribution to teaching requirements and limits. Time commitments for DTF appointments vary between one-fifth and half-time per semester, depending on the scope of the departmental goals and availability of funds, and they normally span a full AY. Equivalence to other TF/TA appointments grants DTFs a degree of formal authorization via a recognized title and a mandate to interact with faculty, administrators, and TFs/TAs regarding teaching. Equivalence also means that DTFs integrate their work into their graduate programs by setting aside adequate time for the job without neglecting other responsibilities for scholarship and coursework. This hiring structure broadens the formal definition of teaching for graduate students to include teaching about teaching, whether the department has or proposes a catalogue-listed course for TFs/TAs on disciplinary teaching methods (as in nine of the twenty participating departments in AY 2008–09, all co-taught by department faculty and DTFs) or has or proposes a non-course-based TF/TA training and development program.

To date, the DTF program has been cofunded by the Bok Center and by the Office for Undergraduate Education. Cost sharing has been facilitated by an external, current-use gift at the Bok Center (ending in AY 2008–09) and expansion of what constitutes teaching from an administrative perspective in FAS. Because of this broad definition of teaching, approximately half the DTF positions have been funded out of the TF/TA teaching appointment budget through the Office of Undergraduate Education. In a few cases, departments or schools outside FAS have either fully funded or shared costs for DTF appointments (see Table 21.1).

Training and Development

The Bok Center provides each cohort of DTFs with extensive training and professional development in the spring prior to, and ongoing throughout, their appointments. A typical year of DTF meetings includes these activities:

- In early May, outgoing and incoming DTFs meet in disciplinary groups to share advice and ask questions. These panel discussions convey the scope of the job and tips for how to begin planning.

- In late May through early June, a two-day orientation program introduces central skills and concepts. The orientation includes interactive sessions on topics such as characterizing teaching cultures, setting goals, planning and implementing programs, handling politically difficult situations, confidentiality, and research on teaching, learning, and faculty/graduate student development.

- In September and November, a series of monthly interactive workshops on common faculty/TA development tools fosters opportunities for practice and feedback. Tools include practice teaching, video-based consultations, class observations, and teaching evaluations.

- In December, DTFs contribute for discussion their own cases based on challenging, puzzling, or successful experiences. These case discussions are a turning point in the program, where DTF meetings shift from prescriptive training to self-directed professional development.

- In January through April, small groups of DTFs work with Bok Center staff to plan professional development sessions of their own choosing. Recent topics have included "creating sustainable teaching programs in departments," "working with TFs/TAs on teaching portfolios," "recent research on teaching and learning," and "faculty/TA development as a career."

These training and development activities aim to build a strong cohort among DTFs and strong connections with Bok Center staff, which in turn enlarges their professional network and facilitates collaboration across departments.

Program Assessment

During the first pilot year of the program (AY 2004–05), assessment methods were informal, consisting of midyear and end-of-year reports and ongoing focus groups with DTFs to discuss the current and future structure of the program. More formal program assessment in AYs 2005–06 through 2008–09 included multiple forms of quantitative and qualitative data.

Methods

In all AYs after 2004–05, DTFs completed quantitative work inventories (capturing numbers and types of DTF interactions with TFs and TAs), pre- and-post surveys and evaluations (addressing expectations, skill areas, and DTF training and development), and self-reports (including midyear and end-of-year reports). In AY 2007–08, DTFs began using the Bok Center's secure calendar and database to inventory and track their work.

In May 2006, the Bok Center and the FAS Committee on Pedagogical Improvement conducted an electronic survey of all recent TFs in FAS, with questions on many aspects of the TF experience; approximately four hundred TFs responded, enabling comparison between departments with, and without, DTFs at that time. In-depth interviews of departmental faculty and administrators were conducted in AYs 2005–06 and 2006–07. In 2008–09, feedback surveys via email took the place of formal interviews with faculty and administrators, although Bok Center and departmental faculty and staff communicate informally on a regular basis.

Quantitative Outcomes

Prior to AY 2007–08, when DTFs began using the same internal database as Bok Center staff, it was difficult to make reliable comparisons between numbers of clients (TFs, TAs, faculty, other or unknown-rank instructors) served. With the use of a common database in AY 2007–08, the Bok Center defined one "participation" as one client attending one substantial teaching development event (for instance, a teaching-related consultation, a video-based consultation, a class observation consultation, a practice teaching session, or a workshop on teaching). Large multistaff events (such as biannual teaching conferences and teaching award ceremonies) and serial programs (such as a small, stable group that meets many times) were not included as participation. Note that the total number of participations exceeded the number of unique clients because some clients participated in several consultations or workshops.

According to these criteria, in AY 2007–08 fifteen DTFs generated approximately 940 participations with TFs/TAs in their departments. For comparison, nine senior Bok Center staff and several postdoctoral fellows/officers generated approximately 1,520 participations—853 with TFs/TAs, 339 with faculty, and 332 with clients of other or unknown rank). Senior Bok Center staff and postdoctoral fellows/officers have worked consistently at capacity and have generated a roughly stable number of total client participations from year to year, including increased participation by faculty. The Bok Center infers that the DTF program has increased TF/TA participation in teaching development work.

In addition to increasing participation, analysis of the May 2006 survey of TFs suggested that the seven departments with DTFs fared better on measures of intellectual community and teaching culture than departments without DTFs (see Table 21.2). The TF survey received approximately 150 responses from TFs in departments with DTFs and approximately 250 responses from TFs in departments without DTFs. Departments with DTFs scored higher on quantity and effectiveness of teaching-related communications, effectiveness of disciplinary teaching workshops and panels, and perceived value of teaching. The differences between departments with and without DTFs were statistically significant at the .05 level for composite scores on teaching-related communications between graduate students and faculty and for composite scores on teaching-related communications in general.

Qualitative Outcomes

Table 21.3 summarizes the prevalence of qualitative program outcomes as themes in interviews with departmental faculty and administrators and

Table 21.2. Measures of Intellectual Community and Teaching Culture on the 2006 Survey of TFs in FAS, DTF Versus Non-DTF Departments

Survey item(s)	Mean (SD)		Responses		
	DTF	No DTF	DTF	No DTF	t, p
Teaching-related communication[a]					
With peers (frequency + effectiveness)	3.52 (1.01)	3.36 (0.94)	141	241	1.6, .11
With faculty (frequency + effectiveness)	2.68 (0.98)	2.46 (1.04)	139	242	2.0, .04*
Peers + faculty overall	3.16 (0.84)	2.97 (0.82)	139	241	2.2, .03*
Effectiveness of workshops and panels[b]	3.01 (1.27)	2.76 (1.16)	85	102	1.4, 17
Value department places on teaching[b]	2.87 (1.11)	2.78 (1.08)	137	238	0.8, .44

Notes: Survey scale (quantity, effectiveness): 1 (very low, ineffective), 2 (low, somewhat ineffective), 3(average, moderately effective), 4 (high, effective), 5 (very high, very effective), (n/a, have not had the chance to use).

[a]Overall scores combining two or more survey items.

[b]Single survey items.

*p < .05, two-tailed t-test.

Table 21.3. Summary of Qualitative Themes in DTF Assessment Data

AY	N[a]	Theme			
		Informal Support[b]	Faculty-TF Interaction[c]	Systematic Opportunities[d]	Liminality[e]
		Faculty and administrator views			
2005–06	6	5	4	6	3
2006–07	10	9	5	9	2
		DTF reports			
2005–06	7	7	5	7	4
2006–07	12	12	8	10	5
2007–08	14	14	9	12	3

Notes: Open-ended interviews and reports were coded according to whether each theme was mentioned at least once as a strength, outcome, or goal of the DTF program in the department.

[a]Number of departments where a faculty member or administrator was interviewed, or number of DTFs completing reports.

[b]Interviews and reports citing one or more forms of informal support for teaching (perceived value of teaching, discussion of teaching, and sharing of teaching materials among peers).

[c]Interviews and reports citing quality or quantity of interactions between graduate students and faculty on teaching.

[d]Interviews and reports citing systematic opportunities for teaching-related professional development.

[e]Interviews and reports citing one or more forms of liminal status (e.g., liaison, link, translator; occupying a gap; being on a threshold).

in reports submitted by the DTFs during AYs 2005–06, 2006–07, and 2007–08. Interviews and reports were open-ended, inviting reflection on goals, strengths, accomplishments, plans for the future, weaknesses, and areas for improvement. Almost all faculty, administrators, and DTFs in all years mentioned informal support for teaching (including perceived value of teaching, discussions about teaching, and sharing of teaching materials among peers) as an important outcome, strength, or goal of the program. Systematic opportunities for teaching-related professional development also appeared in a large majority of interviews and reports in all years. Quality and quantity of interactions between graduate students and faculty on teaching was cited by a majority in all years, with somewhat greater variability.

Liminality, encompassing multiple forms of professional transitions and thresholds, appeared in 20–60 percent of interviews and surveys every year, making it a consistent and substantial theme. Alternative expressions of liminality in the qualitative data included words and phrases such as *liaison, link, translator*; occupying a space or gap in status, expertise, or professional identity; and being between roles or stages. When liminality did appear in the qualitative data, the material was often particularly rich with meaning. Examples are explored in greater depth in the next section.

Discussion

While acknowledging the outcomes described here, the five-year mark has prompted reflection at the Bok Center on why the DTF program works as it does. At the turning point between a fledgling program and a somewhat established one, it makes sense to go beyond documenting outcomes and move toward understanding the processes behind them. The DTF program outcomes demonstrate that an institution can engage doctoral students in transforming the teaching and learning environment. But they do not answer the larger questions: Why had departments not already improved intellectual community and teaching culture prior to the DTF program? Why do graduate students, in the role of DTF, seem to effectively catalyze such transformations?

Risk and Failure

One of the larger social science departments in FAS, SS-3, had for many years been known anecdotally for its difficult, sometimes hostile, teaching environment. (Department names are coded according to disciplinary group and arbitrary number: SS for social sciences, SCI for sciences and mathematical fields, and HUM for humanities). Key faculty members had a reputation for encouraging a utilitarian approach to teaching: get it done but spend as little time as possible. After participating in the DTF program for multiple years, a department administrator (a relatively neutral party in the department and someone with whom the DTF worked closely) offered these thoughts on the program's role in departmental transformation:

> [The DTFs] have filled an important gap between scholarship/research and the leap to teaching. . . . Many faculty members are talented mentors but they differ in terms of what they can give to teacher training. [The DTF] ensures a baseline of quality teaching in the department. . . .

[TF] training was not in the forefront of the faculty's attention before. With the [DTF], it reminds the faculty that it's important. Now we're able to create some progress. It's an incentive for faculty to think about implementing things they may not have found the time for in the past. [The DTF] creates synergy by making it doable for faculty to be more active in [TF] training. [The DTF's work] makes it possible for faculty to share their teaching knowledge with all of the graduate students, not just those teaching in their classes.

This SS-3 administrator may be interpreted as identifying two kinds of liminality: a "gap" separating scholarly work and teaching and a transition (the metaphorical "leap") into beginning to teach. The former is addressed in the next section. The latter speaks poignantly to the lived experience of risk and danger for many doctoral students, also identified by Walker et al. (2008) as the culture surrounding experimentation and failure.

The same administrator noted at another point in the interview that "having [the DTF] here makes it possible for [TFs] to ask . . . teaching questions they might not want to ask the faculty about." A DTF in a related field, SS-6, identified the most important parts of the job as "organizing events and creating spaces in which people feel comfortable talking about teaching [and] developing personal relationships with [TFs] such that they feel comfortable coming to me with issues/problems."

If helping TFs feel comfortable speaking about teaching was important, and if TFs were cautious about talking with faculty about teaching, then the sense of risk associated with teaching appears high. These data suggest that DTFs have contributed to development of "flexible and forgiving" intellectual communities (Walker et al., 2008, p. 126), where risk, experiments, open discussion, and questions related to teaching are tolerated and encouraged.

Kinds of Liminality

Scholar-teacher. The gap between scholarship and teaching that the SS-3 administrator identified suggests an assumption that scholarship and teaching are not connected. This assumption could imply that one simply leaps into teaching at some point, ready or not; that teaching requires little or no formal preparation or training (unlike research and scholarship); that it is merely a craft rather than a subject of scholarly inquiry and discussion. If such assumptions were at play, one would expect measures of the perceived value of teaching to be low. Here the change in SCI-3, as reported by the DTF, is instructive:

I'd hoped that the grad[uate] student disdain for teaching might be supplanted by an enthusiasm, and . . . it has. . . . When I arrived . . . the [Ph.D. student] culture of the department was dominated by . . . advanced students who had only negative things to say about teaching. Now the culture is more diverse, and in the [entering Ph.D.] class . . . we have an unprecedented enthusiasm for teaching and for actively improving the department.

From Bok Center staff knowledge of SCI-3, it is likely that the "disdain" mentioned by the DTF came from a perceived status gap between research and teaching, with research valued higher. The SCI-3 DTF also noted "several measurable, and more unmeasurable, changes in the department that signify the shift [in culture]. To what extent these changes would have occurred regardless of the [DTF] program, and of my efforts in particular, there is no way to know." In SCI-3 alone, such changes are indeed relatively "unmeasurable," but the results from the 2006 TF survey suggest that teaching cultures were, at that time, generally better in departments with DTFs than departments without DTFs (see Table 21.2). Although causation cannot be determined, the qualitative and quantitative data together suggest positive associations between the DTF program and the teaching culture, including the connection between research and teaching.

Apprentice-professional. The qualitative data reveal another form of liminality, the gap in professional status between faculty and graduate students. Some DTFs consciously inhabit this gap. From the threshold of their future as scholars and teachers, they have in some cases been able to address the concerns of their less-experienced peers while applying a growing understanding of the role that departmental structures of authority play. A DTF from SCI-4 commented:

> I see my role as twofold: On the one hand, I have been trying to use my own [TF] perspective to understand where the gaps in the training and information for [TFs] are—and to try to fill them in. On the other hand, I think it is important that I have also helped organize and support the . . . structures that are already in place in my department, and help them become an appreciated, useful, and natural part of a Ph.D. in [SCI-4].

Prior to the DTF program, SCI-4 was one of the first quantitative departments in FAS to require new TFs/TAs to participate in a series of teaching development steps. These steps included a discipline-specific orientation, a practice teaching session, a video-based consultation, and midsemester teaching evaluations. However, the requirements were neither tracked nor enforced prior to having a DTF. Even though the

DTF's job is not to enforce the requirements, organizing and supporting the structures and communicating their meaning has been helpful.

Peer-authority. DTFs and their mentors suggest a third form of liminality, between being a peer and being an authority to TFs/TAs. For example: "[My] strengths are in mediating between departmental administration/faculty and [TFs] . . . in seeing what both sides want, and improving communication between the sides" (DTF in SS-6); "[The DTF] has his ear to the ground better than anyone and it has helped me deal with issues in a much better way" (administrator in SS-4). Liminality may afford privileged access to information from people in positions of both greater and lesser authority, as in the "seeing both sides" and "ear to the ground" metaphors above. Faculty and administrators have the authority to nominate and endorse DTFs and to require participation in TF/TA training, but they may not always have the same liminal access to information as DTFs.

Leading from Liminality

The privilege afforded by the DTFs' liminal status helps make sense of the SS-3 administrator's comments about faculty attention and time: the DTF "reminds the faculty that [TF training] is important"; the DTF provides "an incentive for faculty to think about implementing things they may not have found the time for in the past"; the DTF "creates synergy by making it doable for faculty to be more active [and] . . . to share their teaching knowledge." Unlike the old reputation of the SS-3 department as actively hostile to teaching, an interpretation based on liminality suggests that, prior to the DTF program, the faculty may not have had the right synergy of support, time, and direction to channel their considerable knowledge toward improving teaching conditions for graduate students. Fostering synergies of this kind may be a form of the DTF's leadership.

Walker et al. (2008) advocate strongly for graduate students to exercise leadership on the basis of liminality. They argue for graduate students "to become involved in—and to help lead—a process of self-study and deliberation about [their] doctoral program[s]" because "one of the special strengths that graduate students . . . bring . . . is that they are not yet fully inside the system. . . . Students bring fresh lenses, different perspectives and passions, and an ability to ask unexpected questions about what others may take for granted" (p. 144). However, despite the call for graduate students to "help lead" and the advice to graduate students to "become involved," Walker et al.'s underlying assumption seems to be that faculty are the ones "enlisting [graduate students] as partners" (p. 35), rather than graduate students enlisting faculty as partners.

The evidence from SS-3 raises the possibility, though, that in some cases faculty may be less able to do the enlisting than DTFs. Recall SS-3: problems with intellectual community and teaching culture, such as TF training, were "not in the forefront of the faculty's attention." In other words, faculty perceptions had to shift in order to transform the teaching culture. Heifetz and Linsky (2002) called problems whose solutions require people to change their underlying assumptions, beliefs, and ways of operating *adaptive*. Reframing the problem of changing departmental teaching cultures as adaptive suggests that a stagnant teaching culture may persist not only because faculty are too busy but also because they have to recognize and act on needs they may not yet perceive.

Heifetz and Linsky (2002) also separated the often-undifferentiated concepts of authority and leadership. According to them, authority encompasses one's explicit permission to act in an organization—one's job description and the expectations of colleagues. Authorities are often equipped to implement technical solutions, which do not require individuals to change their intrinsic values, beliefs, or attitudes. Adaptive leadership, in contrast, is evident in actions taken to elicit new behaviors and attitudes from individuals in the organization. This kind of leadership is often more effectively exercised from a liminal position because one does not typically receive authorization to change the accepted culture. Most problems require a combination of technical and adaptive solutions—actions that fall within one's zone of authority and actions that fall along or just outside its margins.

Changing the quality of a department's intellectual community taps deeply held patterns of interaction, structures of collaboration, and beliefs about the relationship between scholarship and teaching. Such changes may be facilitated by a combination of adaptive leadership from liminal positions and technical solutions from authoritative positions. I argue that advising graduate students to take the initiative without granting them any authority, as recommended by Walker et al. (2008), is not enough. Granting formal authority over TF training was also not enough, as evidenced by the lack of implementation after the 1995 Faculty Council mandate to departments.

It is plausible that the DTFs' combination of formal authority and liminal status facilitates adaptive changes in teaching culture. A revealing, though not unique, example of deep change comes from SS-6, as relayed by a senior faculty member and director of undergraduate studies:

> The most striking thing is how [the DTF] has given graduate students and tenured faculty, who would not otherwise, a forum to talk in

public about teaching. [The seminars on teaching] were an absolute revelation. . . . [Faculty members] really thought about it and were able to describe what they'd been doing so successfully as teachers . . . they took it very seriously. . . . Without these seminars, no one would have known how much thought the faculty put into teaching. We need more occasions where faculty give themselves permission to talk about teaching. There are more of them who think about teaching than you would guess. . . . [The DTF's work] made it all right to look interested in teaching. Faculty can't get other faculty to talk about teaching—we need someone else [to organize it].

The "absolute revelation" and the admission that "we need someone else" indicate an adaptive problem. From a liminal position, the DTF was able to create a structure that enabled a palpable shift, not only in interactions between faculty and graduate students but also among senior faculty. Walker et al. (2008) identified "opening classroom doors . . . metaphorically and otherwise" as a powerful activity fostering intellectual community (p. 129). In SS-6, the DTF's efforts helped open the doors on teaching practice in the department.

Perhaps DTFs are uniquely positioned to ask for changes in intellectual community on behalf of their own and their colleagues' formation as scholars and teachers. Their liminal positions, combined with a measure of formal authority, may allow them to appeal to the faculty's sense of stewardship—the need to "prepare and initiate the next generation of stewards" of the discipline (Walker et al., 2008, p. 11). This sense of stewardship is perhaps the "incentive for faculty" that the SS-3 administrator identified.

DTFs in the SS-3 department have continued to facilitate an ongoing transformation in the teaching culture. Recently, the DTF worked collaboratively with the faculty on a new course on pedagogy in the discipline, to be co-taught by a senior faculty member and the DTF. The DTF met one-on-one with faculty in the department about the proposal, presented it at a faculty meeting, and was present for the faculty's vote to endorse and require the new pedagogy course for new TFs. The DTF reflected on the experience: "What I took from the politics of this experience . . . was that convincing such a diverse faculty to pass any measure is a difficult and unpredictable process. But I was also buoyed by how many of them truly respected my opinion, as an advocate for the graduate students."

A faculty member in HUM-7 commented on a similar level of collegial respect: "[The DTF] contributed to the sense of community, as well as helping [the] community think about what kinds of problems they encounter in teaching . . . [and] address those problems." Adaptive change is "difficult," often "unpredictable," and likely to elicit some resistance. To be respected as an advocate and to help the disciplinary community address problems in disciplinary teaching, though, points to a deepening of intergenerational collaboration, another hallmark of a healthy intellectual community (Walker et al., 2008).

A core aspect of the Bok Center's mission is to improve undergraduate education. As an example of closing the circle toward transformation of learning for undergraduates, a DTF from SS-3 commented: "I love working with the [TFs] new to teaching and seeing their eyes light up when they think about what they do in the classroom in an entirely different way. . . . With [the TF training] requirement, younger [TFs] in the . . . department feel like teaching is a more important part of their graduate career. I feel like the manager of a team that tries to go out there and inspire undergraduates to love their classes and their work."

This DTF began to think and act like a steward of the discipline, not only connected to the faculty and to peers but also seeking to inspire undergraduates and improve the teaching and learning environment for everyone in the institution.

Challenges, Questions, and Plans

The DTF program has demonstrated the potential for graduate students to act as agents of change on behalf of intellectual community and teaching culture, not simply on their own but through an institutional structure that taps the creativity, energy, and insights available from their liminal positions. Now the challenge is to continue the program and the process of transformation. Specifically, the current economic downturn threatens the expanded definition of teaching as inclusive of DTF work, which has been an important factor in institutionalization of funding to date. With DTFs in nearly half of FAS departments as of 2008–09, another challenge involves meeting the needs of departments that have not found the program's structure to be a good fit. For example, anthropology discontinued participation because the "department" really consisted of three subareas with too great a scope for one DTF to serve effectively (see Table 21.1). Other departments may not yet have applied to the program for similar reasons. Finding qualified graduate students with time, interest, and no conflict with other funding stipulations has also proven challenging in several instances (see Table 21.1). In light of recent changes in graduate student funding packages and time-to-degree initiatives, this challenge is likely to remain. Some departments have solved this problem by planning one to two years in advance, so that the next DTF to be nominated spends time as an apprentice before assuming the role and can plan to complete other requirements and arrange funding accordingly.

Remaining questions include whether other liminal populations within institutions of higher education, such as undergraduate students, adjunct faculty, or postdoctoral fellows, might contribute to improvements in the cultures of teaching and learning. Are there ways in which institutions can confer formal authority to leaders from those populations, to tap their creative potential for contributing to adaptive change? Or are there other models for empowering graduate students as agents of change? Finally, are there drawbacks or flaws in the notion of deliberately joining formal authority with marginality to encourage adaptive leadership? As the DTFs continue their work with greater awareness of the characteristics of intellectual community, teaching culture, and adaptive leadership, the next five-year cycle of program assessment may provide some answers to these questions.

In the next five years, more data from departments before and after joining the DTF program, including end-of-semester teaching evaluation data, may help clarify the connection between improving teaching culture and improving outcomes for students. These comparisons must be undertaken carefully. For example, no significant difference emerged between the overall mean AY 2007–08 teaching evaluation scores between FAS departments with DTFs and without DTFs. However, comparing such overall scores may not be meaningful given other predictable factors or biases associated with teaching evaluation data—for example, whether a course is an elective or a requirement and whether it is in the humanities and social sciences or in the sciences (Aleamoni, 1999). Launching another survey of all TFs on the cultures of teaching and intellectual community may also yield insights in large-scale transformation relative to the 1996 survey.

Finally, some faculty have requested that the program serve as a more frequent point of connection between chairs and directors of graduate or undergraduate study among the departments, and this suggestion indicates an important new direction for the program. With the potential to form a cohort not only among the DTFs themselves but also among their faculty mentors, the Bok Center plans to create opportunities, such as cross-department symposia, for direct connections among interdepartmental faculty and administrators.

REFERENCES

Aleamoni, L. M. (1999). Student rating myths versus research facts from 1924 to 1998. *Journal of Personnel Evaluation in Education, 13*(2), 153–166.

Austin, A. E. (2002). Preparing the next generation of faculty: Graduate school as socialization to the academic career. *Journal of Higher Education, 73*(1), 94–122.

Border, L. B. (2005). *The Lead Network*. Retrieved March 1, 2009, from www.colorado.edu/gtp/lead/index.htm

Feldman, K. A., & Paulsen, M. B. (1999). Faculty motivation: The role of a supportive teaching culture. In M. Theall (Ed.), *New directions for teaching and learning: No 78. Motivation from within: Approaches for encouraging faculty and students to excel* (pp. 71–78). San Francisco: Jossey-Bass.

Heifetz, R. A., & Linsky, M. (2002). *Leadership on the line: Staying alive through the dangers of leading*. Boston: Harvard Business School Press.

Huber, M. T., & Morreale, S. P. (2002). Situating the scholarship of teaching and learning: A cross-disciplinary conversation. In M. T. Huber & S. P. Morreale (Eds.), *Disciplinary styles in the scholarship of teaching and learning* (pp. 1–24). Washington, DC: American Association for Higher Education.

Nyquist, J. D., & Sprague, J. (1998). Thinking developmentally about TAs. In M. Marincovich, J. Prostko, & F. Stout (Eds.), *The professional development of graduate teaching assistants* (pp. 61–88). Bolton, MA: Anker.

Rohdieck, S. (2009). *Graduate teaching fellows*. Retrieved March 1, 2009, from http://ftad.osu.edu/ostep/gtf.html

Ronkowski, S. A. (1998). The disciplinary/departmental context of TA training. In M. Marincovich, J. Prostko, & F. Stout (Eds.), *The professional development of graduate teaching assistants* (pp. 41–60). Bolton, MA: Anker.

University of Michigan, Center for Research on Teaching and Learning. (2008a). *Engineering graduate student mentors*. Retrieved April 4, 2009, from www.crlt.umich.edu/gsis/egsm.php

University of Michigan, Center for Research on Teaching and Learning. (2008b). *Graduate Teaching Consultants Program (GTC)*. Retrieved April 4, 2009, from www.crlt.umich.edu/gsis/gtc.php

Walker, G. E., Golde, C. M., Jones, L., Bueschel, A. C., & Hutchings, P. (2008). *The formation of scholars: Rethinking doctoral education for the twenty-first century*. San Francisco: Jossey-Bass.